Child Welfare

CLINICAL THEORY AND PRACTICE

Elaine S. LeVine *and* Alvin L. Sallee

The Center Through the Looking Glass   *New Mexico State University*

eb
eddie bowers publishing, inc.

2600 Jackson Street
Dubuque, IA 52001-3342

Design and Production: David Corona Design

Exclusive marketing and distributor rights for
U.K., Eire, and Continental Europe held by:

Gazelle Book Services Limited
Falcon House
Queen Square
Lancaster
LAl, IRN
U.K.

eddie bowers publishing, inc.
2600 Jackson Street
Dubuque, Iowa 52001-3342

ISBN 0-945483-91-0

Copyright © 1999, by *eddie bowers publishing, inc.*

Printed in the United States of America.

9 8 7 6 5 4 3 2 1

Dedication

TO OUR SPOUSES
Jim Thompson and Kathy Sallee.
For their continued encouragement, support, and love.

and

TO OUR CHILDREN
Marshall and Randall Dylan Thompson.
Charles, Shawn, and Joan Sallee.
From whom we learn so much when we listen.

Contents

Part II
Theories of Child Practice 81

Part III

Developing a Treatment Plan
for the Child and Family   185

10 Family Assessment and Case Management 221

11 Selection of Child Treatment Modalities 249

Part IV
Vulnerable Children   293

12   Physical Abuse, Sexual Abuse, and Neglect   296

Part V
Looking Forward   **403**

15   Emerging Roles for Child Welfare Practitioners   **405**

Preface

Although most people readily agree that children are our greatest treasure, a powerful natural resource, it is our contention that society and children's services have fallen dramatically short of meeting the needs of maltreated and special children. Newspapers are replete with cases of children whose needs for basic protection have not been met. An estimated one million documented cases of child abuse and neglect are documented each year by child welfare agencies. In 1995, the victimization rate of children was approximately 15 out of 1000. Unfortunately, the true picture may be much worst as only 28 per cent of children who are harmed have their cases investigated by child protective services (Sedlak & Broadhurst, 1996). Compounding these distressing statistics, many emotionally and physically abused and neglected children are brought into some type of social service care, only to continue the nightmarish existence because our legal, mental health and child welfare systems are not sufficiently refined and organized to protect them until the damaging circumstances are corrected.

Yet, it is not only in severe cases of abuse and neglect that the emotional needs of children are not heeded. Everyday thousands of other children face an array of problems at home, in the schools and the community. Gifted children, children with developmental disabilities and children in new families often experience emotional and social difficulties requiring the services of trained child welfare professionals. Our review of the child welfare literature indicates a main focus is on programs, policies and in clinical discussions a focus almost totally on the adult parent. Few universities offer courses on the clinical concerns of the child. Our review of current child welfare texts reveals little content on practice directly with children. It appears to us based upon thousands of cases, that from training to practice, in both the private and public sectors, few professional child welfare workers are ready and able to listen to the needs of children.

Child Welfare: Clinical Theory and Practice, is written to assist future and present child welfare workers from the professions of social work, counseling, psychology to more effectively recognize and meet the social and emotional needs of children. This book is broadly based upon the classic psychological, sociological, and developmental literature with a focus on working directly with the child and their contextual surroundings.

This text will first help alert the reader to the signals that a child is in need of help. Thus, Part I "Children and Change," identifies children with needs by reviewing statistical indices of childhood disturbances and by highlighting historical and developmental research of expected and maladapted patterns in children. Specialized theories and techniques required to be an effective advocate and worker for children are presented in Part II, "Theories of Child Treatment." In addition to major theoretical underpinnings of the most prominent and effective approaches to child therapy, the reader will find case studies which bridge theory and practice. Part III of the text, "Developing Treatment Plans for the Child and Family," is a practical guide for establishing an individual treatment plan for a child. Means of child and family assessment, psychological testing , and how to work with a child in treatment sessions are discussed in depth. The specific personal and social factors which catalyze emotional disturbances in children are detailed in Part IV, "Vulnerable Children."

We do believe that children are our nations's greatest treasure and a powerful resource that should be preserved. The final and a most important part of this text, Part V, "Looking Forward," overviews prevention and policy strategies. We hope each reader, upon completing this book, will feel more effective not only in recognizing and quelling desperate cries, but also in assuring the well-being of children. All children have a right to grow and flourish to their optimal ability. Healthy children assure the future well-being of our country.

The use of the editorial "we" in this book is appropriate and many people have contributed to its writing over many years. The authors thank them for their support and encouragement. First we thank our students, child welfare workers, children and families who continually provided a reality check and inspiration for us.

A number of people helped in the production, research, editing and typing: Barbara Myers, who's skills have been critical to this project for years, Joyce Tinsley for her editorial work, Robert Ellison, Mary Manzo and James Ott, Sharon Lloyd, and Tom Lemarre for their editing and research efforts. We are grateful to Eddie Bowers for his vision and financial backing.

Many colleagues provided special help with a number of chapters, including, Dr. William LeVine, University of Kansas Medical School, for his review of Chapter 11 and his comments; Elsa Iverson, Indiana University for her comments on Chapters 7,10 and 12. June Lloyd, Department of Health and Human Services, for her over all assistance and Chapter 14; and Dr. Karen Brown, Southwest Texas State University, for contributions on divorce in Chapter 14. Our gratitude to Amando Padilla of Stanford University for his efforts on the early stages of this text.

A special word of thanks to our spouses, Jim Thompson and Kathy Sallee, for their continued encouragement, support and love.

E.S.L.
A.L.S.

About the Authors

ELAINE S. LEVINE is a licensed psychologist, founder of The Center Through the Looking Glass, and has been in private practice specializing in child and family therapy for more than 20 years. She has served as a consultant to numerous child welfare and family service agencies and as an expert witness concerning sexual and child abuse. She also is a college Professor at New Mexico State University. She has authored three books and numerous articles on aspects of cross-cultural counseling and child therapy (with the gifted, abused, and adopted, employing specialized techniques such as reattachment and hypnotherapy).

ALVIN L. SALLEE is a licensed independent social worker, a member of the Academy of Certified Social Workers, and has had a part-time private practice in adoption and family therapy. He is a Professor and Head of the Family Preservation Institute in the Department of Social Work at New Mexico State University. He has authored books, monographs, and numerous articles on social work practice, family preservation, adoption, and foster care. He has served as an expert witness in court concerning children's cases and has staffed mor than 1,500 child abuse and foster care cases. He has completed research and practice with developmentally disabled children and families.

Part I
Children and Change

O ne of the greatest challenges to meeting the needs of children is that this population is so dynamic, changing on so many dimensions. Our views of the psychological and social needs of children have changed dramatically through recent history. Studies of child development are redoubling in number and sophistication, and the effective child welfare practitioner needs a broad understanding of those findings in order to set appropriate goals for child clients and to know when and how to refer them for specialized services. Of course, the state of being-a-child is itself in constant flux, and the effective child welfare practitioner must be exquisitely sensitive to the developmental issues and abilities of each client.

Part I will attempt to sensitize the reader to the dynamic issues of treatment with children. Chapter 1 of this unit presents current data about the children in need of children's services and those who are and are not receiving care. Historical attitudes about children by society at large and in varied service fields will be reviewed in Chapter 2. Special attention will be devoted to discussing the emergence of the concept of childhood. Then, our present understanding of children's psychological needs and capacities will be identified in Chapter 3, which discusses developmental issues.

The major thesis of this book, that children have often not been listened to, is well exemplified in this unit, in which you will learn of the historical maltreatment of children, of the many children whose needs are yet unmet, and, despite great gains, of the present limitations to our understanding of child welfare theories and practice.

Chapter 1
Who Are the Children in Need?

It is often said that a great many children are in crisis and in need of services. The sources of the crisis are multiple. The child may be a product of a disruptive social environment and/or a dysfunctional family. Other crises are provoked by intrapsychic factors such as personality type or sensitive temperament traits. Global estimates concerning childhood problems range greatly. Some epidemiologists base estimates of children's emotional needs upon referral statistics (such as the number of children placed outside of their home in foster care or in-patient care, out-patient community mental health services, and private therapy) and report that between 1 to 5 per cent of children experience significant emotional problems. When children's behavior is systematically observed and when broad questionnaire methodologies are employed to tap attitudes of teachers and parents, at least 7.5 million children in the United States—representing approximately 12% of the Nation's 63 million children under 18—are believed to suffer enough to require treatment. (National Institute of Mental Health, 1990).

In 1995, child protective services (CPS) agencies investigated an estimated 2 million reports alleging the maltreatment of almost 3 million children. More than half of all reports alleging maltreatment came from professionals, including educators, law enforcement and justice officials, medical mental health professionals, social service professionals, and child care providers. Approximately 19 percent of reports came from relatives of the child or from the child himself. Reports from professionals are more likely to be substantiated or indicated than reports from nonprofessionals. Based on reports received and investigated by CPS agencies in 1995, about 15 children per 1,000 children younger than 18 in the general population are likely to be victims of abuse or neglect (U.S. Department of Health and Human Services, 1995).

In one retrospective survey, 26% of females had a sexual experience with an adult before age 13. Only 6% of the incidents were reported to appropriate agencies (Gagnon, 1965). Some experts (O'Brien, 1983) state the average age of the sexually exploited child is 7 years with 75% being females.

Thus, the epidemiological and research designs as well as the definition of children in need of services affects the estimate of children experiencing emotional problems.

In this chapter, we will review a range of descriptive data about children in the United States, with particular attention to the frequency, distribution, etiology, and longevity of the areas of concern. In order to interpret this data base, we will point out the research methodologies employed.

The Status of Children

Demographics

According to the census data, American children under age 15 made up 22 percent of the population in 1990 compared to 28 percent in 1970. (U.S. Bureau of Census, 1992). The graphs in Figure 1.1 (pages 6–7) compare the distribution of the U.S. population by age and sex in 1960 to 1990. In 1960, some baby boomers had not yet been born and the majority were not yet in school. In 1990, the baby boomers from World War II were 26 to 44 years of age (U.S. Bureau of the Census, 1992).

The decrease in the percent of the population under 15 years of age reflects the combined effect of several personal/social factors, which are: a growing preference for two-child families, an increasing proportion of women desiring to remain childless, women delaying childbearing in order to pursue education and careers and subsequently bearing few children, and parents feeling constrained to limit families because of the increasing cost of rearing a child while incomes are not keeping pace with inflation. Although the fertility rate (number of live births per 100,000 women) will probably continue to fall, the absolute number of children is increasing now because the many post-World War II babies are now reaching child-bearing age (U.S. Bureau of the Census, 1992). Even with a decrease in fertility rates, the child welfare worker can be assured that a significant proportion, approximately 15 to 22%, of the U.S. population in the coming decade will be children (U.S. Bureau of Census, 1992).

Not only the number of children but also their demographic characteristics and the nature of families are changing in accord with the new values and demands of American life. The population of children in central cities and rural areas has decreased more dramatically than that in suburban areas and in small cities, as families continue to move to these semi-rural and semi-urban environments. Children of today are a relatively mobile population. In 1978, 53.4% of children ages 3 and 4 and 41.4% of children ages 5 to 9 moved during the previous 3-year period. Children growing up in small cities and semi-rural environments face some different dilemmas than those in large urban areas (U.S. Bureau of the Census, 1978).

In 1985, 79% of births were White, 16.6% were African-American and 4.0% were of other ethnicity and races (U.S. Bureau of the Census, 1989). The majority of children of all ethnicities live in metropolitan areas, rather than rural areas or small cities. However, a larger percentage of Black and Hispanic children live in central cities than White children (U.S. Bureau of the Census, 1992). For these reasons, we may expect Black and Hispanic children to face some different problems from White children because of greater pressures associated with urban living, especially in central city areas.

Later in the text, we will present the position that child welfare procedures must be concurrent with working with children of ethnic minority families. We will outline approaches of pluralistic child therapy in which the child welfare worker orients goals and techniques towards helping the child adapt to her or his and the family's chosen ethnic milieu.

According to Table 1.1 (page 8), we can see that the rate of births in white families has diminished significantly since 1960, yet the rate has increased slightly for African-Americans and quite a bit for other mixed races and ethnicities. The child welfare worker should be familiar with demographic data such as these since they provide indirect information about the values that different ethnic/racial groups place on children and family life.

Family Status

An other important area for the child welfare practitioner to consider is the changing form of family life. Concomitant with rising divorce, the percentage of children living with both natural parents has decreased since 1970. At lease 13 million

FIGURE 1.1

Distribution of the U.S. Population, by Age and Sex: 1960 to 1990 (in percent)

U.S. Population Ages

The population pyramids here show how baby boomer have aged during the last 30 years. In 1960, some baby boomers had not yet been born. and the majority were not yet in school. In 1990, they were 26 to 44 years of age. Now the majority have jobs and families of their own.

Coinciding with the aging of baby boomers, the median age for the U.S. population has risen, from 29.4 in 1960 to 32.8 in 1990. There are more women than men at older ages. In 1990, women outnumbered men beginning at age 40, with the largest differences occurring for those 65 years and over.

As for children, those under age 15 made up 22 percent of the population in 1990 compared to 28 percent in 1970.

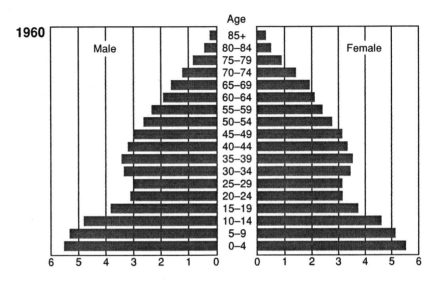

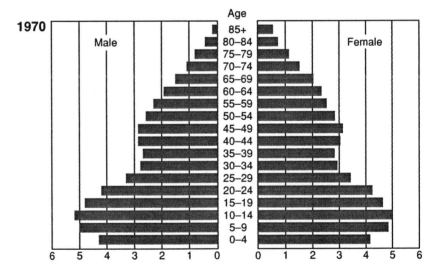

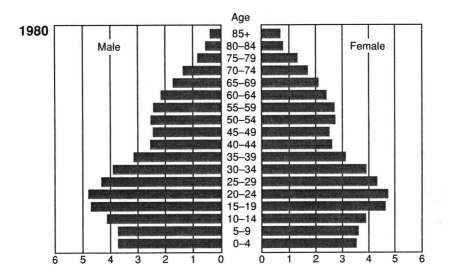

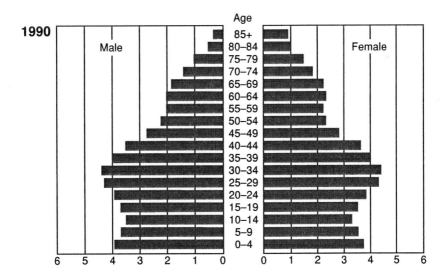

TABLE 1.1

Births by Race: 1960 to 2080 (Projection data from middle series. Numbers in thousands. Includes Armed Forces overseas)

	Percent of total births that are—		
Year	*White*	*Black*	*Other races*
Estimates:			
1960	84.3	14.4	1.3
1965	82.9	15.6	1.5
1970	82.7	15.5	1.8
1975	81.0	16.4	2.6
1980	80.1	16.4	3.5
1985	79.4	16.6	4.0
Projections:			
1987	79.7	16.5	3.8
1990	79.2	16.6	4.2
1995	78.0	17.1	4.9
2000	76.8	17.6	5.6
2005	76.0	17.8	6.2
2010	75.7	17.7	6.6
2020	74.9	17.8	7.4
2030	73.6	18.0	8.4
2040	73.3	17.7	9.0
2050	73.0	17.4	9.6
2080	71.3	17.0	11.6

Source: U.S. Bureau of the Census, 1989, Current Population Reports (Series P-25, Number 1018)

children are living with one parent, and approximately two million are living with neither. As shown in Figure 1.2, in 1990, the majority of White children and Hispanic children lived with two parents, while the majority of Black children lived in one-parent situations. The proportion of White children living with one parent more than doubled between 1960 and 1990, rising from 7.1 to 19.2 percent. For Black children, the proportion living with one parent also more than doubled from 21.9 percent in 1960 to 54.8 percent in 1990. (U.S. Bureau of the Census, 1992).

FIGURE 1.2

Living Arrangements of Children Under Age 18, by Presence of Parent, Race, and Hispanic Origin: 1960 to 1990 (in Percent)

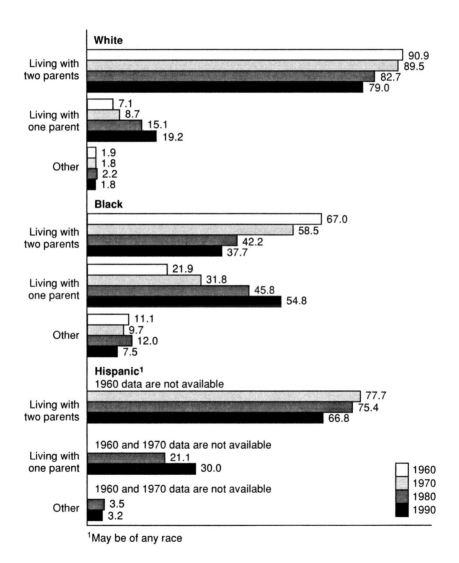

¹May be of any race

Source: U.S. Bureau of the Census, 1992, C3.186: pp 23–181.

Although many divorced individuals with children remarry within five or six years, accumulating research suggests that the psychological loss incurred through divorce and the subsequent child rearing by one parent can create significant stress for children. Moreover, children may experience further stress adjusting to step-parents. As will be discussed in Chapter 14, the psychosocial effects are complex. The divorced parents' adjustment, their availability to the child, economic factors, and the child's temperament make some children more prone to emotional problems following divorce than others. We consider children of divorce to be vulnerable children because they are more prone to problems than other children not experiencing these stress factors in their lives. The child practitioner needs to be aware of the increasing number of children facing this special vulnerability.

Poverty

Another group of special children are those raised in poverty. The poverty rate for families with children declined between 1960 and 1970 but has increased since. African-American families with children present were the more likely to be poor and White families were least likely to be poor. Hispanic families had poverty rates slightly lower than Black families. The same trends influencing family income also influence changes in poverty rate, most notable the growth in one parent families. In 1987, nearly one of every six families with children were living in poverty. Nationwide, over 450,000 children are now homeless, and another two million children are "precariously housed and at imminent risk of homelessness" (National Center on Homelessness and Poverty, May 1990). In Los Angeles County there are an estimated 12,500 homeless children who sleep on the streets, in cars, in parks, under overpasses, in illegally occupied garages, on school grounds, and in shelters (Ninth National Conference on Child Abuse and Neglect, 1991). It is important to note that poverty rates vary significantly according to the gender, ethnicity, or race of the head of household as well as urban or rural setting. As can be seen in Figure 1.3, while 14 percent of the overall population lives in poverty, more than 33 % of Black families and 29% of families of Hispanic origin face poverty every day. In addition, about 50% of all children raised in households that are headed by a female live in poverty. Of these, approximately 37% are white, 59% are Black, and 60% are Hispanic. Interestingly, a considerably smaller proportion of children living with a single male head of household lives under poverty conditions (U.S. Bureau of Census, 1993). In Chapter 13, we discuss in detail the debilitating psychological effects of poverty upon children. Many of these children in poverty enter life with vulnerabilities beginning with low birth weight, illness, and malnutrition. In turn, these physical vulnerabilities can lead to increased rates of mental retardation and problematic personality temperaments.

FIGURE 1.3

Poverty rates for People with Selected Characteristics

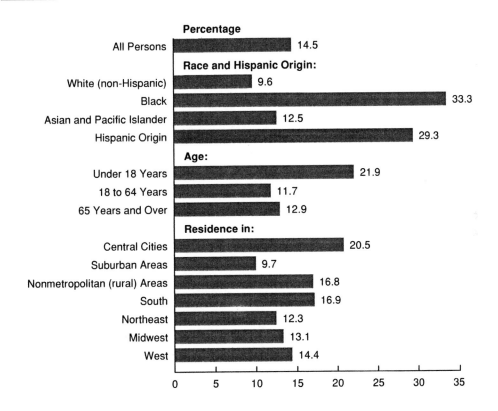

Source: U.S. Bureau of Census, *Poverty in the United States: 1992,* Current Population Reports, Series P60-185 (Washington, DC: U.S. Government Printing Office, 1993).

Substitute Care

Associated with changing lifestyles with the large number of single parents families and large number of poor families in which one or both parents must work,
increasingly larger numbers of children are cared for outside of the home. In 1976
through 1977, approximately 13% of employed women utilized child care for
their 900,000 children. By 1985, 25% of women employed day care for their
children. In addition, children sometimes receive substitute care as a means of
intense psychological or social intervention. Of course, the quality of child care
varies greatly. The child clinician will be called upon to deal with children with
whom adults and peers at day care centers play significant roles in early life. In
these cases, the child clinician needs knowledge of the child-rearing practices of
the supervising adults at the day care center as well as the parents (U.S. Department of Health & Human Services, 1980). Figure 1.4 depicts the types of child
care employed by working women in 1985.

FIGURE 1.4

Child Care Arrangements for Children of Working Mothers: Winter 1985–85 (in percent)

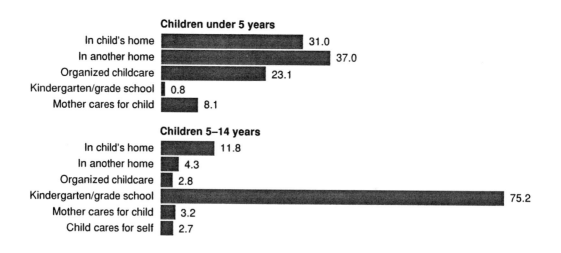

Source: U.S. Bureau of the Census, 1989, Current Population Reports (Series P-23, No. 163).

Table 1.2 presents the number of children receiving various kinds of social and psychological intervention (Young, Pappenfort, & Marlow, 1983). As can be seen in this 1982 survey of approximately 125,000 youth and children, the highest category for residential care was delinquency, followed by dependent and neglected and emotionally disturbed children. Table 1.3 shows the number of children that have been in foster care in 1982, 1988, and 1990. This table demonstrates that the numbers of children placed in foster care have remained relatively constant for the last 20, years, although there has been somewhat less reliance upon group homes and an increasing placement in foster homes and nonfinalized adoptive homes.

Determining when foster care is a source of damage has been a central concern of the Child Welfare League of America and the National Association of Social Workers since the early 1960s (Fanshel & Shinn, 1978). The prediction that children removed from a permanent home were more vulnerable to cognitive and personality problems has received much support. Intensive work with the child in his or her own home is emerging as an alternative to out of home placements. Known as Family Preservation, this approach may include intensive child and family therapy, as discussed in Chapter 13.

TABLE 1.2

Numbers of Children and Youth, 1966 and 1981, by Type of Facility

Type of Facility	Number of Children and Youth	
	1966	*1981*
Dependent and Neglected	60,459	24,533
Pregnant Adolescent	5,835	1,676
Temporary Shelter	1,832	3,893
Delinquent	55,000	40,335
Status Offenders	a	4,754
Detention	10,875	15,423
Substance Abuse	a	1,629
Emotionally Disturbed	13,876	20,397
Psychiatric	8,028	12,683
Total of Children	155,905	125,323

TABLE 1.3

Selected Characteristics of the Foster Care Population in 1982, 1988, and 1990 (percentage)

Characteristics	1982	1988	1990
Type of substitute care[a]			
Family foster home	72.0	71.4	74.5
Non-finalized adoptive home	—	2.3	2.7
Group home	21.5	18.6	16.4
Living independently	0.6	0.7	0.5
Other	5.2	5.7	0.3
Unknown	0.7	1.3	0.3
Age[b]			
Under one year	2.7	5.0	4.9
One to five years	19.8	27.4	31.1
Six to 12 years	29.0	31.1	32.3
13 to 18 years	45.3	34.1	29.7
19 and over	2.9	2.3	1.7
Unknown	0.4	0.1	0.3
Race/ethnicity[c]			
White	52.7	45.5	39.3
African American	34.2	36.5	40.4
Hispanic	6.7	10.1	11.8
Other	4.6	4.2	4.3
Unknown	1.8	3.7	4.2

Source: Tatara, T. (1993). *Characteristics of children in substitute and adoptive care.* Washington, DC: Voluntary Cooperative Information System, American Public Welfare Association.

[a] Data are based on reports from 41 states in 1982, 31 states in 1988, and 28 states in 1990, accounting for 86 percent, 78 percent, and 68 percent of the total substitute care population, respectively.

[b] Data are based on reports from 30 states in 1982, 26 states in 1988, and 23 states in 1990, accounting for 53 percent, 70 percent, and 61 percent of the total substitute care population, respectively.

[c] Data are based on reports from 38 states in 1982, 34 states in 1988, an 31 states in 1990, accounting for 81 percent, 82 percent, and 75 percent of the total substitute care population, respectively.

Frequency of Childhood Problems

Environmental Impacts

While each child has a different level of potential, a child's social and psychological well being is clearly linked to their living environment, that is their home, neighborhood, community, and role models among others. When examining the frequency of childhood problems it becomes abundantly clear that child development is enhanced or retarded by a child's social experiences. Yet our conclusions are not precise because the interaction between a given child and their environment is very complex and therefore we only best describe the impact or outcome rather than the cause or contributing factors to a child's problem (Giovannoni, 1995).

Abnormal Versus Normal

It might seem a relatively easy task to extrapolate these statistics concerning the status of typical and vulnerable children to the frequency of problems. In fact, it is extremely difficult to define the parameters of abnormal child development because experts differ so greatly in their definition of childhood maladjustment. Some believe it is a distinct departure from normalcy. Others view it as an extension of typical range, distinctive only in degree. Still others view maladjustment as a combination of qualitative and quantitative factors differing from the typical (Anthony, 1970). The problem of defining maladjustment is especially difficult among children. Several studies lead to the conclusion that most children show disturbed behavior at some time.

In their now classic epidemiological studies, Lapouse & Monk (1959) and MacFarlane, Allen & Honzik (1956) demonstrated many symptoms of pathology in the general population of children. Shepherd, Oppenheim & Mitchell (1966) surveyed children brought to mental health clinics and compared their symptomatology to a control group of randomly selected children. They reported that the symptoms of the two groups of children were not significantly different, although the parents of the clinic children were easily upset, less able to cope with misbehavior, and more likely to consult others with their problems. Along the lines of these findings, Kanner (1962b) has said that child abnormality may be related more to the "annoyance threshold" of significant others than to any intrinsic quality of the child. McCoy (1976) requested doctoral clinical psychology students to assess children's pathology from filmed segments and parental reports. The judges based their treatment recommendations more upon parental reports than on observation of the child. Thus, it often seems unclear what symptoms the child welfare worker centers upon and whether the therapist treats primarily the child or the referring adult.

In the United States, the most commonly employed methods for classifying emotional disturbances among children are the ICD-10 (World Health Organization, 1994). The ICD-10 is a manual employed internationally. The DSM-IV (1994) was created by a committee of psychiatrists in particular to meet the needs of clinicians in this country. Both are categorical systems, that is, they were created on the basis of descriptions of experienced clinicians of the supposedly essential features for a particular diagnosis. When these descriptions are agreed upon by a wide range of clinicians, it is stated that the evaluation method has "face validity." At present, many of the categories of the DSM-IV and the ICD-10 have only face validity. In addition, a few hold descriptive validity; that is, the cluster of symptoms are commonly seen in only one type of mental disorder. Ideally, the nosology should also be associated with predictive validity; that is, a category should predict other differences such as etiology of the syndrome, biological correlates, family patterns, and response to treatment. Unfortunately, such knowledge remains limited in the field of child therapy. In other words, the major systems of classification in childhood disorders are presently almost completely atheoretical because there are so few disorders for which etiology or treatment has been consistently demonstrated.

These classification systems now widely employed show great advantages over previous systems but are still limited in a number of ways. First of all, neither system is based upon an overall definition of what a mental disorder is. Without an overall definition, there is a lack of clear criterion for the decision on whether or not any particular disorder should be included in the classification system. The DSM-IV does attempt to somewhat address this issue, although no clear definition is provided. Now disorders are conceptualized as clinically significant, behavioral or psychological syndromes. The patterns must be associated with either distress (such as a symptom) or disability (such as impairment in one or more areas of functioning). There must be a behavioral psychological or biological dysfunction that does not reside solely in the relationship between the individual and society. The classification systems are limited not only by the difficulty to finding the task that they attempt to classify, but also by the fact that the system must almost be completely atheoretical because there are so few emotional disorders of children in which the etiology and treatment has been systematically demonstrated. A further difficulty is that the conditions that are normal for one time of life may be pathological at another (for example, bed-wetting at age 2 vs. bed-wetting at age 16). The same symptom may have very different implications at different age periods (for example, school refusal in the early years may indicate separation anxiety; while when it first appears in high school, it often indicates emerging schizophrenia or a major depressive disorder).

A major challenge of the system is to classify a disorder rather than children. In other words, there is a heterogeneity of symptoms within any group of children suffering extrapsychic stresses (such as the sexually abused child or a child of divorce). An effective classification system must glean out clusters of symptoms that correlate and, this cluster must appear significant to clinicians. Moreover, children with one type of disorder when young may be free of disorder or show different conditions later in life. (Rutter, Tuma & Lann, 1988).

Outpatient Data

Data collected from a representative sample of outpatient services (NIMH Survey and Reports, 1979) reveal some different trends than institutional placements. Over 40% of the users were youths under 25 years of age in comparison to the 25% admissions at public and private hospitals. Compared to the overall rate of use of outpatient facilities of 665 per 100,000, the rate of youths was as high or higher. From 55% to 73% of the youths 14 years of age or younger were diagnosed as adjustment reaction and behavior disorders. In comparison to the data of state and private hospitals, a larger number of the adolescent referrals to outpatient psychiatric services are for adjustment reactions. Schizophrenia depressive, and personality disorders are relatively infrequent, while many cases are classified as "other" unspecified conditions. The outpatient facilities show a lack of sex differences by diagnostic category.

Analysis of the Frequency Data on Childhood Problems

The statistics concerning childhood maladjustment are alarmingly high. Although admissions to state, county, and private hospitals are lower for children than adults, some 1 to 2% of the childhood population is experiencing such significant disturbance as to require hospitalization (NIMH, 1991). Moreover, the rate of hospitalization for youths has not decreased in the last ten years at the same rate as it has for adults.

The frequency data demonstrate that among young children, similar types and frequency of syndromes are reported at hospital and outpatient clinics. By adolescence, it seems that clients with more severe pathology are treated in hospital settings, while the outpatient facilities meet the needs of the less disturbed. We will see in a later chapter that hospitalization is rarely recommended as preferred treatment for children. Successful reentry into the family, school, and community is consistently stressed as necessary for effective childhood adjustment. The fact that more than 40% of the users of outpatient facilities are youths is quite interesting but difficult to interpret since the primary childhood diagnosis, whether in an inpatient or outpatient facility, is adjustment reaction. Perhaps, encouragingly, most children receive outpatient care so that they can be kept in their homes. Yet, one wonders under what conditions some children are hospitalized for adjustment reactions, while others receive outpatient care. Minority children are institutionalized in correctional facilities at a rate four times greater than non-minority children. Interestingly, minorities are institutionalized in medical and educational facilities at a rate only 20% higher than white children (U.S. Department of Health & Human Services, 1980). Are there ethnic, social class, or sex biases such that some children receive outpatient assistance, while others, because of bias, are hospitalized? Or perhaps the diagnosis of adjustment reaction is so broad that differences in symptoms of those hospitalized and those receiving outpatient care are masked.

The hospital and outpatient data raise many questions that certainly alert us to the extent of maladjustment among children. Not only is the extent of needs of concern, but the cost of providing such service adequately also must be given serious consideration. Table 1.4 overviews types of care for seriously emotionally disturbed children and the cost per episode. As this table well demonstrates, in patient and residential care is enormously costly to our society (National Mental Health Association, 1989). To the extent that we can find develop out patient and intensive in-home services to assist the children in need, we will be able to provide much longer assistance and will have financial resources available to identify and assist many more children. Some researchers have attempted to determine what happens to the childhood population that has received treatment for maladjustment. Researchers have employed various classification schemes to evaluate the progression of childhood disorders.

TABLE 1.4

Types of Care for Seriously Emotionally Disturbed Children and Cost Per Episode

Type of Care	Description	Cost
Intensive in-home crisis services	Six weeks of intensive in-home crisis counseling may be offered to prevent removal of children from home and to stabilize the family situation.	$1,100
Day treatment	A year of treatment in a day treatment program may be offered to children who are seriously emotionally disturbed. Often, this treatment has prevented the removal of the child from home.	$15,000–$18,000
State hospital	Nationally, the average daily cost in a state hospital for treatment of adolescents and children is $299. The cost per episode would be $38,272 based on an average length of stay of 128 days.	$38,272
Residential treatment facility	Nationally, the average daily cost in a residential treatment facility is $111.67. Because of the incomplete data, this rate is considered an underestimate of the actual cost of the service. Based on an average length of stay of 15.4 months, the cost per episode would be $52,300.	$51,592

Source: National Mental Health Association (1989).

Long-Term Studies of Childhood Problems

Long-term studies of childhood maladjustment take several forms. One type is the follow-up study in which children treated for emotional problems are reexamined and retested some years later. Another type of long-term study is the longitudinal design. In the longitudinal study, the development of a group of children is investigated over a number of years with the goal of identifying factors contributing to health and maladjustment. A third type of long-term study is the retrospective design in which target adults are asked to think back and assess their own or another's childhood.

Follow-up Studies

In the follow-up studies, children with target problems are located and retested a number of years later. O'Neal and Robins (1959) followed up 526 adults who had been seen in psychiatric clinics for diagnosis with no treatment and matched controls some 30–40 years earlier. They reported that a large number of individuals who had been diagnosed as antisocial children turned out to be antisocial adults. Individuals with less severe diagnoses grew up with a range of symptoms of moderate severity. As a whole, the control group of children grew up to be well-adjusted adults. Thus, O'Neal and Robins demonstrate some relationship between child and adult disorders. The relationship seems to be one of intensity of pathology rather than of specific symptomatology. These findings are supported by the follow-up study of Pritchard and Graham (1966) who noted a significant relationship between antisocial children and adults and a significant correlation between childhood neurosis and later affective disorders.

Longitudinal Studies

Several researchers have attempted longitudinal studies of childhood maladjustment. These studies are exciting because they shed light on the relationship between childhood and adult disorders. However, they suffer from several limitations. It is difficult to continue to follow a group of children through to adulthood. Different evaluation instruments must be used at various developmental stages, and the relationship of the findings from testing to testing becomes unclear the older our subjects become.

Moreover, scientific advances tend to render some findings unfashionable or irrelevant before the study is actually completed (Anthony, 1970). Despite these limitations, several interesting findings have emerged. In the Berkeley Study, MacFarlane et al. (1954), evaluated 116 randomly selected children from ages 2 months through 14 years. They demonstrated that most disorders did not persist into adulthood. Douglas and Mulligan (1961) studied the development of 5,000 British children over 20 years and noted that few with significant behavioral disturbances were receiving therapy. Thomas, Birch, Chess, and Hertzig (1960) examined a broad cross section of children and identified normal differences in reaction time and temperament that antedated symptomatology.

Retrospective Studies

Some interesting findings have emerged from retrospective studies in which adults are asked to look back and evaluate their own or their children's childhoods. Clearly, recall studies are subject to much bias, and this limitation must be kept in mind in evaluating these findings. Lapouse and Monk (1958) pioneered this approach in child therapy research by interviewing a cross section of mothers with a 200-item questionnaire. They reported that over half the sample children considered normal had many fears, temper tantrums, and worries. About one-third experienced nightmares, wet their beds, and sucked their thumbs. Similarly, findings of equivalent symptoms among child clinic populations and controls have been reported in a number of retrospective studies (Renaud & Estess, 1961: Shepherd, Oppenheim, & Mitchell, 1966).

What can be concluded from these large- scale studies of childhood maladjustment? First, there is a sizeable number of children with rather severe personal and behavioral problems. The specific symptomatology varies with developmental level. With the exception of antisocial characteristics, most symptomatology expressed by children will not be evident when they mature. However, the tendency toward maladjustment does continue. Maladjusted children are likely to become maladjusted adults. Thus, early identification of childhood problems, removal of causative agents, and treatment are very important. We are "building our case" about the value of child theory when it is used to correct causes of maladjustment. With this point well-emphasized, we will turn to a discussion of the causative factors in childhood maladjustment.

Etiology of Childhood Maladjustment

Genetics

Research is being conducted to ascertain the degree to which childhood maladjustment is genetically based. Evidence from concordance studies (in which emotional disturbance among twins and siblings reared together and separately is compared) suggests that some childhood emotional problems may be inherited. Chess and Hassibi (1978) summarize results of a number of concordance studies conducted about childhood schizophrenia. In sum, children with one schizophrenic parent have 8–10 times higher expectancies for becoming schizophrenic during their childhood. Siblings of schizophrenics have 6–7 times higher likelihood of becoming schizophrenic than siblings of non-schizophrenics. When children of schizophrenics are raised by non-schizophrenic guardians, their rate of acquiring schizophrenia remains similar to that as when raised by the schizophrenic parent. In contrast, children of non-schizophrenics adopted by schizophrenic parents do not show a higher rate of schizophrenia. Thus, development of schizophrenia seems more closely related to genetic disposition than to home environment.

Similarly convincing evidence has been collated about the development of manic-depressive psychosis. Concordance among identical child twins ranges from 50% (Harvald & Hauge, 1965) to 100% (Kallmann, 1953).

Researchers are attempting to understand what types of genetic messages are transmitted in cases of childhood schizophrenia and affective psychosis. An extensive field of research begun by Hill (1952) has suggested that brain wave patterns as evidenced in electroencephalograms are abnormal among some disturbed children. The irregular EEG pattern is particularly characteristic of about 50% of the children diagnosed as hyperactive (Chess & Hassibi, 1978). Differences in blood serum and amino acids have been noted in some studies comparing adult schizophrenics and non-schizophrenics. Interestingly, these studies have not been replicated successfully with children, again suggesting that the adult and child syndromes, though showing similar symptoms, are dynamically different (Goldfarb, 1970). Other experts suggest that genetic predisposition toward maladjustment is expressed through the endocrine and/or nervous system. To some degree, the sympathetic, rather than the parasympathetic, nervous system predominates in children with tenseness and impulsivity (Anthony, 1970).

Prenatal and Postnatal Factors

Certain constitutional factors created by prenatal and postnatal experiences have been linked with a variety of childhood emotional problems. Most of the prenatal studies of childhood maladjustment are retrospective, correlational ones; that is children with disturbance are identified, and their prenatal histories are investigated. The studies suggest that the pregnant mother's nutrition is correlated with infant intelligence (Harrell, Woodyard, & Gates, 1955). Severe malnutrition is associated with infant retardation. Commonly, we encounter infants who suffer from undernutrition and low birth weight and other more serious physiological problems because of maternal alcoholism or drug addiction. Fetal alcohol syndrome is discussed in Chapter 3. The relevance here is that these children manifest a variety of prenatal and postnatal symptoms that are detrimental to their well-being. Further, it is now known that the social adjustment of these children can be affected during the school years.

Maternal illnesses, especially during the first three months of pregnancy, also can affect the embryo's well-being. Viral diseases that are relatively innocuous among adults, such as measles and colds, can cause blindness and deafness. Bacterial infections also are transmitted, although in most bacterial diseases, the infection is transmitted rather than the bacteria spurring congenital malformation. The infant can be born with tuberculosis or syphilis or other bacterial illnesses transmitted through the infected mother's placenta.

Several perinatal factors also affect the neonate's well-being. Anoxia, lack of oxygen during birth, is associated with lower physiological reactivity scores and lower Stanford-Binet intelligence scores years later (Graham et al., 1961). Prolonged and complicated labor is associated with possible later retardation, behavioral disorders, and reading problems (Pasamanick & Knobloch, 1966). Prematurity also constitutes a factor that results in infants being grouped as high-risk for a variety of medical and psychological disturbances (Chess & Hassibi, 1978).

A number of postnatal factors, such as infections of the central nervous system, brain trauma, and malnutrition, affect the child's constitutional well-being.

We have described the physical effects of a number of prenatal and postnatal factors. Although the effect of these factors appears first to be physical, these toxic factors are transformed easily and often to temperament and personal disturbances. If the child's constitution is disturbed, her or his ability to develop effective social relationships may be disturbed.

Family Factors

A number of family factors may be causative in childhood maladjustment. Loss of a parent has been associated with childhood disturbance. When children under 2 are separated from a primary caretaker, they grieve. The degree of reversibility of the despair depends upon a number of factors: whether the separation is permanent or temporary, duration and frequency of separation, and the nature of substitute care (Freedman, Kaplan, & Sadock, 1976). As will be explored in Chapter 3, it is now well-documented that the infant needs a firm attachment to a primary caretaker. Bonding to other significant adults also is important for the overall psychological well-being of the child. The intensity and quality of the bond also is critical (Bowlby, 1969), since these variables communicate to the child the extent to which the child is loved and wanted by parents and other adults.

As mentioned previously, separation or divorce has complex effects on the child. Children of poverty are at risk for maladjustment. In these cases, maladjustment may occur because of the family dysfunction and/or because of nonnurturing environmental conditions that are incurred following divorce or as a result of poverty. Also, parents' physical illnesses have been associated with childhood delinquency (Glueck & Glueck, 1952).

Clearly, pathology in the parent–child interaction can stimulate maladjustment. Much research has been conducted to ascertain the relationship between parents' emotional problems and those of their children, barring genetic influences. Several noncontrolled studies report that mothers with negative feelings toward themselves have children who are frequently ill, withdrawn, and passive (Anthony, 1958; Lewis, 1954). Wolking, Quast, and Lawton (1966) administered the Minnesota Multiphasic Personality Inventory (MMPI) to parents of children in six diagnostic groups. They reported elevations on several MMPI scales for parents of clinical children as compared to controls, but parental profiles and childhood disorders did not match on any dimension. We are becoming increasingly aware of how a child may be caught in a web of a pathological family system. The child's maladjustment may be the only way to cope within a disturbed world. Thus, too much, too little or inconsistent child rearing have been linked to childhood maladjustment.

In general, it does seem that deviance in the family is associated with higher rates of childhood maladjustment. Children with behavioral disorders have three to four times greater probability of becoming psychiatric patients as adults, although the pathognomic patterns are discontinuous (Goldfarb, 1970; Mellsop, 1972). Perhaps you know someone who was raised in a very pathological family environment, yet seems well-adjusted. Although the psychosocial stresses we have listed correlate strongly with childhood maladjustment, many children with great environmental liabilities do not become disturbed. Child specialists puzzle how that could happen. Do these children have more adaptive temperaments and constitutions? Are they receiving ameliorative support elsewhere? Clearly, the relationship between psychosocial stress and childhood maladjustment is not fully understood. The types of family deviance and their effects are voluminous. There are many theories about the effects, but few documented, controlled studies which show how childhood rearing practices sculpture the behavior and temperament of a given child.

In reviewing the finding on etiology, we see that the child's biology and the physical and social environment can be menacing forces. In most cases, maladjustment is probably an interaction of self and environmental factors. Some say stress alone causes maladjustment (Axline, 1969). Others rely on biological explanations (Bender, 1947). Most believe that stress is a trigger that releases constitutional vulnerability (Selye, 1950). As our ability to diagnose childhood disorders is refined, and with more controlled, objective studies, perhaps we may move toward a resolution on this critical issue. This point and the points previously made in this chapter are summarized on the next page.

Summary

Our review of the statistics concerning the status of children reveals some hopeful and some alarming findings. The decreasing birth rate allows for existing services to reach more children than earlier, and we can expect this trend to continue. However, gains have not been uniform. A large number of female-headed, ethnic minority, and inner-city families are locked into poverty, and their children are particularly vulnerable to emotional problems. The data concerning childhood maladjustment create as many questions as answers. About 655,000 children under 18 years of age are admitted to organized mental health facilities (U.S. Department of Health & Human Services, 1980); admission for children has not decreased in the last 20 years as it has for adult clients. Are children getting "more disturbed" or are more children being served? Long-term findings suggest that many children show pathological symptoms during some period of their growing up. We must ask: is it typical for children to show signs of serious disturbances during some period of their childhood? Or, are there a tremendous number of troubled children, many of whom are not receiving therapeutic assistance? Will the symptoms dissipate in time without intervention? Our review of epidemiological studies indicates that some symptoms carry on into adulthood.

Yet, in other cases symptoms dissipate, but the tendency toward maladjustment remains. What exactly is the relationship between the problems of childhood and adult symptomatology? What particular childhood issues has therapy been effective in ameliorating? A major issue is to determine which child welfare strategies are associated with long-term gains for particular problems. In order to assess these issues, we need a system of classification of childhood disorders. We have attempted to demonstrate that our assessments are improving but yet subject to many fallibilities.

It follows that since we are not yet completely clear on the nature and causes of childhood problems, it is extremely difficult to assess the effectiveness of various treatment modalities. At times it appears that we are trying to evaluate the effectiveness of procedures upon phenomena that have not been well identified. A difficult task indeed! The reader is asked to keep these limitations in mind in later chapters of this text. We will present empirical support for our assertions when data exist and attempt to point out when the data are lacking. We also will summarize theoretical, descriptive, and expository writings that hold promise for treatment. It is important to carefully evaluate the validity of these untested premises in work with children.

Chapter 2
Children in Historical Perspective

Children of yesterday
Heirs of tomorrow
What are you weaving?
Labor and sorrow?
Look to the looms again,
Faster and faster,
Fly the great shuttles,
Prepared by the Master.
Life's in the loom
Room for it—room!

Mary Artemisia Lathbury, "Sons of Hope,"
Stanza One, 1841-1913

Concept of Children as Miniature Adults

The idea of childhood as a distinct developmental stage has not always existed. In ancient times, for example, children were regarded as chattel whose primary purpose in life was to be of help to their parents. To achieve this purpose, the children were required from early ages to assist their parents in the fields or wherever else their services were required (Popple & Leighninger, 1996). Instead of trying to understand the child and allowing the child to develop naturally, ancient people attempted to mold each child according to their standards of what a child should be and what the child should know as adolescence approached. Thus, children in Sparta were molded to become soldiers; in other cultures, they were trained to become cultivators of the soil. The concept of childhood did not really exist—children were seen and treated as miniature adults (Kadushin, 1980). The little education provided was in preparation for the responsibilities that the child would assume at maturity.

In many societies, it was common practice for the father to have absolute authority in the decision of whether a newborn infant should live or die. Upon birth the newborn was inspected for physical deformities and for its sex. If the newborn was in any way deformed or, often, simply female, the father could decree that the infant should be put to death or abandoned to die from exposure to the elements. Continuing through medieval times, childhood was not conceived of as a distinct developmental phase. Children were seldom the subject matter of literature or art. As soon as children abandoned swaddling clothes, they were dressed like the adults of their class and treated as little adults. As youths, they were often forced to work at hard labor.

Often by age seven or eight, children were apprenticed to other families, perhaps never to live with their parents again. The family transmitted name and property; it was not a source of human sensitivity. The importance of the family as an institution is a recent social change. The family today is the primary if not sole social institution for children. This change is closely linked to the life expectancy of children.

In the few paintings depicting children in medieval times, the youngsters were often portrayed as emaciated or dead. Aries (1962) explains that children in the Middle Ages were cared for, but so many died that parents were hesitant to commit their attention and love to them. Infanticide and exposure were common practices for almost all cultures through history. Deformed, sickly, retarded children, or twins were exposed to the weather, thrown in freezing rivers, or strangled. The parents' right to kill their children existed in Europe until the 19th century (Radbill, 1980). The lack of public health and medical knowledge resulted in a very high infant mortality rate. For example, in the late 1600s, 59% of the children born in London died before age five, while 64% died before age 10. Because of limited prenatal and perinatal care, many infants were born with significant deformities (Hewett& Forness, 1977), contracted infectious diseases, or fell victims to a wide variety of fatal accidents before age five. To think of children as full beings with a range of feelings and personality would make parents more alert to their children's fragileness and more fearful of their likely death. Thus, children were cherished by their parents at whim or according to economic dictates (Popple & Leighninger, 1996).

Emergence of the Concept of Childhood as Unique

With the advent of the 17th century, the idea of childhood as a special period in which children have unique psychological, educational, and physical needs, came to hold influence. Children became the center of paintings and were dressed in special, more versatile clothing. At this time Johann Amos Comenius, a famous Slavic educational reformer, published *Orbis Pictus*, or the *World in Pictures*, which was the first children's reading material accompanied by pictures. The pictures enhanced children's interest in and understanding of the book. Education was beginning to be related to children's abilities (Hurlock, 1942). The emerging sensitivity to children's needs and abilities increased in vigor in the 18th century. For example, Jean Jacques Rousseau of France, in his now classic *Emile*, published in 1762, described at length the application of his ideal of political freedom to the education of the child. Other notable individuals whose interests in children paved the way for a more humanistic understanding of childhood included the Swiss Pestalozzi and the German physician Tiedemann. Pestalozzi in 1744 published the first scientific record of the development of a young child (Hurlock, 1942). The work based on observations of Pestalozzi's own child was followed by a similar study by Tiedemann in 1787. These two studies were the forerunners of the biographical studies of children which became so popular in the following century (Hurlock, 1942).

Emergence of Children's Services

Study of Children

The first half of the 19th century was marked by little advance in the study of children, but during the latter part of the century a succession of baby biographies increased our knowledge about childhood. For instance, Charles Darwin published his *Biographical Sketch of an Infant* in 1877, while Wilhelm Preyer wrote *The Mind of the Child* in 1882. Both of these books served as models for observational studies of children as well as for the experimental approach to the investigation of developmental processes in children. So influential was Preyer's book

that he is often called the "father of child psychology." Preyer's diary was important because it replaced general observations and anecdotes found in other diaries
with careful measurements of behavior—beginning with the development of
reflexes from birth on.

Another important contributor in the last part of the 19th century was G.
Stanley Hall of the United States. Hall studied extensively the physical and mental
capabilities of children, irrespective of educational issues. Hall aroused popular
interest in the child and is often referred to as the "father of the child study
movement" (Hurlock, 1942).

In 1893, at the time of the International conference on Education held at the
Chicago World's Fair, Hall organized the National Association for the Study of
Children, the first child study society in the United States. In the following year,
a Department of Child Study was formed as apart of the National Education
Association. The child study society movement quickly spread across the nation
as well as abroad with groups being formed in England in 1894, Poland in 1897,
Germany in 1899, and France in 1901. So much interest was generated in this
movement that in 1906 the First International Congress of Child Study was held
in Berlin (Hurlock, 1942).

Child Welfare Programs

Children were first addressed as a separate group in the Elizabethan Poor Laws
of 1601 in England. Orphans, poor and troubled youth were placed in Almshouses
and thus institutionalized. Over the next 150 years the terrible conditions and
harm children suffered while in the poorhouses resulted in the development of
specialized children homes and a move toward deinstitutionalization in the last
quarter of the 19th Century.

During this time, emphasis on the welfare of the child is indicated through
the formation of the Society for the Prevention of Cruelty to Children in 1875;
the establishment of the first settlement house for children in 1887 in New York
City; and the appearance of juvenile courts in Denver, Boston, Chicago, and New
York between 1898 and 1900 (Hurlock, 1942).

In the 1850s, Charles Loring Brace founded the Children's Aid Society to
help the 10,000 to 50,000 homeless children wandering the streets of New York
(Trattner, 1994). The children were "farmed out" to rural families in New York
state and the western frontier. This program was based on the theory that a change

in environment and removal from a poorly functioning family would meet the child's needs (Zuckerman, 1983). Unfortunately, these children were often abused and as many as 60 percent of their placements failed (Popple and Leighninger, 1996).

> Little orphan Annie's come to our house to stay,
> To wash the cups and saucers up, an'
> brush the crumbs away,
> An' shoo the chickens off the porch, an'
> dust the hearth, an sweep,
> An' make the fire, and bake the bread,
> An' earn her board and keep.
>
> James Whitcomb Riley

The development of the concept of protective services for children culminated with the White House Conference on dependent Children in 1909 and the formation of the U.S. Children's Bureau in 1912. The welfare of the child was largely view as health related issues until the 1935 passage of the Social Security Act which through title IV B required services and income support for dependent children. This made preventing and treating abused and neglected children the responsibility of the federal government through the states.

Yet again in reality children were not well served. An American Humane Association survey covering the 1950 and 60s found the majority of services to children were financial in nature and not treatment oriented. Furthermore what services and counseling children received were inconsistent and unorganized. Thus, Child abuse and neglect was "rediscovered" in the late 1960s and early 1970s A number of important pieces of legislation were passed and the term, "battered child syndrome" was first used by Dr. Kempe.

In 1972 title XX was implemented providing millions of dollars for true children services through the states with one, of five goals, the goal of preventing institutionalization of children. The same year National Center for the Prevention and Treatment of Child Abuse and Neglect was established. A dramatic and ever increasing number of reports of child abused began shortly after the 1974 passage of the Federal Child Abuse Prevention and Treatment Act. States were required to have mandatory reporting of child abuse, not only by professionals but by all citizens. Funds were also made available to develop treatment programs and to do research.

The increase in reporting resulted in an increase of out of home placements and an enormous use of foster care. Children became lost in foster care and were many times "in limbo" for the formative years of their lives. States under federal programs were actually financially rewarded for placing children in out of home placements. This coupled with the increased number of abuse referrals resulted in the number of children placed going from 258,000 in 1960 to almost 500,000 in the early 1980s (Sallee, 1991). The advocacy groups successfully sued states for the system abuses of children not placed in permanent homes in a timely fashion resulting in Federal Court orders.

The passage of the Adoption Assistance and Child Welfare Act in 1980 and implemented as title IV E is meant to insure permanency for abused and neglected children by returning them to their homes or placing them for adoption. The Act also provides funding for case management and training but not for treatment. From 1980 to 1987 the number of children in care dropped back down to 250,000 but then began to climb back above the 500,000 level by 1993.

Finally, in 1993 President Clinton signed the Family Preservation Act which provides approximately $1 billion over five years to states to implement programs to work with abused and neglected children in their own families, thus avoiding placement all together. Many veteran child welfare workers know the number one predictor of whether or not a child will enter the out of home system is, if they have already been in foster care.

Services addressing children's well being are still focused primary on changing their parent's behavior or the child's environment and less on the actual treatment of the child's emotions and social development or education. And there are still today policy makers who want to return to the orphanage system for children from poor families. This even though there is twice as many cases of child abuse in institutions than in foster care (Popple & Leighninger, 1996)!

Treatment of Children

From the work of Dorothea Dix 17 state legislatures, the U.S. Congress and other counties were made aware of the deplorable conditions children lived in institutions in the mid 1800s (Haynes & Holmes, 1994). Along with a commitment to the study of normal children, programs emerged forth study of maladjusted children. In 1896 Witmer established the Psychological Clinic at the University of Pennsylvania which was devoted to assisting children who were having problems at school or with their families. In the same year, the Psychiatric Institute was founded in New York City with the same purpose of counseling children who were having adjustment problems. The basic structure of these early clinics has continued until today so that presently there are child guidance clinics in almost every community in the United States (Kanner, 1962a).

The 20th century has sometimes been called the "Century of the Child". More serious study about the child has been completed in this century than in the entire history of the world. Today, we have children's books, children's movies, children's television programs, and special games and toys for youth. Children usually have their own bedrooms, parks, zoos, schools, and organized activities. Clearly, children are considered unique in virtually every country of the world today. As proof of this, the International Year of the Child held in 1979 was observed in every country of the world through meetings devoted to special problems of children. Our interest in children has resulted in a marked improvement in how children are perceived by adults and in the love and attention they receive from parents.

A Complex World

Despite the concern for children that exists today, children still face a wide variety of problems in our technological society. Compared to the past, it looks as though children "never had it so good." Nonetheless, it appears that our concept of childhood is about to change again because of the effects of technology. The child of today plays few meaningful roles in society. The dependency of childhood and adolescence is often extended into the early twenties because youth are nonskilled enough to work in a technological society that demands a high degree of educational sophistication. How are youth to acquire skills to compete in a society where scientific knowledge doubles in less than 10 years? What can the person hope to learn that will last? Thus, in a technological society, childhood and adolescence are extended, but meaningful values are not attached to this new concept of youth.

Feelings of the transience and unsettledness in life are also characteristic of a technological society and are exacerbated by the media. "Fragmentation of the family and kinship group and alienation and anomie are the bitter fruits of a highly individualistic, mobile, and technically oriented civilization" (Specht,

1981, p.9). Through the slick sophistication and the violence and sex on television, children learn a superficial set of values without intellectual understanding and physical maturity to fully integrate what they emulate. Further, parents and teachers often feel lost to define future directions for children (Fullmer & Bernard, 1972). The solution exercised by many youths is to try to "get it now." The child "plays at being big because he is not given an opportunity to be a small partner in a big world" (Erikson, 1963, p. 238).

Children have not had an easy time through most of history (Popple & Lieghninger, 1996). Although time has brought increasing awareness about the state of childhood, growing up continues to be a difficult process. The child coming to the therapist today brings stress unique to her or his developmental stage and unique to our technological age. Some suggest that more children are disturbed today than in previous times because life in a technological age is so stressful and without meaningful roles for children. In order to explore this thesis, it is helpful to review how emotionally disturbed children have been viewed throughout history.

Conceptions of Childhood Problems

Early Explanations of Maladjustment

Given the lack of interest in childhood and the fact that children over seven were considered adults, it is not surprising that there is a dearth of information concerning childhood maladjustment before the 18th century. Shortly before the French and American Revolutions, new doctrines concerning the rights of individuals spurred humanitarian reforms. The mentally disturbed were considered physically ill and deserving of humane treatment. Even so, it was assumed that maladjustment represented underlying physical illness. Attention focused upon observable physical handicaps, and children's subjective feelings were little understood (Hewitt& Forness, 1977). It was believed that the best one could do was to teach the maladjusted child to control his physically based maladjustment with moral integrity. Kanner (1962a, p. 97), using biographical material, describes the case of a seven-year-old child by the name of Emerentia who in 1713 was taken to the local minister to cure her behavioral maladjustment. Let us read the case of Emerentia.

Case 2.1   The Case of Emerentia

This 7-year-old girl, the offspring of an aristocratic family, whose father remarried after an unhappy first matrimony, offended her "noble and Godfearing" stepmother by her peculiar behavior. Worst of all, she would not join in the prayers and was panic-stricken when taken to the black robed preacher in the dark and gloomy chapel. She avoided contact with people by hiding in closets or running away from home. The local physician had nothing to offer beyond declaring that she might be insane. She was placed in the custody of a minister known for his rigid orthodoxy. The minister, who saw in her ways the machinations of a "baneful and infernal" power, used a number of would-be therapeutic devices. He laid her on a bench and beat her with a-cat-o-nine-tails. He locked her in a dark pantry. He subjected her to a period of starvation. He clothed her in a frock of burlap. Under these circumstances, the child did not last long. She died after a few months, and everybody was relieved. The minister was amply rewarded for his efforts by Emerentia's parents.

Beyond Moral Intentions

Although the case of Emerentia may be extreme, it does show the callousness involved in caring for children who went against the wishes of their parents. With increasing interest in the 1800s in human rights and scientific rigor, methods for assisting maladjusted children besides religious and moral training were sought. A turning point was the treatment of the "Wild Boy of Aveyron" by one of Pinel's pupils, Jean Itard. Pinel (the great reformer of French mental institutions in the 1700s) found a totally unsocialized and nonverbal boy believed to have been raised by wolves. Itard, greatly influenced by his teacher's humanitarian ideals, believed he could help the boy. Although it was later believed that the Wild Boy was severely retarded rather than raised by animals, Itard showed that with consistent attention over several years, the child could learn basic skills and rudimentary language (Alexander & Selesnick, 1966). Thus, Itard demonstrated that with patience, teaching, and persistence, one could systematically affect a child's behavior.

In the 1800s children's behavioral problems were considered to be caused by physical malfunctions, and rational ways of helping children modify their maladjusted behavior were not yet developed. As a whole, the primary form of treatment continued to be punitive. Kanner (1962b), for instance, summarizes an 1838 case study by Esquirol. To teach a 7-year old to stop her temper tantrums and excessive masturbation and to punish her for saying she wanted her mother to die, the child was told that a flour-water mixture was arsenic, and she was forced to swallow it. Eventually, she was sent to a convent and apprenticed to a jewelry cutter. The treatment was considered a success as the parents were pleased to find that their daughter became submissive and attended church regularly on Sunday.

By the mid 1800s, the punitive orientation to treatment was muted by a more humanitarian appreciation of the child. The relationship between the child rearing and child development was given greater consideration. For example, in 1841 Descuret wrote of a boy who lived with a nurse during his first two years of life. Descuret puzzled that the boy became pale, refused to eat, and did not respond to adults when returned to his natural parents. Eventually, Descuret recommended that the nurse be brought to the home, at which point the child seemed to recover immediately. Once recovered, he was gradually separated from the nurse, first for a few hours, then for an entire day, followed by a week, until finally the child adjusted to the absence of the nurse (Kanner, 1962b). As Kanner (1962b) notes, this example marks the era when explanations for maladjusted behavior began to be sought on other than theological or moralistic grounds.

By 1880, several texts on childhood insanity were authored in Germany, France, Ireland, and Great Britain. In each text, the disorders were described as irreversible, the product of heredity, degeneracy, parasites, masturbation, or overwork (Kanner, 1962b). Despite this general pessimism about the long-term outcome for maladjusted children, a psychodynamic orientation was emerging. The effects of separation, fear, and deprivation were noted, although systematic conceptualization about these factors would wait another 20 years. Interest in the classification of childhood disorders also emerged in the mid 1800s. In the text *Pathology of the Mind*, Maudsley (1800) devoted a chapter to classification of childhood psychosis, attempting to correlate symptomatology with developmental status. Efforts were made to distinguish emotional disturbance and mental retardation. Seguin, a student of Itard, proposed guidelines for systematically identifying and curing retardation through practical education. Seguin brought his ideas to the United States in the late 1800s and was responsible for establishing a number of centers to assist in the education of the mentally retarded (Hewitt & Forness, 1977).

The stage was set by the late 1800s for important developments in child care. Infant and child mortality rates decreased significantly. Adults were more committed to aiding children in their overall development. Scientists looked for logical explanations of human behavior. Understanding of childhood disorders would now mushroom in three main directions: (1) the development of systematic theories of child psychology, (2) the design of special treatment facilities for children, and (3) the application of principles of child behavior to education.

Development of Techniques for Child Therapy

Psychoanalytic Approach.   Some sophisticated writing on child psychology began to emerge in the late 1800s, as indicated earlier. In 1887, Frank Emminghaus published a systematic treatise on child psychiatry. The case histories of their children's development by Darwin and Preyer influenced later theorists, especially Sigmund Freud, who published his systematic theory of infantile sexuality in 1905. Freud did not conduct therapy with children, but in 1908, he directed a father through letters to treat his son, "Little Hans," for horse phobia (Freud, 1928). As you are most certainly aware, voluminous publications from case reports to texts were stimulated by Freud's work. G. Stanley Hall stressed the importance of studying normal development in order to understand childhood maladjustment. He founded the *Pedagogical Seminary* in 1891, a journal devoted to the study of typical childhood behavior. Beginning his career under Hall, Gesell published the first comprehensive outline of normal child development in 1925 (Alexander &Selesnick, 1966).

By the second decade of this century, a number of theorists proposed methods of child treatment based upon psychodynamic suppositions about the causes of their emotional stress. Leo Kanner, generally viewed as the "father of child psychiatry," was instrumental in identifying various syndromes of maladjustment and treatments for those disorders. He also closely studied the history of the treatment of emotionally disturbed children. Hug Hellmith, a Viennese psychoanalyst, published a systematic theory for treating children in 1919. In the 1920s, Melanie Klein greatly influenced the direction of child therapy by presenting a systematic play therapy approach. She pointed out that infants feel a range of emotions from anger to joy and that the mother becomes the primary object of support and hostility. She also emphasized that it was not the child's daily routine, but rather the child's subjective perception of reality, that caused emotional disturbance. Klein maintained a strict analytic view advocating direct interpretation of the unconscious experiences of the child. In the 1930s, Anna Freud developed a theory of child therapy that veered from the strict analytic stance advanced by her father. In numerous writings, she specified ways in which child and adult analysis should differ. Shortly afterward, David Levy and Frederick Allen introduced "relationship therapy" with children. They recommended that the therapist become an ally of the child, assuming a permissive attitude. In structured play, the child was encouraged to reenact specific situations believed to be traumatic. Thus, much emphasis was placed upon appropriate nurturing of the child. As we shall see, a number of theories for child therapy have been advanced since these early writings. Some of the theories are based upon principles very similar to those proposed by the early child therapists, while others are antithetical to the initial approaches to child therapy. We will note in later chapters how few of these approaches have been well-documented.

Behavioristic Approach.   An approach to child therapy quite different from that proposed by Freud and other analytically oriented child therapists was the behaviorally oriented work of John B. Watson, who is sometimes called the "father of behaviorism." Beginning in 1917, Watson devised a series of new experimental techniques for studying children. One of these techniques was conditioning reflexive behavior, and Watson demonstrated that a fear response could be conditioned in a child. At the initiation of Watson's experiment a child, known as "Little Albert," was a normal, healthy child of nine months with no fear of animals. Watson allowed "Little Albert" to play with a white furry rat. Once it was established that the child demonstrated no fear of the rat, a loud gong was sounded when Albert approached the rat. The loud sound elicited a startled response in the child, who began to cry. After a few pairings of the loud sound (Unconditioned Stimulus) and the rat (Conditioned Stimulus), the child would cry (Conditioned Response). This conditioned fear response generalized to other furry animals and objects. On the basis of this finding, Watson argued that all phobias are conditioned in the same fashion as Albert learned fear of the rat. Thus, Watson proposed that phobias and other maladjusted behaviors were due to conditioning, not to the presence of underlying internal conflicts and repression as put forth by Freud.

A student of Watson's, Mary Cover Jones, also developed a variety of methods for eliminating children's fears based upon conditioning principles (Jones, 1926). Later, Mowrer and Mowrer (1938) described the treatment of bed wetting by conditioning techniques. From this beginning, the behavioral modification techniques advanced by Skinner (1938) and Bandura (1969, 1977) became commonplace.

Today, a wide variety of behavioral therapies are available for the treatment of maladjustments in children (Fischer &Gochros, 1975). Behavioral modification techniques have been shown to be effective in eliminating childhood fears, school-related behavioral problems, and a host of other problems. Possibly the greatest use of behavioral approaches is with mentally retarded and autistic children. We will discuss the behavioral treatment approach in more detail in Chapter 5.

Medical Approach.   A third approach to child treatment that evolved at the turn of the century was medically oriented. In the 1940s, Lauretta Bender emphasized the importance of the child's biological nature. She stressed the physiological basis of maladjustment and recommended minimal insight therapy. She relied heavily on drug treatment and electroshock therapy (Chess& Hassibi, 1978).

Child Guidance Clinics.   Concomitant with the interest shown in therapeutic work with children in the early 1900s was the establishment of special treatment facilities for children with behavioral problems. In 1909, the National Committee for Mental Hygiene established by Clifford Beers, Adolph Meyers, and William James launched the "Child Guidance Movement." The purpose of the Child Guidance Movement was to establish special clinics for children in which psychiatrists, psychologists, and social service personnel worked as a team to help children and their parents (Kanner, 1962b). At the same time in Chicago, a philanthropist by the name of Mrs. W. F. Drummer commissioned Dr. William Healy, a gynecologist and general practitioner, to study the causes and treatment of delinquency. Healy published a text on the **Individual Delinquent** and, with Drummer's continued financial support, established the first Institute for Juvenile Research (Freedman, Kaplan & Sadock, 1976). Delinquents were not considered "bad" by Healy but rather as wayward youths. Under Healy's guidance, the protective care for delinquents was to continue for several decades.

Special guidance centers for assisting normal children with everyday kinds of problems also emerged in the early 1900s. For instance, Frank Parsons began steering a vocational guidance movement to help match children with careers (Dimick &Huff, 1970). From the turn of the century to the mid 1940s, the child guidance clinics grew in number (Chess & Hassibi, 1978; Dimick & Huff, 1970). Some of the more important clinics and their theoretical thrusts are summarized as follows:

- The Yale clinic of Child Development was established by Arnold Gesell in 1911 to study the stages of normal development.

- Vocational guidance clinics were established by Parsons in Boston in 1908 and shortly thereafter by Eli Weaver in New York public schools.

- The Judge Baker Guidance Center in Boston was established in 1917 under Healy's directorship to assist delinquent youths.

- The Phipps Clinic in Baltimore was founded in 1913 and was headed by Adolph Meyers to provide outpatient treatment for youngsters. At this clinic, Watson carried out his study of fear conditioning in "Little Albert."

- In 1937, a special adolescent unit was established at Bellevue Hospital in New York, setting the standard for inpatient child care.

- After World War II, inpatient care for children was expanded to a number of hospitals. Establishment of these inpatient facilities was spurred by an outbreak of encephalitis lethargia, which resulted in a number of behavioral disorders among infected children.

The growth of the child guidance clinics seemed to terminate around mid-century. Kanner (1962a) reported that a minimum of 500 centers was functioning in 1930; a 1960 survey (Freedman, Kaplan, &Sadock, 1976) identified fewer than 300 clinics. Perhaps the clinics attempted to do too much and failed in their own and others' expectations. Clearly, the vocational guidance centers were negatively influenced by the Depression. Also, the clinics may have become places for dumping the unwanted and profoundly disturbed children of a community. The movement could also have been curbed by shocking exposes such as that of the President's Committee on Mental Health in 1960, which documented extremely dehumanizing conditions in a number of residential treatment institutions (Hewin & Forness, 1977). Nevertheless, there is little doubt that history will credit the early Child guidance Clinic Movement for providing leadership in the care and treatment of the whole child from a perspective that the child thinks and feels in ways different from adults.

Today, the Child Clinic Movement has been subsumed in some respects into larger enterprises such as the growth of community mental health centers which appeared after 1963 and continue to the present.

Individual Differences and Education. The relationship between cognitive and emotional functioning continued to perplex the child experts. Beginning in the 1890s, Alfred Binet, working in Paris, became concerned with ways of assessing the intellectual level of children thought to be retarded or slow learners. At the urging of the minister of public instruction, Binet, along with Simon, a French psychiatrist, assembled a test consisting of 30 tasks ranging from the ability to follow a moving, lighted match to naming of simple objects, repeating sentences, arranging objects by weight, and using three words in a sentence. The test also required the child to complete simple arithmetic problems and to define abstract words such as "character" and "reputation." The first version of the Binet test appeared in 1905 and was subsequently revised in 1908. Using the test, Binet was able to differentiate between "bright" and "dull" children in about one hour per child. The Binet method proved to be more economical, efficient, and objective than previous methods used to assess intellectual development. The scale was introduced into the U.S. in 1910 by Goddard who was at that time administering the Vineland Training School for the retarded in New Jersey. Soon thereafter, Louis Terman of Stanford University developed an American version of Binet's scale. This test became available for widespread use in 1916 and is known as the Stanford Binet Intelligence Test. The test was useful for children as young as three years and extended through adulthood. The publication of the Stanford Binet and other tests of intelligence spurred much research on intelligence because the tests promised objectivity and the potential for studying facets of the child's intellectual growth and adaptation to the environment.

Out of the recognition of individual differences in intelligence grew a movement for individualized instruction. John Dewey stressed that children learn through self-discovery and urged that educational curriculum be organized to allow children to learn through that method. Further, many states enacted legislation to promote the education of the retarded and other handicapped individuals. In Europe a movement known as Heidpadagojik arose, the intent of which was to make teachers aware of the problems and feelings of their pupils. The relationship between school and family was also recognized. In the 1920s, a visiting teacher program was initiated in which 205 teachers in 34 states visited homes to secure school-family cooperation (Kanner, 1962a).

With the recognition that the proper education of a child requires an understanding of child psychology, the Child guidance Movement, which was weakened in the Depression, was renewed within the schools. School counselors served largely an educational/vocational role in the 1930s and 1940s. Their function of guiding adolescents toward wise career choices was expanded after the 1950 launching of Sputnik. Mention of elementary school counselors began in the 1940s, but it was not until the 1960s that many counselors were trained and placed in the elementary schools. With rapid technological changes occurring in our society, school counselors have become less concerned with matching jobs and student personalities. Counselors' and school social workers' roles have now expanded to include consulting with teachers and parents, coordinating services, and counseling with students (Dimick & Huff, 1970). They increasingly find themselves needing to know about patterns of child maladjustment and methods of short-term treatment.

Summary

We have seen that tin earlier times, infanticide and cruel treatment of children were common. We have come to understand that childhood is a special state. Exploitation of children has diminished. Humane treatment and education has greatly expanded. Yet, we also know that the child in today's technological age has few meaningful roles to play and has the stress of rapid change to adapt to. How much has the child's lot improved?

The development of the concept of childhood, shifts in economic, political, and social institutions, and the solution of protective services to children have all helped to place an emphasis on children in our society. The treatment of children is part of the larger human service system. Early concepts of treatment involved physical abuse and neglect. Only within the last hundred years have we developed scientific explanations of child maladjustment. By the 1950s, countless theories of child therapy evolved, but few were well documented, and some are not based upon sound developmental principles. Yet, "in the midst of wrangling over what is or is not valued therapy or good therapy or properly trained and functioning therapists, the reforms of Dorothea Dix and those who came before and after her seem at times to melt away in the face of continuing wasting away of countless mentally ill in poorly equipped and badly cared for mental hospitals and other facilities" (Howells, 1975, p. 467). The need for sound therapeutic techniques still exists despite our increased understanding of children.

In subsequent chapters, we will present evidence about etiological factors associated with specific syndromes, and you will learn of the complexity of these causative agents. Some practitioners suggest a singular treatment approach for all kinds of childhood disorders. It is important to ask whether these holistic approaches will hold up to the test of time. When etiology is oversimplified, the suggested treatment that follows may look, sublimely logical but be harmful to children by not recognizing the vicissitude of forces impinging upon their lives.

In order to understand the complexity of forces acting upon children, we now look at some of the findings from the field of developmental psychology that are of practical relevance to the practitioner. Later we will address the means of treating and researching childhood problems found in childwelfare practice.

Chapter 3
Relevant Developmental Issues

At one time it was believed that children reacted passively to events around them. Today, we know differently. The infant from birth possesses many modes of functioning. These include reflexes and other motoric responses, sensory thresholds, perceptual abilities, and affective and cognitive response styles that enable the very young child to actively approach, avoid, select, and organize the stimulation around the child. These same modes of functioning permit the child to act upon the environment. At birth the infant's responses are innately determined, but these are quickly altered through experience and learning.

This chapter overviews the developmental issues of relevance to child theory and practice from birth through adolescence. One chapter is not enough to communicate in detail all aspects of child development, so the processes deemed essential for the child welfare practitioner will be discussed. Other developmental processes will be discussed to clarify or facilitate insight into childhood maladjustment and treatment approaches.

Through out our study of child develop it is important to recognize and respect developmental diversity (Schriver, 1995). A child's development must always be taken in context. Culture, environment and conditions help us individualize each child in relationship to the normed developmental task or level. One dimensional understanding of a child's development may result in an inaccurate assessment and ineffective treatment.

Early in the 1900s, it became apparent it was necessary to understand normal development and process before one could identify and treat problem patterns. Child specialists once thought that after we identified normal development sequences, we would clearly understand the abnormal sequence. This has proven to be not true. The literature on developmental theory is, for the most part, separate from writings on child psychopathology and child clinical practice. This is an unfortunate circumstance. Children with behavioral problems can be better served by practitioners with expertise in developmental therapy who can translate research literature about children to the practical problem of treating children with problems.

Developmental Theory

Developmental theorists study how individuals change across time. Like other theorists, their work is rooted in the scientific study of behavior and seeks to understand a wide variety of questions concerning how the person changes from conception to death. The developmental theorists should be concerned with every aspect of development.

For the sake of convenience, we can summarize the activities of developmental theorists into three broad categories. The first of these has to do with the study of physical processes which include body changes and motor development. At one time, this area constituted a very active focus of study, and as a consequence we know much about the milestones of motor development in infants and children. The second category is cognitive and language development. This is an extremely important area in the study of child behavior, and we will have much to say about this in a later section of this chapter. This category includes all the mental processes that are used to gain knowledge or to become aware of the environment, such as perception, imagination, memory, judgment, morals, thinking, and, of course, language. The final category is psychosocial development. This area focuses upon personality and social development. Of particular interest here is the impact on the child of the parents and family members. Also of interest is the effect other individuals such as peers and teachers have on the child.

Although the work of developmental theorists may seem fragmented because, for example, they focus on the acquisition of a particular speech form by children of a certain age or on father–child relationships, there is agreement that development is holistic and that the child cannot be understood just from the examination of any single perspective. This is an important concept to understand since it implies that childhood behavioral maladjustments can be understood only when the total child and her or his environment are considered.

At one time, some developmental psychologists emphasized the inborn capacities and limitations of each person. This focus on "nature" or hereditary aspects contrasted with other psychologists who emphasized the importance of "nurture" or environmental factors, such as the influence of family, school, neighborhood, and culture on the child. This continuing debate over whether inherited or acquired traits are greater determinants of human behavior is called the nature–nurture controversy.

Most theorists today agree that both nature and nurture are essential to development and that the interaction between them is of crucial importance to the development of any individual. For example, most theorists believe that intelligence is determined by the interplay of heredity and such aspects of the social and physical environment as schooling and nutrition. Despite this usual acknowledgment of the interaction of nature and nurture on setting the limits of intelligence, some psychologists, such as Arthur Jensen (1969), maintain that one's genes are more important in determining intelligence than is one's environment. We all are acquainted with the heated debate that Jensen has created since he initially espoused his ideas in 1969 in the context of whether Head Start programs could elevate the school performance of African–American children.

Another area where we have seen the appearance of the nature–nurture controversy is in whether mental illness is genetically or environmentally determined. It is generally conceded today that some people are born with a predisposition toward schizophrenia or manic-depression. Evidence of the genetic predisposition to mental illness comes from studies of monozygotic twins (Cohen, Allen, Pollin,& Hrubec, 1972; Gottesman & Shields, 1972). If one twin becomes schizophrenic or manic-depressive, chances are (estimates range from 20% to 80%) that the other twin will have serious psychological problems too. On the other hand, the likelihood of dizygotic twins both becoming schizophrenic or manic-depressive is much lower than with monozygotic twins. In many cases, however, one identical twin is schizophrenic and the other is not mentally ill. Since monozygotic twins have identical genes and usually very similar environments, some specific, if hidden, environmental circumstances must have a large impact. The usual conclusion drawn from these studies is that genes make some people more vulnerable to mental illness than others, but personal experiences determine whether a person actually becomes mentally ill or not.

Another distinction that merits attention here is the one between maturation and learning. Maturation results from the aging process, while learning is produced by experience. Specifically, maturation is a series of autonomous internal processes that result from biochemical information transmitted via the individual's genes. The genetic mechanisms that control maturation determine the traits that typify a species and the sequence in which those traits emerge. Maturational effects are most clearly seen during childhood in the unfolding of motor abilities. Table 3.1 presents age norms for various motor skills. As can be seen from the Table, by about age 24 months, most children have mastered the essential motor skills that are required for effective functioning. The point that requires emphasizing is that maturation determined the sequence with which particular skills will appear, and this sequence usually is invariant. Thus, earlier skill development in a sequence is essential to the development of later skills (e.g., crawling usually precedes walking in infants).

Learning, in contrast, refers to changes within the individual that occur because of specific experiences. Some learning experiences are obvious; for example, a child acquiring the skill of reading with the help of a teacher who promises a gold star for good performance. Other examples of learning are less obvious, as in the efforts of an infant to walk by imitating others for the purpose

TABLE 3.1

Age Norms (in Months) for Motor Skills

Skill	When 50% of All Babies Master the Skill (in Months)	When 90% of All Babies Master the Skill (in Months)
Lifts head 90 degrees when lying on stomach	2.4	4.9
Rolls over	2.8	4.7
Sits propped up (head steady)	2.9	4.2
Sits without support	5.5	7.8
Stands holding on	5.8	10.0
Walks holding on	9.2	12.7
Stands momentarily	9.8	13.0
Stands alone well	11.5	13.9
Walks well	12.1	14.3
Walks backward	14.3	21.5
Walks up steps	17.0	22.0
Kicks ball forward	20.0	24.0

of obtaining a bright shiny object that cannot be reached by crawling. The essential thing to remember here is that learning requires experience with a problem, a teacher or model, and some degree of practice. Further, learning and maturation interact to determine when a learned response will first be observed in a child. Assisting a child to walk, although important, will not facilitate walking until a child is maturationally "ready" to walk, which requires that the child possess the muscular strength and coordination to put together all of the movements required in walking.

At one time theorists argued over which was more important—maturation or learning. As with the nature vs. nurture controversy, it is now generally conceded that both maturation and learning interact in development. The critical thing to note is that for a practitioner to be effective in understanding child behavior, he or she must have knowledge of both the genetic/maturational factors and the environmental/learning aspects of development. Both components interact to determine whether a child's behavior is appropriate for her or his age group. Further, the way in which treatment is oriented for children must take maturational/learning factors into consideration. This point will become clearer later when we discuss the topics of cognitive and language development.

Implications of Child Development for Practice

Anyone who works with children is aware of the importance of a developmental framework (Longres, 1995). A child may express one set of symptoms at one stage of development and entirely different symptoms at another developmental level. For example, at age five, an anxious child may experience night terrors; if the source of anxiety is not removed, the same child at age 13 may employ runaway behavior as a means of dealing with stress. Because of a child's biological disposition, personal stress may be greater at one developmental level than another. Thus, learning to walk may create significant stress for a frail child. Similarly, learning to keep a bed dry may create difficulties for other children with poor bladder control, especially if they sleep deeply and do not awaken easily. It is not clear whether there are upper time bounds, that is, "critical periods" for the development of skills so that if appropriate stimulus conditions are not provided within that time frame, the skill will never evolve. Perhaps there are critical periods for the acquisition of some skills (such as language) and not others (such as learning to swim). There do appear to be lower limits determined by central nervous system maturation for the age appearance of each skill. Thus, no amount of verbal stimulation leads to speech within the first half year of life. The early verbal stimulation plays a role in preparing the ground for later language acquisition, but the acquisition must await neurological development (Lenneberg, 1967).

Thus, syndromes of child maladjustment are shaped by the age and stage of the child and the equilibrium between the child's growing needs and the environmental potential for satisfaction of these needs. The effective child practitioner must keep in mind an understanding of the major stages in language, cognitive, and social development. It is essential that the therapist keep note of the restrictions imposed by age on the child in each of these realms. Knowing these limitations, the practitioner can be more effective in intervening with children and families.

Language Development

During the early years following infancy, all normal children, and even many youngsters with below normal intelligence, master the language spoken around them. One might infer that language is a simple system, or pattern of elements, that is easily analyzed and explained. In fact, on examination, language proves highly complex, indeed so intricate that the area of language acquisition has begun to generate much interest among developmental theorists. Still, we know relatively little about the acquisition of language and how communication develops as accurately and as completely as it does in children.

Vocalization

Let us begin with the question of how language is learned by children. Children normally do not begin to speak meaningfully until after the first year of life, but such real speech is preceded by various forms of vocalization and reaction to vocalization in others. For example, Trevarthen (1977) found that a nine-week-old-baby boy made small cooing sounds in response to his mother's repeated, rhythmic baby-talk questions. The baby responds to the sound of the human voice, and the adult treats the baby's cooing and babbling as meaningful responses. That hearing speech stimulates the baby is shown by the fact that deaf infants stop babbling at about six months of age; whereas, hearing infants continue to diversify their babbling experimentation (Lenneberg, 1967).

The content of children's vocalization changes rapidly during infancy. For the first two or three months of life, cries and grunts predominate. Then, at about three months, cooing begins. Whereas crying involves little more than the blowing of air along the vocal tract by the infant, cooing is sound produced by the articulatory organs, mainly the tongue. Infant cooing sometimes sounds "vowel like" but differs from adult vowel production both functionally and acoustically. Social babbling develops after cooing and often sounds like an effort to communicate in a foreign language. Some observers have noted that bawling in infants appears to follow the intonation patterns of adult speech involving the use of questions and declarative statements (Miller & Ervin, 1970). Others have shown that infants in their babbling imitate the pitch, loudness, and intonation of adults (Weir, 1972). While babbling probably plays some role in later speech, the course of development between babbling and more sophisticated language does not appear to be direct. Baby's first words usually are made up of the sounds they babble most, and some children continue to babble for several months after they begin to produce real speech.

During the cooing and babbling stage, the infant makes many more sounds than he or she will actually use in the production of later language. Some sounds drop out as one's native language is acquired. At the same time, though, single sounds are transformed into groups called phonemes, the raw materials from which all later speech will be composed. In a general way, phonemes correspond to the usual vowel and consonant sounds of a language. The letter *b*, for example, is pronounced somewhat differently in bat and tab. That the infant recognizes the sound *b* in both words is part of the competence of the child speaker as well as listener and is important in the acquisition in language.

Newborn babies can distinguish between sounds such as *ba* and *ga*; *r* and *l*; and *p*, *b*, *d*, and *t*. They can discriminate among vowel sounds (Eimas, 1974, 1975; Trehub & Rabinovitch, 1972; Trehub, 1973). The first consonant type sounds a baby makes are usually those produced in the back of the mouth, such as *k* or *g*. Conversely, the first vowel type sounds, such as *o* or *u*, are produced in the front of the mouth (Kaplan & Kaplan, 1971). In their babbling, babies are able to produce the sounds of all languages.

In addition to the development of phonemes, the child must learn the relationship of language to meaning, which is called semantics, as well as the rules to follow in producing permissible constructions which is called grammar. The study of grammar is divided into two parts—syntax and morphology. Syntax concerns itself with how words are combined into phrases and sentences, while morphology examines the formation of words themselves. A child who has mastered the semantics and the grammar of a particular language then reflects her or his linguistic competence in that language.

Communication

The ability to communicate, however, entails more than just linguistic competence. Appropriate communication entails knowing what to say as well as how and when to say it and thus demands that the speaker be sensitive to the person(s) with whom he or she is communicating as well as to the context in which the communication occurs. In recent years, the study of language acquisition has shown us that linguistic competence is achieved fairly early in the development of the child; whereas, the broader ability to communicate effectively continues to develop well into adolescence.

Sentence Development

The first word that children almost everywhere produce sounds very much like *mama*, and it is believed that *mama* appears in so many diverse languages because it is derived from the natural nasal-like murmur that infants make when sucking (mmmh-ah). The single word mama is usually learned by infants by about the age of nine months. Shortly thereafter, the infant begins to acquire a variety of other single words usually grouped into three categories. These categories include single words for animals, foods, and toys. So rapid is the acquisition of words by the child that by the age of 24 months, the vocabulary has multiplied many times so that by two years the child usually has a vocabulary of approximately 250 to 300 words.

By the age of 18 months or so, most children are producing dozens of words, usually spoken one by one. At various moments young speakers will be heard uttering such recognizable sounds as "doggie," "cookie," "come," "more," and "no." These brief utterances are called holophrases to indicate that the child's single word may refer to something beyond the usual delimited meaning of the single word. In saying "mama," a child might simply be naming the mother, or may be asking that the mother come closer, or that he or she wants milk given to her or him by the mother, or that he or she desires to be changed. In other words, holophrases can be interpreted in many ways, each of which can be meaningful both to the child and to the listener.

Within a few months after uttering her or his first meaningful one-word sentence, the child will begin to produce pairs of words that make some type of statement. Careful observation has shown that the transition from two one-word sentences to a functional two-word sentence is a gradual one. After beginning to use a few single words, the child will string them together, pausing between each. Then, the location of the pause will gradually change so that the child will begin saying "baby" and "chair" together but will soon combine them to form a two-word sentence, "baby chair" (Bloom, 1973).

Once children begin to produce two-word sentences, their use expands at a very rapid rate. It is as if children suddenly discover the power to express an almost unlimited set of ideas and cannot resist doing so. One case study has shown that more than 1,000 new and distinct two-word utterances per month appear during this phase of development (Braine, 1976). Brown (1973) also has pointed out that by the age of 36 months, some children are so advanced in the construction process of their language that they are able to produce all the major varieties of English simple sentences up to a length of 10 or 11 words.

The Child's First Conversations

Although children communicate their assertions and requests from a very early age, there is an unmistakable one-sidedness to these communications. It is not until the age of two or so that real interchange, the beginning of conversations, emerges. The child's first experience with language interactions comes through her or his association with parents. As soon as children begin to talk at all, parents seem to promote the idea of taking conversational turns and alternating the role of speaker and listener. Parents usually require the infant to produce words in communicating with them once the child has begun to acquire a vocabulary. Further, in teaching conversational skills, parents often model both sides of a dialogue so that their children can learn through observation how conversation should take place (Ervin Tripp, 1973). For example, parents may model the child's role as well as their own in an effort to teach turn taking, creating such dialogues as:

> PARENT: What's the doggie doing?
>
> CHILD: The doggie is eating.

By this means, the child begins to acquire turn taking skills and learns that conversation proceeds in alternating between speaking and listening.

Child/Adult Communication

Anyone who has ever tried to talk to a young child conversationally knows very well that one cannot speak to a child as one does to an adult. One problem is simply getting the child's attention. Adults use a variety of devices for this purpose, such as using the child's name at the beginning of a sentence ("Johnny, look at the horse."), using exclamations (such as, "Hey, Johnny!"), repeating portions of what they have said in order to capture and hold the child's attention (for example, "Yes, horsey!"), or looking or pointing at the objects they are talking about (Snow, 1972).

Adults also simplify their speech in various ways when talking to young children (Snow, 1972). Articles and possessives are frequently omitted so that these words occur least frequently when adults talk to 2 year olds, more frequently when they talk to 10 year olds, and most frequently when talking to other adults. Adults also avoid pronouns when talking to young children, repeating the relevant noun instead. For example, an adult might not say, "See the boy. He is riding the horse." Instead, an adult might say to a young child, "See the boy. The boy is riding the horse." Presumably, these devices make it easier to understand what is being said.

By the time children reach the age of five or so, their conversational competence is impressive and as similar in many respects to communication among adults. Most major grammatical forms have appeared, and the child already possesses an adequate vocabulary. However, the child's language is rather egocentric and remarkably concrete.

In a 1926 study, Piaget (1951) asked children to teach other youngsters how to use mechanical devices, such as a syringe. Children under six years of age did very poorly at instructing others. They were unable to see the problem from the listener's point of view. The children used vague gestures and pronouns such as "this," "something," "here," or "there." This experimental arrangement has been repeated by Glucksberg, Krauss, and Higgins (1975). These researchers found that children between the ages of four and five years were unsuccessful in describing a series of squiggled lines to other children. Often these 4- and 5-year-olds would give idiosyncratic names to or neglect important details of the squiggled lines. It appears these 4- and 5-year-olds are egocentric; that is, they are locked into their own perspective, unable to assume the point of view of someone else, and unable to find out what the other already knows and needs to know. Accordingly, they communicate with difficulty. Not having the sense of what the other child knows, they oscillate between providing unnecessary information and failing to provide crucial information. It is as if they were always entering the conversation in the middle, not sure of what has been said or what needs to be said, or of what could not possibly be understood. On the other hand, 7- to 8-year-olds are capable of taking the position of another child, communicating with precision, acting flexibly to clarify a point, and recognizing the important features of both the speaker's and the listener's roles. These older children are able to suppress their own point of view and adopt instead the perspective of others for the purposes of effective communication.

Thought and Language

How are thought and language related? Does the child first get an idea and then try to find words to express it? Or does a child's language ability enable him or her to think new thoughts? Are 6-year-olds more likely to know what they mean than how to say? Do they talk to themselves in order to figure out what they think? Piaget believes that cognitive development precedes language. In other words, cognition makes language development possible. As support for his thesis, Piaget (1974) asked children to crawl and then to describe what they did. Even the 3-year-olds in his study could crawl without hesitation, but it is not until age five or six that the children could describe what they did when they crawled. Most of them mistakenly said they moved both hands together and then both knees, or the right-hand with the right foot and then the left hand with the left foot. Even adults sometimes have difficulty with this task. Piaget argues that having the necessary motor skills and vocabulary does not mean a child has the necessary cognitive ability to understand and explain what he or she has done.

Piaget's position can be contrasted with that of Whorf (1956) and Sapir (1921). Both Whorf and Sapir argued that an individual's experience in language shapes one's thoughts. According to Whorf and Sapir, each culture has a unique world view that is transmitted from generation to generation through the medium of language. For example, Eskimos have a number of words describing various states of snow and ice that denote distinctions in quality that English-speaking individuals might not make. According to the Whorf–Sapir hypothesis, one's way of thinking reflects the structure and vocabulary of one's language. If this hypothesis is correct, children should begin to reason very differently once they have begun to talk. Moreover, since the world's languages differ markedly in many ways, children in one culture should begin to think differently from those in remote and linguistically distinct cultures. Overall, little evidence substantiates the idea of thinking across cultures or the Whorf–Sapir hypothesis.

Another contrasting position from that of Piaget is reflected in the work of Bruner (1964), who believes that by kindergarten, language ability affects almost every aspect of a child's thought and behavior to the extent that language becomes a means not only for representing experience but also for transforming it. In this view, Bruner is similar to the Russian psychologist Lev Vygotsky (1962). Vygotsky holds that the beginning of symbolic thinking, which occurs at about age two, is largely interrelated with language development so that they influence each other in their development.

Both Bruner and Vygotsky argue that at some point during early childhood, language helps form ideas. Although there is no definitive answer to which position is correct, it is clear that both language development and cognitive development are essential in our understanding of child development.

Implications of Language Development for Practice

Our review of language development has pointed out that the ability to speak is integral to the ability to understand. Therefore, the child practitioner must always be very cognizant of the child's linguistic abilities. The therapist, in working with young children, must obviously keep in mind the child's limitations in language development. Young children are able to comprehend more language than they are able to produce. Further, they have not mastered all of the adult conventions of social speech such as turn taking. They may have difficulty in describing sequences of events, how they feel, or what they think, or in completely under-standing what is being asked of them by adults, especially strangers. Given these limitations though, practitioners can work effectively with young children if communicative demands are not excessive and if the practitioners are oriented to the developmental level of the child.

Cognitive Development

Due largely to the ground breaking work of the Swiss psychologist Jean Piaget (1976) and his colleagues, we now know much about the development of cognition in children. According to Piaget, adult intelligence is qualitatively different from that of a child, but all levels of intelligence are defined in terms of "adaptive thinking and action." Children arrive at the adult stage by passing through the four major stages of conceptualization. These are the sensorimotor, preoperational, concrete operational, and formal operational stages. Piaget holds that the ages at which individuals attain the various stages are somewhat variable and depend on environmental influences, but that the sequence of development is always the same. Thus, the formal operational stage can be attained only if a child has progressed first through the sensorimotor, the preoperational, and the concrete operational stages and only in this order. This progress begins in infancy with the processing of sensorimotor information and progresses to the formal operational stage, typically attained by mid adolescence.

A large and growing body of research tends to support the Piagetian view that the sequence of cognitive development is universal. Although not every person may attain the highest stage, individuals of every culture and background pass through the same stages. It is important to know a little about each of these stages since they do set limitations on therapeutic work with children. Accordingly, each stage will be described in more detail.

Sensorimotor Stage

In the early stages of infancy, behavior occurs as though the world were perceived as a continuous moving and changing series of objects and events. Young infants appear not to perceive permanence in objects. They behave as though they believe that objects disappearing from their sight no longer exist. The maxim "out of sight, out of mind" appears to be literally true for infants. They can be engrossed in playing with a toy or a person; then, when that object disappears from sight, they behave as though it no longer exists. This behavior begins to change during the closing months of the first year. At this point, infants cry when left by their mothers. One of the major cognitive achievements of the sensorimotor period is the establishment of object permanence, the ability to be aware of the existence of objects even when they are not in sight or within a range where they can be touched, smelled, tasted, or heard. Another major cognitive achievement during the sensorimotor period is the acquisition of a notion of causality. During this period, infants begin to note the results of their actions and to anticipate certain results before they occur. For example, infants learn to play and to get attention by throwing their toys out of their crib. When they knock a toy out of the crib, they may look to the floor in anticipation that it will fall, and they also may anticipate an adult's reaction of picking up the toy and returning it. Spatial concepts also are established during this period as infants learn how to gain access to every part of their home.

During the first two years of life, infants make remarkable progress in their thinking about the world. Their concepts develop from perceiving the world only interims of immediate sensorimotor experience to gaining a notion of object permanence, causality, and space. Although infants in their first years of life do not acquire the ability to clearly represent the world internally, Piaget feels that the sensorimotor stage is significant because infants construct all of the cognitive substructures that will serve as a point of departure for the development of perception and thinking. During this stage, there is a continuous progression from spontaneous movements and natural reflexes to acquired habits and to behavior clearly reflecting intelligence. Thus, adaptive thinking, which is the basis for adult intelligence, has its foundation in the earliest years.

Piaget (1976) presents evidence for two forms of cognitive adaptation during the early stages of infancy: accommodation and assimilation. By accommodation, Piaget means the infant's ability to adapt to external stimuli rather than to respond mechanically to these stimuli. By assimilation is meant the integration of stimuli into the infant's existing cognitive structures. In the case of an infant, accommodation is a motor activity involving a shaping of a new behavior; in the case of an 8-year-old, the accommodation is conceptual. Thus, children must accommodate their former concepts of, for example, sugar to include the concept of sugar in a dissolved state in order to understand, or assimilate, what actually occurs when sugar is dissolved in water. A younger child, who is not able to accommodate the concept of sugar in this manner, believes that the sugar disappears.

Other behaviors that emerge during the final months of the sensorimotor stage are deferred imitation and complete object permanence. Children now can imitate a behavior hours or days after they have observed it, and they also have formed a mental image of an object so they can follow it through a series of complex displacements even if they cannot see it. Thus, infants during the latter part of the sensorimotor stage are no longer fooled when objects are hidden from their sight. They no longer look for them in the place where they were last seen, but rather trace the movement of the objects and look in new locations where they believe them to be.

The Preoperational Stage

Between the ages of about two and six, children develop the ability to use symbols. Language development is a significant component of this stage, and there also is the emergence of symbolic play, dreaming, and deferred imitation. Mastery of symbolic function means that children are able, by themselves, to produce abstract representations. Symbolic function is evident when children are able to imagine that the kitchen table is a tent in the woods, when they have dreams and nightmares, and when they are able to imitate Superman several hours or days after they have seen their hero on television.

Once children become capable of symbolic thought, they learn to use thousands of words, as well as many objects and gestures, to represent ideas, actions, and things. It then becomes easier for them to remember the past, imagine the future, and deal with the present. During this period of cognitive development, creative play is a favorite activity of the child's. Children are now old enough to pretend but are not able to distinguish fantasy from reality very well. Imagination becomes more apparent with each passing year. Whereas the 1-year-old might play with a cup and saucer as two independent objects, the 2-year-old might place the cup on the saucer and pretend to drink, and the 3-year-old transforms the cup and saucer into almost anything. For this child, the cup and the saucer could just as easily become a race car, a spaceship, or a house. By the end of the preoperational period, at approximately age six, the imaginary objects can be invisible, existing solely in the child's mind.

Another consequence of preoperational thinking is that children during this period have trouble understanding cause and effect, partly because they center on one aspect of an event rather than on the relationship between events. As a result, a child who falls down might blame the sidewalk, while another child might blame a child nearby but not close enough to have caused the fall. Because children during this period do not understand chance, they sometimes interpret the phrase, "It was an accident," to mean "Don't blame me." Thus, a child might very well hit her younger brother deliberately and then protest, "It was an accident." Parents who understand the cognitive characteristics of children during this period will realize that the child who deliberately hits a sibling is not lying when saying that it was an accident.

Another interesting phenomenon to consider during this period is the child's thought processes that reflect egocentrism. By egocentrism, we mean that the child's ideas about the world are restricted by her or his own narrow point of view. This means only that the child is naturally self-centered, not that the child is selfish. Egocentrism appears in different forms at various ages. During early childhood, for example, it is expressed in the child's difficulty imagining what it would be like to be someone else. Children assume that everyone reacts to the world as they themselves do. Children's descriptions of natural phenomena often show egocentric thought, as when preschool children declare that it has snowed so that they can make a snowman or that the grass grows so that they will not hurt themselves when they fall.

Children's egocentrism makes many young children think that everything in the world is alive, just as they are. This view is referred to by developmental psychologists as animism. Animistic children might bump into a table and then punish the table for hitting them, or when they drop a stuffed toy, they might begin to cry because they think they have hurt the toy. Similarly, the child during this period might ask questions such as "Why does the radio talk so loud?" Other children might egocentrically reason that because they themselves make many things from blocks, sand, sticks, and the like, everything living, including themselves, is made in a similar fashion. Children whose thinking is influenced by this artificialism might try to manufacture a toy out of sticks or a puppy out of mud, or might imagine God creating the world by building a fire to make the sun. Both animism and artificialism seem amusing to older children and parents who prefer scientific explanations of natural phenomena. However, preschool ideas probably make sense if one does not know or believe in the rules and findings of science. Indeed, many have suggested that the preoperational child's concepts are very similar to those folktales, myths, and some forms of religion and philosophy.

The limitations of preoperational thought often make it hard for children during this period to understand death, illness, or divorce. Children often blame themselves for these events. For example, a 4-year-old boy might think he killed grandma by disobeying her, or that God made his tonsils infected because he said a bad word, or that his father and mother are separating because he soiled on the carpet. Explanations to relieve the child's anxiety should be phrased in terms the preoperational child can understand. One little girl heard that her grandmother had died of old age, so she refused to eat any cake at her own birthday party, crying, "I don't want to be five; I don't want to die like Grandma." In such situations, parents face less difficulty in explaining death to children when they use religious ideas of afterlife since children often more readily accept the idea that Grandma died because she was ready for heaven than understand the more scientific facts related to the gradual deterioration involved in the aging process. Similarly, preschool children who are told that their parents are divorcing because they no longer love each other may wonder whether the parents will fall out of love with them as well. It is important to explain to children in these circumstances that love between parent and child is a bond that cannot be severed by divorce or weakened by time. By about the age of six, the child's social understanding grows and egocentrism declines. Similarly, children by this age can maintain and express internal representations of objects and events. When they have reached this age, children enter what Piaget calls the period of concrete operations.

Concrete Operations

It is during this stage that children begin to form notions of class, relations, and number. While preoperational children can use the language symbol *doggie* to stand for a specific dog, they also use the word *doggie* interchangeably with the dog's name to identify all other dogs and perhaps bears, foxes, and wolves. In other words, they cannot distinguish between using *doggie* for a single member of a class and for the class as a whole. Between the ages of 6 or 7 and 11 or 12, children emerge into the "age of reason" in that they develop the ability to internalize actions and to reason in an elementary fashion. They can deal with classes and can manipulate them in a manner analogous to elementary arithmetical operations. In this way, they understand that apples and oranges are part of the broader class of fruit and that boys and girls fit within the logical class children. Furthermore, they can reason that when boys are removed from the category of children what is left is girls. During this period, children become able to deal with the concept of time and can learn to read the clock and to understand historical time. Reasoning is internalized so that children can work out problems in their heads rather than attempting to solve them in the trial and error fashion that characterizes the preoperational stage. During the period of concrete operations, children become aware of constants in their environment and recognize them as such, even in the face of seemingly contradictory perceptual evidence. One of the best examples of this phenomena is the conservation of quantity. Piaget believes that most children under 7 years old do not fully understand that when liquid from beaker B is poured into a narrower beaker, A, or a wider one, C, the amount of liquid remains the same. However, by the time children are 7 or 8 and have attained concrete operations, they know the amount of liquid is conserved. They will explain that even though the column of liquid is higher in beaker A than beaker C, this is made up for by the fact that A also is narrower. Moreover, the child will note that the amount remains the same, because the transformation of shape can be reversed by pouring the liquid back into the original beaker, B. Piaget holds that the ability of the child to conserve reflects the development of a new system of coordinated mental operations. With increasing age and experience, these operations are generalized to a wide variety of situations.

The development of concrete operations also affects the child's social relations and moral judgments. In studying children's understanding of games with rules, Piaget found that before the age of about 7, children tend to regard such rules as sacred, untouchable, and of "transcendent origin." Older children, on the contrary, regard rules as a result of agreement among contemporaries and accept the idea that rules can be changed by means of a democratic consensus. At this earlier age, children also have a touching faith in the potency of words. Many playground fights are justified with the assertion, "He called me a name." The fighting potential of particular insults depends more on local custom than literal meaning. For example, when a normally well behaved boy suddenly attacked another boy in the classroom, and when the teacher told him he should know better, he explained, "He said my mother wears combat boots, and you know I couldn't let him get away with that." As children grow older, they realize that they can combat words with words. They are likely to answer an insult with another insult rather than with a blow. If a younger or less articulate child begins to get the worst of a verbal duel, he or she often resorts to physical fighting or responds, "Sticks and stones may break my bones, but names can never hurt me." This is a defense that makes the victim feel better and exasperates the attacker, proving again the power of words.

Formal Operational Thought

Progression from concrete to formal operations occurs during early adolescence (between ages 11 or 12 and 15). Before adolescence, the child has an earthbound, concrete, practical problem-solving approach. In the period of formal operations, the adolescent is able to reason with logical propositions as well as with concrete objects. Further, adolescents are able to speculate, hypothesize, and fantasize much more readily and on a much grander scale than children who are still tied to concrete operational thinking. By the end of adolescence, many young people can understand and create general principles or formal rules to explain many aspects of human experience. Consequently, Piaget calls the last stage of cognitive development, attained at about age 15, formal operational thought. This is the stage at which the adolescent begins to build systems or theories, in the largest sense of the term, about literature, philosophy, morality, love, and the world at work (Inhelder & Piaget, 1958).

Formal operations enable one to use "hypothetico-deductive," or formal, reasoning. Faced with a problem, one can now think through all of the logical combinations of factors that might account for a situation, deduce the consequences of each of these possible hypotheses, and then test to see which is correct. Acquiring formal operations also enables one to think at a new and higher level about such topics as social justice, beauty, or philosophy. Piaget believes that these new powers of reasoning often lead adolescents to engage in speculation about hypothetical, political, or social systems, or to develop strong emotional commitment to abstract ideals.

In addition to having the ability to be logical and imaginative and to see the hypothetical and the possible, most adolescents demonstrate another cognitive characteristic—adolescent egocentrism. Adolescents are long past the egocentrism of the preoperational thought typical of preschool children, who assume that everyone thinks the same way they themselves do, and that the world and all of its wonders are put on earth for them to enjoy. By adolescence, young people know quite well that others can have different opinions, and they also know that their personal existence is largely irrelevant to the forces of nature. They are fully aware, for instance, that it does not rain because they forgot their umbrella, even though they may curse the heavens instead of themselves. Nevertheless, the particular limits of adolescent judgment and logic make young people susceptible to egocentrism of another kind. Instead of believing the physical world centers on them, adolescents believe that the psychological universe revolves around them. That is, they believe that their unique thoughts are universally held and, at the same time, that they alone understand human experiences. It is not unusual for adolescents to inform their parents or other adults that they alone know what it is to be in love, to hate someone, or to be fearful of something.

Often, adolescents also create for themselves an imaginary audience as they fantasize how others will react to their appearance and behavior. Although adolescent boys and girls know that people are not usually thinking the same things about them as they themselves are thinking, they sometimes have trouble realizing that they may not be the center of others' thoughts and concerns. For instance, adolescents often are so preoccupied with their physical appearance that they assume that everyone else judges the final result. Anticipation of a favorable judgment can cause teenagers to enter a crowded room with the air of regarding themselves as the most attractive and admired human beings alive. On the other hand, sometimes something as trivial as a pimple on the chin can make them wish that they could enter the room invisibly. It often takes several years before this egocentrism declines and the individual can walk into a crowded room without the look of one who thinks he or she owns the world or the fearfulness of one who imagines contempt in every gaze.

Elkind (1974) has suggested that sometimes egocentrism can lead from the possible into the impossible. One example that Elkind gives is the foundling fantasy. In the foundling fantasy, the young people imagine that they are the offspring not of their actual parents, but of much wiser and more beautiful people who were forced to give them up in infancy. Many fix their attention on any of their physical characteristics that their parents do not have and decide that adoption is the most plausible explanation for the discrepancy. Another example is the personal fable through which adolescents imagine their own lives as heroic or even mythical. They see themselves destined for great fame and fortune, discovering the cure for some disease such as cancer or authoring a masterpiece. Thus, adolescent thought processes are usually a mixture of the abilities to imagine many logical possibilities and to deny reality when it interferes with hopes and fantasies.

Implications of Cognitive Development for Practice

The child practitioner needs a clear understanding of the typical processes of cognitive development in order to understand that children think differently from adults in many ways. At specific stages, they hold notions of the world that are erroneously adult standards. It is reasonable that an infant in the sensorimotor stage holds an egocentric value orientation. At that stage, "right" is what feels good and "bad" is what hurts. Later, around age five or six years, in the preoperational stage, children can integrate some understanding of right and wrong providing it is explained very concretely. It is unreasonable to expect most children to perform formal operations, that is, sophisticated interpretation, before about age 11 or 12 years. Understanding can be facilitated within limits by using experiential approaches. Thus, insight therapy, as typically conducted with adults, will have little meaning for most children under 11 or 12 years. Experiential learning, as in play therapy, is more appropriate.

In subsequent chapters, we will present approaches to therapy that claim effectiveness in helping children gain a handle on complex, interpersonal issues. These approaches are only effective if geared to the children's cognitive developmental level. An approach that is effective at one age may be too complicated for younger children and too simple for older children. It is important to keep in mind that the young child has a limited sense of causality. It may be too much for the child to be presented with an intricate set of attributions concerning her or his role or that of her or his parents, in the difficulty they are experiencing. In short, the practitioner must probe for the child's level of understanding and begin there in establishing the intervention process.

Social Development

The child is expected to learn particular social skills such as using a toilet, dressing, and sharing toys at given developmental levels. The social skills differ greatly from one culture to another. Thus, toilet training begins at about six months in Japan and at about two years in most U.S. cultures. Children first learn from their parents the social skills that they must develop to get along. The quality of the relationship with the parents will affect the child's ability to learn those skills and will transfer to the child's relationships with others. By studying children in foundling homes, Ribble (1945) and Bowlby (1951) illuminated the importance of the infant's continued contact with the primary parent. Bowlby (1951) identified stages of "anaclitic depression." When infants are separated from a primary parent, they protest, then express despair, and finally (if mourning is unresolved) become detached. Detachment may be so great that the child fails to eat, to thrive, or even to survive. We now recognize that these early researchers confounded effects of separation with effects of institutionalization. However, later research supports the tenet that infants need much stimulation and affection. The quality, if not the consistency, of early parenting is critical (Freedman, Kaplan, & Saddock, 1976).

Gender Issues

A body of literature important to development stems from research conducted by Carol Gilligan among others relevant to women's development, particularly in the adolescence and early adult phases. By taking a different perspective, Gilligan and others point out that girls and women develop a "different voice" due to theme—often gender related. For example, girls emerge from the first three years of life with a basis for empathy as an intergral part of the self in a way boys do not (Schriver, 1995).

Family and Environment

In time, siblings and extended family members exert influence upon the child's social development. By school age, peer influence becomes critical. As presented in Table 3.2, Freud (1953) identified critical social developmental tasks each child must conquer and has pointed out possible psychological effects of dealing with those tasks. Also in Table 3.2, Erikson (1963) helps us see how the child's solutions to those tasks affect the child's sociability. Moreover, we can identify operational behaviors that suggest a child is entering a particular psychosocial developmental level (Freedman, Kaplan, & Sadock, 1976).

Infant.   In infancy, passive protection by significant others is not enough. Social growth requires active stimulation of the genetically determined sequence. The handling of the infant's oral needs will serve as a primogenitor of trust with others. A mutuality needs to develop between the caregiver's way of giving and the baby's way of accepting. If feeding is unsatisfactory (for example, if the child is separated from the mother without a proper substitute or if the child is under-nourished), the child may grow up with a feeling of loss, of not trusting others, or of being unloved.

TABLE 3.2

Stages of Psychosocial Development

Age	Freud	Erikson	Target Behaviors
0-4 weeks			impassive phase
16 weeks			spontaneous smile
			aware of strange situations
24 weeks	oral	trust-vs.-mistrust	separation anxiety
36 weeks			stranger anxiety
40 weeks			responds to social play
			such as peek-a-boo
52 weeks			cooperates in dressing
12 months			
15 months			throws objects
			begins to choose, to refuse
18 months		autonomy-vs.-shame	carries or hugs special toys
	anal		
2 years			
			dresses self
3 years			domestic mimicry
			states own sex
			understands taking turns
	phallic		
4 years		iniative-vs.-guilt	plays cooperatively
5 years			plays competitively

Toddler. In the toddler stage, toilet training serves as a paradigm of general training practices. The child must learn self-control to accommodate social demands. If successful, the child continues to grow with a feeling of autonomy and pride. If not, the child feels doubt and shame. Erikson (1963) tells us that there is a limit to the amount of shame one can endure. If a child feels extremely ashamed, the child tends to reject those feelings and to doubt those around him or her.

From age two to school age, mobility is a key facet of the child's socialization. The child learns to move independently and vigorously. If efforts toward autonomy are encouraged, the child grows in initiative. If the child's independence is discouraged, or if the child feels no support when faltering, self-doubt increases. The child may vacillate between desires to individuate and to remain an infant protected by the mother (Mahler, Pine, & Bergman, 1975).

School Age.   During school age, cognition can flourish. If intellectual pursuits are gratifying, the child becomes increasingly industrious. Imagination flowers; friendships build. If efforts at mastery are thwarted, the child begins to see her or himself as inferior and to act out perceived inferior roles. Competition is expected at this age. The child learns to share, but may do so with some difficulty. How the competition is dealt with will help determine whether the child develops a moral system based upon an appreciation of human rights and needs or a rigid moralism. Sexual identification develops during this age, and it also is greatly influenced by social relations. If curiosity is met with age appropriate replies, the child acquires a positive sense of wonder about life. If curiosity is rebuffed or treated as taboo, the child experiences discomfort (Freedman, Kaplan, & Sadock, 1976).

Parents with problem children often want to know which child-rearing practices "really work." They want to know the "right way." In studying children's social development, we are struck with the dynamic interaction between the characteristics of the child (age, sex, temperament etc.) and physical and social demands. We can chart the general effect of some social factors upon the child's socialization. There is a correlation between extremes of child-rearing practices and pathological personal and social development in children (Chess & Hassibi, 1978). On the whole, the factors contributing to maladjustment are so complex that we cannot elucidate a direct link between style of child-rearing and a child's psychosocial development. In the rest of this section, we will focus on two aspects of child-rearing, the parent–infant bond, and sex role development because they are exemplary and central aspects of normal child development.

The Parent–Infant Bond

The future of an infant is perhaps most importantly determined by the relationship that is established between parent and child commencing with the birth of the infant. The term parent–infant bond is intended to emphasize the psychological fastening that occurs between the infant and the primary caretaker. Sometimes the bond is referred to as attachment. This bond is revealed by the infant's tendency to maintain close contact with that person. Thus, the infant maintains contact with his eyes; the infant stares intently at his mother; and his eyes follow her as she goes about her chores. As the infant becomes more mobile, he or she tries to maintain physical proximity with the mother. If the child is for some reason unsuccessful in maintaining physical proximity with the mother, the child shows obvious signs of distress. This has come to be known as separation anxiety (Ainsworth, 1973).

The bond between parents and infant does not develop automatically. Contrary to popular belief, there is no maternal or paternal "instinct." The question of interest, then, is what factors control the bonding relationship. The most significant variable seems to be early physical and social contact with the infant. Not too many years ago, the usual hospital routine following birth involved the mother's quick glance at her infant at delivery, a short visit with the infant within the next 12 hours, and then about 30 minutes with the baby at feeding every four hours, except at night. Today, it generally is conceded that mothers should have immediate and extensive contact with their infants following delivery. The results of one study (Kennell, Jerault, Wolfe, Chesler, McAlpine, Kreger, Steffa, & Klaus, 1974) have shown that mothers given extended contact with their infants, in comparison with mothers who had the traditional amount of contact with their infants, spent more time soothing, cuddling, looking at, and picking up the infants when they cried. The infants thrived under this attention and scored better on tests of physical and mental development at one year than did the babies who did not have the extended contact. Differences continued to be apparent even at 2 years of age. Mothers who had had more contact with their infants at birth spoke to them more and gave them fewer commands and more encouragement than did the other mothers.

The importance of early mother–infant contact is perhaps best seen in situations of premature infants. Usually when the infant is born prematurely, the mother is allowed only limited access to the infant because of its precarious health for several weeks or months. Quinn and Goldberg (1977) and Leifer, Leiderman, Barnett, and Williams (1972) found that mothers of premature infants are less involved emotionally with their babies than are mothers of full-term infants. They are less inclined to cuddle their babies or hold them. This diminished maternal response after postpartum separation may last as long as nine months (Brown & Bakeman, 1977) and may be a contributing factor to later child neglect and abuse (Hunter, Kilstrom, Kraybill, & Loda, 1978; Klein & Stern, 1971).

The importance of father–infant bonding cannot be ignored. Although the emphasis on attachment to mother is well researched, it is known that the father's presence is as effective as the mother's in making babies feel secure. For instance, a study of Lester, Kotelchuck, Spelke, Sellers, and Klein (1974) indicated that infants whose fathers took an active role in their care were more likely to show an interest in exploring their environment.

A final aspect of the parent–infant bond of importance to the child welfare worker is that children who do not develop a strong parent–infant bonding run a higher risk of being abused or neglected by one or both of their parents. "'Difficult'" children are more likely to be abused than are other children, and parents are more likely to perceive their offspring as "difficult" if a strong bond has not been formed between parents and the infant. Predictors of poor bonding and subsequent child abuse include parents who have difficulty looking their infants in the eye or in touching them, parental disappointment over the baby's sex, and displeasure with the infant's physical appearance (Kempe & Kempe, 1978).

Those parents who were rejected themselves as infants are more likely to be abusing parents. They seem to lack the capacity to establish a strong bond with their own offspring. Thus, the cycle of child abuse repeats itself from generation to generation. The worker must be attentive to disruptions in early parent–infant bonding. These disruptions may be the cause of subsequent problem behavior later in the child's life. In a later section, we discuss strategies for rebonding the parents to their child.

Sex Roles and Stereotypes

Parental attitudes and behavior may very well be the determining factor in the development of young children's conception of femininity or masculinity. Children learn about gender very early. Most two-year-olds know whether they are boys or girls, identify strangers as daddies or mommies, and know that Daddy has a penis and Mommy has breasts. By age three, children can consistently apply gender labels (Thompson, 1975).

These accomplishments do not mean that children understand that gender is biological. Until age four or five, they are likely to think sex differences depend on clothes, hair, or maturation, rather than on biology, believing that a girl would be a boy if she cut her hair, or that a boy might become a girl if he wore a dress. One preschooler visited the neighbor's new baby who was having a bath. Later, her parents asked whether the baby was a boy or a girl. "I don't know," she replied, "it's so hard to tell at that age, especially when it's not wearing clothes" (Stone & Church, 1973)

Given the prevalent notions about female and male behavior in our society and the degree to which colors, clothes, and toys for infants are classified almost exclusively by sex, we assume that boys and girls are treated differently from birth. A number of studies do show different socialization practices for females and for males. Nevertheless, reviews of the research concerning early socialization conclude that, on the whole, the sexes are treated very similarly during the preschool years. Maccoby (1980) concludes that there are two general areas that differ in the socialization of boy and girl children. First, boys are handled somewhat more roughly than girls, and parents indicate more concern about their daughters' physical well-being. Second, boys are physically punished more and given more direction than girls.

One study leading to such conclusions was carried out by Minton, Kagan, & Levine (1971), who observed the interaction of nearly 100 mothers with their two-year-olds in the homes of these individuals. Both lower-middle and middle-class mothers were rather intrusive, interrupting their children every 6 to 8 minutes to reprimand or command them. Sons were reprimanded and physically punished more frequently than daughters, and the lower the educational level attained by the mother, the more inclined she was to be intrusive.

Besides being punished more in general, boys also seem to be punished more than girls for behaviors deemed inappropriate for their sex. The masculine role in our society is regarded with greater respect and status. It is more clearly defined than the feminine role, and there appears to be greater pressure on boys than girls to conform to sex-appropriate standards. When asked to respond to sex appropriate behaviors for boys and girls, parents of young children responded more negatively to opposite sex choices for boys than for girls (Lanky, 1967). Girl children who climb trees and play with toy soldiers are tolerated to a much greater degree than little boys who cry, play with dolls, or like to play at dress up (especially if it involves dressing up in Mommy's clothes).

Because they are punished for exhibiting sex-inappropriate behaviors, it is not surprising that boys are more consistent in their adoption of sex-typed behaviors and adopt them earlier than girls do. When asked whether they would like to be boys or girls, young boys are far more likely than young girls to select their own sex. It is not until the age of 10 that a majority of girls state that they prefer to be female. These results may occur because girls have observed the greater advantage accorded to males and state a preference for their own sex only as a

result of preadolescent social pressures. An alternative explanation is that because girls are not punished as frequently as boys for sex inappropriate choices,
they are therefore less fearful of expressing their honest preference.

A number of theories have been devised to explain sexual identification. We
will examine the three most prominent theories of sex role development: the
psychoanalytic approach, the social learning approach, and the cognitive developmental approach.

The Psychoanalytic Approach.   Freudian theory, which will be discussed in
more detail in the next chapter, assumes that physical differences between the
sexes predestine them to radically different personality configurations. Psychoanalytic theory stresses the importance of early development in shaping lifelong
patterns of behavior, and it does not view sex roles as flexible. Biological and
psychological aspects of individuals are the organizing properties for sex role
identity which, once crystallized, will be maintained for life. According to the
psychoanalytic position, sex role differentiation appears during the phallic stage
of development which involves the resolution of the Oedipal complex (for boys)
and the Electra complex (for girls). In this view, a boy desires his mother and
becomes a rival of his father. Aware of the father's greater strength and power and
fearing castration, the boy renounces his desire for his mother, identifies with his
father, and thus completes his gender identity when he passes through this third
stage of psychosexual development, around the age of five or six. In this manner,
a boy who probably spends most of his time with his mother as his primary
caretaker still manages to identify with and pattern his behavior after his father.
Girls, on the other hand, do not need to switch their identification from their first
love object—their mother. According to Freud, they do, however, go through the
phallic stage, during which they develop penis envy and desire their fathers. Little
girls, like boys, resolve the competition with their same-sexed parent by identifying with that parent and behaving in a sex-appropriate manner. The sex-role
identity attained at this period will be maintained throughout life, and fixation
at this stage may cause lifelong patterns of abnormal sex-role identification.
Although Freud was the first to report the increased interest in sexual phenomena
in children around the ages of four to six, his postulation of the Oedipal and the
Electra complexes has proven difficult to test empirically. Furthermore, behaviors observed during this period can be explained by alternate hypotheses. Especially damaging to the psychoanalytic interpretation is the known flexibility of

sex-role behavior over the life span, as well as the recent trends indicating that traditional sex-role differentiations are breaking down.

Social Learning Approach.   Social learning theorists such as Bandura (1977) and Mischel (1968) have emphasized the significance of social contingencies and external environmental influences as the main shapers of gender identity. Patterns of reinforcement, verbal instruction, the behaviors of models, and the publicly observable consequences of the model's behaviors (vicarious learning) are the means through which children acquire sex role identification. Through observation of anatomy, children learn that there are two types of individuals, or two sexes, and that all of the forces in the environment indicate that people are differentiated on the basis of these physical characteristics. Children come to have a broad concept of femaleness and maleness on the basis of their experiences. Sex differences are learned, and once this learning takes place, a child's identification is formed.

The social learning approach emphasizes the flexibility of sex-role behavior and the potential for changing sex-role stereotypes. If the environment is constantly shaping behavior, then alterations in the environment can lead to alterations in attitudes and behaviors of females and males. From this perspective, social changes may lead to changes in early sex-role socialization practices. Further, sex-role identity is not seen as being laid down indelibly in the first five years of life as is true in the psychoanalytic theory, nor is it seen as being so intimately linked to anatomy.

Cognitive Developmental Approach.   On the basis of Piaget's cognitive theory, Kohlberg (1966, 1969) has explained sex role development as a cognitive phenomenon. Whereas social learning theorists view the environment as being the organizing force in sex-role identity, cognitive developmental theorists see the organizing force as being the interactions between an individual and the environment. A child's general cognitive level shapes her or his social responses. Sex-role development progresses through three stages, beginning with the formation of gender identity—rather than culminating in it as postulated by psychoanalytic and social learning theories. Gilligan's research with female subjects differed from Kolberg's work in the area of moral development (Gilligan, 1982). She believed that girls are not deficient but rather different in their responses to moral issues as children (Schriver, 1995). The stages advanced by Kohlberg are as follows:

1. Gender identity. The child recognizes that he or she is either male or female.

2. Gender stability. The child recognizes that boys invariably become men and girls become women.

3. Gender consistency. The child recognizes that the attributes of being either female or male will not change with changing situations and personal motivations.

By at least age three, the child can accurately label her- or himself and can label the gender of others with some correctness. By age four, the child is partially aware that gender cannot change. It is not until about age six, however, that a firm concept of sex identity is established, based primarily on physical differences of the sexes. This progression follows the more general pattern of cognitive development, and the constancy of gender maybe a special case of object constancy. Once basic gender identity has been established, the child actively seeks to shape her or his behavior to match sex identity. With age, the child also relies more on social functions to determine appropriate sex-role behavior. Thus, sex-role behaviors are influenced by parents, peers, and the social roles played out by men and women in our culture.

Conclusions About Sex Role Research.   Recent trends indicate that traditional sex-role differentiations are breaking down. Greater numbers of individuals are experiencing discontinuities between early sex-role socialization and later life experiences. Females who have been socialized consistently and strongly to favor traditional feminine activities and interpersonal behaviors are likely in later life to experience circumstances or opportunities calling for more traditional masculine role behaviors. Social movements such as women's liberation can be expected to accelerate societal redefinitions of traditional sex roles. Additionally, the changing status of women is having an impact on attitudes about sex roles in young parents and affecting the manner in which they socialize their children. With more and more women entering the work force (almost 50% of mothers of children 18 years or younger), it appears certain that growing numbers of children will develop less rigid attitudes about appropriate sex-role behaviors.

A concept, androgyny, has been developed to counter the misconception that femininity and masculinity are exact opposites—an assumption that leads a great many people to believe that, unless one follows the feminine role, the more masculine one becomes, and vice versa. Androgyny, strictly speaking, is the state of having both female and male sexual characteristics and has come to be used in connection with a person's defining herself or himself primarily as a human being, rather than as female or male (Bem, 1974, 1975). In this sense, androgynous men and women share many of the same personality characteristics, instead of following the traditional sex role patterns. For instance, traditional males rate significantly higher than traditional females on a personality trait labeled "dominant ambitious," but androgynous females and males score about the same, because the men see themselves as less dominant than the traditional male does, while the women see themselves as more dominant than the traditional female does. Androgynous people of both sexes are nurturing and independent, and neither sex tries to be unemotional or passive.

People who are flexible in their sex roles and able to display the best qualities of both traditional stereotypes are more competent and have a higher sense of self-esteem than people who follow traditional sex-role behavior (Spence & Helmreich, 1978). This suggests that it is good to encourage children to develop all their potential characteristics, letting them engage in rough and tumble play outside as well as quiet play in the doll corner. Instead of saying, "Boys don't cry" or "Girls don't fight," we should simply apply the same standards to both sexes, either advising, "Children should settle their own arguments," or "Nobody fights," as the situation demands. Or as Lever (1976) observed, when a dispute over the rules broke out on the playground boys continue to fight, while girls eventually give up in order to sustain the relationships (Schiriver, 1995).

Disruption of Normal Developmental Processes

We have confined our overview of normal developmental issues to those topics that are of importance to all children. A growing body of literature identifies factors that disrupt typical developmental processes and can result in abnormal child behavior.

Physical Factors

For instance, certain constitutional factors created by pre- and postnatal experiences have been linked with a variety of childhood emotional problems. Many studies attest that the mother's nutritional status during pregnancy is correlated with infant intelligence (Harrell, Woodyard, &Gates, 1955). Significant malnutrition is associated with infant retardation. The mother's overall health during pregnancy has also been correlated with the baby's birth weight (Erickson, 1978). The low birth weight itself is not pathological, but often may signal undernourishment which can lead to organic lags. Following this logic, low birth weight of a full-term baby is more serious than low weight associated with prematurity as the former is more likely to signal undernourishment.

A number of toxic substances, called teratogens, can be transmitted through the mother to the newborn. The mother's illnesses, especially during the first three months of pregnancy, can affect the embryo's well-being. Viral diseases that are relatively innocuous among adults, such as measles and colds, can cause significant organic impairment, such as retardation, blindness, and deafness. Bacterial infections also are transmitted, although inmost bacterial diseases the infection itself is transmitted rather than the bacteria spurring congenital malformation. The infant can be born with tuberculosis, syphilis, or other bacterial illnesses transmitted through the infected mother's placenta. Nicotine and a number of other drugs are teratogens leading to prematurity, underweight, undernourishment, and/or malformations in a number of children (Erickson, 1978). Toxemias, such as preeclampsia, which affect about 5% of pregnant women, disturb the embryo's overall health (Chess & Hassibi, 1978).

Several perinatal (during birth) factors affect the neonate's well-being. Anoxia, lack of oxygen during birth, is associated with difficulties in development and intellectual functioning (Goldstein, Caputo, &Taub, 1976; Drillien, 1970). Prolonged and complicated labor is associated with later retardation, behavioral disorders, and reading problems (Pasamanick & Knobloch, 1966). Premature babies are a high-risk group on a number of vital dimensions (Chess & Hassibi, 1978). A number of postnatal (after birth) factors such as infections of the central nervous system, brain trauma, and malnutrition affect the child's constitutional well-being.

We have described the constitutional effects of a number of pre-, peri-, and postnatal factors. Although the effect of these factors appears first to be physical, these toxic factors are easily and often transformed to temperament and personality disturbances. If the child's constitution is disturbed, her or his ability to develop effective sensorimotor functions will be disturbed. Remember the sensorimotor acquisition is a prerequisite for development of later cognitive ability. Thus, factors in the child's development because of prebirth and birth experiences may impede expected development.

Since determination and treatment of the physical factors that enhance and impede development are primarily the purview of medical researchers, we will not discuss these in more detail. In the rest of this text, we consider in depth the temperamental and psychosocial factors that affect child development, as it is within these areas that the child welfare worker may have the greatest impact.

Social Factors

A number of social factors may disrupt normal development. For example, loss of a parent has been associated with disturbance in normal growth patterns. When children are separated from a primary caretaker, they grieve. The degree of reversibility of the despair or impairment of development depends upon a number of factors such as the age of the child, whether the separation is permanent or temporary, the duration and frequency of separation, and the nature of substitute care.

Severe physical illnesses of parents can affect children's development (Glueck & Glueck, 1952). Factors such as divorce and remarriage also may change developmental patterns. We will speak more specifically about how such psychosocial stresses affect children in Part IV on children with special concerns.

Clearly, pathology in the parent–child interaction can stimulate maladjustment. Much research has been conducted to ascertain the relationship between parents' emotional problems and those of their children, barring genetic influences. As explained in detail in the chapter on family therapy, the child may be caught in the web of a pathological family system. The child's maladjustment may be the only way to cope with a disturbed world. Too severe, too lax, or inconsistent child rearing has been linked to childhood maladjustment.

Developmental Psychopathology

The more we understand about normal variations in development, the more we are able to determine which behaviors and reactions are indicative of problems in children. Psychologists specializing in the understanding of childhood problems as a deviation from normal development are considered specialists in "developmental psychopathology" (Cicchetti, Toth, & Bush, 1988).

Work in developmental psychopathology offers new insights into various syndromes among children, for example, depression in childhood. Historically, researchers and therapists believed that children could not suffer depression because they did not conceptualize experiences, particularly guilt and worry about future events, as do adults. We now understand that children do experience some symptoms equated with depression. At elementary school age, children have been noted to experience dysphoric mood, pessimism, as well as self-doubts. As many as two-thirds of elementary-age children with dysthymic states may develop major depressive disorders over the next five years.

With the development of metacognition, that is, the children's ability to reflect on their own cognitive processes, their capacity to report as well as to experience depressive symptoms increases. Thus, by late childhood and early adolescence, many children experience the self-blame, self-depreciation, and helplessness often associated with adult depression. Therefore, developmental psychopathology points out that children may experience depression, but that this depression may be quite different in quality from that of adults (Rutter, Izard, & Read, 1986).

As another example of how developmental studies are assisting our understanding or childhood psychopathology, developmental psychopathologists recently have been successful in elucidating various kinds of anxiety states in children. We now understand that a number of these anxiety states, such as attachment disorder, separation anxiety disorder, and withdrawal disorder, are related to developmental issues. Others, such as obsessive–compulsive disorder, appear to have a very strong genetic component and are similar in psychologica structure in both children and adults (Campbell, 1986, Rapoport, 1989).

bImplications about Disruption of Normal Development on Practice

In reviewing the findings on disruption of normal development, we see that the child's biology, temperament, and physical and social environment can be menacing forces that impede normal development. Some say stress alone causes maladjustment; others rely on biological explanations. In most cases, maladjustment is probably an interaction of self and environmental factors. Most believe that stress is a trigger that releases constitutional vulnerability (Selye, 1950).

According to the developmental perspective, competence results from the successful resolution of life tasks that are salient at given periods. A successful resolution of issues at one stage increases the likelihood of subsequent successful task resolution. Because early structures are incorporated into later structures, an early deviation may cause much more disturbance to emerge in following developmental stages. In general, then, the younger the child at the point of psychological or physical trauma, the more pervasive the effects. Collaterally, the earlier the trauma or significant deviation from development is identified, the more successful is therapeutic intervention in delimiting the effects.

The developmental perspective to psychopathology emphasizes the overall interrelationship of cognitive, social, emotional, and biological domains. The interrelationship signals the need for a multi-system approach to the assessment and treatment of children (Cecchetti, et al., 1988). As we explore the various theoretical approaches to child therapy in the next unit, you will be aware that each theorist makes certain assumptions against what is empirically known about child development. As mentioned previously, too often the findings of child development have not been applied to the practice of child welfare.

Summary

This brief overview of child development demonstrates how intricate are the biological, physical, and social forces that lead to the adaptation or maladjustment of a particular child. Thus, an effective assessment of a child needs to consider the child's overall physical, cognitive, and social development in the context of the family and larger social environment. Clinical intervention may be aimed at various spheres of the child's development and various factors in the child's world. Since no simple set of determinants explains the child's behavior and temperament, the tasks of the child welfare worker in both assessment and intervention are highly complex, requiring a critical synthesis of empirical data about child development and child therapy and astute sensitivity to the developmental capacities of a given child.

Part II

Theories of Child Practice

As pointed out in Part I of This text, the concept of the child as the focus of child practice has evolved within the last 100 years, spurred by Freud's revolutionary thinking that emotional disorders were often rooted in childhood trauma. Since that time, a vast literature of theoretical expositions and case studies concerning effective means for ameliorating stress in children has developed. Most of these writings and case studies fall into one of the four major theoretical stances to therapy: the psychoanalytic/psychodynamic, behavioral/cognitive, humanistic/psychosocial (Maluccio, 1995), or family therapy. The major writings about childhood applications of these theoretical tenets are summarized in Chapters 4 through 7. Each of these reviewed major approaches to child practice reports documented effectiveness according to case study analysis and some empirical research. However, experimental verification of each of the theories is limited. At this point, one theory of child treatment cannot be proven more effective than any other. Rather, it appears that some combination of the worker's training and temperament plus the temperament of the child and specific nature of the child's problems determine the effectiveness of the theoretical modality. Thus, the child welfare worker needs a working familiarity with each of the four major approaches to child treatment.

Of course, trying to integrate and apply all of these approaches is an overwhelming task. It would be ideal if one could integrate the best of each of these approaches into an omnibus theory, but this goal is not viable because several of the approaches rely upon opposing principles and, thus, cannot be philosophically integrated.

Much of the clinical and theory development in the helping professions has been developed for adults. But, children are not miniature adults, they are developing human beings with unique needs, qualities and characteristics. Therefore work with children should take into account three special features; children are highly susceptible to external influences (both positive and negative), children act out their feelings, and children who come to the attention of child welfare workers are usually "involuntary clients" (Maluccio, 1995). When applying theories for child practice the child welfare worker assesses the individual child's age, socioeconomic status, ethnicity, physical health, family structure, and other psychosocial factors.

In Chapter 8, we have attempted to summarize the important principles that do cut across the varied theories of child treatment and to offer some guidelines for selecting an appropriate theoretical stance for a particular child. In essence, we have attempted to outline a systematic, eclectic approach to child counseling that facilitates the practitioner's listening and responding broadly to the child's and family's needs. Throughout Part II, you are presented with numerous clinical examples of the varied theoretical approaches. Chapter 8 ends with an extended case of how we attempt to listen to our child clients.

Chapter 4
Psychodynamic Contributions to Child Theory

While very few child welfare workers will ever use psychoanalysis, many related professions are based in part on the principles of Freud's work or in response to it. Therefore we believe it is critical to understand the evolution and principles of psychoanalysis, as a major theory in treating childhood issues.

Psychodynamic psychotherapy is based upon principles of psychoanalysis as elucidated by Freud and his students. Trained in the traditional approach to medicine in Europe's finest medical school of the late 1800's, Freud's research focused on observation rather than experimentation as reflected in his practice of psychoanalysis (Schriver, 1995). Psychodynamic psychotherapy assumes that human behavior is determined by the combined effect of one's inherited constitution and temperament and early experiences, particularly with parents, during the infancy and toddler stages of development. Humans are conceived of as systems whose energy is expressed in drives such as the life urge, or libido, and death wish, or destrudo. Most early behavior is motivated by unconscious drives. The development of these unconscious drives, in the id, is shaped by attachment to significant others. The ego analysts, such as Margaret Mahler, accept Freud's precepts about id development but emphasize that conscious processes also are an important domain of human behavior. The child grows from primarily unconscious thought (id experiencing) to secondary conscious thought (ego) through a series of psychosocial stages. Constitutional disturbances and environmental trauma interfere with the child's growth through the stages and with the equilibrium of the id and ego. If the disturbance is tolerable and the constitution strong, the ego may be able to defend against stress, and growth continues. If the constitution is somewhat vulnerable and the stress is repetitive, neurotic symptomatology characterized by inappropriate or overuse of defense mechanisms develops. If the disturbance is severe and/or chronic and the constitution weak, the child may exhibit psychotic symptomatology characterized by primitive id and ego functioning.

The child analytic theorists extend Freudian thought by breaking down Freud's oral stage into several more discreet phases. Moreover, they recognize that some. emotional problems are unique to children. The child's symptoms are symbolic, but the symbolism is age-specific. The child analysts have described critical differences between adult and child clients based upon their differing language ability and cognitive and physical development. Emotional disturbance is viewed as a defense against unconscious conflicts between impulses that are characteristic of a developmental stage and pressures in the environment that the child has internalized. The child analysts believe that the child will not suffer maladjustment unless he or she has internalized stress.

Further, the child analysts attempt to explain how psychoanalytic theory must be modified when working with children. They believe that, as is true when conducting therapy with adults, *talking through* helps a client resolve conflicts. However, they point out that free association is not possible. Instead, the child therapist encourages the child to use play to express motivations and conflicts. In play, the child reproduces her or his precepts of conflict within the family. These precepts may or may not coincide with the actual family interaction, but the analyst believes that it is these "introjects" (subjective perceptions) that cause the child stress. It is the introjection, not reality itself, that must be modified (Smirnoff, 1971). A number of specific ways of treatment follow from these psychoanalytic principles, as will be discussed later in this chapter.

Freud's landmark writing about the case of "Little Hans," in which Freud trained a father to help his son overcome a phobia of horses, paved the direction for psychoanalytic work with children, but it remained for a number of Freud's followers, such as his daughter, Anna Freud, Melanie Klein, and Margaret Mahler to describe explicitly how psychoanalytic child therapy could be conducted. As we shall see, the child psychoanalysts range greatly in principles and techniques. Yet, each accepts some basic tenets of analytic thought.

Melanie Klein: Principles of Child Psychoanalysis

Writing about child therapy as early as 1932, Melanie Klein postulated new concepts about the developmental stages of and psychic dynamics in children and offered a systematic means for conducting child play therapy. Klein believed that the first year of life is most critical in the child's personality development. She labeled the first five months as the Paranoid–Schizoid Position and age 6 months to 1 year as the Depressive Position.

The newborn does not sense a difference between her or himself and the mother, and thus Klein viewed the infant as in a dim state of awareness. The developing infant learns that all of her or his needs cannot be met. Sometimes the newborn is not fed when hungry. Sometimes the infant experiences discomfort. Thus, he or she feels many fears and anxieties so that Klein perceived the newborn in a somewhat paranoid state.

The depressive phase that occurs from age 6 months to 1 year is catalyzed by the weaning process (Klein, 1937). The infant experiences much anxiety and anger about being left alone. The infant learns to internalize, "introject," central facets of her or his life that are absent. At first, the infant introjects parts of these significant persons, "objects," in the environment. So, the infant introjects the mother's breasts or face. Klein strongly believed that the newborn has a sense of sexual relations so that the infant also introjects partial images of the sexual act. Gradually, the infant learns to introject whole objects, such as a precept of the mother and a precept of the father.

The infant tries to introject only good objects. Thus, he or she learns how to not internalize, to "project," perceptions that he or she perceives as bad. Therefore, the child may introject the "good breast" if the mother is supportive and nurturing or project the "bad breast" if the mother is cold or her milk is not good. If a newborn grows through the depressive position with basically positive feelings about the objects, the infant will introject a positive ideal object. The positive ideal object serves as a basis of the infant's developing ego and superego, protecting the infant against anxiety and helping to deal with her or his own aggression.

Sometimes processes of introjection and projection become confused or fragmented. The infant may introject bad objects in an effort to control them or project good objects to make the outside person seem safe. If the infant is angry at the parents because many of her or his needs are not met, the infant may never introject whole positive images of the object. Instead, the infant continues to introject "split" precepts, accepting only part of the object he or she experiences as safe. Because of "splitting" of introjects and projects (i.e., only internalizing part of the precept of an object), the disturbed infant does not develop healthy id and ego functioning. The child has an inability to tolerate frustration and to inhibit sexual impulses and does not see others accurately and completely. The infant may be overly aggressive or riddled with anxiety and guilt.

Changes in the infant's family will not help the disturbed child, because the child's introjects are split and disturbed. These confused and split introjections and projections, then, are the target of therapy. Klein wanted to help her child clients introject accurate perceptions of the objects in their lives and to reduce the splitting of significant objects into all positive or all negative introjection and projections (Smimoff, 1971).

Klein developed a systematic play therapy approach to help her child clients understand their motivation and develop more realistic images of others and themselves. At first, she conducted therapy by visiting the homes of her child patients. Later, she saw children in her office (Alexander & Selesnick, 1966). She presented toys of a "primitive kind"—little wooden people, trees, houses, paper, pencils, scissors, running water, and tumblers (Klein, 1960). She believed that if the therapist adopts a very neutral stance, transference occurs in which the child reacts to the therapist as the child perceives significant persons in her or his life. Each repetitive activity in play therapy is viewed as a representation of the child's unconscious conflicts. The more impulsive the play, the more likely it represents a past conflict (Feigelson, 1974). Klein advocated immediate and direct interpretation of the child's unconscious play activity. She felt that children would understand her statements unconsciously and was not deterred by the lack of overt response to her interventions. Her interpretations dealt with themes, such as the child's desire to kill the mother, father, or siblings; to incorporate the mother's breast or father's penis; or the child's interest in the primal scene. She believed play material and play activity held symbolic significance. For example, a child might view sticks as penises, bumping toys as sex, water as a symbol for sperm, fear of water as a fear of castration, and nose picking as an anal attack on the parents. She cautioned, however, that the therapist needed to know the child before interpreting the meaning of play objects and activities. The key to the symbolic import of the toy is not in the toy itself, but in the child's use of the play material (Klein, 1960). She felt that deep interpretations about the child's introjects enabled the client to develop more integrated views of her- or himself and to be more spontaneous and less inhibited (Smirnoff, 1971).

Klein defined the role of the therapist as one of friendly reserve. The therapist participates as little as possible in the play situation, but instead notes interpretations from a neutral, distant perspective. Klein's only adaptation of interpretation with children was the use of the child's vernacular. She interviewed mothers prior to therapy and asked them for the special words which the child used to describe excremental processes, sex, genitals, and masturbation. An example of Kleinian interpretation follows:

Case 4.1   The Case of Rita

"Rita (age 2 years, 9 months) put a triangular brick on one side and said, 'That's a little woman'; she then took a little 'hammer,' as she called another long-shaped brick, and hit the brick box with it exactly in a place where it was only stuck together with paper, so that she made a hole in it. She said, 'When the hammer hit hard, the little woman was so frightened.' Hitting with the hammer stood for coitus between her parents which she had witnessed until she was two years old." Klein's interpretation was, "Your daddy hit hard like that inside your mummy with his little hammer, and you were so frightened" (Klein, 1960, p. 162).

Although many analysts adopt Kleinian approaches in dealing with adult clients, her system of child analysis has been subject to much criticism. Many feel she is amiss in not focusing upon the child's actual relationship with the parents. She presented a singular, sexual view of children's motivation and was not open to other evidence. Kanner (1962a) discusses Klein's Case of Little Erma, who was seen in unfinished play analysis for 575 hours over 2 years. He writes sardonically:

> We are told she suffered from megalomania, paranoia, pseudologia, severe depression, sadistic and cannibalistic impulses, masochism, homosexual tendencies, anal love desires, a desire to be seduced and a few other signs of an extravagant and uncurbed instinctual life.—Her parents did not bring her back for the 576th play session (1962a, p. 239).

Even if we choose to disregard many of her interpretations, Klein helped clinicians see that children's behavior could be analyzed and that clinicians could interact with children in a therapeutic manner that is distinct from parenting or

teaching. We should give Klein credit for developing a system in which children's behavior can be interpreted to them. Moreover, she helped clinicians see that children do experience emotions of anger and anguish. Importantly, she emphasized that children's subjective perceptions of reality must be taken into account if we are to assist them.

Margaret Mahler: A Poignant View of Growing Up

Beginning her writings in the 1940's and continuing to the present, Margaret Mahler (1968) has built upon the more viable constructs of Kleinian analysis. She has refined explanations of children's development during the first two years of life. Her stages of autism, symbiosis, individuation, and rapprochement are described below.

Mahler explains that the newborn strives to replicate the homeostasis experienced in the mother's womb. From birth to 2 months, the newborn is in an autistic state, a state of absolute primary narcissism (i.e., the infant is totally preoccupied with her or his own well-being). The newborn feels no differentiation between her or himself and the primary nurturing figures. Mahler explains that this autistic phase is normal and healthy. If the child's needs are comfortably met during this time, the child moves smoothly into the symbiotic phase at about age 2 months.

From about 2 months to 1 year of age, the infant is in a twilight state of symbiosis. During this period, infants are only vaguely aware of the boundary between themselves and their nurturing figures. Mahler explains that the mother and other nurturing figures also experience the symbiotic state. The child and parent feel a mutual physical and psychological dependence.

From a period of about 16 months to 3 years, the child enters into the stage of separation/individuation. Concomitant to the child's development of locomotion, the infant moves into the differentiation subphase of separation—individuation. He or she develops a clear sense of self. Gradually, the child develops into a practicing subphase. The child tests the environment and the mother. Thus, the child plays games of hide and seek, or may refuse to cooperate with the parent's request. Through such "practicing," the child learns to function in an autonomous fashion.

While the child is pulling away from the mother, the child also wants to maintain close ties with the mother. "As the toddler realizes his or her power and ability to physically move away from his mother, the toddler now seems to have an increased need and a wish for his mother to share with him every new acquisition of skill and experience" (Mahler, 1968, p.25). If the nurturing figures encourage these explorations and remain supportive, the child develops positive feelings about functioning on her or his own.

Some mothers overprotect and over control the child during the individuation phase. Others are very rejecting of their children once they begin to assert themselves. These mothers may feel rejected by their children's stubbornness, refusal to cooperate, or tendency to run away, and so these mothers withhold any support to their children once they enter the individuation phase. Children who experience faulty upbringing at this stage may become overly dependent and shadow the maternal figure or become insulated from others because of the fear of engulfment. If the parent–child relationship is satisfactory during the separation–individuation phase, the child achieves a sense of autonomy.

Around age two, the child then moves into a rapprochement phase. Object constancy consolidates, and the infant can tolerate more time away from the primary caretaker. The father becomes important as a channel to the excitement and challenges of the external world. Comfortable with her or his own boundaries, the child approaches the parenting figures more affectionately and consistently. A "honeymoon" state in the parent–child relationship may continue for several years. It ends when the child enters school and begins to struggle with feelings of competence and adequacy.

Mahler has used her paradigm of infant psychosocial stages to explain the etiology of neurosis and psychosis. She postulates that the autistic child's development is blocked within the first few days of life. If the infant experiences physical ailments, social trauma, or poor mothering, the infant may perceive the mother as bad and be blocked to her. The child functions in the totally narcissistic state in which he or she was born. Psychosis may occur if the child does not successfully enter into the individuation stage. The psychotic child remains in a symbiotic state in which her or his sense of self is dimly perceived. The growth to individuation may be blocked by malfunctions of biological systems or by inadequate mothering. Some children may be predisposed not to use effectively their mother's nurturing. Neurosis may develop if movement through the individuation phase has been traumatic because the parent is over- or under-protective. The neurotic child longs for reuniting into the safety of the symbiotic phase, but does not want to lose identity. Thus, the child wavers between longing for symbiosis and fear of reengulfment (Mahler, 1968). The following case example illustrates Mahler's unique style.

Case 4.2 The Case of Violet

Violet explored the insides of the piano in a way that made one feel that the piano represented the mother's body: it was reminiscent of the way in which an infant of about ten months will carefully examine and inspect the mother's face and her body, in his attempts to differentiate himself after his emergence from the symbiotic phase. . . . For instance, one day, before a Christmas vacation, Violet chose to play a Clementi sonata on the piano. She took all the repeats over and over again, and thus did not bring the piece to an ending. The interpretation was made to Violet that she did not want the piece to come to an end, just as she did not want her time with the therapist to come to an end. Violet's crying and tantrums indicated that this interpretation was correct (Mahler, 1968, pp. 204–205).

Mahler bases the direction of her therapy upon her evaluation of the child's development. If the child is very autistic, Mahler views therapy as a "beginning period." The primary task of the therapist is to establish contact with the child and then to move the child through a symbiotic parenting stage, finally encouraging the child's striving for autonomy. If the child is psychotic, Mahler attempts to create a corrective parenting experience. The therapist provides support akin to healthy symbiotic parenting. The therapist allows the child much freedom, intercedes in any self-destructive play, and reassures the child that he or she is safe and loved. Once the child feels close, the therapist gradually gives her or him feedback that it is all right to pull away, that the therapist will remain a friend although the therapist and child must function as separate beings. With the neurotic child, the therapist must replay the traumatic separation, offering feedback that encourages the child to assert her or himself and allowing the child to ask for assistance when needed.

Mahler offers a broad conceptualization of early development; however, she does not delineate specific therapeutic approaches derived from her developmental framework. Her theory allows for broad psychodynamic descriptions of a client. Although very eloquent, the relationship between these abstract descriptions and effective therapeutic interventions is not always clear.

Anna Freud: Elucidation of Psychoanalytic Psychotherapy

Anna Freud began extending her father's writings to child analysis in the late 1920s and developed a coherent system for child therapy by 1940. Like Melanie Klein, she perceived child therapy as distinct from adult analysis because of children's developmental and conceptual limitations. However, her proposals for dealing with these developmental limitations differed radically from Melanie Klein. Whereas Klein believed analysis could be completed through play, Anna Freud felt analysis of the unconscious was not completely possible and often not necessary. Because the child's superego was not fully developed, Anna Freud proposed that a complete transference relationship would not develop. Children would sometimes see the therapist as a parent figure, sometimes as a real figure, and sometimes as a projection of themselves. Anna Freud suggested that the techniques of child therapy must be tailored to the degree of pathology and the degree of ego and superego development.

She agreed with her contemporaries' assessment of the importance of psychosocial stages of development and incorporated the stages posited by Klein and Mahler into her theoretical framework. She viewed the infant as moving through the stages of autism, symbiosis, and separation/individuation. She accepted Klein's tenet that from birth to 3 or 4 months of age, infants were in a need fulfilling stage in which the object is partly introjected. From about 4 months onward, the child develops object constancy, which allows for a positive inner image of the object to be maintained irrespective of satisfaction or dissatisfaction. She stressed the importance of the object-centered phallic and oedipal stages as identified by her father, Sigmund Freud, which are characterized by possession of the opposite-sexed parent and jealousy and cruelty toward the own-sexed parent. Anna Freud perceived the period of latency and preadolescence as a very important time in which the child learns control over her or his body. She believed that children's personal growth could be stymied by internal or external events at any stage, but she stressed that a certain amount of ego regression is expected and normal. Development of aspects of personality is uneven so that a degree of egocentrism and disequilibrium is typical in childhood.

Anna Freud proposed that since development is uneven, maladjustment cannot be diagnosed through the child's impaired functioning. Further, she proposed that the presence of suffering is not a reliable index of pathology because a certain degree of anxiety is a normal facet of development. Instead, Anna Freud maintained that maladjustment must be assessed by looking at the relationship of the child's id, ego, and superego functioning. Maladjustment is signaled if: the id is out of ego control; the id is in conflict with the superego; the ego control is rigid, allowing limited spontaneity; regressions are permanent; anxiety is internalized regardless of external events; frustration tolerance is low; and ability to sublimate and master anxiety is limited.

The goal of child therapy as perceived by Anna Freud was the alleviation of anxiety and neurotic symptomatology. She felt that this goal is difficult to accomplish because the child cannot free associate, because the ego is not fully developed, thereby limiting transference, and because the child does not voluntarily seek or understand treatment. On the other hand, she believed that the child's instinctual desire to grow was the therapist's greatest aid in therapy. Although the child may not choose to get well, the child will choose to develop. The successful child therapist exploits the child's natural desire for growth and autonomy.

A diagnostic procedure recommended by Anna Freud (1965) provided a comprehensive internal and external profile of the child. The external profile included referral symptoms, description of the child, family history, and information about significant environmental influences. The internal profile consisted of a personality assessment. The child was analyzed to determine whether he or she had developed to his or her age-adequate psychosexual stage. Regression, fixation points, and levels of aggression were noted. Ego functions, as evidenced by memory, speech, control of motility, and reality testing, were examined in detail.

To Anna Freud, the first step of child therapy is the establishment of a warm, positive relationship—what she referred to as a "positive transference relationship." The therapist provides the motivation for therapy by winning the child's respect and pointing out how therapy will help the child grow. The therapist then acts as an "auxiliary superego" to help the child evaluate the consequences of her or his thoughts and acts. The therapist encourages the child to discard ineffective defense mechanisms and teaches more appropriate sublimations. The therapist does interpret transferences and resistances when clearly present; however, Anna Freud believed that most children's problems reflected difficulty dealing with a reality, rather than replication of events from the child's past. Thus, Anna Freud, unlike Melanie Klein, would not offer deep interpretations to children experiencing reactive stress, e.g., maladjustment spurred by external events such as divorce or death in the family. In cases of reactive stress, the therapist encourages the child to function more effectively in reality. Only when symptoms are deeply rooted and exacerbated by internalized distortions does the therapist attempt systematic analytic uncovering of id material. For example, if a child in play therapy competitively bumped two toy cars against each other, Melanie Klein might react by interpreting the behavior to the child as a reflection of her or his repressed sexual fantasies. For most children, Anna Freud would view this activity as indicating the child's realistic concerns about the dangers of life. Only when consistent sexual conflict is apparent would Anna Freud venture a "deep interpretation."

Whereas Melanie Klein developed a theory for conducting psychoanalysis with children, Anna Freud presents a model for doing psychoanalytic psychotherapy. Freud explained that psychoanalytic psychotherapy was more appropriate for the majority of childhood disorders which are reactive, precipitated by external stresses. In sum, psychoanalytic psychotherapy encourages the child's natural urge for growth. The causative factors of the child's distress are carefully considered. The therapist looks for means of aiding the child in overcoming issues and tapping her or his own potential.

Techniques Common to the Psychodynamic Approaches

A child welfare worker employing psychodynamic psychotherapy assumes that the child's symptoms and behaviors are complex and carry many meanings. He or she knows the child's language is concrete and that the dialogue between the therapist and the child is often action, the language of play. The worker becomes a player under the direction of the child. As the player, the worker represents the transference aspect of the treatment relationship. The child welfare worker, as the observer, represents the therapeutic alliance aspect of the relationship. The initial or immature alliance is based upon a positive relationship with an adult. The adult worker becomes a trusted, helping person, a person who will follow and whose lead can safely be followed. Then, the child gradually becomes more willing to do psychotherapeutic work. The child begins to expose the way he or she relates to significant others in the world. In child psychodynamic work an alliance with the child is not enough. An effective therapeutic alliance also must be built with the family.

Psychodynamic treatment is centered upon techniques that enable "uncovering" (that is, to "uncover the blocked off internal life") in order to provide insight to the child. The techniques to facilitate uncovering include

- confrontation where the behavior in question is made evident and explicit

- clarification, during which the experience is further exemplified

- interpretation, in which the unconscious meaning is suggested to the client. Effective interpretation gives the child a human context for his or her disturbing feeling

- working through, which involves the repetition and elaborated exploration of the meaning of the insight, its relationship to the child's symptoms and problems of daily living

The child welfare worker is quite alert to making interventions that may come from the transference relationship; that is, derivatives of meaningful and significant relationships of the past emerge in the treatment situation because of the therapeutic alliance. Interventions about the wishes, fears, and memories of experiences often can be most powerfully accomplished by looking at the dynamics of the living relationship of worker and child (Chethik, 1989). In other words, by making interpretations about the nature of the worker–child relationship, the worker facilitates deeper uncovering. Eventually, with insight and catharsis, the child client becomes free from the bondage of past emotional pain.

Summary

The historical contribution of psychoanalytic theory to the field of child theory is enormous. The psychoanalysts proposed a number of constructs about psychosocial development that are accepted broadly by child specialists:

1. Childhood is critical in the development of human personality.

2. Aspects of child personality are biologically determined.

3. Much motivation is physiologically and unconsciously catalyzed.

4. Acceptance and love in childhood are necessary for healthy personality development.

5. Family and cultural conditions can prevent or distort the normal expression of unconscious drives.

6. Childhood traumas can become deeply entrenched, blocking further development.

7. The sex drive is natural and powerful.

8. Using play, children's unconscious motivation can be understood.

9. Unconscious drives can advantageously be brought to the surface of the conscious so that they are understood and controlled.

10. By analyzing and interpreting children's motivations, crippling anxieties and defenses can be redressed.

Many child therapists hold that psychodynamic explanation remains a very viable way of explaining, predicting, and modifying children's behavior. Anthony (1970) writes:

> There is also no other set of constructions as clinically useful in elucidating different aspects of personality development. . . . The theory is at its best when showing how instinctive motivation operates in the production of thoughts and feelings and it contains an elaborate and sophisticated theory regarding the ways in which the instincts lead to thoughts and feelings and then on to behavior (pp. 706–707).

The major criticisms of psychoanalytic child theory are leveled at the abstraction of the terms, some of which are not clearly defined and consequently cannot be empirically tested and at the lack of specific psychotherapeutic techniques construed from the theories. Other criticisms are based upon an incomplete understanding of analytic thought. For example, many claim that psychoanalytic precepts must be employed for years in the therapeutic process before clients demonstrate significant change. However, Anna Freud helped us understand that through psychoanalytic psychotherapy, reactive maladjustment, spurred by external stress, maybe treated rather rapidly. Moreover, therapists of varied persuasions agree that true personality reconstruction requires years of intervention. Critics of psychoanalytic therapy are apt to claim that insight is not necessary for behavioral change. The psychoanalytic psychotherapists do perceive insight as an important facet of the therapeutic process even though insight may not be a prerequisite for symptom removal. Insight allows clients to understand and control their motivations and operate freely and spontaneously. Many psychoanalytic psychotherapists, such as Margaret Mahler and Anna Freud, recognize the importance of other therapeutic techniques. Besides interpretations, they stress the importance of the therapeutic relationship and of a corrective emotional experience within the therapy hour. Another criticism concerns the validity of interpretations (e.g., especially those symbolic interpretations recommended by Klein). These criticisms seem valid. It is quite a jump from a child playing with pick-up sticks to an interpretation of the child wanting to incorporate the father's penis. On the other hand, the ineffectiveness in child therapy is often due to poor or inaccurate interpretations rather than the use of interpretations per se. Before a clinician can effectively employ analytic approaches to child therapy, the therapist must become very knowledgeable in analytic thought so that the interpretation of a client's psychodynamic responses recognize the depth and complexity of human motivation and stress. Analytic techniques can be a powerful contribution to the child therapy armamentarium if the therapist is scholarly in her or his approach to the theory and cautious and deliberate in using the techniques.

Chapter 5
Behavioral and Cognitive Contributions to Child Theory

The behavioral and cognitive approaches to be discussed in this chapter differ markedly from the psychoanalytic approach (Schriver, 1995) discussed in Chapter 4 and from the psychosocial approach to be taken up in the next chapter. Some psychologists believed that if psychology was to be accepted as science then they should study only what they could see and measure (Berger, 1988). The behavioral approaches are linked directly to the psychology of learning and have their roots in the work of Pavlov, Watson, Thorndike, and B. F. Skinner (Zigler & Stevenson, 1993). The cognitive approaches are tied to the newer developments in cognitive psychology with roots in information processing, linguistics, and problem solving. Some readers may wonder about the appropriateness of discussing both the behavioral and cognitive approaches within one chapter, and some disagreement regarding the nature of their relationship can be found in the literature (Ledwidge, 1978). Our premise here is that they do possess certain similarities, and that over the years, some of the concepts from cognitive theory have been incorporated into behavior therapy. Leading cognitive behaviorists such as Mahoney, who wrote *Cognition and Behavior Modification* (1974), and Meichenbaum, the author of *Cognitive Behavior Modification* (1977), refer to cognitions or "self-statements" as classes of behavior. Thus, whereas psychotherapy was and still is considered to be the process of changing a person's mind through verbal methods, changing an individual's self-statements involves changing behaviors—the goal of behavior therapy. Because of this similarity, both approaches are included in this chapter, although they are discussed separately.

Behavior Theory

Historical Foundations

Behaviorism began as a revolt against the subjective influence prevalent in psychology at the turn of the century. John B. Watson in 1913 argued for a scientific psychology based on the objective study of behavior. In establishing behaviorism as the modus operandi of psychology, Watson adopted Pavlov's classical conditioning model as the way in which psychologists should proceed in their study of behavior. According to Watson, all behavior was learned through the principles of classical conditioning. Today, this model of conditioning is called respondent, Pavlovian, or classical conditioning.

Watson was joined by numerous other American psychologists in his call for an objective, scientific psychology based on behavior. Edward L. Thorndike, as early as 1898, for instance, was advocating a psychology based on the Law of Effect. According to Thorndike's Law of Effect, a behavior is learned as a consequence of the "satisfying state of affairs" or reward that follows the response. Similarly, a response ceases to occur if followed by an "aversive state of affairs" or punishment (Thorndike, 1898). One major advocate of both behaviorism and the Law of Effect has been B. F. Skinner. In his now classic book, *The Behavior of Organisms*, published in 1938, Skinner argued that although respondent conditioning was important, more of our everyday behaviors are shaped through operant conditioning. This is a conditioning paradigm in which the rate of the desired response or behavior is contingent upon the consequence. Focusing on operant conditioning as the major type of conditioning, Skinner and his students have sought to show that principles of learning discovered in the laboratory are applicable to a wide range of behavioral problems. The application of these principles to behavioral problems is known as behavior modification or behavioral engineering.

In addition to the operant and classical conditioning models, another approach can be included under the auspices of behavior theory: social learning. This approach, developed primarily by Bandura (1969), claims that much behavior can be learned on a vicarious basis through the observation of the behavior of others. The technique of modeling is used, often in conjunction with various operant procedures, to gain therapeutic effects.

Behavior Therapy: Principles and Techniques

Behavior therapy is based on the premise that all behavior is learned and that behavior can be changed through the principles of learning. Behavioral therapists propose that behaviors judged to be adjusted or maladjusted are learned according to one or more of the three behavioral approaches (respondent, operant, or social learning). The subjectively felt outcome of well-adjusted behavior is a sense of personal well-being. The subjectively experienced outcome of maladjustment is anxiety. To the behavior therapist, therapy is a special learning environment. The client is not viewed as sick, but rather as lacking in adaptive skills. Behavioral therapy stresses that clients are capable of and must ultimately assume an autonomous, effective way of living. As the client learns to respond appropriately, maladjustment and subjectively felt anxiety decrease. The behavioral child therapist is concerned with identifying the links between the environment and the child's responses. The behavior therapist is willing to actively intervene and to change the stream of events in the client's life. Target behaviors are increased and decreased using a variety of techniques within a supportive therapeutic relationship (Keat, 1974). The client's autonomy is increased as a result of learning (Fullmer & Bernard, 1972).

The first step in behavior therapy as in other approaches is to establish a comfortable therapeutic relationship (Schwartz & Goldiamond, 1975). The client must feel open to talk to the social worker about the extent and ramifications of the problem for which help is being sought. Then, the behavior therapist works with the client to clearly identify those behaviors to be changed and to define the desired behaviors. Those factors that maintain the dysfunctional behaviors or that prevent the occurrence of functional behaviors are then identified. Next, the resources that are available in the client's environment, or elsewhere, are discussed. Finally, the practitioner considers those procedures or techniques that are most likely to have an effect on the identified behaviors (Fischer & Gochros, 1975).

One of the distinguishing features of behavior therapy is that the intervention techniques used can be evaluated as to their effectiveness in a variety of settings and with different types of problems (Pinkston, Levitt, Green, Linsk, & Rzepnicki, 1982). Before the intervention is introduced, a baseline of desired target behaviors or dysfunctional behaviors is carefully developed. This baseline is obtained by noting the frequency of these behaviors over some definable period of time, such as hours, days, or weeks. With the introduction of the intervention technique (which is itself clearly operationalized), this record of behaviors is maintained and provides both social worker and client with an indication of the relative effectiveness of the intervention.

The behavior therapist has a wide variety of techniques from which to choose and, as mentioned above, selects the most appropriate technique as a part of the assessment process. These techniques are based on the principles of either the operant, respondent, or social learning behavior theory approach.

Operant Conditioning Techniques.   These techniques involve the processes of reinforcement and punishment. Reinforcement maintains and increases the probability of a behavior; whereas, punishment decreases the probability of a behavior. Both reinforcement and punishment involve either adding something to the environment (positive reinforcement or punishment) or removing something from the environment (negative reinforcement or punishment). As a general rule, positive reinforcement is the technique of choice, although the others also can be very effective under the correct circumstances (Fischer & Gochros, 1975).

Reinforcement Techniques.   In the use of reinforcement, it is important to determine what is reinforcing for that particular child. In early behavioral therapy, a limited number of reinforcers were used, e.g., food, praise. It is now recognized that a variety of reinforcers are feasible, and these vary for each client. Thus, praise may be reinforcing for one child, but another might feel embarrassed if, for example, he or she is praised in front of peers. This attention then actually serves as a punishment and has the effect of decreasing the frequency of the desired behavior. Keat (1979) recommends asking children about their likes and dislikes before implementing behavioral counseling. A list of the child's preferred reinforcers is known as a "reinforcement menu." Some unusual activities such as being left alone, watching other people, or reading may be potent reinforcers to some children.

Once the child's reinforcers are determined, they can be systematically applied by parents, teachers, or in some cases by the child. Among older children, a token or point system can be implemented. Tokens can be given each time the appropriate behavior is carried out. The token can later be "cashed in" for the reinforcer the child prefers. Token systems have been effective in many different settings, including homes, institutions, and schools. In addition, they seem effective in dealing with a wide range of problem behaviors (Kazdin, 1977).

In many cases, it may not be sufficient to simply tell the child what behaviors are desired and which ones will be reinforced. The desired response may not be part of the child's behavioral repertoire. In these cases, the reinforcement technique of shaping can be used. Small steps of the desired behavior or successive approximations are reinforced as they occur. For example, in some cases of primary encopresis, the child needs to learn appropriate toilet behavior. Each of the steps involved in this behavior, such as attending quickly to body signals, going to the bathroom, removing clothes, sitting down, and releasing sphincter control are reinforced.

Extinction in behavior theory refers to a situation where the consequences that previously reinforced or punished a behavior no longer occur. As a result, the behavior either increases or decreases. A characteristic of extinction is the extinction curve, an increase in undesirable behavior before the client is able to discriminate the new contingency system. For example, a child demands much parental attention, displaying temper tantrums at bedtime and insisting his parents not leave the room until he goes to sleep. Extinction of the parents' attention was carried out which resulted in the child crying for 45 minutes the first night, 20 minutes the second night, 10 minutes the third night, and finally no crying. Extinction should be used with caution, preferably in combination with reinforcement. Differential attention is given in which the undesirable behavior is ignored and the desirable behavior reinforced. Children's aggression has been treated successfully this way (Pinkston, et al., 1982).

Another reinforcement technique is that of behavior rehearsal, which involves the child practicing the complex verbal and/or physical desired behaviors in the safe therapeutic environment. Thus, the rehearsed behavior is systematically reinforced in vitro. In time, the child will feel confident to express this complex repertoire in the natural environment, and parents and teachers can be alerted to reinforce this behavior when it occurs in vivo.

Contingency contracting is a reinforcement technique which involves the child client, social worker, and other participating adults (for example, teachers) drawing up a written agreement specifying the therapeutic process. The contract includes the child's goals, the desired behaviors, and preferred reinforcers. If the contract is broken by any party, a joint meeting is held to determine the reason for the broken contract. Renegotiation takes place. Contingency contracting usually involves the use of positive reinforcement, although punishment-based techniques are sometimes used.

Punishment Techniques.   These techniques are used to decrease the future probability of undesirable behaviors. As with extinction, no punishment techniques should be used alone, without teaching appropriate replacement behaviors, as the result may be withdrawal by the client or the development of some emotional problems. One punishment technique involves the presentation of an aversive event (something that is unpleasant to the individual). Extreme cases of self-destruction and aggression can be decreased by this intervention (Lovaas & Bucher, 1974). Response cost involves removing an event to decrease the future probability of a behavior (compared with negative reinforcement which also involves removing a reinforcing event but with the intent of increasing a behavior). Response cost works particularly well in combination with a token system. Hall, Panyon, Rabon, & Broden (1972) reduced whining, complaining, and crying by removing free tokens contingent upon the occurrence of these behaviors. Time out is another form of punishment. The child is removed from a reinforcing situation following an occurrence of the undesirable behavior. This is a technique that has been effective with aggressive, acting out children (Bostow & Barley, 1969).

Respondent Conditioning Techniques.   A number of techniques have been developed from the respondent model of behavior theory. Many of these techniques are based on the concept of counter conditioning; the assumption is made that some emotional responses cannot occur at the same time as other responses; in other words, they are incompatible.

Systematic desensitization is probably the most widely used and best known respondent technique based on counter conditioning. A response of relaxation is paired with an anxiety producing stimulus such that the bonding results in the stimulus evoking relaxation rather than anxiety. In the therapeutic application, the child is taught to relax during situations that elicit anxiety and maladaptive responses. The originator of systematic desensitization, who referred to the underlying principle of this technique as "occupational inhibition," was Joseph Wolpe (1961). Using the method with adults, Wolpe described the process of desensitization as the method consisting of

> presenting to the imagination of the deeply relaxed patient the feeblest item in a list of anxiety evoking stimuli—repeatedly, until no more anxiety is evoked. The next item in the list is presented, and so on, until eventually, even the strongest of the anxiety evoking stimuli fails to evoke any stir of anxiety in the patient (p. 191).

Keat (1974) recommends that a potent way to teach children how to relax is through systematic deep breathing exercises. The breathing exercises can be practiced individually or in group sessions. Practicing isometric exercises also is effective in helping some children learn to identify and create relaxation. Once the child learns to identify the subjective feeling of relaxation and knows how to create these sensations, he or she can pair relaxation with the anxiety-producing situations. The child insomniac can practice deep breathing upon retiring; or the child who is afraid to speak in class can practice isometric hand clinching before beginning to deliver a speech and during the speech if any anxiety reappears.

Wolpe's (1969) approach of systematic desensitization has the broadest research and empirical support of any behavior therapy technique and has been successfully implemented with children. However, several child behaviorists (e.g., Erickson, 1978 and Keat, 1974) have pointed out that it is difficult to teach children to relax systematically, construct a fear hierarchy, and imagine specific scenes. Keat (1974) suggests that it often is more effective with children to practice the increasingly anxiety producing situations in vivo rather than in vitro, relying upon the child's imagination. Thus, Lazarus, Davison, and Polefka (1965) successfully treated a child with a school phobia by gradually exposing the child to the school environment, systematically reinforcing the approach to school behaviors.

Another widely used respondent conditioning-based technique is assertion training. Here, the intention is for the client to reduce the anxiety that inhibits expression and at the same time increase assertive behaviors. The expression of assertive feeling then inhibits anxiety (Wolpe, 1969). The child who is bullied by peers may be taught how to look angry and how to fight. Assertion training often consists of a combination of techniques, for example, the use of positive reinforcement and modeling.

Social Learning Techniques.   Modeling procedures can be used to teach both new skills and new ways of combining old skills. Modeling results in new behaviors being elicited which can then be reinforced using operant techniques such as positive reinforcement. Feedback, which stresses the positive aspects of the client's performance, and rehearsal by the client also can be used in combination with modeling and reinforcement. This combination has been used successfully for parent training programs (Nay, 1979). Bandura (1969) has carried out extensive research on the use of modeling for a variety of behaviors and its effectiveness as an intervention technique appears to have been confirmed.

The case of Michael which follows exemplifies the use of humanistic core conditions and modeling of spontaneous behavior to assist a rigid, withdrawn child. The authors have coined the term "expansion training" (Kaczmarek & LeVine, 1980) for the eclectic approach demonstrated in this case that is particularly suited to anxious children. The primary principles of expansion training can be summarized as:

1. The social worker avoids reflection, insight, interpretation, and other feedback that may reinforce anxious thinking.

2. The social worker models spontaneous, playful behavior in the counseling sessions and assures that such behavior does not merit punishment.

3. The social worker does not actively involve parents or teachers to reinforce or monitor the child's behavior. Changes are gradual, appropriate, and self-reinforcing.

4. The social worker verbally reinforces any active and spontaneous behavior that the client exhibits in sessions (as long as it is not dangerous to the client or to others), whether or not the behavior is goal directed.

5. The social worker designs one or more relatively innocuous conflict situations in the counseling sessions and then models alternative ways of handling those dilemmas.

6. As counseling progresses, the social worker models conflict situations that more closely illustrate a client's concern and again models alternative behavior for handling the dilemmas.

The case provides a brief overview of the symptomology leading to Michael's referral by his classroom teacher to the school counselor. The activities of several exemplary sessions are then over viewed.

Implications of Behavior Therapy

A number of studies have demonstrated that learning principles derived from early experimental research with animals and humans can provide a clear and systematic way of helping children modify inappropriate behavior and learn more appropriate alternatives. Research about the efficacy of the behavioral approaches is strong. Some profoundly disturbed children have been helped by behavioral approaches when all other therapeutic techniques have failed (Lovaas, Koegel, Simmons, & Stevens–Long, 1973). One of the most powerful features of behavior therapy is that the method of continuously monitoring behaviors (partly made possible because of the observative nature of child behavior) allows for constant and precise evaluation of the efficacy of treatment (Pinkston, et al., 1982).

Case 5.1   The Case of Michael

History

Michael, an 8-year-old boy, was referred for counseling by his father, a school counselor. Michael was an only child who lived with his father and stepmother. Michael's father was concerned about his son's lack of friends, maintenance of a power struggle in the home, and rigidity in completing tasks.

Before our meeting, Michael had participated in a client-centered, peer-counseling group, where he initiated a power struggle. According to the group facilitator, Michael used the group to discuss his own issues. He talked about his lack of friends and accused the other group members of not liking him. Michael became emotional, sometimes screaming at his peers, often crying and ventilating hostility toward his father. "I hate my father. I have the world's worst father." After two sessions, Michael became an unwilling group member. He complained about coming and used the excuse that he was falling behind in his schoolwork. In the words of the group facilitator, "I was not pleased with the results."

Michael's third-grade teacher reemphasized his lack of friends. According to her, Michael was hesitant to approach other children, but when he did, he tended to alienate his peers with "his subordinate attitudes and his agitated behavior." Michael rarely went out for recess, and on the few occasions when he did, he played alone.

Sessions II and III

The practitioner decided to follow Michael's lead in determining the activity to use for modeling spontaneous behavior. His favorite classroom activity, drawing with colored markers, was his choice. Michael's first drawing was a desert landscape that took him two sessions to complete. He outlined the mountains, the sun, and the moon before he proceeded to methodically color them, using predominantly blue, brown, and black.

Atop the highest mountain peak, he drew a rock and a yucca tree, both placed precariously near the edge. After he had completed the picture, Michael wrote the words Help, OK, and Never.

Michael gave rigid attention to detail and took a very careful approach to drawing. Whenever he took a marker from a box, he would slip a pencil in its place. He would stop the tape recorder while drawing because he could not draw and speak simultaneously.

During this session, the practitioner purposely did not put the caps back on the markers as a way of demonstrating more spontaneous behavior. Michael slapped the practitioner's hand and stated, "You don't leave caps off markers. They'll dry up." The practitioner also noticed that Michael froze when he accidentally drew on the table. He wiped the table clean immediately because he believed that he would be reprimanded. During both sessions he left after only 20 minutes had elapsed. (continued)

Session IV

The practitioner concentrated on modeling freer methods of drawing. Michael had begun work on a house when the practitioner dumped all of the markers onto the table and began to make bold strokes on the paper.

> PRACTITIONER: I am going to draw with my eyes closed.
>
> MICHAEL: You cheat; you just make lines.
>
> PRACTITIONER: I make whatever I feel like making.
>
> MICHAEL: You never know what you're making until you're done.
>
> PRACTITIONER: I don't like to know what I'm making. It's fun to figure it out when I'm done. And if I don't really make anything, that's all right too.
>
> *Time passes (15 minutes).*
>
> MICHAEL: I want to make what you're making, it looks more interesting.

Michael put the house drawing aside and began to draw with his eyes closed. He also started to imitate the practitioner's choice of color. Then Michael exhibited spontaneous behavior beyond simple imitation by drawing with three colors at once. The completed picture was a conglomeration of circular colored lines that were thickly massed in the center and thinly massed as they moved away from the center. Michael finished the session by writing the word happy on his drawing. The practitioner had to remind him that the session was over.

Session V

Because Michael had shown fear when he accidentally wrote on the table, the practitioner decided to model an alternate way of dealing with a similar situation. The practitioner broke one of Michael's favorite markers on purpose.

> MICHAEL: What happened to the marker?
>
> PRACTITIONER: It was on the floor and I stepped on it. It was an accident—no big deal.
>
> MICHAEL: Won't it cost a lot of money to get another?
>
> PRACTITIONER: Not really.
>
> MICHAEL: This sure is your bad luck day.
>
> PRACTITIONER: Bad day—no. It was just one of those things that happens. It's really no big deal.

In this session Michael remembered having drawn with his eyes closed, and he expressed a desire to repeat the experience. The practitioner followed Michael's lead and ended up with a series of multicolored marks on her paper. Michael looked at the practitioner's picture and decided the marks were actually "dots." Taking a black crayon, he quickly connected the dots to form a creature with two distinct heads, one on each side of the paper, that joined in the middle of the paper. Each of the appendages was given an eye and Michael proudly announced that he had drawn a "dragon walking backwards."

Results

The practitioner saw Michael for 30-minute sessions each week for one semester. It was difficult to find a measurable index to monitor results. His curriculum had been individualized, and it was not possible to compare the number of assignments given and the number completed. The only index available was the number of times that Michael went out to recess. In February, before counseling was initiated, Michael did not go out to recess at all. Even though his teacher sent him out, he would sneak back into the room to work on assignments. By the end of the semester, Michael was attending recess at least twice a week. Because the practitioner saw Michael during the recess period, the maximum number of times he could go out was four. Also, when Michael did stay in from recess, it was increasingly done to complete art projects, a favorite pastime of his.

The practitioner did not actively involve Michael's parents in the counseling process. Michael's parents, however, did seek out the practitioner at the close of the semester to discuss the changes they observed in their son. Michael's five-year struggle with his stepmother had eased considerably. He gradually learned to verbalize his difficulty in adjusting to changes. Now when Michael loses in a game of Monopoly with his family, instead of throwing a tantrum he says, "No big deal."

A major criticism of the behavioral approach is that the techniques are necessary but not sufficient to ameliorate a range of maladjustment. Some argue that the behavioral approaches are needlessly tedious because they do not exploit children's ability to think. These critics argue that through understanding and/or cognitive restructuring (to be discussed in the next section), complex responses can be rapidly taught. They believe behavioral approaches are limited because they emphasize the development of discrete response sets. Yet, no one could argue that the extinction of extremely maladaptive behavior and development of new appropriate behavior is not an important gain. The issue, then, is not whether behavior therapy works, but how its effectiveness can be extended by combining it with approaches that focus on clients' developing a broad range of new attitudes, behaviors, and emotions. One way in which this combination has taken place has been with the development of the socio-behavioral approach (Thomas, 1977) which uses techniques derived from behavior therapy and social psychology. Another development has been that of cognitive behavior therapy.

Cognitive Behavior Therapy

Recent years have witnessed a sharp resurgence of interest in cognitive processes. Essentially, cognitive psychologists are interested in studying and understanding complex mental processes such as imagery, symbolic representation of external events, and verbal coding of experience. Perhaps the most dramatic development in behavior therapy in the 1970s was the emphasis on cognitive processes in behavior therapy. The terms "cognitive behavior therapy" and "cognitive behavior modification" are used frequently to describe this recent development. The procedures that have received most attention in the recent development of cognitive behavior therapy and that merit the most attention because of their importance are referred to as cognitive restructuring. The essential notion of cognitive restructuring is that emotional disorders are the result of maladaptive thought patterns, and the task of therapy is to restructure these maladaptive cognitions.

The maladaptive thought patterns include the characteristically negative interpretations of the self, world, and future as described by Aaron Beck (1982) in his study of adult and childhood depression. Other cognitions that are the target of change are negative self-schema, that is, very negative sets of beliefs and propositions about the self. Still others focus on the attributional style of the child. The attributional style refers to the cognitions the child uses to explain the causes of events. For example, some children will feel the causes of their distress are uncontrollable, while others feel that the causes are something they can control. Others see the causes as due to luck, while others attribute the causes to their competency. Of course, it is easier to cope if one's attributions are not discouraging to the self. Thus, if children learn to see events as controllable, or due to external factors, they may find them easier to manage and change than if they view those events as caused by uncontrollable elements or caused by their own intrinsic limitations. Relatedly, some cognitive behaviors attempt to reshape feelings of helplessness. Let us now examine some of the various techniques that fall under the general rubric of cognitive restructuring techniques.

Rational-Emotive Therapy

Albert Ellis (1962) was one of the first psychotherapists to explore use of cognitive restructuring in his "A, B, C" approach to therapy. Ellis explains that we usually perceive the events at point "A" as causing the negative reactions at point "C." For example, a child may perceive others' teasing on the playground (point "A") as causing him or her to be alone (point "C"). Ellis proposes that it is the child's interpretation of point "A," "Nobody likes me" or "I'll never have any friends" (point "B"), that causes the undesirable state at point "C."

A	B	C
Teasing on Playground	"I must be awful." or "No one ever likes me." or "I can't defend myself." or "Kids always pick on me." etc., as if to say, "I am awful."	Child now hesitates to interact with others at school; or child now acts differently from other children, dressing peculiarly,

When clients experience maladjustment, to Ellis it is because their self-cognitions at point "B" carry a highly charged self-criticism, "catastrophizing" the consequences at point "A." Programmed with a new cognitive interpretation of the event, the negative consequences will be attenuated.

A	B	C
Teasing on Playground	"Oh, well, who wanted to be friends with them?" Or "So they tease me, that's not so awful." Or "Lots of kids get teased." Or "Teasing is attention, and I like attention."	Child still seeks company of others and withdrawal from awkwardness with peers does not generalize.

Ellis' (1962) approach is very directive. He capitalizes upon clients' desires to please the practitioner. He suggests, persuades, and bombards the clients with feedback aimed at restructuring their self-cognitions (Freedman, Kaplan, & Sadock, 1976). In the Case of Charlie, Keat (1974, pp. 76–77) employs Ellis' Rational-Emotive Therapy to restructure Charlie's self-destructive messages about his repaired and practically unnoticeable cleft palate.

Case 5.2   The Case of Charlie

PRACTITIONER: Let's see what the other children are saying to you. What do they call you?

CHARLIE: Usually two names. Either Bugs Bunny or Lippy.

PRACTITIONER: How do you feel when they say this?

CHARLIE: Bad.

PRACTITIONER: Let me guess what you're telling yourself. "Other kids call me Bugs Bunny or Lippy, so I must be pretty funny looking."

CHARLIE: Yeah.

PRACTITIONER: What's so great about what they think? How do they rate to say how you look?

CHARLIE: Don't know.

PRACTITIONER: Well, they're not really so hot. Let's see about the Bugs Bunny bit. Look at my teeth (practitioner shows his crooked teeth). Whose do you think are worse? Mine or yours? (Some practitioners use a mirror at this stage to show the client how he looks.)

CHARLIE: Yours.

PRACTITIONER: Okay. That's the reality of it. My teeth are worse off than yours. Now what's so bad about yours?

CHARLIE: Not much.

PRACTITIONER: Right. You know the saying "sticks and stone"?

CHARLIE: Yeah.

PRACTITIONER: What's the rest?

CHARLIE: You know it.

PRACTITIONER: Yeah. But I want to hear you say it.

CHARLIE: What's that again?

PRACTITIONER: "Sticks and stones will break my bones but . . ."

CHARLIE: Yeah.

PRACTITIONER: What's the rest?

CHARLIE: Names will never hurt me."

PRACTITIONER: That's it. But that's not what you're telling yourself. Names do hurt you now. But they shouldn't. So now, what do you say?

CHARLIE: Names won't hurt me

PRACTITIONER: That's right. And also, I feel sorry for others who have to pick on you to feel good. It's really their problem if they need to make fun of you.

In this case, four attitudes were *restructured cognitively*. The child was (1) told not to value others' opinions so much; (2) confronted with reality; (3) told alternative sentences to say to himself; and (4) taught to project the pathology onto the other children rather than absorbing it as his problem. By using oneself as a guide to one's self-esteem, the child has a more stable means for evaluating himself. In reality, some of the most physically beautiful people consider themselves ugly, such as Marilyn Monroe. Through cognitive restructuring, unsure children can learn that physical attributes are basically what a person tells him or herself they are. Perceptions are, of course, influenced by environmental feedback, but the crucial dimension is what the person tells him or herself.

Emotive Imagery

Another technique of cognitive restructuring is to present *emotive imagery* to the child (Lazarus, 1976). Images can be physically drawn or verbally presented that help children conceive of their behavior or attitudes in new ways. Thus, if a child were afraid of a class bully, he could be encouraged to see the bully holding a baby bottle, saying his threats in a baby-tone.

Or if a child were afraid of speaking in class, he would be encouraged to see himself as some force with whom he identifies. For example, he would see himself as Splinter, leader of the Teenage Mutant Ninja Turtles, speaking to his clan of turtles, who are anxious to learn from him.

Paradoxical Intention

Another means of attaining cognitive restructuring is *paradoxical intention*, in which the practitioner greatly exaggerates and encourages the child to overuse her or his symptomatology. Symptoms help a client to avoid dealing directly with stressful events. Paradoxical intention seems to facilitate adaptation because it encourages a client to move through a conflict situation and stop the unending repetition of the *approach-avoidance behavior*. Marshall (1976) presents several creative examples of the use of the paradoxical intention with children:

- Ask a child who says, "I don't know" frequently, rather than looking at the consequences of her or his acts, to develop a list of "Rules for Not Knowing."

- To the silent child or one who talks but does not share the true content of his or her feelings, practice being silent.

- To the child who tends to dismiss her or his inappropriate behavior as "not important," make a list of "How to Have Fun."

- With manipulative children, have them teach you "Rules for Not Winning."

- To the mistrusting children, tell them not to come to therapy since you are sure you cannot make it worth their while.

As another example, Caron (1980) worked with a child who had developed a habit of urinating 10 to 15 times per hour. The child constantly asked to use the bathroom whether at home or at school. The behavior seemed to be maintained because it created a sense of power in the child. He felt he had maximal control over his significant adults. The practitioner challenged the child, "I bet you couldn't go to the bathroom 20 times in an hour. You've never been able to go that often. Let's keep a record. If you can go 20 times in an hour, then I'll be really impressed." The child was placed in a double-bind. If he accepted the practitioner's challenge, he would be cooperating and thus would lose his power over the practitioner's desires. In the first therapy session, he asked to use the bathroom four times. The challenge was reinstated in the next session. "I'm really disappointed you couldn't use the bathroom 20 times in our last session. I really thought you could do it." The client did not ask to use the bathroom during the entire session. The new behavior quickly generalized to other environments.

Self-Instructional Training

This technique, developed by Meichenbaum (1977), became very popular. The method resembles Ellis' (1962) approach since it holds that irrational self-talk is the cause of emotional disorders. To make the technique applicable to children, Meichenbaum borrowed from the theorizing of Luria (1961), who has written on the developmental sequence by which children develop internalized speech and exert verbal symbolic control over their behavior. According to Luria, the behavior of children is first regulated by the instructions of adults; eventually, children acquire control over their own behavior through the use of overt self-instructions which they ultimately internalizes covert self-instructions. The steps involved in self-instructional training are as follows:

1. The child is trained to identify and become aware of maladaptive thoughts (self-statements). For example, the child may fear the dark and believe that harm will come to him or her when the lights are turned off. The practitioner assists the child to identify this fear of the dark and the self-statements made by the child about dark rooms, etc.

2. The practitioner models appropriate behavior while verbalizing effective action strategies. These verbalizations include an appraisal of task requirements, self-instructions that guide graded performance, self-statements that stress personal adequacy and counteract worry over failure, and covert self-reinforcement for successful performance. For example, the social worker may model that he or she is not afraid of a darkened room by saying out loud, "I am a brave person. I can take care of myself in the dark." Then, the practitioner may model that he or she can control the situation by turning lights off and on. Finally, the practitioner may model various methods of self-reinforcement for remaining in a darkened room without experiencing fear.

3. The child is then told to perform the target behavior first while verbalizing aloud the appropriate self-instructions and then by covertly rehearsing them. The social worker now provides feedback to the child concerning his or her performance as well as aiding in sharpening his or her positive self statements.

If the training has been successful, the self-statements will replace the previous anxiety inducing cognitions associated with the situation. Meichenbaum (1977) has shown that the method of self-instructional training can be used successfully to reduce diverse anxiety-related problems, to enhance creativity, to develop methods of coping with stress and pain, and to increase self-control in impulsive children.

Implications of Cognitive Behavior Therapy

The basic premise of the cognitive behavior methods of therapy is that children as well as adults react not to the actual but to the perceived environment. These perceptions may be inaccurate or irrational, in which case emotional distress may be the result. Further, this approach recognizes the importance of what people say to themselves in determining their behavior. Thus, the focus of therapy is on changing the things that people say to themselves, implicitly if not explicitly, which lead to ineffective behavior and emotional disturbance.

It is important to point out that both the theory and actual application of cognitive behavior therapy are incomplete. Numerous questions concern the best way to facilitate cognitive restructuring in children. For instance, what is the best way to teach self-statements to children? Is cognitive restructuring more effective with some types of childhood disorders (phobias) than with others (attention deficits)? Also necessary are studies that focus on the development of an explicit technology for maximizing generality across behaviors and environmental settings, and that has long-term consequences. In addition, because of cognitive behavior theories' tendency to emphasize personal change, more emphasis needs to be placed on how strategies for affecting social factors can be integrated into the theoretical framework. Nevertheless, despite these questions, cognitive behavior theory promises increased efficiency and popularity in the future.

Summary

Behavioral and cognitive theories, in stark contrast to psychoanalytic theory, view human behavior as determined through modeling and reinforcement (Schriver, 1995). The cognitive and behavioral approaches to child therapy are based upon the proposition that children's adjustments can be significantly enhanced by identifying and modifying discreet overt behaviors and discreet cognitions. Almost all behaviorists and cognitive behaviorists rely upon a variety of approaches that include conditioning, cognitive restructuring, and modeling. Other approaches see the child's intrapsychic life or the child's interaction with the environment as the critical point of intervention.

We have seen that significant advantages of the cognitive/behavioral approaches are that (1) the principles are operationally defined, and (2) because the target of change is clearly operationalized, it is easier to measure change. The practitioners who hold primarily a cognitive behavioral thrust have much to offer the field of child welfare and their techniques are useful to practitioners in all persuasions.

Chapter 6
Humanism and the Psychosocial Perspective

In contrast to the psychoanalytic and behaviorist approaches to child therapy, other practitioners prefer to take a more socially oriented approach (Newman & Newman, 1995). These approaches focus on the individual as a social being and attempt to understand the family and other relationships that have molded the child's personality and behavior. The socially oriented approaches to child therapy are well articulated by the psychosocial theorists such as Alfred Adler and Rudolph Dreikurs, by various humanists such as Virginia Axline, Clark Moustakes, and William Glasser, and by the gestalt approach of Virginia Oaklander.

The Psychosocial Approaches

Adler's Theory of Individual Psychology

You probably recall that Alfred Adler was one of Sigmund Freud's earliest disciples. He was a charter member of the Vienna Psychoanalytic Society and later its president. However, Adler developed ideas at variance with those of Freud and the Vienna Society, discrediting the importance of psychic determinism and emphasizing social influence. He resigned as president of the Vienna Society and formed his own group which became known as Individual Psychology (Hall &Lindzey, 1970). He inspired the establishment of an experimental school in

Vienna where neurotic as well as normal children were counseled in joint sessions with parents and teachers (Belkin, 1980).

Adler's break from analytic thought because of its emphasis upon psychic determinism led to several important theses of great utility to the child practitioner. From his theory of personality emerged techniques of use in adult and family therapy. A number of his students, Dreikurs and Soltz (1964) and Dinkmeyer and Caldwell (1970), extrapolated his tenets to develop useful child therapy techniques.

Basic Principles of Adlerian Child Theory.   Adler proposed that people are inherently social beings. They are motivated primarily by social rather than sexual desires. A good demonstration of Adler's (1958) position in this regard can be seen in his reinterpretation of the Freudian concept of the Oedipal complex:

> . . . it is supposed that children have a tendency to fall in love with their mothers and wish to marry them and to hate their fathers and wish to kill them. Such a mistake could never arise if we understood the development of children. The Oedipus Complex could appear only in a child who wishes to occupy his other's whole attention and get rid of everyone else. Such a desire is not sexual. It is a desire to subjugate the mother, to have complete control over her and to make her into a servant. It can only occur with children who have been pampered by their mothers and whose feeling of fellowship has never included the rest of the world (p. 126).

Because of early experiences, each person is a unique creative being. Adler pointed out that children feel inferior because of their limited physical and cognitive capacities. They strive for superiority, to become competent in personal and social realms. If children meet a number of discouraging situations at home and at school, they become disheartened. Out of their successes and failures, children develop a "style of life," a patterned means of seeking superiority. This style of life is well-established by age four or five.

Much of Adler's research focused upon the roles children adopt within the family. He believed that the eldest child possessed considerable freedom in determining a style of life. Adler proposed that most first-born children achieve feelings of superiority through socially sanctioned achievement. However, the eldest suffer feelings of stress because their power in the family is dethroned through the birth of younger siblings. Subsequent children have less choice in their style of life. Characteristically, they do not choose the same pattern as the eldest because this leads to rivalry and frustration. The youngest child typically experiences some feelings of inferiority by virtue of his or her size and age. Current research has supported some of Adler's predictions about children's roles, but research demonstrates that a number of factors besides the child's position in the family contribute to the child's personality development and personal goals and attitudes (Hall & Lindzey, 1970).

Adler introduced the idea of family intervention when treating disturbed children. In family conferences, he would discuss the target child's and other family member's styles of life. Then, he would host a discussion among family members about ways each one could help the maladjusted child develop socially appropriate behaviors.

Dreikurs' Extension of the Theory of Individual Psychology Dreikurs' extension of Adlerian principles leads to some very effective means of therapeutic intervention. Dreikurs (Dreikurs & Soltz, 1964) developed a system for characterizing children's faulty goals. He built upon Adler's construct that children intuitively strive for superiority. If they fail to achieve a sense of superiority through socially acceptable means, they will select one of four faulty goals. They may strive for attention, that is, instead of seeking a place in the world by cooperation, they seek to be noticed, regardless of whether the attention meets others' needs or their own long-term goals. Some children deal with feelings of social inferiority by seeking power. They feel superior if they win, regardless of the consequences of that winning upon themselves or others. Still other children will seek revenge. They build a style of life centered upon "getting even" with others that they perceive are acting superior. Still other children compensate for feelings of inferiority by displaying inadequacies. They obtain recognition by becoming incompetent, beseeching for help. Each of these faulty goals may be pursued actively or passively. In the active stance, the goal is directly sought. In the passive stance, the lack of activity leads to achieving the faulty goal. Table 6.1 lists the faulty goals and some typical active and passive means of achieving them.

Once the purpose of a child's misbehavior is established, the social worker can work with the child's family and school so that the faulty striving for superiority no longer leads to the desired goal. For the attention-getter, passive and active attempts to be noticed are ignored. For children with a faulty goal of power, the power struggle must be systematically avoided. Dreikurs recommends that the recipients of the child's struggle for power (e.g., parents, and teachers) simply not respond. He has even recommended that parents remove themselves from the

TABLE 6.1

Examples of Faulty Goals to Compensate for Feelings of Social Inadequacy

Type of Faulty Goal	Active Examples	Passive Examples
Attention Getting	Gets good grades simply for the attention, not because the child wants to learn; always wants to perform for family and friends.	Is excessively quiet; loses or gains an inordinate amount of weight; doesn't turn in class assignments.
Power	Always wants to be the leader; openly defies parents, teachers, and other authorities.	Soils and wets after physiological skill for continence is obtained; refuses to cooperate, to answer a question, or to complete a chore.
Revenge	Physically attacks siblings and other children; is destructive to others' property; makes hurtful comments, embarrasses others, or does not keep confidences.	Sets others up for attack, for example, provoking a sibling into a fight or destructive activity, then refusing to acknowledge her or his own role; encourages peers to report on one another's misbehaviors.
Displaying Inadequacy	Frequently, openly critiques self; frequently asks for help; makes jokes at one's own expense.	Withdraws; cries frequently; forgets to complete assignments.

Source: Dreikurs & Soltz, 1964

environment when in a struggle for power with the child. By this means the child recognizes that parents cannot be controlled. For those seeking retaliation and revenge, Dreikurs believes the use of restitution is most beneficial. If a child destroys property, he must mend it or find a replacement. If a child hurts another's feelings, she must apologize. Dreikurs also recommends the use of "natural consequences." In many cases, a faulty goal leads to aversive situations. If the adults allow the consequences to occur naturally, the aversive effects provide control over the behavior. For example, if the child breaks confidences of other family members, it is decided in a family meeting that confidences will no longer be told to the child until the child again wins the trust of others. If the child "sets up" another's misbehavior, he or she is held responsible for the other's act. Dreikurs sees the displaying of inadequacies as a most serious faulty goal. If not remediated, the child who displays inadequacies eventually no longer feels any personal power. The social worker should encourage these children to act constructively. Any constructive act reverses the trend of increasing feelings of inadequacy. Important individuals in the child's life must refuse to accept statements of the child's inadequacy as accurate. These children must be encouraged to seek their competencies, and their successful, assertive behavior should be reinforced. Sympathy from others (e.g., "It's not your fault you're clumsy, not everyone can be coordinated at your age.") fosters the child's belief that he or she can gain a noticeable place in the world by being inadequate.

Implications of Psychosocial Approaches

In general, the Individual Psychology paradigm helps the social worker identify the social factors that contribute to or maintain maladjustment. If these social factors can be clearly identified, remediation becomes a relatively direct task. The precepts and techniques of individual psychology can be mastered readily and can be taught to parents. Dinkmeyer & McKay (1976) have packaged materials called Systematic Training for Effective Parenting (STEP) for teaching Adlerian–Dreikurian principles to parents. Through the use of text, charts, and worksheets, principles of individual psychology and techniques for avoiding power struggles and using natural consequences are taught in about eight weeks. Based upon the proposition that behavior is not fully determined by the psyche, the techniques of Adlerian–Dreikurian therapy are highly congruent with those of behavioral tenets of reinforcement. In the individual psychology model, much behavior can be explained and predicted with a few basic tenets that provide a comfortable means of communication between lay people and practitioners.

Humanistic Contributions to Child Theory

Although the tenets of humanistic child theory were not eludicated extensively until the last 20 years, threads of the concepts were used by earliest child clinicians. As explained in Chapter 4, Anna Freud rejected the then strongly held assumption that all meaningful therapy required the development and interpretation of a transference relationship. She emphasized the therapeutic benefit of a warm relationship between the practitioner and child. In the 1940s, Allen (1942, 1963) outlined the qualities of a facilitative therapeutic relationship with a child. He stated that the practitioner needed to begin "where the patient is" and guide the child toward a more creative acceptance and use of him or herself. He described child therapy as an experience in living rather than a corrective, remedial relationship.

According to the humanistic approach, human nature is perceived as being essentially loving, cooperative, wise, and health-seeking. The humanistically oriented practitioner facilitates the client's exploration and discovery of her or his feelings and development of autonomy. Personal growth, rather than the abatement of illness or the reduction of symptoms, is the objective of this approach.

The basic principles of humanistic psychotherapy are applicable to children and adults alike. The humanist maintains that all individuals are motivated by personal growth, wanting to actualize their potentials. Personal growth can be thwarted, however, if "significant others" (family and others with important impact upon one's physical and psychological needs) are judgmental and non-accepting. Once thwarted, individuals tend to mask their personalities, attitudes, and beliefs. They hide themselves either by withdrawing or by acting out. Therefore, maladaptive behavior occurs whenever individuals through social pressure lose confidence in themselves. Their growth and self-actualization is stunted and indirect.

It follows that humanistic therapy must provide an atmosphere of complete acceptance. If the therapeutic climate is warm and accepting, the clients will no longer limit their potentials and will begin discovering answers to their dilemmas (Rogers, 1951). In a very accepting atmosphere, clients will ponder the existential dilemmas that confront each one of us: What is the purpose of my life? How much control do I have over my life? Why must I die? (Axline, 1969).

A number of theorists have been responsible for translating the basic humanistic tenets for use in child therapy. Axline (1969) developed a nondirective system of play therapy that fosters a therapeutic atmosphere of acceptance. Ginott (1961), Dimick and Huff (1970), and others help to specify the personal qualities the practitioner must project in successful play therapy. Moustakes (1973), Glasser (1965), and others have helped to operationalize the nature of the existential dilemma in child therapy. A special application of humanistic theory to child therapy that we shall discuss is gestalt techniques.

Personal Qualities of the Humanistic Child Practitioner

The humanists have identified a number of personal qualities in practitioners that contribute to a positive, warm atmosphere in therapy. These qualities have been tested experimentally in adult therapy-client dyads (Truax & Carkhuff, 1967). They are accepted by most humanistic child practitioners, but are not thoroughly validated against child client populations. In their widely accepted text on child counseling, Dimick and Huff (1970) summarize the important qualities of the humanistic practitioner.

Unconditional Positive Regard

The practitioner expresses unqualified acceptance and faith in the child and his or her potentialities. This faith is conveyed by encouraging the child to make personal decisions and by accepting and appreciating everything the child says and does. The practitioner listens carefully and communicates a desire to understand. All of the practitioner's verbal and nonverbal messages establish an atmosphere of, "I hold your peculiarities, your loves and your hates, your mannerisms and your habits in esteem and honor as I do all aspects of your self" (Moustakes, 1959, p. 6).

Many words are synonymous with unconditional positive regard respect, prizing, altruistic love. To communicate unconditional positive regard, the social worker must hold an underlying commitment to others, a belief in children's intrinsic good nature, and an optimism that the children can change.

Empathy

The practitioner must communicate that he or she appreciates the child's feelings. The practitioner symbolically takes on the child's role so that he or she can reflect understanding about the child's feelings. The practitioner is not sympathetic; that is, he or she does not excuse or sanction the child's bad feelings. Nor does the practitioner become an advocate of the child against outside adversaries. An example of an empathic response would be, "You're feeling really bad that your brother keeps breaking your toys." The social worker would not respond, "Your brother is really mean. I don't blame you for wanting him to be out of the family."

Genuineness

The social worker communicates a flexible, open manner. The practitioner admits his or her effort and shortcomings. The practitioner discloses about feelings of vulnerability. The humanistic practitioner may say to a child, for example, "I really missed you when you didn't come to our appointment last week"; or "I'm really feeling frustrated. I'm not sure how to show you that you can trust me." The social worker does not stand in judgment of the child. For example, the practitioner would not say, "The trouble with you is—." Rather, the practitioner shares with the child. The practitioner might say, "How can I help you change the way you're handling those upsetting circumstances?" The social worker is profoundly serious in purpose and intensely absorbed in the helping process. The practitioner's voice, touch, and genuine concern communicate active involvement with the child.

Concreteness

The worker's language is relevant to the child. The practitioner does not talk down to the child, but communicates clearly, guarding against hidden or double messages. (p. 6).

Ginott (1961) writes that the major therapeutic cement of child therapy is the practitioner's modeling of effective ways of being. To the extent that the social worker is emotionally stable, warm, and open, the child will find the therapeutic environment one in which he or she can grow. To Ginott, the humanistic child practitioner is a "responsible anarchist." The social worker does not impose values on the child, but models responsible living and commitment to the child. The practitioner encourages the child to break the shackles of unfair socialization and to make a commitment to personal growth.

Nondirective Play Therapy

A number of humanistic child practitioners believe that if a practitioner provides a warm, supportive atmosphere, children will resolve their own difficulties. Axline (1969) is the major spokesperson of this nondirective play therapy stance. Axline stresses that the potential to grow and to resolve one's dilemmas is within each child. If the social worker provides a sound therapeutic climate, the child will resolve spontaneously his or her conflicts. Axline lists eight steps that are necessary to create a sound play therapy milieu:

1. **Accept the child as he or she is.** The social worker should never evaluate or judge the child. The social worker should not teach the child about the consequences of his or her acts, nor should the social worker attempt to offer answers to the child's dilemmas.

2. **Establish a positive relationship.** The practitioner should endeavor to make the play therapy sessions an enjoyable experience. The social worker communicates pleasure to be with the child and likes the child just as is.

3. **Be permissive.** The social worker should allow for a free expression of feelings. The social worker should not sanction or disapprove of any feelings the child presents.

4. **Reflect feelings and content.** As the child plays, the practitioner observes attentively. The worker mirrors the child's comments in a manner that facilitates insight. As one reads case studies of Axline and her students, it is apparent that she particularly mirrors the child's affect. Thus, if a child says, "I want to play with the doll house now," Axline may simply watch attentively. If the child says, "I need to play house," the social worker might respond, "The playhouse is important to you."

5. **Let the child be responsible for his or her choices.** Again, the worker interferes as little as possible. If a child wants to smear finger paints on his or her clothes, the social worker simply responds, "You want to smear paint now." The worker would not ask questions such as, "What will your mother think if your clothes are dirty?"

6. **Consistently communicate to the child that in play therapy the child can and will lead.** If the child wants to terminate the session early, it is terminated. If the child wants the social worker to play with him or her, only then does the practitioner participate.

7. **Allow the child to explore feelings at her or his own pace.** The practitioner should not attempt to hurry the counseling process by reminding the child of what has happened previously or by prompting the child to try to resolve dilemmas.

8. **Establish only those limits that are needed.** The social worker would not, for example, discuss an injunction against hitting at the initiation of play therapy. This limit would only be raised if the child continued to assault the worker. Similarly, the practitioner would not demand that the child help clean up the playroom.

Axline's (1969) reflective stance is illustrated in the case study excerpt which follows:

CHILD: I want to drink from the nursing bottle.

PRACTITIONER: There it is, over on the shelf. Drink from the nursing bottle if you want to.

CHILD: Know what?

PRACTITIONER: Hmm?

CHILD: I want to crawl on the floor and drink my bottle.

PRACTITIONER: You want to act just like a baby. Well, go ahead. (Child hesitates.) You don't know whether you should or not.

CHILD: Me little baby.

PRACTITIONER: You like to be a little baby.

CHILD: Ummhumm. (Child continues to suck on the bottle for the rest of the hour.) (p. 174)

In sum, in nondirective play therapy a child's behavior and affect are accepted as much as possible within the limits of the child's and social worker's physical safety. The practitioner is actively attentive, but is a responder, never an initiator of the therapeutic process. Axline (1969) presents many case studies in which children seem to "work through" their hurts and find answers to their own dilemmas within accepting environments. Other practitioners, such as Moustakes and Glasser whom we discuss next, argue that the atmosphere of acceptance can be maintained while the practitioner is more active. They propose that the therapeutic process is enhanced by supportive, active therapeutic intervention.

The Existential Dilemma

Several humanistic child practitioners emphasize the importance of dealing with existential dilemmas in child counseling. Moustakes (1959) writes that the root of children's maladjustment is "submission and denial of the self." The child relinquishes his or her uniqueness. His play therapy is aimed at assisting children to rediscover their unique values and beliefs and reestablish a purpose to their lives that is based upon those unique competencies. To accomplish this goal, Moustakes (1973) offers feedback to his child clients that helps them see their unique attributes and encourages them to make active decisions about their lives.

Further, he explains that the most meaningful feedback can be offered within the therapeutic relationship. The practitioner shows his or her reactions to the child: "When you do that, it has no consequence upon me." "When you stick your tongue out at me, I feel like going away." The practitioner helps the child client clarify values. "Yesterday you said you'd like to be a scientist; today, you said you don't like school. How can you become a scientist if you choose not to go to school?" The practitioner encourages the child to be responsible, to look at the consequences of his or her acts and to make conscious decisions that are consonant with the child's long-range goals.

The following is an excerpt from a play session with a seven-year-old withdrawn and anxious girl.

> PRACTITIONER: In here, if you spill and mess, it is all right. . . . As long as you don't mind, it doesn't bother me. (She spills water on the floor and sand on her dress. She looks at the practitioner and begins to laugh.)
>
> PRACTITIONER: In here, you can laugh about messing. But what about at home?
>
> CHILD: No. There I have to keep clean.
>
> PRACTITIONER: Your mother doesn't like you to get dirty.
>
> CHILD: When I play with mud, I keep away from my mother. I try to wash it off before she sees me, but sometimes she catches me and screams "K-A-R-E-N."
>
> PRACTITIONER: So, at home there are some things your mother doesn't like you to do?
>
> CHILD: Yes, many things.
>
> PRACTITIONER: You are not always free to do what you want to do.
>
> CHILD: No. Not free.
>
> (Moustakes, 1975, p. 38)

Glasser (1965) writes further about the importance of teaching the child to make wise decisions. He states that children experience problems if they fail to receive love. Without love, their self-worth diminishes, and they make poor choices. Not just delinquent children, but all troubled children (underachievers, anxious, depressed, etc.) make poor choices.

Glasser stresses that a practitioner must become actively involved with the client in order to foster feelings of hope and worthiness within the child. Then, the practitioner prompts the child to make a judgment about what he or she is doing that leads to feelings of failure. Following this identification of the problem, the practitioner helps the child verbally design better choices. The practitioner requests a commitment from the child to try these new choices. The practitioner contracts with the child about the consequences that will ensue if he or she breaks the commitment. In Glasser's Reality Therapy, the practitioner communicates love, but does not allow the child to escape responsibility for designing a more meaningful, productive life.

The Case of P. W. demonstrates an active humanistic stance in child therapy. The social worker relates personally and intimately with the child. The social worker also plays the role of a significant other, "the stranger," in P. W.'s life, thereby encouraging P. W. to learn new ways to relate to his father, whom he perceived as a stranger.

Case 6.1   The Case of P. W.

When I first met five-year-old P. W., he was very withdrawn and would not even tell his parents or teacher when he needed to use the bathroom. He cried often and seemed to tremble when spoken to. When Mrs. W. first brought P. to see me, she had told him nothing about me. She deceived him by stating, "I'm just going around the corner, I will be right back." When Mrs. W. left, P. had a look of terror on face and began sobbing. I brought him to my office and held him while he cried. I responded, "It seems like you don't know whether to believe your mother or not. You feel really scared; you don't know if she's coming back."

Over the next few sessions P. sat idly in the middle of the room and looked at me. I set out some toys that I thought might be of some interest to him, but he did not respond.

One day, I brought out a music box, opened it so that the music would start, and P. inched toward it. I explained, "I would be glad to teach you how to run the music box, and you can use it whenever you are here." P.'s eyes lit up. I showed him how to wind up the music box and how to open it. He began to ask some questions, and I discovered he could express himself very well.

In play therapy, P. frequently took adult male figures and buried them in play dough. Employing a toy castle, he would often throw "the mean man" in the dungeon for a million years and set him on fire.

During the sixth session, I suggested to P. that we become "explorers." We began walking farther and farther away from my office, and I would reinforce P. for his new assertiveness, "Look how brave and strong you are. Look how much you are learning to do." Gradually, P. would walk blocks away from the office with me. His confidence generalized to other environments. He began speaking in class and over the next several months learned his alphabet and numbers from one to ten.

One game that P. W. initiated he entitled, "The Stranger." We would go to utility tunnels underneath the office building. P. requested, "You play the mean stranger. You try and get me." I would chase P. up and down the tunnels. Finally, P. would turn around and shoot me, thus getting rid of the mean stranger. I began asking, "Poor me, I don't want to be a mean person. What can I do to be nice?" P. eventually responded that "to be nice, you have to let me know you."

This game initiated dialogue about how frightened he was of his father. He felt father spent little time with him, seldom expressed his ideas and thoughts, and did not offer comfort or warmth to P. P. was encouraged to express his feelings about his father over a number of sessions. Once P. better understood his feelings about his father, P. and his practitioner role-played new ways of approaching him. P. learned to express intimate feelings to his family. His openness was paralleled by increased spontaneity and assertiveness. He became increasingly successful at academic tasks and began to form friendships. Gradually, his father responded to P. W.'s approaches, and they developed a more comfortable and open relationship.

Gestalt Techniques

An especially socially oriented perspective that draws from humanistic tenets of child therapy is gestalt. Akin to other humanistic theories, Fritz Perls, the originator of gestalt therapy, proposed that a key aspect of good mental health is personal growth. The gestalt practitioner further believes that humans strive to complete gestalts, to interact as integrated wholes with the environment. When a person is restricted or rigid, he or she is unable to complete gestalts. The neurotic individual plays roles rather than living spontaneously, projects onto others what is incomplete in him- or herself, and remains "stuck at an impasse" (Perls, 1969). Therapy focuses upon increasing a client's awareness, thereby enabling a client to "break through" an impasse and live more spontaneously. When the client can react spontaneously, with few roles, that client feels in harmony with the self and the environment and is personally healthy.

The gestalt practitioner typically employs provocative "games" (also called "experiments" or "gimmicks") to help clients accept responsibility for, redefine, and reintegrate themselves with the environment. These games, such as "role reversal" and "empty chair technique" can be particularly appealing to older children because they provide an activity base to verbal therapy (Belkin, 1980).

Shostrom (1967) uses gestalt terms to describe some role-playing, non-spontaneous life stances that some children adapt. Shostrom talks to children and their parents of "Freddy-the-Fox," who begins life as a crier to get others to take responsibility for him, "Tom-the-Tough," who uses hate and fear to control people, and "Carl-the-Competitor" who views winning as the most important goal in life.

Although many propose that gestalt techniques are particularly viable with children, little empirical research documents this position. Gannon (1972) reported that a gestalt group was effective in increasing openness of high school students. A variety of stimulating games and language gimmicks adapted for child and school counseling are outlined in Passons' (1975) text. In Chapter 11, we describe many of Oaklander's (1978) creative techniques that fall within the gestalt tradition.

Comparing the Humanistic and Psychosocial to the psychodynamic and Behavioral Approaches

The early approaches to child therapy were dominated by psychoanalytic theory. The strict application of analytic principles to the child therapy process led practitioners such as Melanie Klein to look for the symbolic, primarily sexual, content in a child's play. The early child analysts often worked with their clients several times each week for a period of several years in order to foster and interpret transference so that the child could gain more insight about repressed impulses toward family members and the self.

Gradually, child analysts such as Anna Freud realized that children are not simply "little adults," and the process of therapy must be uniquely designed to meet their needs and their developmental levels of conceptualization. Anna Freud and other psychoanalysts have stressed the importance of and the unique ways a child practitioner can establish a "positive therapeutic alliance" with a child. With a positive therapeutic alliance, insights can be provided that prompt change.

The demands for psychotherapeutic services, the extensive commitment required for psychoanalytic psychotherapy, and new findings in developmental psychology have created an increased emphasis upon environmental interventions to curb childhood disorders. Through the work of Skinner, Bandura, and others, principles derived in laboratories have been extended to modify children's behaviors. The behavioral approaches provide quick, efficient ways that practitioners, parents, teachers, and children themselves can learn to increase appropriate and decrease inappropriate behaviors. The behaviorists have demonstrated that not all insight leads to behavioral change, and that insight may not be necessary for behavioral change. By skillful manipulation of environmental contingencies, children can be helped to change a variety of discrete behaviors as well as pervasive life styles.

No one argues about the success of behaviorism in modifying a range of childhood symptomatology, but many cry, "What has become of the child, the child's feelings and right to make personal decisions?" The socially oriented approaches emerged as a third force to counterpoise the depersonalizing, dehumanizing qualities of the strict analytic and strict behavioral stances. The humanists propose that the child must be treated as a unique person first, object of scientific study second. The humanists have been quite successful in identifying core therapeutic conditions that help a child client feel that he or she is being treated like a unique person rather than an object of scientific investigation. Many believe that the humanists are defining therapeutic qualities that undercut effective behavioral and analytic therapy as well.

Summary

To the humanists, children need acceptance from others as a basis for their accepting and valuing themselves. With self-esteem, children will be socially productive members of society. They will learn to fulfill their needs in ways that do not deprive others of their abilities to meet their own needs. With acceptance and positive self-esteem, children will want to be close to others. They will cooperate and accept differences in others. With self-esteem, they will make wise decisions. The analysts first wrote of the "corrective therapeutic experience." The humanists have concentrated on defining the therapeutic qualities and interventions that create a warm, accepting atmosphere. Few practitioners of any theoretical persuasion would argue against the core conditions established by the humanists. Most would laud the humanists for their attempts to operationalize the therapeutic qualities that are conducive to client growth.

Criticism of the approach takes several forms. Many believe that the core conditions of an effective therapeutic relationship which are central to humanistic thought are very vague. How can these core conditions be taught? How does the practitioner really know if he or she is enacting them? As a whole, the work of Truax and Carkhuff (1967), Carkhuff and Berenson (1977), and associates demonstrate that these qualities can be taught. However, little of this critical empirical research has been conducted with children. Extensive compilations of research suggest that the humanistic approach to therapy is a necessary, but not a sufficient, condition to facilitate client gain. The humanists disagree, but their lofty language and abstract theories make empirical testing of client gain difficult.

Chapter 7
Family Therapy

Family therapy is a very potent means for assisting many child clients. It assumes that children do not and cannot have complete autonomy over their behavior. Children are a part of a family system, and they will act in ways consonant with the social rules laid down by their parents. Family preservation services, as a growing influence in child welfare, make extensive use of family theory and therapy. Just as children are diverse so are their families, in fact, today diverse families may be more typical than traditional nuclear families. Child welfare workers often come in contact with a vast variety of families. Children live in single parent, adoptive, gay and lesbian, and multiracial families (Okun, 1996).

Compared to other therapeutic interventions, family therapy is a relatively recent innovation for assisting children. During the social diagnostic period (1910–1930), social work was distinctive among the helping professions for emphasis in treating the family unit. Then, a shift in focus to the individual almost totally pushed family therapy out of social work practice until the 1950s (Sherman, 1981). In the 1950s, under the leadership of Gregory Bateson and Don Jackson, family therapy gained prominence among psychologists and psychiatrists. Family therapy combines two bodies of knowledge, personality dynamics and social systems, and thus draws upon theories of psychology and sociology. Just as its theoretical base derives from two sources, so the goals of family therapy are two-sided: to increase autonomy of individuals in the family and to facilitate smooth functioning of the family unit. Family therapists attempt to explain and treat the external struggle of family members for connectedness and separateness (Janzan & Harris, 1997). Behind the basic premise that personal growth can be facilitated by assessing and working with a client's family, family therapists differ widely in theory and technique. A survey of 300 established family therapists revealed differences in their practices ranging from use of family therapy as an extension of individual therapy to only working with family units; from seeing few dangers involved in family therapy to elaborating upon many constraints for its use; and from offering insight interpretations to family groups to emphasizing behavioral prescriptions (committee on the Family Group for the Advancement of Psychiatry, 1970).

On the whole, family therapists tend to build their approaches from either psychoanalytic or systems theory. Those ascribing to an analytically oriented family therapy use family interviews to diagnose the etiology of a child's problem. Through family interviews, they decide how much of the child's difficulties are self-perpetuating because of internalized emotional problems and how much the child's problems are serving as an expression of the parents' pathology. The analytically oriented family therapist then designs individual and small group procedures to help the child and the parents deal with their part of the family difficulties. Thus, family sessions serve primarily as diagnostic sessions that provide clues to interpretations that will be made in individual therapy with the child or parents. They interact and affect one another, and a child's disturbance is viewed as fulfilling a psychologically meaningful function for the system. Therefore, changes in the child, the "identified patient," necessitate changes in the entire family system. Otherwise, changes in the child will result in the appearance of new symptoms in other family members or the further destruction of the family as a unit.

Since the psychoanalytic approach to family therapy draws primarily upon principles we discussed in previous chapters, we will not discuss these procedures in detail in this chapter. Rather, most of this chapter will concentrate on the techniques of systems approaches to family therapy. The reader who wishes to conduct analytically oriented family therapy will nevertheless find many of the suggestions of the family systems theorists applicable.

Major Contributors to Family Systems Thought

As stated earlier, family therapy combines knowledge of personality dynamics and social systems. Creative synthesis of divergent ideas is needed for this task. Since the 1950s, a number of very creative social scientists from varied fields, such as medicine, social work, anthropology, psychology, psychiatry, and communications analysis, have contributed to our repository of understanding about families in therapy. Let us mention some of the major figures in this field. Their relationship to one another temporally and historically is presented in Figure 7.1. Then, in following sections of the chapter, we will present three schools of family therapy and ways that their thinking has been united into an organized view of how family systems function and malfunction.

Gregory Bateson

In the 1950s, Bateson And his colleagues were instrumental in identifying patterns in family communication that can lead to emotional distress in individuals and disturbance with family functioning. Highly regarded is Bateson's theory about how members of families are often placed in "double binds" (that is, no-win situations) by inconsistent communication (Bateson, Jackson, Haley, & Weakland, 1956). Bateson, et al., (1956) suggested that schizophrenic youth often were raised by parents who communicated to them in an inconsistent manner. He coined the term "schizophrenogenic mother" for the parent who he believed provoked schizophrenia in her child because her verbal messages were confusing for the child to follow. Bateson, et al. (1956) stated that schizophrenogenic mothers create double binds for their children. They communicate untenable requests so that no matter how the child responds, the child receives negative feedback and/or absence of reward. For example, a schizophrenogenic mother might say, "Come here, Johnny. Sit on my lap. You never show your mother you love her." When Johnny comes to his mother's lap, she retorts, "You're too dirty. Get off." Johnny is in a double bind. If he had originally told his mother that he did not want to come to her (because he was dirty or just because he did not want to come to her), she would have responded, "You are bad; you don't love your mother." Johnny goes to his mother and is rejected. There is no way of Johnny's escaping negation by his mother in this interaction. Through language analysis, such as the "double bind," Bateson's work established the importance of communication in healthy and maladaptive families.

Don Jackson and Associates

In his psychiatric family practice, Jackson (1959) noted that families sought balance or homeostasis in how members relate to one another. For example, the aggressiveness of one family member might be balanced by the gentleness of another. When one family member changes or leaves, the balance is upset, and everyone will change to create a new homeostasis. Jackson was a key member of Bateson's Palo Alto group that began family therapy while studying communication patterns of schizophrenic families. Jackson's focus on the dynamics between persons was based upon his belief that behavior and communication are the same. Jackson believed that family rituals and members' repetitive ways of communicating are evidence of a family's homeostasis. Further, because families seek homeostasis, they are slow to change. Change in family systems is a complex process which requires that all members adapt to a new balance.

Lyman C. Wynne

Wynne (1961) expanded upon Jackson's premise that families are slow to change. He suggested that some families create a facade of mutual support, "pseudomutuality." They espouse regard for one another, but in actuality are rigid and tolerate little divergence. Individual growth is hampered in families operating with pseudomutuality.

Murray Bowen

Bowen (1966), trained at the Menninger Clinic, suggested that it is helpful to think of the family system as possessing an ego in a fashion similar to employing the construct of ego to explain individual psychodynamics. He agreed with Wynne (1961) that healthy families allow individuals to be autonomous. Bowen (1966) states that members of healthy families identify with a group ego and have a sense of connection with one another. Many unhealthy families are characterized by "undifferentiated ego mass" in which members lose a sense of autonomy. The family members' identities fuse together. Their lives are enmeshed, and there is little intimate contact with people outside the family. Also unhealthy are families in which members are highly "disengaged." In disengaged families, members feel little identification with a family ego mass. Most intimate contacts are with individuals outside the family.

The concept of triangulation, when one family member tells a third person what he or she thinks of another family member, was developed after 12 years of work with Bowen's own family. Bowen detriangled himself from a series of enmeshed family interactions during a trip home to discuss the family business (Anonymous, 1972). Bowen noticed that effective family systems therapists applied systems theory to their own families. They would return from workshops to develop a better working relationship with their own family members. In the chapter on family assessment, we review Bowen's system of family analysis in more detail.

James Bell

Bell (1964) studied extensively how members seek autonomy and control in families. He emphasized that children modify parents' behaviors by their moods, activity levels, etc. In unhealthy families, members struggle overtly and/or covertly for power and control. In maladaptive families, children express frustration in having to follow rules and claim rules infringing on their freedoms are unfair. Parents, in turn, feel unappreciated and frustrated that they cannot exert more control. Healthy families are characterized by sharing, cooperation, and spontaneity.

Bell's treatment involved group counseling in which open communication among family members is encouraged. Bell (1964) explained that families in group counseling grow through various stages. Intervention is carefully planned in coordination with each stage. Serving the family as a group allows for treatment in a social context.

Robert MacGregor

MacGregor (1962) contributed greatly to the field of family systems theory through interdisciplinary models for intervention. Based upon his need to serve children and parents in southeast Texas who traveled many miles, MacGregor assembled a team of psychologists, social workers, and psychiatric residents to provide intense two-day family treatment sessions. In order to assist a family in distress, he recommended that a team of therapists work with the entire family, part of the family, and groups of families, according to their need. He called this multi-level approach to intervention "Multiple Impact Therapy."

Richard Speck

Speck (1967) extrapolated MacGregor's principles and developed techniques for working with an extended family in family therapy. Speck stated that certainly all individuals living with a troubled youngster needed to participate in therapy. He believed further that other significant family members that lived outside the home but had affected the family's values and beliefs needed to participate in therapy. The influence of these family members is felt and reacted to even if they are not present, and a new healthy pattern is best established if they are present in therapy. Speck (1967) encouraged critical family members to attend family meetings. With the cooperation of the extended family, a large "social network" is built that can help in the improvement of an emotionally disturbed family member.

Jay Haley

Haley (1963), an influential member of the Palo Alto Group, agrees with Bell that the primary cause of family dissension concerns control. The usual conflict in families is about rules and who will set the rules. The conflict is particularly severe if the ones who make the rules will not admit that they hold the power. As a communication analyst, Haley has provided sophisticated descriptions of the indirect verbal and nonverbal communication patterns that family members adopt in order to gain covert control. Haley states that a family member with a "symptom" gains control and achieves his or her goal through the symptom, but in doing so perpetuates the covert control characteristic of the family conflict. For example, a wife who is ostensibly dominated by her brusk, aggressive husband may gain attention and feel some control through hypochondriacal symptoms. Although her symptoms win her some attention, they eventually frustrate and alienate family members. As a consequence, she feels further unappreciated and powerless, and the family conflict continues.

A major purpose of family therapy is to realign control and power. Initially, the therapist assumes control in order to realign forces. Haley believes that if the family therapist assumes control discreetly through paradoxical maneuvers, some borrowed from Milton Erickson, then family members believe the changes are their own ideas and therefore do not resist.

Virginia Satir

A social worker trained as a Gestalt therapist under Fritz Perls, Satir (1967, 1972) has added a humanistic orientation to family therapy. She believes that difficulties in families are created by a combination of individual and group factors: low self-esteem of one or more family members; poor communication patterns; and/ or rigid roles. Satir (1967) identifies four types of persons who seem to frequently communicate in nonproductive ways. The "placator's" remarks indicate that he or she feels no good. Continually, the placator seems to be saying, "You are right; forgive me." The "criticizer" tends to center all communication by blaming someone else. The criticizer's covert message is that others are no good. Some family members are "intellectualizers." By being extremely reasonable at all times, the intellectualizer denies the family members' feelings. Finally, the "irrelevant" one communicates in a dizzy, distracting manner. When family members adopt these faulty communication patterns, successful resolution of difficulties is hampered.

Satir's family therapy involves use of very active techniques (role-playing, other gestalt-type games) to help family members become aware of their roles in families. She also imparts information that educates the family members about maladaptive roles they are assuming. She uses communication exercises to help family members learn more open and direct ways of communicating with one another.

Richard Bandler and John Grinder

The base of clinical research by Bandler and Grinder was in analyzing the communication patterns of very successful psychotherapists, including Milton Erickson, Fritz Perls, Albert Ellis, and others. Gradually, Bandler and Grinder expanded their work to study healthy and nonproductive communication patterns in and out of therapy. Collaborating with Satir (Bandler, Grinder, & Satir, 1976), they refer to the faulty stereotypical communication patterns that families adopt as "calibrated" patterns. Calibrated interpersonal communications are characterized by incongruency. For example, a specific individual's verbal communication may differ from his or her nonverbal communication. In calibrated communications, listeners tend to mistake part of a message for the whole message. For example, a listener may block out conflicting parts of a message and hear only that part that he or she wants to hear. Calibrated communications are further characterized by "mind reading." A listener assumes that he or she understands an abstract message and does not ask for further clarification. Bandler, Grinder, and Satir point out that we often speak in "nominalizations"; that is, we employ an abstract noun to stand for a multitude of feelings. Unfortunately, such nominalizations are often misunderstood. Thus, a wife may say that she wants more "freedom." A jealous husband assumes that this means she wants to have relationships with other men. She means that she wants to work outside the home. The husband would never have considered this "freedom." They both "mind read" that they know what the other feels. A final characteristic of calibrated communication is that a listener forms rigid, fixed generalizations about other's messages. It is the family therapist's role to uncover calibrated communications and to model and encourage open and spontaneous expression of ideas and feelings.

Salvador Minuchin

Minuchin (Minuchin, Montalvo, Guerney, Rosman, & Schurmer, 1967) has developed a popular, practical application of family system theory based upon his work with low socioeconomic families at the Philadelphia Child Guidance Clinic. Empirical research, a dedication to training, and practical, direct systematic techniques may account for Minuchin's popularity in the late 1970s and 1980s (Nichols, 1984). The basic structural concepts are boundaries, subsystems, power, and alignments. The model is useful for a number of child problems as it takes into account the individual, the family, and the social context.

Every family has a structure that is revealed when the family is in action (Minuchin, 1974). Boundaries regulate the amount of contact between family members and the outside world. Small children repeatedly interrupting parents when they are talking indicates minimal boundaries.

Subsystems help the practitioner understand the functions of the family. If an emotionally abused child is looked to for leadership in a family, then the child is the executive subsystem, rather than the mother or father. Subsystems are determined by emotional boundaries, allowing autonomy of individuals yet permeable to ensure affection (Minuchin & Fishman, 1981).

Structured family therapists believe it is important for the therapist to avoid becoming part of the family, while at the same time to gain trust by accommodating to the family's usual patterns of behavior. Assessment techniques are used to activate existing but dormant structures and to alter alignments and shift power in and between subsystems. Restructuring is concrete, forceful, and dramatic, which again may account for the popularity of this approach.

Nathan Ackerman

Nathan Ackerman, an early leader in family therapy, applied psychoanalytical theory learned while working with children at the Menninger Clinic to family practice. As the chief psychiatrist at Menninger Clinic, he followed the traditional model of the 1940s of the psychiatrist working with the child and the social worker assisting the mother. Dissatisfied with this model, he requested that the therapist see both the child and the mother together (Nichols & Schwartz, 1995). He believed the therapist's role is to "stir up" the family interaction so family members break out of traditional roles and begin to relate to each other on deep levels of feeling and understanding (Ackerman, 1966). To accomplish this, he insisted that all persons living in a family attend all family sessions.

He established "emotional contact" with all family members before encouraging an open expression of feelings. Open and honest expressions were shared by the therapist as well. He emphasized the intrapsychic effects upon individual members by the family as a whole. The family helps shape a member's needs and desires and feelings of security and self-fulfillment.

Families may appear unified; however, below the surface, they can be split into competing emotional components. The practitioner helps the family understand the factions, interactions, and individual feelings that lie behind the dysfunctional symptoms of individual family members. As each individual understands what he or she is feeling, doing, and thinking, each member can change patterns of behavior, thereby achieving deep intimacy (Thorman, 1982). Ackerman, who died in 1971, did not use a set of techniques but rather became deeply emotionally involved with families he treated, creating procedures for the individual family problem. At times, he worked with extended family members; at other times, he saw members individually. This creative and very flexible process makes it difficult to learn Ackerman's approach (Nichols, 1984).

Carl Whitaker

Colorful, radical, strong-willed, and provocative are terms used to describe Carl Whitaker's family therapy. Trained as a psychiatrist, Whitaker began using co-therapists with couples and children in the mid-1940s. Whitaker let his unconscious direct the therapeutic process to realign family power in more constructive patterns. He did not employ structure or a preplanned strategy (Whitaker, 1976). Whitaker's work has no clear theoretical base, which may be why his work is not as well known as other pioneers of family therapy. His emotional "goading" of individual family members aids them in understanding their immediate experience in an environment of warm support. Although his treatment is flexible and unpredictable, he views the common problem of families as their inability to share their feelings (Nichols & Schwartz, 1995). He employed a variety of paradoxical and provocative approaches to encourage family members to drop facades and defenses and to express themselves openly to one another. In accord with basic humanistic tenets, he believed that an openness among family members allowed the family to function more adaptively.

Major Therapies

We have identified three major schools of therapies that have grown out of or are based upon the above theorists' work, These are (1) solution-focused therapy, (2) systemic family therapy, and (3) externalization of blame. We will present each school and then discuss what may determine a healthy family versus a dysfunctional family.

Solution-Focused Therapy

The solution-focused model grew out of the strategic therapy model, particularly the Mental Research Institute model of family therapy. Developed in an effort to keep therapy brief, it focuses on the attempt of the therapist to help the family find another more contemporary solution to its issues rather than focus on the problem. The model assumes clients want to change, yet the solutions they are attempting are limited (Atwood, 1996). Solution-focused therapists borrow from the constructivists the notions that people create their reality and that there are exceptions to the times when the problem presents itself. During spaces of time between the occurrence of the problem, building blocks in the construction of a solution can be accomplished (de Shazer, 1986). The most notable leaders in the solution-focused model work out of the Brief Family Therapy Center in Milwaukee and include Steve de Shazer, Insoo Berg, Evel Lipchik, Michele Weiner–Davis, and Bill O'Hanlon.

The solution-focused model is based on two assumptions. The first is that of strengths and possibilities which create self-fulfilling prophecies and can lead the clients to change their behavior; the second is that small changes are usually all that is needed to make improvements because small changes will snowball into larger changes (Nichols & Schwartz, 1995). The therapist works with the client to set achievable goals and focus on either achieving a solution or deciding that the problem is something else (Atwood, 1996). The two questions used most in therapy are the "miracle" question and the "exceptions" question. The exception question looks at the times when the behavior did not exist or in the future when the behavior would not be there. The miracle question asks if a miracle happened and the problem were solved, how would they know, and what would be different (Nichols & Schwartz, 1995). These questions help families address their goals.

A major innovation of the solution-focused model is the questions which allow clients to focus on skills they use when their problems do not exist. Second, this model builds on the clients' strengths as a resource for solutions. The therapy usually lasts only five to six sessions.

Systemic Family Therapy

A markedly different model of family therapy gained recognition in Europe in the late 1970s. Promoted by a group in Milan, Italy, the model uses infrequent, intense sessions with families who live great distances from the clinical setting. The best results were in treating anorexics and chronic schizophrenics. Developed by a group of practitioners, Selvini Palazzoli, Cecchin, Boscolo, and Prata, who had purposefully isolated themselves from Western therapists, the model is built upon the work of Gregory Bateson. The model relies on the notion that behaviors developed over time are a result of the family's adaptation. and that the meaning of the behavior rather than the behavior is of importance (Nichols & Schwartz, 1995).

The therapists formulate hypotheses about the nature and meaning of the behavior while observing a team member interview the family behind a one-way Mirror. They develop "circular questions" that address the systemic nature of the behavior. Initially, a format for interventions that were strategic and paradoxical was used with families. Cecchin and Boscolo split from mainstream systemic thinking in the 1980s and focused on the questioning process. The therapist tests the hypothesis of the team with the family through the circular questioning process, which allows the family to agree or dispel the hypothesis. The questions add new information into the system for the team and family to ponder. The therapist and the team remain in a neutral position to their hypothesis rather than forcing the hypothesis on the family. This approach is appealing to Western therapists who have held staunchly to the belief that families should decide the direction of change (Papp in Simon, 1987; Hoffman, 1989). Family members' intentions are positively noted (Nichols & Schwartz, 1995).

As this approach was studied and refined by Westerners such as Carl Tomm, Lynn Hoffman, Imber–Black, and Peggy Pap, they developed an emphasis on the questions themselves as interventions. The questions are designed by the team to bring about new revelations within the family. More recently, the teams have come out from behind the minor, using a co-therapy model to reflect their discussions about the meaning of the behavior and the team hypothesis in front of the family (Hoffman, 1989; Anderson, 1988). The reflecting team requires the family to process their responses to the hypothesis and discuss it with one other in front of the therapists or team.

The systemic school growing out of the Milan model has had a significant influence in the field of family therapy. There are four important aspects of this contribution: (1) the importance of the historical evolution of the problem within the family system, (2) the therapists' trust in the families to identify their own solutions and decrease their need to force families to change in preconceived ways, (3) the increasing appreciation of focus on the meaning of the families' behaviors, and (4) the art of interviewing through the use of a circular questioning process which defines the positions of family members in relationship to one another and the beliefs they have about their family's past, present, and future.

Externalization of Blame

In the late 1980s, an Australian, Michael White, had a great impact on the family therapy field. The model used by White builds on the systemic and solution-focused models with more of a social work philosophy by addressing the oppression of families. White attempts to empower families by externalizing the blame. The model assumes that people feel oppressed by their problems and, much like the solution-focused family therapy model, that through a positive approach, families can expand or explore the times where the problem did not dominate them (Nichols & Schwartz, 1995).

White draws on the work of Gregory Bateson and other social constructivists. He proposes the families' views of themselves and the world are constructed around certain stories about themselves that focus on negative aspects or what he calls "problem saturated descriptions." This view often dominates the family

(White, 1989). Therapy helps people distance themselves from the old perception of the problem and locate, generate, or resurrect alterative stories that offer a new sense of self and a different relationship with the problem. The problem is treated as a separate entity that can exist outside of the family. The family is in charge; they are not controlled by the problem. The concept of blaming the victim, employed by society to tell the family what they did wrong, is transformed by helping families to organize to escape the oppression of the problem, other people or systems.

We have reviewed major ideological advances in family therapy. In this new and rapidly growing field of practice, at least 43 distinct family therapy models have emerged. For a more complete analysis of the similarities and differences among the major models of family therapy, the reader is referred to *Mind in Therapy* (Keeney & Ross, 1985). A genogram overview of the major family therapies was developed by David Sallee (Sallee, 1991), which helps to make sense of the evolution of this field (see Figure 7.1). Chapter 10 of this text provides an in-depth discussion of means for assessing healthy families. Next, we provide some general discussion of the concomitants of healthy and maladjusted families. Then, we will discuss general principles of systems intervention.

Determinants of Family Health

Combining the ideas of the varied scholars in family studies, we can gain an overview of the characteristics of healthy families and those that are functioning poorly. Healthy families are characterized by openness and clarity of communication. Members speak precisely to one another. There is a minimum of lecturing or "talking at" one another. People listen and compromise. Leadership is assumed in direct fashion and is shared according to the family needs and strengths of the members. The family is a source of support and encouragement of self-worth and autonomy for its members.

Of course, as pointed out by Satir (1972), all families experience crises, particularly with significant life events, such as pregnancy, childbirth, adolescence, the reaching of adulthood and marriage of children, menopause, grandparenting, and death. In healthy families, crises are met with much mutual support and the flexibility and resiliency needed to make necessary decisions.

FIGURE 7.1

A Genogram of Family Therapy

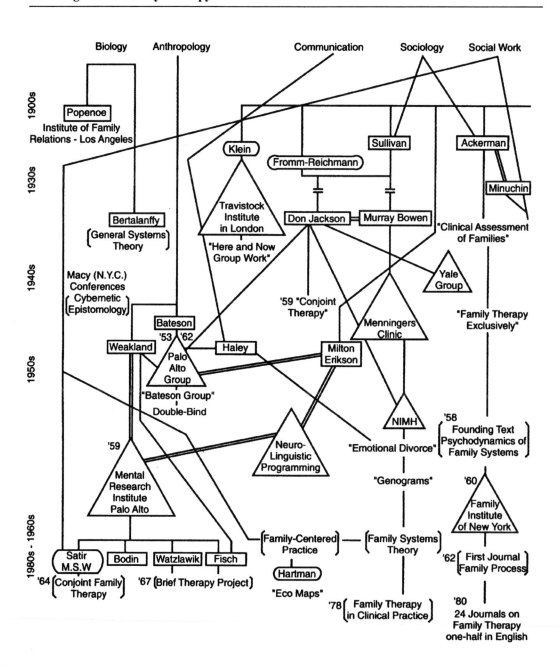

FIGURE 7.1

A Genogram of Family Therapy *(continued)*

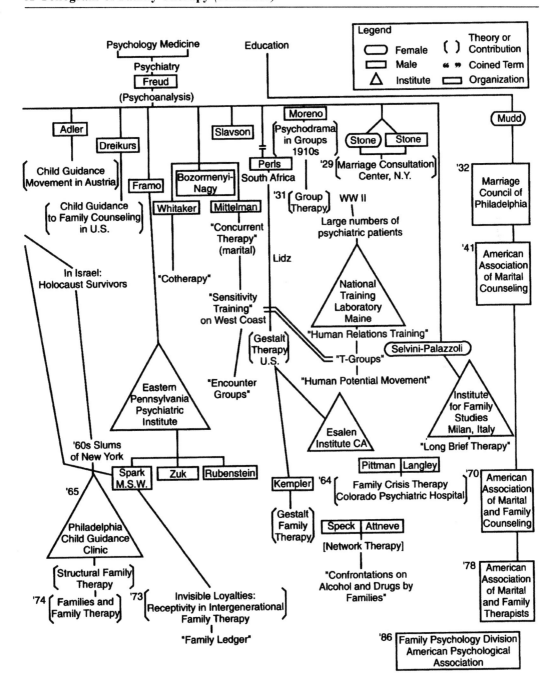

In contrast, in maladjusted family systems, communication is often unclear or confusing and inconsistent. Members hold "hidden agendas," trying to obtain power and get their needs met covertly. The family is not characterized by a balance of autonomy and support among members. Instead, members may be overly dependent on one another, that is, fused in identity; or they may feel alienated from one another, demonstrating little mutual empathy and trust. Coalitions may form in which some family members are antagonistic to others. Rather than sharing because of a sense of mutual respect and support, affection and sex are used to bargain and manipulate.

Maladaptive patterns are often self-perpetuating. Members feel hurt and misunderstood and rely upon their inappropriate roles and styles of communication to cover their hurt feelings and to regain some sense of power. As a consequence, members often assume rigid roles. Satir (1972) characterizes four such rigid parent roles. She describes the family "tyrant," who constantly criticizes and attempts to dominate others. The family "martyr" communicates in a placating style and is always deferring his or her needs for others, but eventually tries to make others pay through guilt and attention for the sacrifice. The "great stone face" communicates primarily in an intellectualizing mode. The stone face is always extremely reasonable to cover his or her feelings of tenderness, fear, and anger. The great stone face hides feelings in order to not be vulnerable in the destructive family system; but, of course, the stone face frustrates others so that they burst forth with the anger which the stone face so much wishes to avoid. Satir also speaks of the inappropriate rigid role of being the "pal." The pal indulges the spouse and children even when discipline or asserting for one's rights is a more appropriate response. Other family members quickly lose respect for the pal and feel their own sense of self-worth diminishing because they are not responding in a loving fashion to the pal.

A review of the clinical child literature suggests that in maladjusted families, children as well as parents often assume rigid roles. We will discuss the terms "family pet," "family baby," "peacemaker," and "scapegoat" as first coined by Ackerman (1971) to characterize these inappropriate, rigid roles.

The "family pet" is showered with love and attention. However, if the pet role is extreme, the child may not learn to cope with difficult situations outside the family network. Also, if this role is exaggerated, other family members may actually or subjectively feel that they lack affection. These members then assume antagonistic family roles characterized by jealousy and negativism.

The common role of the "family baby" can become so entrenched that even as an adolescent or adult, the child is considered a baby by all family members. Of course, a baby is protected, and his or her misbehavior is tolerated. So, the child placed in a rigid baby role comes to expect protection throughout life, and his or her autonomous behavior is limited. If the child's baby role is extreme, other members of the family may not receive the protection that they need. For example, one of the authors (E. S. L.) worked with a 25-year-old mother who had physically abused her two children, resulting in the death of one of them. It was learned that the mother was one of twins. Her sister was born second and was very weak. The sister required much special nursing as an infant. Throughout her childhood, the sister's baby role was rigidly maintained. In time, the client was expected to assume responsibility and care for her twin sister. In fact, it was assumed that she would work full-time through her adolescence and young adulthood so that her twin sister could attend college without having to worry about money. By adulthood, the client's rage was intolerable. She projected this upon her own children, and thus the familial pathology continued into another generation.

Another rigid family role expected of some children is that of the "peacemaker." The peacemaker diminishes family stress through a variety of maneuvers, such as creating a joke in stressful situations or assuming blame for the family difficulties. The problem is that in time, the peacemaker and other family members begin to assume that the peacemaker is at fault. The peacemaker experiences inappropriate guilt and feelings of failure. Once the peacemaker begins to label him or herself as a failure, he or she begins to act like a failure and more negative consequences ensue.

Another rigid family role for children is that of "scapegoat." A scapegoat is the object of displacement for another or several other family members' feelings of guilt. The scapegoat is punished so that the other members feel relieved of their responsibility and anxiety. Often, the scapegoat reminds the displacing family member of his or her own traumatic past. The scapegoat, in time, accepts and plays out the rigid role assigned to him or her.

Therefore, in troubled families, members relate to one another in rigid patterns. Unique needs are met through disguise and manipulation. The problem in the maladjusted family is in the system, the network of relationships. The family comes to therapy because a member, usually a child, has developed extreme symptoms in order to cope with the pathological system. To the family therapist, the member with the untenable symptoms is the "identified patient;" whereas, the actual client is the family unit

Principles of Family Systems Therapy

The principles underlying family systems therapy are drawn from its tenets concerning healthy and maladjusted patterns of family interaction. Framo (1979) summarizes these ideas into seven principles that we expand upon below:

1. Families have unique bondings, rules, communication networks, and myths.

2. People act differently in their family systems than in other environments. The family environment is a unique environment. Employing the principles of Gestalt psychology, we could say that the whole of the family is different from and greater than a combination of the individuals comprising it. The family operates with a personality characterized by particular norms, values, and roles.

3. Families seek homeostasis. Once a system of relating is developed, the family resists efforts of anyone to change it. Changes in families necessitate action to break through the homeostasis.

4. Family members can "drive each other crazy." Some members, the "identified client," develop symptoms in order to reduce the stress in the family. The problems of the individual client is actually present in all family members. The family projects its stress onto the identified client.

5. Family symptoms may be passed through many generations. The trouble in families is the "attempted solution" that is used in a repetitive, rigid fashion. Families get caught in systems needing change. Due to the pull toward homeostasis, change is resisted. Pathological solutions can become entrenched through years and generations.

6. If the identified client changes, another member of the family may become maladjusted as he or she absorbs the family stress. In family

systems theory, the child brought to therapy is viewed as a symptom, not the cause of the family stress. As the child changes, he or she will affect the way all family members relate.

7. Effective therapy requires a realignment of the ways all members relate to one another. It is more efficient for the worker to intervene with the whole family system so that the basic sources of the stress are ameliorated. In that way, another family member will not become an identified client, and a new harmonious homeostasis can be built.

As stated earlier, family systems therapists differ in the techniques they employ in order to work with family members. All will use techniques that facilitate open communication. The therapist models clear communication (Satir, 1967) and helps break down calibrated communication by challenging rigid assumptions and unclear nominalization (Bandler, Grinder, & Satir, 1976). The therapist creates an atmosphere in which members feel free to express themselves. Bell (1964) begins family therapy with a joint session with parents in which he gleans their version of the difficulties, including children's developmental history and education. Then, Bell explains, in family therapy, he will serve as a moderator, encouraging all family members to talk. Bell then brings together all family members over age four and re-explains his role in the therapeutic process.

The family systems therapist uses techniques to help members become more aware of the family dynamics, myths, and rigid roles. Some family therapists are more directive and controlling in order to accomplish this aim than are others. Satir (1972) describes herself as a resource person who is not omnipotent, God, parent, or judge. She sees herself as an "official observer" who gives the family feedback about how members express their autonomy and individuality, what roles are played either overtly or covertly by family members, and whether individual members are congruent in their verbal and nonverbal communication as well as in their behavior. Family therapists point out examples of rigid role-taking and how they serve to block individuals' personal growth. Gradually, the therapist entreats family members to give one another feedback about how it feels to be in those roles. A variety of exercises and worksheets may be used to facilitate family members' awareness of the family dynamics.

Some family therapists exploit the power inherent in the social worker's role to increase family members' awareness of group dynamics (Haley, 1963; Minuchen, et al., 1967; Whitaker, 1976). Haley (1963) states that the social worker initially makes new rules for the family that will make them aware of how the family functions. The homework assignments and injunctions are designed to break up coalitions and neutralize the effects of symptoms that led to covert control. Finally, the family systems therapists are instrumental in fostering behavioral changes in the family unit. They prompt members to act in new ways (insight is of secondary importance). They offer behavioral prescriptions. For example, the therapist may tell family members to hold nightly discussion groups (if communication has been limited), to go out on a family picnic (if alienation is high), or for each member to spend one evening out without other family members present (if fusion is intense). The therapist offers new rationalizations for old problems. By "reframing" the problem, using different explanations to describe a phenomenon, members may be willing to tackle the problem in a new way. Thus, a family may come to therapy with a presenting complaint that family members are not loving to one another and are spending little time together. The therapist might reframe the problem by stating, "Actually, your problem is that you love each other so much that you are afraid to hurt one another's feelings. I want you to get together for a family conference each evening and lovingly tell each other what you feel and what has been bothering you." The therapist may use behavioral contracts to further ensure that goals are direct. Some family systems therapists use paradoxical statements and behavioral prescriptions to prompt family members to work through resistance to change associated with the family homeostasis. Some paradoxical verbal approaches include:

- *Go-slow approach.* The therapist tells the family that they are trying to change too fast. The paradoxical intent is that the clients will resist and therefore change faster.

- *Using resistance.* The therapist asks family members to accentuate their symptoms, to continue doing what they are doing, but to do more of it. For example, a woman who is hypochondriacal ought be told to go to bed, not do any work, and not speak to anyone if she feels the slightest bit ill. The paradoxical effect is that by accentuating the symptomatology, covert maneuvers are made overt. Clients become more aware of their actual motivations and resist the therapist's injunctions, thereby assuming power more directly.

- *Pleading ignorance.* The therapist acts as if he or she does not understand what is happening in a family interaction. This forces family members to assume more responsibility in the session and to openly explain maneuvers.

- *Paradoxical decompensation.* A client with a debilitating problem is asked to demonstrate the symptomatic behavior in the therapy hour, but in an exaggerated fashion. For example, Carl Whitaker (1960) tells of a family counseling session in which the identified patient was an adult male schizophrenic who believed he was Jesus Christ. Whitaker told the client that his trouble was that he had not been baptized. Whitaker proceeded to recreate the original Biblical baptism scene, having family members serve as Mary, John the Baptist, etc. The client soon asked Whitaker to stop the proceedings and stated that obviously his family members were not biblical characters, and he was not Jesus Christ. Thus, the effect of the paradoxical decompensation can be that the exaggerated symptom does not serve its manipulative purpose in the therapy hour so that the client stops it.

- *Benevolent sabotage.* The therapist collaborates with one member of the family to stage a reaction to other family members in order to break rigid relationship patterns. For example, in a private session with a mother who has been placed in a role of family martyr, the therapist might suggest that the mother return home from the session complaining to the family that the individual therapy upset her so much that she cannot do any work. Whenever family members demand something from the mother, expecting her to play a martyr role, she responds that the therapy was so disconcerting that she simply cannot do a thing. The paradoxical sabotage helps the family member break rigid role expectations without directly defying the family rules.

Case 7.1   The Case of Brad's Family

It was easy to tell that Mrs. Jackson was upset when she first called. Her son, Brad, age 9, was having problems in school. Mrs. Jackson was simply terrified that Brad was going to "follow in his brother's footsteps." Ruth, Brad's school counselor and Mrs. Jackson's friend, had referred her. Ruth also was a vigilant member of our agency's board of directors. Mr. Jackson was the chief of police of a small town in the county. All things considered, the family was scheduled for a counseling session the same evening. Mrs. Jackson was told to bring the whole family so work could begin immediately on this "serious problem."

The family arrived early. Chief Jackson had insisted that Butch (18) and Brenda (16), Brad's siblings, attend. They were both acting unhappy to be there. Chief began in a loud, stern voice, "I will not stand for it." Mrs. Jackson began to sob; Brenda looked out the window; Butch looked for an ashtray; and Brad looked at the floor. When the chaos died down, Mrs. Jackson announced that a teacher had witnessed a marijuana cigarette falling out of Brad's locker. Butch laughed, and Brenda said, "Mom you didn't tell me about this." Then the Chief's pocket pager beeped, and he got up and went to find a telephone. I asked everyone else to wait outside while I talked to Brad. His mother seemed relieved.

Shaking my head, I asked Brad if it was always like this in his family and offered him a Coke. He nodded and declined the offer. After some casual conversation I said, "Some kids I see in here get in trouble to get help for their families, but you seem different. You're smart and you don't seem to be crazy. Am I right so far? ("Yeah.") Now I don't know if you're innocent or guilty of the 'crime,' but you are in trouble with your dad and mom. They think you're turning into your brother, so they'll bug you for weeks, months, or even years. I've seen parents like them push kids into proving them right. You probably don't want it, but I might be able to help you get them off your back. You'd have to promise me that you wouldn't tell them what we're up to. If you did tell them, I'd have to lie, and who do you think they'd believe? Think about it for a while."

The family was called back in. Chief said he had to leave in four minutes. Since Brad had agreed to the plan, I proceeded by instructing the family to do all it could to prove Brad guilty for the next few days before our next session. "After all," I said, "it is better to be cautious when the stakes are this high. We have to nip this problem in the bud." Another session was set for a week later.

The second session was spent talking about other problems in the family. They had grown tired of trying to prove Brad guilty and argued that it was unfair. I told the family that my consulting psychiatrist had recommended that Brad meet with me every other day for individual therapy. In this way, we could get at any underlying problems. Since it was important that Brad knew that the whole family wanted to help him, I continued, they must take turns driving him the 15 miles to the agency. Eventually all agreed to the treatment plan.

The individual sessions began. We talked about the weather, sports, minor problems, and occasionally about different ways to act in his family. We also climbed out the window now and then and walked to the ice cream store. After six such sessions, Mrs. Jackson and Chief were convinced that whatever I had said to Brad had helped, and that they didn't want to bring him over anymore if the therapy had worked. Even the school counselor was pleased. Just to make sure everyone was convinced, I cautioned them that change takes time and saw Brad for six more sessions. At follow-up, Mrs. Jackson reported that "everything" was fine and asked what we had talked about. Neither Brad nor I would say. Ruth remained watchful over the agency's services, and we continued to get referrals from the chief's police department.

In the Case of Brad's Family (Heath, 1981), you read of the use of many of the specialized techniques developed by the family systems therapists. Note that the family sought therapy because of the disturbing behavior of their child, Brad. This child might have been placed in individual therapy, but the therapist gleaned information about the family which indicated that the child's symptomatology was primarily a reaction to profound disturbance in the family system. Therefore, the therapist chose to aim therapeutic intervention at changing family roles and communication styles.

In the Case of Brad's Family, the therapist placed focus upon problems in the family system as a whole. The therapist is concerned about members' stereotypical expectations of one another and about the general commotion in the family unit. The therapist intervenes in the family system by changing alliances. He forms a covert pact with Brad, the identified patient, so that Brad and the therapist agree to convince family members that they must prove Brad guilty. Also, notice the frequent use of paradoxical statements. The therapist states, for example, "You probably don't want it, but I might be able to help." No matter what Brad says, he is complying with the therapist. If he refuses help, he validates the therapist's statement. If Brad accepts the help, he is developing a therapeutic alliance.

Issues in Family Therapy

The family therapy literature is extensive, and empirical studies of its effectiveness are increasing (Knopf, 1979). For example, in one controlled study, family systems intervention increased the number of positive responses among family members, decreased the frequency of undesirable behavior, and facilitated more spontaneous interaction among members (Hardcastle, 1977). There is a need for empirical studies which tie down the precise psychological problems for which family therapy is preferred.

There is also an emerging awareness to the diversity in families and new theoretical perspectives such as feminism (McGlodrick, Giordano & Pearce, 1996). The range of issues in which social workers utilize family treatment in child welfare includes, single parent, adoptive, gay and lesbian, AIDS, low income and multiracial families (Janzen & Harris, 1997).

The early family therapists believed that all children's problems were best dealt with by intervening in the family system. Some still subscribe to this position, but a number now agree that the difficulties of the identified child patient may become so internalized that individual therapy is preferred. In other cases, family members besides the identified child may be so disturbed that individual therapy with them must precede effective family intervention (Framo, 1979). Wynne (1961) suggests that family therapy is contraindicated if conditions prevent the establishment of a working relationship with the family. Ackerman (1966a) specifies further conditions. He states that family systems intervention is not preferred if one or more of the following conditions exist:

- There is an irreversible and malignant trend towards break-up of the family.

- One or both parents are psychopathic.

- One or both parents are consistently dishonest in therapy.

- A valid family secret might be revealed inappropriately in therapy.

- One or more family members have rigid defenses that may break under family therapy.

- Organic disease prevents participation by one or more critical members.

- The family expresses an unyielding prejudice against family therapy intervention.

Some see a goal conflict in family therapy. The practitioner hopes to increase individual autonomy, but also aims to facilitate family harmony. Sometimes these goals are incompatible. For example, an adolescent may feel that to be happy he or she needs to live in his or her own apartment. The parents, on the other hand, feel better if the adolescent comes home early each evening. In this situation, there is a conflict between the adolescent's need for autonomy and the parents' need to protect the adolescent. The family therapist must be honest with the family about his or her beliefs in what will facilitate family growth.

Some practitioners and theorists question the ethics of paradox and manipulation by the family systems therapist. It has been suggested that the paradoxical meaning may be confusing to very disturbed clients who have been raised on and are vulnerable to double binds. The family systems therapists employing these approaches reply that their use of indirect techniques is appropriate because they are benevolent in helping their clients. They see their double binds as therapeutic, having the long-term effect of increasing a client's sense of autonomy and control. The reader needs to consider the ethics of this important issue before deciding to use or not use particular techniques of the family systems approaches.

Summary

Family therapy in child welfare grew out of the recognition that the family is the primary unit for all children, even the worse cases found in the field. As such to effectively work with children a good understanding of the theories and therapeutic interventions used to know and work with families is important for all child welfare workers.

A systems approach to family therapy began in the 1960s when a few maverick therapists began to treat entire families. This approach is based upon the principle that the family is a system that has a unique structure and thus resists change. Those workers adopting an analytic framework in family therapy employ different techniques than those who prefer a systems approach. The analytically oriented family therapist holds the individual as the primary client. The family systems theorist sees the total system as the difficulty. Analytically oriented therapists use family meetings to form interpretations about individual psychopathology. Family systems theorists use the group sessions to point out inappropriate processes and how members relate to one another. They point out double and unclear messages by members and ask them to clarify their meanings. They help identify rigid roles assumed by family members. Homework assignments are given in which members are asked to play new roles. At times, the family seeking homeostasis refuses change. Therefore, paradoxical techniques may be implemented. By exaggerating the rigid maladjusted pattern of relating to one another, new dynamics among members emerge, and the symptomatic way of interacting can be diminished.

Family theorists agree that families function better when members are aware of the group dynamics, communicate spontaneously and openly, and assume direct responsibility for behavioral change. All family theorists agree that childhood maladjustments often are a manifestation of parents' problems or problems in the family as a whole. Thus, the effective child welfare worker always is concerned about the family and draws all or part of the family into therapy as necessary. Family therapists have been very creative in their development of therapeutic techniques. The effectiveness of these techniques and the conditions under which they are preferable to other therapeutic interventions are presently under empirical investigation.

Chapter 8
A Synthesis of Theories and Application

Our review of the major theories and therapy for children reveals a multiplicity of ways to conceptualize childhood issues and a variety of techniques to facilitate personal growth. Since each of these theories of childhood personality development is based upon partially untested assumptions about the nature of human beings, the absolute validity of the theories cannot be ascertained. Rather, the theories must be evaluated according to their consistencies thoroughness, expansiveness, and usefulness. Although our review of each theory of childhood personality and therapy is brief, we have tried to delineate each one's respective strengths. Each provides a profitable means of conceptualizing the problems of some children. Each has been found to predict some children's behavior. Each has been widely employed by child welfare practitioners.

Almost a century ago, practitioners committed themselves to the ideal of prevention of insanity in childhood and eradication of delinquency in adolescence (Richmond, 1917). Yet, with the theoretical advances in child theory and therapy, much remains to be done. Kanner (1973, p. 219) coined the expression "salvation of the splinter group" to describe those who zealously support a new therapeutic technique as the answer to all childhood problems. Some believe that the explanation of childhood issues lies in infantile sexuality; others expound that the key is a faulty mother–child relationship; some propose that the answer is inappropriate conditioning; still others hold that childhood problems are neurologically based. Kanner (1973) asks:

> Have the theories brought about the abolition of fratricide, tyranny, greed, and prejudice? They have not.—This is because the basic goal has been split off into

a variety of single approaches, each claiming the sole possession of the key to redemption. Ideals degenerated into ideologies, the Golden Rule into ironfisted injunctions (p. 218).

It would seem most profitable to integrate the various approaches of child welfare counseling and therapy into an overall system so that clinicians could select systematically the best approach to employ with a given child. No doubt, accepting only some aspects of each theory and removing those tenets from their respective whole minimizes the overall meaning of those constructs. However, if the constructs are placed in a new inclusive paradigm, they gain in their expansiveness and overall usefulness. Unfortunately, a total integration does not presently seem possible because the theories are based upon such differing assumptions about humans and discrepant views of how people change. Some of the theories are descriptive, and the techniques of child therapy that flow from them are means of fostering natural growth. Other theories are explanatory, attempting to show positive factors that predict childhood behavior. The techniques emerging from those viewpoints are more directive. A full integration of these theories will require a broader paradigm about human behavior that works concomitantly to explain behavior and mental events. It seems that a total integration of the theories of childhood personality development and child therapy is not yet possible. Yet, the effective child social worker needs to be open to discoveries emerging from various approaches.

We think that some principles can be drawn from the theories of child counseling, and psychotherapy to aid the child welfare worker in his or her selection of techniques. We are not suggesting that these principles constitute a new theoretical integration of all the approaches. Rather, we present these principles as guidelines that recur throughout the varied theories reviewed in preceding chapters.

Principles for Assisting Children in Crisis

1. *Early life experiences are critical.*

The newborn reacts to various stimuli with a circumscribed set of responses. The newborn watches, smiles, coos, cries, and kicks. The infant may respond to light, food, warmth, hunger, surprise, and a variety of other stimuli within the same limited repertoire of behavior.

The newborn's perceptual and psychomotor skills specialize soon after birth. The infant learns to distinguish him- or herself from the environment. Responses become more specific. The infant may cry without kicking, smile without cooing. The infant learns to focus attention more specifically on given objects and events. Responses are tailored to particular people and occurrences. Thus, the child smiles more to the presence of the mother than to strangers. The child wants to control responses in order to obtain desired reinforcement from the environment. Cooing may bring the desired attention of one parent, while crying impacts significantly the responses of another. Increasingly, environmental factors modify the child's behavioral repertoire, and responses become specific to particular environmental cues.

2. *The infant is born with certain constitutional traits and vulnerabilities.*

Infants differ along a series of dimensions from birth, and often these differences persist throughout the life of the individual. For instance, some infants are more distractable than others; other infants show more marked activity levels than most; still other infants appear to be far more affected by new objects or people in their environment Also true is that infants and children differ in how they experience and express elation and sadness as well as in their openness to others. It is important to recognize individual differences in working with children since each child brings to therapy a unique set of characteristics that must be dealt with by the therapist.

3. *Growth proceeds in an orderly fashion.*

The burgeoning research in developmental psychology demonstrates that growth in the physical, cognitive, psychomotor, and psychological spheres emerges in a predictable, interlocking order. For example, a child must develop a certain degree of physical muscular strength before he or she can demonstrate the psychomotor skills of grasping and holding objects. Similarly, a child must develop abstract cognitive skills before he or she can begin to develop a depth of emotional reactions. Being empathic of others necessitates a sophisticated cognitive ability of conceptually "taking on" another's role (Mead, 1934). Developing a conscience, that is, feeling good about one's positive acts and guilty or remorseful about wrongdoings, requires the complex cognitive abilities of being able to remember and evaluate one's past acts and to predict future consequences.

4. *Children develop through successive stages whose order is relatively immutable. The exact age at which children pass through the developmental stages varies from child to child.*

The exact age a child passes through a developmental stage and masters specific skills depends upon an interaction of the child's biological makeup and social environment. The keener the child's perception, the more spontaneous and relaxed his or her temperament, and the more stimulating and supportive the environment, the more rapidly and easily the child passes through developmental levels of growth.

5. *A certain amount of anxiety in childhood is expected.*

Whenever an individual attempts a new and challenging task, he or she experiences a degree of anticipatory anxiety. This psychologically felt anxiety is associated with physiological changes (such as increased arousal and quicker reaction time) that mobilize the person to maximize performance. Thus, anxiety is part of a holistic, organismic response that allows a person to invest his or her best efforts for new challenges (Selye, 1950). If a child feels no anxiety, the child is not testing limits and growing to potential. What the child welfare worker is alert to and attempts to ameliorate is massive anxiety that is chronic and not associated with challenges but instead overwhelms the child and impedes action.

6. *The well-adjusted child is characterized by spontaneity, creativity, self-awareness, curiosity, caring of others, autonomy, and a positive and realistic self-concept. Children do not, however, demonstrate all of these traits all the time.*

The different child theorists vary in their definitions of children's mental health. Some speak of positive self-concept or self-esteem; others speak of positive family and social relationships; still others focus upon the child's ability to meet his or her needs in an adaptive fashion. However, when one reviews clinical work from each of the persuasions, the mentally healthy child is described in similar terms of being spontaneous and curious, with a positive ability to care for others and for self. Of course, no child can exhibit these traits at all times. Furthermore, under times of crisis, it is expected and appropriate that the child would display reactive emotions and behaviors such as depression, nightmares, and acting out, that are part of the organism's recuperative efforts against stress.

7. *The maladjusted child is characterized by one or more of the following traits that are present so much of the time that the child's overall psychosocial development is impaired: withdrawn behavior, impulsiveness, self-destructive behavior, inability to obtain positive reinforcers from significant others, negative and unrealistic self-concept, lack of identity, discouragement, and lack of initiative.*

As stressed previously, all children display reactive (that is, nongrowth enhancing) behavior at times. It is self-protective to react to stress by temporary withdrawal or acting out. Furthermore, no one is well-adjusted all the time. The maladjusted child is one who behaves in reactive ways for extended periods of time. Because of their chronicity and intensity, these behaviors no longer serve self-protective functions but instead are self-destructive. Thus, if a child's pet dies, it is an expected response that the child will grieve the loss by crying, withdrawing, and other reactive behaviors. These reactive behaviors allow the child to discharge the hurt and elicit support from others. Contrast this response with that of a child who says she hates school, cries every morning on the way to school, and is reclusive and withdrawn during the school day. This protracted reaction no longer serves a successful discharge function. Nor does it help this child deal with the stress she feels about school. The child must attend school and is not focusing upon constructive ways of approaching it. Furthermore, her reactions become frustrating to others and may elicit criticism from them. The intensity, duration, and chronicity of child's reactions indicate maladjustment.

8. *Children raised in warm and supportive environments characterized by consistency in discipline are more likely to be well adjusted.*

There can be no perfect formula for raising children. Children are born with certain constitutional traits and vulnerabilities and born into particular familial and social environments. The most effective child-rearing techniques for a particular child will be very individualistic, based upon the child's needs, ways of enhancing the child's particular strengths, and the expectations of the family and culture in which the child lives. Thus, a child of aggressive temperament may respond well to firm discipline. A very sensitive child with strong esthetic interests may flourish in a quiet environment that gently encourages the child to explore and use his or her capacities.

Yet, despite the child's idiosyncratic needs, all children profit from encouragement and support. A warm and supportive environment helps develop a positive view of oneself. While punishments and restrictions can curb nonproductive and maladaptive behaviors, reinforcement and support are required to help a child grow and enhance his or her strengths (Rogers, 1951; Azrin & Foxx, 1971).

Once an appropriate style of child-rearing is identified, it is important to maintain it with some consistency, for inconsistency and erratic discipline and expectations can be very confusing to children and prompt emotional disturbance (Bateson, 1972). Of course, the child-rearing should be modified as the child grows and the child's needs change, but these modifications should be logical to the situation and systematic rather than haphazard and frequent.

9. *Children's healthy development is facilitated by an open communication with parents and significant others.*

A distinguishing characteristic between human beings and all other animals is the extent to which humans rely upon cognitive abilities. A child's overall well-being is critically dependent upon the development of cognitive abilities. For the baby, communication verbally and nonverbally with one's caretakers is the primary mode through which the child learns to think about him- or herself and to interpret the environment (Chess, et al., 1978).

As the child grows older, open and frequent communication helps the child refine his or her understanding of the world. Healthy families are characterized by open, clear, and frequent communication. These families are able to help one another with their problems and to work through conflicts. In disturbed families, communication is closed and/or confusing, and the children's abilities to expand their cognitive abilities are impeded (Satir, 1972).

10. *Children need a balance of evaluative feedback concerning their socially appropriate and inappropriate behaviors and acceptance for their individuality.*

Much humanistic child-rearing literature stresses the importance of supporting the child, praising his or her accomplishments, and encouraging his or her individuality. Other child-rearing specialists write of the importance of setting appropriate boundaries and limits (Mahler, et al., 1975; Spock, 1960). In fact, all children need both encouragement and limit setting. Children are not born knowing all the appropriate limits to their safety and the expectations of their culture. Thus, it is the caretakers' responsibility to set guidelines and maintain them. However, when the environment is supportive and encouraging, children have a desire to please and to model appropriate behavior. Thus, when a child is supported and encouraged from birth, less limit setting is needed, and the child is more likely to grow to his or her potential and to be a productive member of the family and society (Adler, 1927).

11. *Children's maladjustment may occur as a consequence of constitutional vulnerabilities, disturbed family life, life crisis, natural disasters, and/or faulty learning. If of intense magnitude and duration, any one of these factors could result in maladjustment. However, most maladjustments are caused by a combination of such factors.*

The child welfare worker must create a dynamic explanation of the child's behavior by integrating therapeutic observations of the child with those of peers and family members and by piecing together background information provided by family and school. In order to ascertain the etiology of the child's maladjustment, the child welfare worker must rely upon some theory of childhood personality development that offers a full explanation of how psychosocial factors affect the child. Analytic, behavioral, and humanistic theories attempt to answer such questions, and the reader must decide which paradigm seems to provide the most fruitful explanations. Clearly, the child welfare worker must be very scholarly in his or her understanding of the theoretical framework employed, because he or she will use that theory to build important formulations about the child. It is crucial that the perceptions and interpretations reflect accurately the child's dilemmas. If not, therapy might increase the child's confusion.

12. *A necessary concern for child welfare is a warm and supportive relationship between the child and social worker in which the child feels respected, accepted, and understood.*

Although the different child theorists stress varying formulations of the causes of a child's problem and employ different techniques for ameliorating the problems, all concede that successful therapy is dependent upon first establishing a trusting relationship with the child. The child must view the social worker as someone who has his or her best interests in mind before the child will begin to disclose about problems, to listen to the practitioner's interpretations or advice, or to model the practitioner's behaviors or suggestions. Children will not automatically trust the social worker because they are told that the social worker is a helpful person. The trust must be earned. In the initial sessions, if the child welfare worker listens very carefully and is supportive and nonjudgmental, an ambience of being understood is created, and the child will begin to trust the practitioner and the counseling setting.

13. *An important ingredient in counseling with children is activity (e.g., play therapy, role-playing), which can be used as a medium for expression of ideas and reinforcement for appropriate behavior.*

Many feel unsure about how to communicate concepts with young children of no or limited language facility. Some falsely assume that since these children cannot talk, they do not understand concepts. They view analytic and cognitive therapy approaches as inappropriate for the preverbal child. The effective child social worker can bridge the language barrier and communicate constructs to young child clients through the use of activity. The social worker observes the child's play pattern and then verbalizes observations and interpretations about the meaning of those patterns to the client; or the social worker may engage the child in specific activity so that the practitioner can demonstrate dynamic principles that will be helpful to the child.

14. *Effective child counseling and therapy include work with parents and others significant to the child.*

The child may spend only an hour weekly with the social worker but the majority of time with family and school personnel. The child, more than the adult client, must be a respondent to the significant adult figures in the family and school. It is logical, then, that the child welfare worker's effectiveness is increased when the social worker's treatment approach is consonant with the approach of other significant adults in the child's life. Child theorists disagree somewhat upon how these significant adult figures should be brought into the counseling process. Some suggest that they be viewed as "consultants" to the child welfare worker and that they should help plan a treatment strategy (Moustakes, 1973). Others recommend bringing the parents into treatment themselves (Klein, 1960). A number of child theorists stress the value of having at least some of the sessions as family sessions in which systems issues are addressed. What is clear is that the impact of family and significant adults in the child's life should not be ignored. We believe that the social worker must assess the level of the parents' psychological functioning in order to determine the best way to include them in the counseling process. If one or both parents are very disturbed, individual counseling for them may be appropriate. Dependent upon the particular case and the social worker's theoretical persuasion, the worker must decide whether to serve as a consultant and/or teacher to the significant adults or whether to bring them into the counseling process.

15. *Child welfare workers often must seek ways of incorporating other support systems (e.g., school, human services department, juvenile justice system) into the helping process through case management if the child is to be served.*

We have stressed throughout this text that the needs of children are often not listened to. The effective child practitioner must be a child advocate and, as such, cannot restrict clinical practice to the office. It is crucial to understand how the child functions at school since the child spends so many hours of his or her life in that environment. If the child's home or social environment is disruptive, then the practitioner best serves the child by enlisting the aid of appropriate agencies. Because these agencies often are riddled with bureaucratic complexities that block effectiveness, the practitioner must remain engaged with the agencies, following up on referrals to assure that the appropriate services are provided.

16. *Analytic approaches are designed to foster a child's spontaneity and self-awareness. Analytic approaches are most appropriate when a child has reached a developmental level where he or she can conceptualize about personal and family dynamics.*

If the child's problem seems deeply tied to the child's overall personality so that the conflicts are internal and self-sustaining, analytically oriented uncovering techniques may be preferred. For example, if a child demonstrates excessive fear of her father and other males, it may be necessary to help her understand the inappropriate dynamics concerning her father and other males that she has integrated. It is in this particular kind of problem that analytically oriented therapists view their strength in assisting child clients.

17. *Therapeutic approaches from the theory of Individual Psychology are designed to foster social competence and caring for others. This often is accomplished when group therapy is conducted for the child and significant adults.*

In the Individual Psychology approach first advocated by Alfred Adler, the therapeutic situation is oriented toward an examination of the client's interpersonal relationships. Here, the child's evolving lifestyle is studied. The child is helped to become aware of his or her social interests and to learn cooperative strategies for social interaction. Further, the ordinal position of the child within the family constellation frequently provides valuable information about how the child relates to others in the family. As a result, the child's self-esteem is enhanced so that neurotic striving for superiority over others is eliminated and replaced by cooperative social behaviors.

18. *Humanistic approaches emphasize the development of positive and realistic self-concepts. This approach claims particular effectiveness in maximizing a child's potential and creativity.*

Within a warm, supportive environment, the child is prompted to try new responses. Within an accepting play therapy environment, the child can test the consequences of various acts and thereby refine his or her discrimination. Thus, for example, a humanistic approach might be very effective for a five-year-old with the primary symptom of encopresis, which is signaling an over-controlled, rigid personality and suppressed anger toward perfectionistic parents. Within the permissive, accepting relationship, the child can explore ways of expressing suppressed anger and behaving spontaneously.

19. *Behavioral therapies are oriented toward the elimination of self-defeating, self-destructive, and/or socially inappropriate behaviors, and the shaping of autonomous, assertive, and socially appropriate behaviors. A strength of this approach is its applicability for children of any age.*

For infants and children who have regressed to primitive behaviors, behavioral modification is very effective. Through systematic reinforcement, grossly simplified and inappropriate behaviors can be shaped into more complex behavioral repertoires. Working with children at this state of development, the practitioner initially responds somewhat like a parent, satisfying basic needs for hugging, feeding, etc., and thereby reinforcing bonding. Gradually, the therapist encourages the child to initiate autonomous behavior. Systematic behavioral reinforcement techniques help the therapist reinforce this autonomy.

Sophisticated behavioral approaches may be useful for older children with behavioral maladjustments. Techniques such as shaping and modeling can encourage a child to learn new adaptive behaviors. For example, the encopretic child can be taught positive and assertive ways to respond to parents' requests. In short, if the child is basically adjusted, but has demonstrated discreet maladapted behaviors, behavioral approaches which lead to quick, definable gains may be preferred. Thus, behavior modification might be the treatment of choice for a nail biter or a child who is afraid to speak in class but appears otherwise adjusted.

20. *Family theorists recommend systems intervention when a child's problems appear to be enmeshed in disturbed family relationships.*

In some cases, maladjustment does not seem to be internalized into the child's personality structure. Rather, the identified behavior seems to be a situational response to faulty family relationships. In these cases, family systems intervention is preferred. Generally, verbal children ages eight or older are able to comprehend and integrate their experiences derived through sophisticated, language-oriented family systems approaches.

21. *Cognitive restructuring therapies argue that language plays an instrumental role in the child's adjustment. By modifying the child's internal speech, subjective comfort and appropriate behaviors can be fostered.*

As children develop cognitively, they begin to integrate more complex precepts of their relationships to their environment. With increasing cognitive development, the child's sense of conscience emerges. By about four years of age, the child begins to evaluate the consequences of his or her actions, and the rudimentary aspects of morality begin to appear in the child's behavior. With the concomitant acquisition of language during early childhood, the child is able to communicate with others at a level different from the preverbal child. With the ability to communicate with others, the child can learn to "take on" the role of others and to internalize how others feel in given situations. Thus, by the time the child reaches the age of four or five, he or she is able to empathize with others. By modifying self-speech, the child can be taught positive feelings about self and others, and behaviors will change accordingly. This is the basic theoretical tenet of cognitive restructuring therapies.

22. *Regardless of which therapeutic approach is selected, the social worker, with the child and significant others, must identify target goals and means of measuring progress toward those goals.*

It is incumbent upon the child welfare worker to assume responsibility for identifying target goals and to relate these to all critically involved parties. Too often, therapy has proceeded without a clear understanding by the parties involved of the goals of the sessions. In such cases, the child may be unaware of the purpose of the therapy and unaided or confused by it. The purpose of therapy should be explained to the child over a number of sessions to assure the client's understanding and cooperation.

At times, the parents' implicit goals may not be consistent with those of the practitioner or child. Differences in goals may be especially apparent if a referral is placed by an outside agency. In such cases, for example, the practitioner may view the most adaptive goal for the child to change some aspect of the family dynamics, while the parents may initially want to maintain a status quo and want the child only to change. When the critical parties hold different goals for the counseling, an essential aspect of the early counseling should be to work toward the establishment of compatible expectations. Equally important as the transmittal of goals to the child and significant others is the practitioner's use of explicit goals to help guide in the solution of therapeutic techniques and to chart progress. Of course, the goals may change as the practitioner gleans more information about the family and/or as the child and family change. It is important for these changes to be discussed with family members.

23. *Therapy, regardless of approach, is not static. The techniques must be modified as the child approaches the target goals.*

The theory and techniques employed in therapy with children should be continually reevaluated and modified to fit the child at each stage of development. Thus, the intervention may, for example, begin with systematic behavioral shaping of a variety of behaviors, move to a humanistic approach in which the child is given freedom to try and test out the consequences of new learnings, gradual evolve into a rational discussion of the effect of the child's acts, and culminate in a mutual discussion of the dynamic forces the child must cope with at home and at school.

24. *Considering the multiplicity of human variation and the complexity of maladjustment, the practitioner should draw upon a variety of theories and techniques.*

Although good research about counseling outcomes with children is limited, available research indicates that effective counseling can occur when the child practitioner adopts any one of the major theoretical persuasions. Furthermore, techniques associated with particular theories appear best suited for children suffering specific syndromes. Thus, phobic children respond quite well to desensitization techniques. Family therapy appears essential in cases of limited child abuse in which the goal is restoration of the family. It is our contention that a child practitioner artificially limits effectiveness if he or she employs one approach to the exclusion of all others. We recommend adopting a systematic eclectic approach, in which the theory and techniques employed are based upon a judicious understanding of the child's needs and problems and the empirical research about the clinical theory and techniques under consideration.

25. *It is the practitioner's responsibility to evaluate the client's progress after termination of the therapy relationship. A significant limitation in the field of child therapy is the failure to evaluate the intermediate and long-term effectiveness of other approaches.*

Any aid the child welfare worker provides to a child in feeling better about himor herself, in functioning better at home and with peers, and in performing at school is most worthwhile. However, as Klein (1960) explained, many of children's psychological problems go into periods of latency, especially during the middle elementary years. Thus, the ultimate effectiveness of the clinical interventions with children rests upon the children's abilities to function as productive and content adults. Yet, there are only a handful of longitudinal studies of the effectiveness of child therapy. If child practitioners would assume responsibility for assessing the long-term gains of the clinical interventions, we would quickly gain a wealth of data about which intervention approaches hold enduring consequences for given children and which psychosocial problems are most amenable to our clinical techniques.

Application of Principles

In this chapter we have synthesized a general set of principles that emerge from our review of the major theoretical approaches to child therapy. In this section, we want to illustrate the application of these principles by means of a case analysis. The Case of Todd Wilson that follows was taken from the files of the author (E. LeVine) who worked with Todd for a period of two years. The case was selected because all the principles can be illustrated. Actual case material is presented first, followed by discussion that highlights the application of various principles. We hope that this interspersing of case material and discussion proves helpful to the reader who wishes to have a better idea of how child therapy is actually conducted.

Case 8.1   The Case of Todd Wilson

Mrs. Wilson called me requesting an appointment for her son. She had been referred by Ms. Nivers, the child welfare adoption worker and by Mr. Dillion, the school social worker. Mrs. Wilson stated that her six-year-old, Todd, had experienced significant personal problems since he was an infant. "He has always been difficult for me to manage. Now things are absolutely out of hand. The teacher called Mr. Dillion yesterday and said that she cannot handle my son in her special education class. He is destructive with class material and hits and kicks other children. The teacher also said, 'He won't listen to anything I say.'"

An overview of Todd's social history was elicited from the mother during the phone conversation. Todd, a child adopted in infancy, lived with his mother, who, when Todd was 2 years old, divorced his adopted father. Subsequently, when Todd was 4, the mother remarried; her husband adopted Todd, thereby becoming his second adoptive male parent. At the time that therapy began, Todd's family consisted of his parents and an older sister. Todd also visited with his first adopted father, whom he called "Dad," one weekend monthly. His relationship with all family members was stormy. He would defy their injunctions and state that he "couldn't stand them." Despite medication with Ritalin (recommended by the mother's psychiatrist), his attention span was very short (maintaining given activities for less than two minutes at a time).

Because the crisis precipitating Todd's referral to therapy concerned his school behavior, I decided to visit him in the school environment.

> In this initial contact, Principle 11 is implemented. The therapist begins to integrate a dynamic explanation of the child's behavior by gleaning varied information. As outlined in Principle 7, some signs of maladjustment are evidenced, such as impulsiveness, destructive behavior, and inability to obtain positive reinforcement.

My first encounter with Todd was observing him playing with his peers on the school playground. Todd kicked a peer who would not hand him a ball (even though it was not Todd's turn). The teacher reprimanded Todd. He ran to the corner of the playground and covered his ears, closed his eyes, and shouted, "I don't want to hear about it. I won't listen."

> Principles 14 and 15 are implemented. The therapist quickly involves signifi-cant others into the therapeutic process. The therapist seeks information from parents and teachers and establishes rapport with them so they will be willing to cooperate in the therapeutic programming for Todd.
>
> Observation of Todd at school further illustrates aspects of Principle 7, that maladjusted children may reveal discouragement and lack of initiative. Todd's behavior suggested that he had difficulty discerning the needs of others. When his request for the ball was not met, he reacted by closing his eyes and covering his ears.

A full psychometric battery was administered at the initiation of therapy. Physical signs of the mental status exam generally appeared typical except that Todd constantly moved his hands and legs in an awkward, frenzied fashion. Orientation and judgment were appropriate, but some distorted thinking was apparent. Todd spoke of "alligators in my stomach that are eating at one another" and of "wanting to die."

Todd's performance on the WISC-R demonstrated an above-average ability to deal with conceptual tasks. His high scores on the Similarities and Compre-hension subtests were viewed as good prognostic signs indicating his ability to conceptualize and thereby profit from verbal therapy.

Aptitude testing revealed that Todd had achieved reading and numerical skills typical at the pre-primer level. Learning disability testing indicated some minor difficulties in figure-ground discrimination (corroborated by a relatively de-pressed score on the Block Design on the WISC-R) and significant auditory discrimination problems. Upon further auditory screening, Todd's auditory dis-ability was localized as a problem in attending that was exacerbated by back-ground noise. His ability to discern sounds and integrate them was intact when he concentrated well.

His answers to the Rorschach, Children's Apperception Test, Sentence Comple-tion, and Draw-a-Person Test portrayed a very anxious child who viewed the world as hostile, difficult to understand, and impossible to change. Todd saw himself as helpless, the subject of unfair attack, and unlovable. On the Draw-a-Person Test, he drew himself in miniature compared to other family members and without hands. Of further note, he drew earmuffs to cover his ears. His mother and sister were characterized by large mouths with sharp, jutting teeth. To the sentence completion item "Dad and Mom," he answered, "hate me." To the sentence fragment "My family," he added, "goes around in circles."

Todd's emotional and behavioral problems seemed primary and more profound than his academic difficulties. Observation, interviewing, and psychological testing created a portrait of Todd as a highly distraught youngster whose anxiety and low self-esteem led to difficulty concentrating and performing at school. He seemed to feel so afraid of and to be so unable to defend against interpersonal difficulties that he withdrew into personal daydreams, literally and symbolically covering his ears.

> Principles 1, 2. 3, and 4 are demonstrated. Through results of the psychometric battery, the therapist begins to identify life experiences and constitutional traits leading to Todd's maladjustment. The mental status and psychometric results enable the practitioner to identify Todd's levels of development in the cognitive, affective, and behavioral domains. Information about his developmental accomplishments and lags will aid in the selection of appropriate therapeutic techniques.

I called Mrs. Wilson's psychiatrist to learn more about the medication he prescribed for Todd. The psychiatrist had recommended a minimal dose of Ritalin, "primarily to take the edge off of Todd's rambunctiousness." The psychiatrist indicated that physical examination of Todd revealed minor sign of hyperactivity and therefore the psychiatrist had not recommended further testing for organic impairment.

> Here, Principle 15 is carried out. Advice and support are sought from another support system relevant to the family, Mrs. Wilson's psychiatrist.

The following treatment plan was established:

1. **Curb destructive behavior to other persons and objects.** This goal would be accomplished by systematically shaping and reinforcing socially appropriate behaviors within the therapy hours and by instructing parents and teachers to carry out a similar procedure.

2. **Once aggressive behavior is minimized, establish a therapeutic alliance in which Todd and the practitioner begin to relate to one another in an open, supportive fashion. A humanistic therapeutic stance would aid in accomplishing this goal.**

3. Encourage Todd to talk and sort out his feelings about varied family members. Todd would be particularly prompted to explore his reasons for feeling that family members hated him and were attacking him.

4. Help Todd learn new ways to respond to family members, school personnel, and peers so that he could receive more positive responses from them.

5. Aid Todd in developing a more positive, realistic self-concept. This goal involved Todd's learning to value his competencies and to recognize and change his self-defeating patterns.

Observable evidence of growth towards these goals would include:

1. Less reprimanding by teacher and parents for aggressive, destructive behavior.

2. A decrease in fidgety behavior.

3. An increased ability to spontaneously explain the sources of his distress.

4. Less covering of his ears.

5. Understanding of ideas and directions when stated only once.

Since it was hypothesized that Todd's school problems were secondary to his emotional distress, it was predicted that his auditory learning disability would decrease, and his school performance increase as gains in therapy accrued.

These goals were discussed with Mr. and Mrs. Wilson and weekly therapy sessions ,with Todd were initiated.

> Principle 22 is fully employed. Short-term and long-term goals were established. Means of monitoring progress towards these goals were delimited. The target goals were discussed with and agreed upon with Mr. and Mrs. Wilson.

The first few times Todd came to psychotherapy, his behavior was highly uncontrolled. He moved around the room in a wild fashion, grabbing a bag of blocks and pounding them against the floor and walls. I explained to Todd that he was "free to use the play therapy as you wish, the only rules are you cannot hurt yourself or me." Soon afterward, Todd looked defiantly at the practitioner and started to throw the blocks at her. She rose calmly and explained that since the rule was broken, play would have to end for the day.

In the next session, frenzied activity and block-throwing continued. After about 10 minutes, Todd stopped, looked at me, and swung the bag of blocks at himself. The play therapy injunction was repeated for Todd. "You may not hurt yourself or me while you are in here. I'm going to help you take care of yourself until you learn how to care better for yourself. Therefore, our session must end for today." Todd protested and began to cry. I held him and stated, "I can see you are sad and need some help. I offer to help you just as long as you need, but we are finished playing for today." Todd and I sat quietly next to each other for about 10 minutes. We engaged in some casual conversation. At the end of this period, Todd was less agitated, and the session was terminated.

> Principle 13 is shown here. Activity in the therapeutic process is provided by working with Todd in a play therapy milieu.
>
> Principle 19 also is employed. One aspect of the early treatment would be behavior modification of Todd's obstreperous behavior. The practitioner used the play therapy situation and her attention as contingencies to modify Todd's self-defeating, self-destructive behavior.
>
> Then, Principle 12 was initiated. Once limits were established, the practitioner offered support and warmth in order to build a therapeutic alliance. Todd's basic needs for protection, physical, and emotional support were met, and he would gradually be encouraged to display more autonomous, self-directed behavior.

Over the next few sessions, Todd involved me in a number of punitive play themes. Through symbolic games, he would put me in jail for a "hundred thousand years." Several times a session, he would place her in a "spanking machine" and severely reprimand her. "I'm pouring boiling hot water all over you." The practitioner would respond, "Oh, I'm so sad . . . I must be so bad. What have I done that is so bad? . . . How can I be better so that I won't have to be in a spanking machine anymore?"

> As is true of some maladjusted children, explained in Principle 7, Todd did not demonstrate a clear sense of identity. In fact, at times he seemed to project onto and confuse his ideas and feelings with the practitioner's. Initially, the practitioner did not attempt to make insight interpretations about Todd's punitive play. Todd's self-perceptions were so blurred that it would be difficult for him to comprehend that he was displacing his frustrations about himself onto the practitioner. Thus, as explained in Principle 18, the practitioner maintained a humanistically oriented psychotherapeutic approach. She responded to Todd's play,

rather than interpreting it. Gradually, she helped him understand how an individual who is so severely punished might feel. Importantly, the practitioner suggested to Todd that he could change. He could learn behaviors so that punishment against him would diminish.

In the next six sessions, Todd progressed to play in which good and bad were dichotomized, such as in games of war and cowboys and Indians. Sometimes, Todd would be the "good guy," but generally he chose to be the "bad guy" and instructed the practitioner to play the "good" role. Regardless of whether he adopted the good or bad role, Todd always won the game. The practitioner pointed out to Todd that it was very important to him to win. Then, she tried to help Todd understand his developing view of the world. "To you the world is made up of good guys and bad guys. You want to win and don't know whether to be good or bad in order to win."

> Todd's play of dichotomized good-bad themes reveals some growth toward adjustment as explained in Principle 6. Todd now portrays a clear sense of himself in relationship to the practitioner, and he struggles to define his identity as good or bad. The practitioner continues the humanistic stance. She offers warmth and acceptance and reflects the content and affect of Todd's play. Thus, she encourages Todd to check the effects of his newly acquired world views.

In the next four months of therapy, Todd began to request that I put him in the spanking machine and lock him up for a hundred years. I responded, "You feel very bad about yourself. You think you should be punished. I think you are a Special friend. You are my special friend. I would like to help you if you are sad, but I won't lock you up. You can change if you are sad, and I'll help you." Todd insisted defiantly that the practitioner lock him up. I consistently refused repeating the previous explanation.

> As described in Principle 18, the practitioner maintained a humanistic-existential stance over the next few months. She communicated her acceptance and caring for Todd. This catalyzed an existential dilemma in their relationship. Todd seemed to be asking, "How do people care for one another? Are you going to punish and scorn me?" The practitioner employed some concepts of Individual Psychology as discussed in Principle 17 to demonstrate to Todd that she was committed to him. It would behoove Todd to change in some ways, and the practitioner would not cooperate in play and talk that was destructive to Todd. She understood his negative feelings and was willing to help him sort them out

through further play and communication. Implied also was that the therapist would not reject Todd regardless of whether he maintained this intensity of friendship or became more intimate.

Todd began to invent games involving family members. He requested that the practitioner play his sister. Then, he would get angry and throw the sister in the spanking machine. Then I would query, "What did I do wrong? How can I get out of here?" Todd said that the sister was bad and took his toys. She responded, "I'm glad you told me. I'll try to do better." Later, he stated, "You always get what you want from Mom." The sister (practitioner) answered, "I don't think so. Mom won't let me stay out as late at night as I want to." Todd continued to sort out his attitudes about his sister through this role-playing. In time, his anger toward her began to dissipate as evidenced by his developing play themes in which he and his sister went swimming and shopping.

> As stated in Principle 23, therapy is not static. As Todd's adjustment is fostered, new therapeutic techniques are appropriate. As described in Principle 21, rational, cognitive approaches helped Todd analyze and reassess family dynamics.

Todd began placing the practitioner in the role of "Pop," his second adopted father. He developed a game where he would stab Pop with an imaginary knife and the practitioner, playing Pop, would cry bitterly. Then he would take the same knife and stab himself and would not be hurt at all. He was joyful about his game, and the clinician responded that it was really important to him to be able to upset Pop and to not get hurt himself.

One day, a plane roared overhead and Todd explained, "That's my father flying that plane." He had never used the word "father" before; he had always referred to his current male parent as "Pop." Thus, I asked him several questions about his father—"What is your father like?" Todd responded, "He is safe—my father is safe. My life is a whirlpool, but my father is safe." As his feelings about his father were explored, it became apparent he was referring to his biological father. This came as a surprise since Todd had never before mentioned his biological father whom he had no knowledge of. It seemed that he had created an entire image of his natural father that was ever-present in his imagination, The image affected him as much as his adopted male parents whom he called "Dad" and "Pop," respectively.

As explicated in Principle 21, Todd continued to develop, and his language, cognition, and symbolic communication became increasingly important. The practitioner needed to be sensitive to the meaning he attached to words. His language, which he now used in a highly sophisticated fashion, held keys to the nature of his conflicts. The practitioner used Todd's language to help identify his underlying conflicts. Gradually, using a cognitive restructuring approach, she helped him change the meaning of some of his terms so that he could feel better about himself.

From about the eighth month through the twelfth month of psychotherapy, Todd often requested that I play the role of Pop as he endeavored to work out his conflicts about his parents and confused and negative feelings about his own adoption. She willingly consented to play the role of Pop but asked also to play his father. Todd continued to be very angry towards Pop, stabbing him with a knife. Once, when the clinician played his father, he cried out, "Where did you go? I'm no good." In many therapy sessions, the following theme was played out by the practitioner in the father role: "Todd, I love you, but I just couldn't take care of you. I asked that you be adopted because I loved you and wanted you to have a good home."

The practitioner now combined analytic and cognitive restructuring approaches as defined in Principles 16 and 21. She asked to play father because she wanted to facilitate Todd's uncovering deeply repressed conflicts. Todd's deeply rooted traumatic anxiety, that he was no good because his natural father rejected him, was uncovered. The practitioner then began to help him redefine himself as good, giving him new symbolic explanations about why his natural father had given him up for adoption.

In similar fashion, his angry feelings towards his mother were worked through. When I played the role of mother, he would first attack her with pillows and other objects and then hug her. She (the therapist) responded, "I don't know whether you love me or hate me."

A similar analytic and cognitive working-through was conducted concerning Todd's reactions to his mother. As posited in Principle 24, a variety of theories and techniques were employed to help Todd deal with the varied facets of his personal dilemmas.

In a psychotherapy session that occurred about a year after initiation of therapy, Todd stated, "You be the mother and I'll be the father. I don't want to be the little boy anymore." He proceeded to play the role of father, calling the practitioner "honey," taking her hand and flirting with her in an adult fashion.

At this point, several discussion sessions with the parents were initiated. The mother explained that Todd often played an adult role with her. When Pop was out of town, Todd would state, "Now I can be the man around the house."

In a few emotionally tense sessions with the parents, the mother began to identify that in some ways she was reinforcing Todd for playing this adult male role. She was placing upon him many of her unsatisfied needs in her marital relationship.

Her relationship with Todd had many sexual overtones. He loved to wrestle with her, liked to watch her get dressed, and would walk naked into her room in the mornings saying such things as "Look at me, Mom."

When these interactions were discussed, concomitant with the parents' discussion of their relationship, the mother began to view her own behavior as inappropriate. Therefore, the advisability of marital therapy was agreed upon.

In the marital therapy sessions, the couple worked hard to reduce their conflicts with each other and to become more effective in meeting each other's needs. The mother began to modify her behavior towards Todd, making it clear to him that his special role in the family was that of son, not surrogate husband.

> Todd's play seemed to indicate some concern about his sexual identification and/or confused role in the family. Through the application of Principle 20, the practitioner met with the parents to see whether this recent play therapy session indicated internalized conflict or Todd was responding primarily to stress in the family system. As explained in Principle 14, the therapist must decide whether to serve as a consultant to the parents or to bring the parents into therapy. In this case, diagnostic discussion sessions with the parents illuminated a need for marital therapy.
>
> Marital therapy helped foster Principles 8 and 9 in Todd's home life. Marital therapy increased the consistency in discipline and appropriate support that Todd received. Principle 10 also came into play after Mrs. Wilson's needs for companionship were more successfully met by her husband. Now she was able to give Todd realistic feedback for his behavior: support when appropriate, reprimands when necessary.

At this point, one year and three months after therapy had been initiated, Todd was much calmer and able to express his feelings more spontaneously. He bounded into his session about Christmas time, picked up a bag of blocks and exclaimed, "Remember how I used to use these? I used to throw them around the room. Now they are Santa Claus' bag. Come sit on Santa Claus' lap and tell me what you want for Christmas." The practitioner was aware that Todd's request would probably provoke sexual feelings, but she was ready and felt it was appropriate to deal with them. When she sat on his knee, Todd stated, "Can I spend the night here with you?" The practitioner stated, "What about Mrs. Claus?" Todd became visibly upset, stating, "You make me so mad!" He got on his sleigh and went back to the North Pole. He carried on a conversation with Mrs. Claus in the corner of the room, then he returned on his sleigh and stated, "Well, I can stay with you now because Mrs. Claus and I have gotten a divorce." I responded, "Divorce isn't that easy. I can see we need to talk about divorce quite a bit more, Todd. Your mother has been divorced, and this must be hard for you to understand." Over the next few sessions, Todd and I discussed his confusion about male and female relationships, and about his mother's need to get a divorce. "You were a very little boy. Just as little boys are too young to go to work and do other things grown-ups do, little boys are too young to cause divorce. Your parents caused their divorce and that was sad for you. Now, you've gotten these sad feelings out, and you can go on and grow up and put this all behind you."

The new family system, that is, a better relationship between his parents, helped Todd stabilize his behavior and his role in the family. However, some of his concerns lingered. From the initiation of therapy, Todd had expressed feelings of being "no good" and of being abandoned by his parents. Now he hinted that he somehow feels tied into his parents' relationship problems. Principle 5 points out that all children experience anxiety. Todd's sensitivity to his parents' marital discord probably intensifies natural Oedipal strivings.

Todd now communicates well in a dialogue fashion. The play serves primarily as a platform for identifying his remaining conflicts. After the conflicts are identified through play and role-playing, therapy is conducted in an almost strictly verbal fashion.

A cognitive approach is implemented in therapy. The logic and illogic of his perceptions are discussed. He is offered a metaphor about "little boys" to help him restructure his thinking concerning his role in his mother's divorce.

After a year and one-half of psychotherapy, Todd returned to a regular educational classroom. In the regular classroom, Todd's behavior continued to improve. Therapy was continued for several more months, so that it was clear that gains toward all target goals established at the initiation of therapy were firmly maintained.

At biannual follow-up sessions, gains were maintained. At the final, three-year follow-up, he was performing above average in all school work. He was participating in several sports and was particularly effective at football. He spoke with delight about his three "good pals." His parents reported that he continued to be very active, but that his energy was now constructively channeled.

> Here we see that Principle 22 is followed. Todd's progress toward therapy goals is charted. Specific target goals such as decreased reprimanding by significant others, decreased fidgety behavior, and increased ability to talk about his feelings and to concentrate are achieved. In addition, secondary goals of improved school performance are noted.
>
> Of course, as explained in Principle 5, Todd is not completely free of anxiety. However, Todd exhibits many overall signs of adjustment elaborated in Principle 6 such as spontaneity, self-awareness, autonomy, curiosity, and caring for others.
>
> Finally, the therapist is committed to Principle 25. Effectiveness of therapy is reevaluated every six months for three years following termination of therapy.

Summary

The effective child welfare worker, often in partnership with other child therapists, is able to use a multiplicity of ways to conceptualize children's issues and a variety of techniques to facilitate change. In this chapter we have presented a synthesis of theories and their applications. The twenty-five principles we have drawn from the major theories presented in the previous chapters are guides for maximizing the application of the theories the child welfare worker (or the therapists they may work with) to employ. In the Todd case these principles were illustrated based on a real life child welfare case.

Part III

Developing a Treatment Plan for the Child and Family

S o far in this text, we have been speaking of the child in theoretical terms. When the child welfare worker meets the child client, the abstract of children's issues and theoretical approach to child treatment must be translated to specific goals and procedures. The intent of Part III of this book is to help set forth concrete strategies for assisting each child with needs. An essential part of developing treatment plans is to identify the working hypotheses about the nature of the child's problems. Then, the practitioner can decide what type of treatment to provide for the individual and for the family. Chapter 9 overviews the means of assessing the nature of the child's problems. Chapter 10 overviews means of assessing the family as a unit. Chapter 11 discusses specific ways of setting up treatment to meet the needs of the family and the child.

Chapter 9
Child Assessment

Two processes are involved in clinical child welfare assessment. The first refers to the assessment of the gravity of the child's problems. Here, the worker attempts to determine how the overt feelings of discomfort interfere with the child's personal growth and adaptation to the environment. The second aspect of assessment is evaluation of the predisposing and precipitating conditions. The child welfare worker attempts to ascertain how familial, school, physical, intrapersonal, and/or interpersonal factors contribute to the child's problem.

Done well, assessment facilitates communication. Most importantly, the results obtained from our assessment help us determine the course of action. Despite this important function, many professionals view assessment with some degree of doubt especially in the area of intellectual assessment. The prevailing negative attitude about psychological assessment and especially standardized testing often is so potent that new findings in the field are not evaluated objectively. A lesser number of professionals defend the use of assessment and may not be open to criticism about psychological evaluation. It seems that the topic occasionally is difficult to discuss objectively. We feel that it is important to begin this chapter by sharing our view of assessment.

Given our definition of assessment (diagnosing the gravity of the child's problem and the predisposing and precipitating conditions), we believe a child welfare worker must assess but *not* label. Child welfare workers differ in how systematically they acquire expertise in assessment techniques, but if the therapeutic procedures are to be based upon client needs, then some assessment of the client's problem is required. We see the need for a relatively systematic assessment procedure. When the procedure is systematic, it is easier to obtain knowledge about all the needs of the child's development (physical, cognitive, affective), and the chances of missing a potentially important variable diminish. The procedure need not be excessively formal, for it often is impossible to gain information from children in a formalized structure. What we recommend is that the child welfare worker be guided by a relatively systematic format so that the child welfare worker knows what information he or she will try to obtain at appropriate points in the assessment interview(s).

Used appropriately, the assessment devices are guides for the worker, but they can be misused. For example, it is misuse to assess a child and not propose a plan for therapeutic or remedial help. In this case, assessment labels a child without providing needed intervention. For example, we all have heard statements such as "Johnny is so hyperactive that there is no use putting him into a regular school classroom." Conscientious social workers do not support such uses of assessment since it is a social worker's responsibility to be of assistance rather than to reinforce inaction.

Results of assessment are ill-used if all children are compared to a single norm. Cultural, class, sex, and socioeconomic factors as well as the child's individual temperament must be considered in any effective assessment procedure. In assessing ethnic minority children, issues of relative reliability and validity must be carefully coordinated.

Naturally, the worker should not employ tests that he or she is not skilled to administer. This latter misuse of testing is rarely mentioned, but does occur. Many assessment instruments require much training in their administration and interpretation, and it is the worker's responsibility to be certain that he or she possesses prerequisite skills. There is a difference between a "reading" knowledge and an "administrative" knowledge of assessment devices. The effective child welfare worker needs a broad reading knowledge about the types of assessment devices available. This broad knowledge is necessary for understanding psychological reports and research articles, and for communicating with other professionals and clients' parents and teachers. The social worker need not and is rarely trained to know how to administer assessment instruments. For psychologists it is better that they know the fine points of administering and interpreting a few tests than to have superficial knowledge in the administration of a broad range of instruments.

We have organized this chapter by first discussing diagnostic interviews and the kinds of information the child welfare worker will want to obtain and observe from parents, teachers, and the child. Then, we review a number of psychometric instruments. Rather than simply listing tests, we divide the review of assessment devices into the domains of screening for organicity and cognitive assessment (including intelligence, achievement, early childhood, and learning disability testing) and social and personality assessment (including measures of overt behavior and standardized and projective personality testing). By this organization, we hope to show how a battery of test results can be combined to shed light on a child's problem areas and how such information can be employed in identifying the most constructive means of intervention. We cannot provide an extensive review of the reliability, validity, and administrative procedures of each device, but we attempt to familiarize the reader with the types of instruments that can comprise a child assessment battery. We also will present the strengths and limitations of various test formats.

Assessment Interviews

Gaining Background Information from Parents

Depending upon one's theory base, the amount of background information desired will vary. Nevertheless, we have demonstrated earlier that most childhood issues are catalyzed by a combination of biological and psychosocial stresses. Certain background information is critical to understand these stresses.

Some social workers like to have parents fill out a written questionnaire about the child. They may use this written questionnaire in place of or as an adjunct to the verbal interview.

Some workers prefer to ask parents for background information in structured interviews. In these background interview sessions, it is important to be open and nonjudgmental with parents. The child welfare worker will want to withhold possible interpretations about the child's problems until all necessary background information is obtained. If interpretations are offered early, parents may have a tendency to offer only background information that fits into the proposed interpretation. It is helpful to ask parents to give very concrete examples of target difficulties. That way, the worker is able to better discriminate problems that are the child's from those that are the parents'.

An informal parent interview is conducted like a brainstorming session. The social worker encourages parents to generate all information that may be relevant to the child's present functioning. The worker does not judge the ideas presented, but does encourage parents to be as operational as possible. Later, after these interviews are terminated, the social worker looks for consistency in the parents' statements in order to formulate themes about how the child and family function (Chess & Hassibi, 1978). A broad range of questions about the child's past and present functioning in the physical and social domains should be gleaned. Combining information about the mother's pregnancy, progress through developmental landmarks, illnesses, and medical exams, the child welfare worker can begin to form hypotheses about the potentiality of organic impairment. Naturally, if organicity appears likely, the social worker will refer the child to a medical professional for further assessment. The worker also will ask questions to determine the child's social relationships with family members, peers, and other adults. By asking about the client's relationships with siblings and other peers as well as parents and other adults, about how the child deals with responsibility at home and in other environments (doing chores, following directions, etc.), and about specific disruptive behaviors (temper tantrums, abstinence, etc.), clear themes about the child's strengths and problems emerge. For example, the social worker may learn that the child gets along well with parents and other adults, but does not relate well with siblings or peers; or the clinician may discover that the child's relationship with all family members is stormy, but that the child's social behavior at school and in other environments is consistently appropriate. In the first example, the child welfare worker begins to suspect that the child's problems center upon personal/social difficulties relating to other children. In the second example, the social worker would formulate the hypothesis, awaiting further substantiation, that the child's difficulties are intimately tied into problems in the family system. In one way or another, it is very important that the child welfare worker obtain information about the client's functioning in each of the developmental domains.

Very possibly, parents' recall of developmental landmarks may be somewhat distorted; and of course, they present their view of the child's problems, which may not coincide with the opinion of the child or of other significant adults. Although some information may lack absolute accuracy, very unusual behaviors tend to be remembered with relative precision. If the responses are viewed as the parents' perceptions of the child, not as absolutes, meaningful trends emerge about how the parents view the child's problem and their role in provoking or ameliorating the child's stress.

Interviewing the Child

In the initial sessions with the child, the social worker wants to glean information about the child's perception of his or her problems, remembering that the child may have a perception of coming to therapy different from the parents'. Social workers agree that great skill and patience are required for assessment sessions with children. Freedman, Kaplan, and Sadock (1976, p. 1038) explain that the worker must be a "responsive human being. It is virtually useless to push diagnostic questions at a child who is unready or unable to lower his guard." By "responsive human being," Freedman, Kaplan, and Sadock (1976) mean that the worker waits for a cue from the child that allows asking a relevant question. Thus, if a child asks, "Where is my mother now?" an opportunity is available to learn more about the child's relationship with his or her parents. Similarly, if a child says, "I have a toy like that at home," questions about the child's daily activities might be asked. If specific questions need to be asked quickly (for example, if the child is experiencing some crisis at school that requires prompt resolution), it is usually helpful to begin by asking simple questions first to help the child feel at ease. Questions about likes and dislikes, pets, hobbies, etc., can facilitate communication (Chess & Hassibi, 1978).

Information about the child's overall development falls into eight primary areas: size and appearance, social/emotional adjustment, motility, coordination, speech, thinking processes, cerebral functioning, and sensory acuity. Some of this information can be obtained by direct observation, while short activities and games may help determine other developmental data. Table 9.1 presents the major areas in a child's mental status examination, that is, the major developmental areas that need to be investigated (Goodman & Sours, 1967), and some activities or observations that help in making the assessment (Keat, 1974).

On the basis of a directed observation of the child conducted along the guidelines suggested in Table 9.1, the social worker can gain needed information about cerebral functioning, the so-called "hard" signs and "soft" signs of organic pathology. The "hard" are indicative of specific brain damage and include disorders of ocular muscles, indifference to pain, lack of tactile sensation, and convulsions, especially those with associated vertigo or vomiting (Chess & Hassibi, 1978). Neurophysiological referral is in order if these signs are present. "Soft" or nonfocal signs are sometimes indicative of organicity, but do not imply anything

TABLE 9.1

Mental Status Examination with Children

Target Area	Specific Indicators	Significant Activities
Size and Appearance	Nutrition Color of Skin Dress Habits Mannerisms	
Social/ Emotional	Friendliness Happiness Maturity for Age	Is child easy to engage in conversation? How does child handle separation from parents?
Motility	Hyperkinesis Hypokinesis Tics	Does child sit still when asked to for three minutes?
Coordination	Posture Gait Balance Gross Motor 　Coordination Apraxia	Ask child to walk stairs and to throw a ball to an object 　while hopping. Pick up sticks, make a fist, play jacks, unwrap candy, use 　a toothbrush, play "Simon Says"
Speech	Dysrhythmnias Pitch Modulation Neologisms Mutism Aphasia	Have child name things in room. Have child repeat a sentence, give meaning of a sentence.
Thinking Pattern	Fragmentation Bizarreness Merging Concepts Lapses of Attention Cognitive Errors 　(attaching literal 　meaning to 　figurative words) Idiosyncratic Views Blurring of Reality and Fantasy Obsessions Repetitive talk Dysphasia	Name and hide objects. Have child find them sequentially.
Sensory Acuity	Vision Hearing Taste Agnosia	Hold up fingers at various distances. Note ocular muscle. Ask child to identify when he/she hears stop as you approach. Ask about any negative feelings for foods. Ask about any "scary" experiences. Have child close eyes and 　touch and identify common objects. Note any indifference to 　pain or loss of tactile experience

about the area of neurological malfunctioning. "Soft" signs include hypotinicity (flaccidity and limpness of muscles), fine and gross motor coordination difficulties, signs of aphasia (absence of speech), dysphasia (disrupted speech), agnosia (difficulties in tactile recognition), and apraxia (problems with coordination) (Hynd, Snow, & Becker, 1986; Goodman & Sours, 1967). The presence of several of these "soft" signs signals the need for further psychophysiological testing, especially if these results confirm findings from the parent interview (Chess & Hassibi, 1978).

If neurological consultation reveals no organic syndromes to underlie these "soft" signs, it is then important for the social worker to work with teachers, speech pathologists, and other related professionals to help remediate the motility, coordination, speech, or acuity disorders. Since the child's physical and psychological development are intimately interwoven, remediation of psychomotor difficulty is integral to therapeutic gain. Clearly, the child's emotional harmony is hampered if he or she is unable to play or compete with peers at psychomotor tasks or if sensory/ motor deficits hamper effective adjustment to school.

If the systematic observation of the child reveals that most difficulties are in thinking processes, the child welfare worker will want to contact a psychologist to explore the extent of the thinking disorder. Psychometric testing may be helpful in this regard.

Since a child is usually brought to counseling because his or her behavior is quite disturbing to some significant adults, many social workers like to observe the child and significant adults interacting at the initiation of therapy. By watching how significant adults and the child interact, the social worker may gain new hypotheses about how they are provoking disturbing responses from one another.

Summary of Interview Data

Regardless of theoretical orientation, the child welfare worker needs information from the child and significant adults about the child's overall functioning, strengths, and problem areas. Specific questioning about developmental history aids the social worker in assessing the probability of organic impairment and in targeting problematic areas of personal and social functioning. Observation of the child, significant adults, and their interaction provides essential information about intrapersonal problems related to emotional and physical development and interpersonal difficulties that are provoked by maladaptive patterns between the child and significant adults.

Because the child's and significant adults' behaviors and attitudes will change as therapy is implemented, the informal interview process should continue through various phases of intervention so that new information and procedures can be incorporated into the management plan as needed.

Psychometric Instruments

Psychometric instruments can offer another sample of a child's behavior. At best, these results offer further clinical hunches for therapy. If there is a discrepancy between the parents' report of a child and clinical observation, or between the child's stated feelings and overt behavior, test results may suggest the motivational factors underlying the child's behavior. Some tests can be useful for screening organic pathology. Others help delineate the relationship between emotional and academic problems. The results are most likely to be helpful when the test is selected wisely to help shed light on a specific concern.

When a psychologist tests a child, it is very important for them to allow plenty of time to establish rapport. Generally, adult test examinees are motivated verbally by suggesting that the test is important or asking them to do their best. With younger children, tests may not seem as intrinsically important. To a preschool child, testing may be an alien experience. These children are likely to be frightened by the social worker telling them they must do their best. Often the child's performance depends upon the relationship with the psychologist. The child is willing to cooperate with the social worker's requests because of the rapport between them. Some behaviorally oriented practitioners attempt to increase the child's motivation to perform well by offering a reinforcement after completing segments of the task. This approach works well with many children, providing standardization procedures are not compromised in the process.

Children's performances also are contingent upon how interesting they find the work to be. They look at the task like a game and want to quit when the game is no longer fun. The social worker must be sensitive to the child's level of interest in the task. Generally, it is a good idea for the psychologist to terminate the testing when the child's interest wanes as indicated by increasing fidgeting, changing the subject, or negativism. Several testing sessions may be required to obtain a valid measure of the child's true functioning.

The child's response to the test situation often is as important as the actual answers to the questions. The child welfare worker will want to know the child's response to the first question as an indication of how the child responds to novel tasks. Also important are repetitive response patterns. Of course, these response patterns should be considered in relation to the child's overall behavior, but do provide one more clue under relatively standardized conditions about how the child thinks and behaves. Thus, how the child responds to not knowing an answer and being wrong may be clues about how the child responds to errors at school and at home. If the child frequently requests assistance, this may suggest that the client is hesitant to act on his or her own and may indicate strong dependency ties. If the child frequently asks, "Am I right?" the tester might postulate that the client needs much reassurance or is questioning her or his judgment. The child may respond differently to one test than another, and certain tentative conclusions can be drawn from this behavior. For example, a child may work fast and smilingly on an achievement test and very haltingly on the Rorschach. In this case, the social worker may hypothesize that this child prefers structured tasks. Thus, the therapist notes all test behavior and adds this to other assessment findings.

A vast number of tests are available, and the reader should be familiar with the **Mental Measurement Yearbooks** which review all standardized tests in print (Buros, 1972). In the remainder of this chapter, we will attempt to overview types of assessment devices widely used today. Our review is by no means exhaustive. We have attempted to organize this review around functions served by the tests: screening for organic problems, cognitive assessment, and social and personality assessment. Some tests are used for more than one of these functions and may be mentioned more than once. In many cases, numerous books have been written about a single instrument, yet we have time and space to write only a few paragraphs. Our review will emphasize how a child welfare worker might benefit from the type of test results, and we will refer you to further reading in the various areas.

Screening for Organicity

We have stated that "hard" or "soft" signs of neurological impairment may be obtained through the clinical interview with the child and his or her parents or other significant adults. A number of psychological instruments can offer further confirmation of organicity. We will review two, the Bender–Gestalt and Wechsler tests, which child practitioners often use. The reader is reminded that many other screening devices are available. Then, we review briefly neuropsychological batteries that are administered by child practitioners who specialize in assessing organicity in children. We demonstrate that the organic assessment devices range greatly in reliability. The combination of test and administrator sophistication determines the precision in identifying organicity.

Bender Visual–Motor Gestalt Test

Psychometrists commonly use the Bender–Gestalt Test (Bender, 1962) as a rough means of screening for organic brain dysfunction among children. The nine cards with geometric designs were developed by Lauretta Bender in 1938 based upon the belief that there is a tendency to perceive and complete the designs according to principles biologically determined by sensorimotor patterns of action. Children before age four scribble with little resemblance to form. Lines are drawn in primarily radial directions with few horizontal movements. Around preschool age, children begin to form loops. Circles are drawn for dots. By age six, good reproduction of form is expected. Bender (1938) posited that children with organic brain syndrome draw on more primitive levels than expected by their chronological age; that is, she believed that organic brain syndrome would be demonstrated by infantilized or regressive drawings. She further posited that these "errors" are distinct from the distortions of an emotionally disturbed child.

Koppitz (1964) developed an objective scoring system normed to 1,200 public school children between the ages of 5 and 10. Administration is in three phases. In the first phase, the administrator simply states, "I have nine cards with designs on them for you, to copy. Here is the first one. Now go ahead and make one just like it." The child copies the nine designs handed to him or her in turn as the directions are repeated. In the second phase, the child is requested to draw as many designs as can be remembered. In the third phase, the child is presented with a design seriously distorted in the first phase. If the child makes the same error again, card is laid next to the child's drawing, and the child is asked if he or she can perceive the difference between them. In the Koppitz (1964) scoring system, points are given for regressive drawing that may be indicative of organicity. In general terms, the scoring system attempts to discriminate the following types of errors:

Errors Indicative of Organic Brain Syndrome

Rotation

Distortion

Fragmentation

Oversimplification

Use of angles for curves

Perseveration

Collision and overlap of form

Circles for dots

Lines that do not meet

Errors Indicative of Psychological Problems

Overabundance of vertical movement

Fluidity of pattern

Loss of boundaries between designs

Destruction of the gestalt by elaboration

Embellishment with own ideas

First few forms good, then deterioration

Figure 9.1 is a reproduction of the nine cards of the Bender–Gestalt. Following this reproduction are protocols completed by two 5-year-old children. Protocol A was produced by a child diagnosed as brain damaged, while Protocol B was drawn by a child referred to counseling because of her insomnia and frequent tearfulness. Naturally, this brief review of the Bender–Gestalt does not prepare us to present a scoring of these protocols, but it might be helpful for the reader's broad understanding to visualize how Bender–Gestalt protocols differ in production. On Protocol A (Figure 9.2), completed in eight minutes, several factors associated with organicity are demonstrated, such as fragmentation and oversimplification, distortion, and overlap of form. In addition, dots are not clearly formed, and angles and curves are not differentiated. In Protocol B (Figure 9.3),

FIGURE 9.1

Nine of Wortheimer's original patterns used by him for research in visual gestalt psychology have been selected and are offered to the individual to be examined for copying. Figure A Is used as an introductory figure (with permission). Published by the American Orthopsychiatric Association.

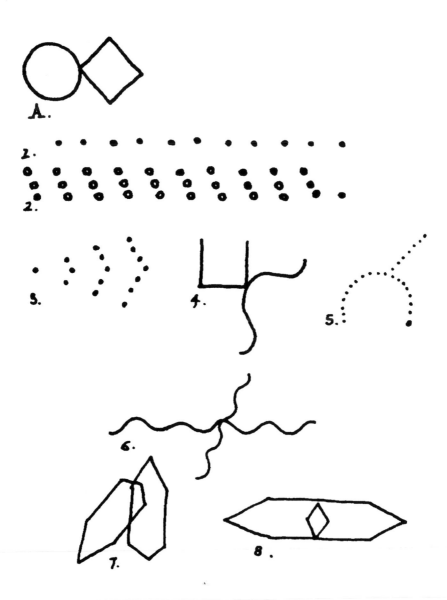

FIGURE 9.2

Bander–Gestalt Protocol A

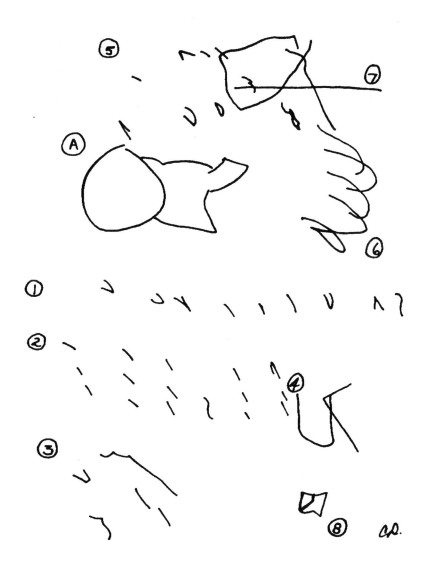

FIGURE 9.3

Bender–Gestalt Protocol B

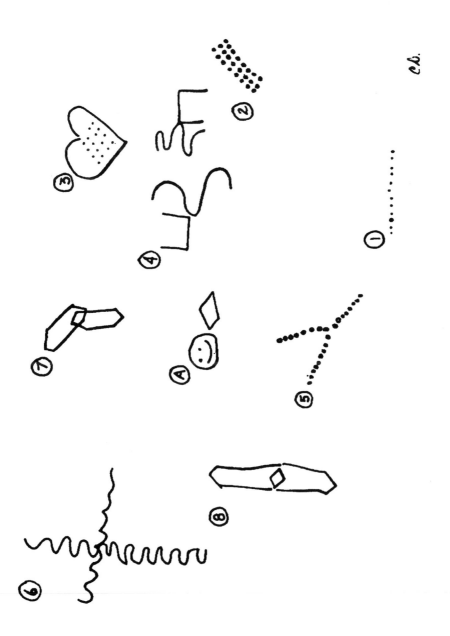

forms are rather meticulously completed, but in many cases appear overworked. Protocol B showed many erasures. Note that Figure 4 of the Bender was attempted twice. Dashes and circles are carefully formed, but at times circles are made rather than dots as in the original cards. Notice the child's embellishment, such as the heart around Figure 3 and the face in Figure A. The child preceded these embellishments each time by stating, "I didn't do that one right." The child worked slowly and meticulously at the task (a total of 20 minutes), yet did not place the drawings in the sequential order (as if she were so concerned about completing each drawing correctly that she did not pay attention to the broader gestalt).

The validity studies of the Bender–Gestalt Test have not been totally favorable. Tolor and Schulberg (1963) reviewed 30 years of research and reported that the test did not have high validity coefficients with organicity. Practitioners often disagree with conclusions that cast doubt on the Bender–Gestalt Test. Our recommendation is that the instrument be considered only as a rough screening device for organic brain syndrome (Chess & Hassibi, 1978).

The Wechsler Subtest Scatter

A series of intelligence tests developed by David Wechsler has been used to screen for organicity. The tests used with children are the Wechsler Intelligence Scales for Children or WISC-Ill (Wechsler, 1991), which is normed for children between the ages of 6 and 16 years, and the Wechsler Preschool and Primary Scale of Intelligence* or WPPSI-R (Wechsler, 1990), which was developed for children ages 4 to 6 years. Each test was standardized on a broad cross-section of the population (Anastasi, 1976). Both scales require considerable training to administer and interpret. The skill of the test administrator can greatly affect how the child performs on the test.

The use of the WISC-III or WPPSI-R in identifying possible organicity lies in the comparison of subtest scatter. The WISC-III is comprised of 12 subtests. The Verbal scale is made of the following subtests:

1. information
2. comprehension
3. arithmetic
4. similarities

   5. vocabulary

   6. digit span

The Performance scale includes:

   7. picture completion

   8. picture arrangement

   9. block design

   10. object assembly

   11. coding

   12. mazes

There are three additional tests, symbol search, digit span, and mazes, that can facilitate determination of processing, speed, freedom from distractibility, and perceptual organization. The WPPSI-R also is comprised of 12 subtests, most of which are modifications of the WISC-III tasks. The Verbal subtests include

   1. information

   2. vocabulary

   3. arithmetic

   4. similarities

   5. comprehension

   6. sentences

The Performance subtests are

   7. animal house

   8. picture completion

   9. mazes retest

   10. geometric designs

   11. block design

   12. animal house retest

In general, a 15-point discrepancy between the Verbal and Performance scale scores, especially if the Performance exceeds the Verbal scale score, is suggestive of possible organic pathology. The test protocol is more suspect if block design, object assembly, and digit symbol are the lowest performance subscales (suggesting possible right-hemisphere damage leading to difficulty interpreting figures), if the similarities subscale is significantly lower than vocabulary (suggesting concreteness that is characteristic of organic brain syndrome), and if digits backward is considerably poorer than digits forward (suggesting difficulty in transposition, also characteristic of some organic brain syndrome) (Friedman & Barclay, 1963; Lutey, 1977). Experts study the Wechsler protocols for more subtle indicators, such as noting the number of rotations and Perseveration of the geometric designs subtest of WPPSI-R. The interpretation of organicity from the Wechsler tests is covered extensively in Lutey (1977) and Sattler (1974). In this chapter, we simply want to illustrate that with specialized training in interpretation of the Wechsler tests, they may serve as relatively reliable screening instruments of organicity. Over time, the greatest use of the Wechsler tests may not be as measures of global IQ, but rather as more discreet measures of intellectual thinking processes.

Clinical Neuropsychological Assessment

Although the child welfare worker would not administer neurological tests, she or he will often make referrals for neurological evaluations when organicity is expected. This branch of human neuropsychology emphasizes use of objective psychometric methods in the assessment of higher cortical functioning to determine the presence and nature of organic impairment. Both psychological (memory, cognition) and neurological (sensation, perception) levels of analysis are included (Meier, 1974). Originally the domain of physicians (neurologists and psychiatrists), it is now common practice for therapists of varied clinical backgrounds and advanced training to administer and interpret neuropsychological assessment batteries such as the Reitan (1964), Gardner (1979) batteries, or Luria–Nebraska (Golden, 1981) batteries.

The clinical neuropsychological assessment batteries are employed to identify the nature and extent of brain damage. Ideally, the results suggest directions for treatment and remediation of sensory or learning disorders. Thus, if a child welfare worker suspects organicity to be a cause of a client's behavioral or academic difficulties, the worker may refer a child for further clinical neuropsychological assessment.

When neuropsychological assessment first began to be practiced in the 1940s, instruments were employed simply to identify the extent of impairment. With our increased understanding of the specialization of various cortical loci, clinical neuropsychological assessment has become exceedingly complex. A number of sophisticated instruments are administered to identify the area as well as the extent of brain damage. For example, the Radian (1964) battery integrates results from the Wechsler–Bellevue (Wechsler, 1944) Wide Range Achievement Test-Revised (Jastak & Jastak, 1965), several other standardized instruments plus a number of tests developed by Reitan. The Reitan battery and Luria–Nebraska (1981) have been significantly more effective than chance in diagnosing organicity later confirmed by surgery. These batteries also are useful since they can be used effectively in localizing the source of brain damage.

Not all clinical neuropsychological assessment batteries are concerned with identifying the point of brain lesion. Others attempt to target the type of impaired functions. Thus, Gardner's (1979) battery provides a means for identifying the sensory and motor processes impaired in minimal brain dysfunction. His battery includes selective use of a parents interview form, Wechsler Intelligence Scale for Children (Wechsler, 1974) standardized tests of coordination and visual and auditory processing, plus several tests he has developed, particularly the Steadiness Tester. The Steadiness Tester requires the subject to place a stylus in holes of a metal board, and the number of times the stylus touches the perimeters of the holes is recorded. The instrument is used to diagnose steadiness and impulsivity. It also can be employed to determine the effectiveness of amphetamine treatment for a given client by determining a baseline steadiness rate, administering the medication, and retesting in six hours. The Reitan and Luria–Nebraska also have been helpful in identifying attention deficit and learning disability disorders.

It is important to recognize the importance that age plays in the manifestation of symptoms resulting from brain damage. It cannot be assumed that brain damage will have the same effect in an adult, a school-aged child, and an infant. Clearly, the pattern of impairment may vary as a function of the age at which the injury is sustained. The behavioral effects depend upon the learning and intellectual development that has occurred prior to the injury. Research on infants (Hynd, et al., 1986) and preschool children indicates that at these age levels the brain-injured tend to be deficient in all intellectual functions (Graham, Ernhart, Craft, & Berman, 1963). Another study by Graham, Ernhart, Thurston, and Craft (1961) of young children with a history of prenatal or birth trauma demonstrated lower

IQ test performance on a variety of standardized intelligence tests. It is suggested that the intellectual impairment may be due to the diffuseness of the brain damage or to critical deficiencies in language and/or attentional control which hinder the acquisition of cognitive abilities.

Summary

The broad screening for organic assessment is not highly reliable, so referral for neurological evaluation should be considered when organicity is suspected. The assessment of neurological impairment is very complex. Reliable neuropsychological instruments require much training to administer and interpret. The age at which the damage occurred, the age at which the children are assessed, and the duration of the pathological condition are all critical in the interpretation. For the most part, the child welfare worker will conduct only rough screening for organicity based upon her or his observation and broad testing of the child. It is important for the practitioner to be aware of the range of neuropsychological tests available so that referrals can be made when appropriate and so the practitioner can understand reports returned from these referrals.

Intellectual Assessment

Intelligence is an ill-defined term used to describe mental ability. Operationally, the term is defined as the score on a test of intelligence. Some of the numerous tests of intelligence will be discussed here. Before beginning our discussion, it must be noted that the question of measuring mental capacity has been heatedly debated by social scientists and politicians alike. The central issue of this debate concerns the inheritability of intelligence and the possible bias in the tests that favor white middle-class children. Repeatedly, the issue is raised of how test scores are analyzed by educational personnel. There is no question that IQ scores have been misused in a variety of ways: to maintain students in special education classes; to track ethnic minority students into vocational rather than academic programs; and to overgeneralize about favorite students' capabilities. These are just a few of the abuses perpetrated with these tests. Yet, used judiciously, the tests have long been an aid to child welfare workers. Here are two examples of cases in which IQ results combined with other data served functional purposes.

A couple is referred because their three-year-old daughter has been slow to learn to talk. The mother was ill with an unidentified flu virus during the first trimester of pregnancy. The parents are worried that their daughter may be retarded. You have the daughter assessed with a battery of tests, including a mental status exam and a Weschler Intelligence Test, and record lags in gross and fine motor coordination and an intelligence score 1.5 standard deviations below the mean. You note that the child's attention span is extremely short, from one to two minutes' duration. You help the parents identify an educational nursery-school program to work on the problems identified and to increase intellectual stimulation. You recommend further neurological testing. You plan a systematic behavior modification program to be administered by the parents to increase the daughter's attention span.

Seven-year-old Johnny is referred upon the recommendation of the teacher. During the assessment session with the parents, they explain that Johnny is a delight at home, always quizzical and willing to assume responsibility. At school, Johnny is not completing work and is engaged in much attention-seeking behavior such as blurting comments without being called upon and moving his desk around, thereby creating much noise. In the initial interviews with Johnny, he tells you that he does not have any problems, but he just does not like school. Johnny surpasses expected developmental landmarks on all mental status areas examined and is a verbally facile child. You decide to have an intelligence test and several psychological inventories administered. The inventory results suggest that Johnny is a very ingenious child who likes to work independently and plays with only a few close friends. He enjoys the company of adults. The WISC-Ill (Wechsler, 1991) results reveal an IQ of 130 with exceedingly high subtest scores on similarities and block design. You recommend that Johnny be placed in a program for gifted children and/or be given opportunity for self-directed, small group study.

School Age Scales

A large number of IQ tests are available for the child welfare worker's assessment. The Wechsler Intelligence Scale for Children III (WISC-111) and Wechsler Preschool and Primary Scale of Intelligence (WPPSI-R) provide reliable measures of a number of skills associated with intelligence for children ages 6 to 17 and 4 to 6, respectively (Wechsler, 1967, 1974). In addition, the Stanford–Binet Intelligence Scale 4th edition (Terman & Merrill, 1973) frequently is used with children, even as young as two years of age. Like the Wechsler scales, the Stanford–Binet is a standardized test that has been shown to have high test reliability and validity. The test, unlike the Wechsler scales, yields a single IQ score which is the composite of both verbal and performance items.

Many child welfare workers should regard the intelligence tests not only as a standardized test of intelligence, but also as a platform for behavioral observation and clinical interview. The tests allow the examiner to observe the child's work methods, approaches to problem solution, activity level, self-confidence, persistence, and ability to concentrate. Obviously, the qualitative observations made in the course of administration should be interpreted with caution because they are less standardized. The value of the administration as a clinical interview will depend to a large extent on the skill, experience, and sophistication of the examiner, as well as on his or her awareness of the limitations imposed by the test on this type of observation.

Both the Wechsler tests and the Stanford–Binet require much training to administer. Testing must be done individually, and generally requires at least an hour. A number of short-form tests have been modeled after these scales. Most of the short-form tests elicit answers through a single sensory channel (Palmer, 1970). Thus, all questions may be verbal or pictorial. Often, the breadth of skill measured and thus the reliability of the score is diminished with these short-form instruments. One such instrument is the Peabody Picture Vocabulary Test (PPVT), which was constructed by Dunn (1965). The PPVT can be administered to children from 2 years to 18 years and consists of a series of 150 plates, each containing four pictures. As each plate is presented, the examiner provides a stimulus word orally, and the child responds by pointing to the picture on the plate that best illustrates the meaning of the stimulus word. The test requires only 10 to 15 minutes to administer. The raw score can be converted to mental age, deviation IQ, or percentile. The PPVT correlates moderately well (in the 60s) with individual and group intelligence scales. Although useful as a quick assessment instrument, especially with handicapped children, the retarded; and in some cases ethnic minority children, the PPT is limited because of reliance on verbal knowledge only. The Leiter International Performance Scale (Leiter, 1959) is a nonverbal test of intelligence that can be used to evaluate children with sensory or motor deficits who have difficulty speaking and reading. Among the tasks included in the Leiter are matching identical colors, shades of gray, forms, or pictures; copying a block design; picture completion; number estimation; spatial relations; memory for a series; and classification of animals according to habitat. The test is administered without time limitations, and the score can be converted to mental age and IQ. Correlations with the Stanford–Binet and Wechsler tests are usually between .50 and .90. The Leiter is purported to be relatively culture free, although this claim and the adequacy of standardization have been questioned (Sattler, 1974).

Another short-form test is the Columbia Mental Maturity Scale (Burgemeister, Blum, & Lorge, 1972). Originally developed for use with cerebral-palsied children, this scale consists of 92 items, each of which is made up of three, four, or five drawings printed on a large card. The child is required to identify the drawing that does not belong with the others. This test requires no verbalization and is not dependent upon the child's vocabulary as is the PPT.. The test is lauded for the usefulness of the approach (Sattler, 1974).

Infant Scales

A number of scales have been developed to assess infant cognition. Two of long-standing usage are the Cattell Infant Intelligence Scale (Cattell, 1940) and the Bayley Scales of Infant Development (Bayley, 1969). The Cattell is a downward extension of the 1937 Stanford–Binet and is appropriate for infants aged 2 years to 30 months. Because of infants' restricted behavioral repertoire, most of the tasks are essentially motor. Standardization of the instrument is old (1930) and limited to 274 infants of middle-class families. In many settings, the Cattell scale has been replaced by the Bayley Scales of Infant Development (Bayley, 1969). This instrument has been designed to assess the developmental status of children between the ages of 2 months and 2 years. The Bayley Scales consist of three components. The Mental Scale samples such functions, as perception, memory, problem solving, the beginnings of verbal communication, and rudimentary abstract thinking. The second component, or Motor Scale, measures of gross motor abilities such as sitting, standing, walking, and manipulatory skills of hands and fingers. The final scale, the Infant Behavior Record, is completed by the examiner after the other two parts have been administered. This scale is designed to assess various aspects of personality development, emotional and social behavior, attention span, persistence, and goal-directedness.

As a whole, the infant scales are not as reliable as scales of intelligence for older children and adults. Importantly, they are generally not good predictors of later performance on intelligence tests since intellectual development is susceptible to many intervening factors (e.g., illness or loss of a parent) that make long-term predictions deficient. However, there is some evidence that infants with very low scores do perform poorly when retested with the Stanford–Binet or Wechsler series at a later age (Erickson, 1978). Perhaps the value of the infant scales is that they are most helpful in the early detection of sensory and neurological defects, emotional disturbances, and environmental deficits (Anastasi, 1976).

Summary

Used judiciously, the intelligence scales can aid a practitioner in determining whether a child's adjustment difficulties are related to unusually high or log cognitive functioning. Perhaps more important than the actual IQ scores, these instruments can serve as a standardized format against which to view the child's cognitive and overall functioning.

Academic Assessment

Child welfare workers frequently see children whose academic performance is below that expected for their age and grade level. Many schools employ educational specialists who are trained in diagnosing the specific types and possible causes of learning deficits. Yet, in some cases, these children are not identified in the schools, and it falls upon the child welfare workers to identify the child's academic problems for the school personnel. Moreover, sometimes school counselors and diagnosticians assess a child's educational lag and then refer the child to a social worker because they believe that the primary block to the child's academic performance is emotional. Or the school personnel may refer a child with academic deficits to a social worker because the child's frustration with learning has prompted inappropriate school behavior, such as not completing assignments, refusing to come to school, or reacting to school tasks by crying, stubbornness, attention-getting behavior. For a variety reasons, then, the child welfare worker should be familiar with the principles of academic assessment and types of instruments available. For a very extensive review of individual and group tests of school aptitude and achievement, the reader may wish to consult Anastasi (1976). We now will elaborate on the basic principles and purposes of these instruments.

Reading Tests

A very large number of academic difficulties can be traced to reading problems. Most school activity is dependent upon reading comprehension. A child with a reading deficit struggles to complete assignments, may not be able to follow written instructions, may not understand what is written on the blackboard, and may miss many items on exams despite knowing the correct answer, because he or she cannot read them. It is no wonder, then, that many children with severe reading problems behave inappropriately in school. They have few means of constructive involvement in the academic tasks.

Two achievement tests commonly employed in the schools that include measures of reading skills are the California Achievement Test (Tiegs & Clark, 1970) and the Metropolitan Achievement Test (Durost, Bixler, Writestone, Prescott, & Barlow, 1971). However, since these written tests require students to read complex sentences and passages in order to respond, those children with extreme deficits may become very distraught and little meaningful information may be obtained from these instruments.

A number of individually administered oral reading tests have been developed that allow examiners to assess the child's reading competence in a more informal fashion. Oral tests such as the Durrell (1955), Gray & Robinson (1967), and Woodcock (1973) are comprised of several sections. The child's listening comprehension level is tested. Then, the child's ability to read single words is examined. The child then reads passages orally beginning with paragraphs containing words more basic than his or her tested sight vocabulary. Gradually, the subject is asked to read and answer questions to passages containing higher level vocabulary so that an "independent level" of reading (the child can read this material on his or her own), an "instructional level" (the child can read this material with the teacher's support and assistance), and a "frustration level" (the child experiences too much difficulty for productive learning to occur) can be evaluated (Lemer, 1971). The oral reading tests are an efficient way of assessing the child's encoding, decoding, and comprehension skills and thus help pinpoint types of reading difficulties.

Achievement Tests

A variety of standardized achievement tests such as the Wide Range Achievement Test (Jastak, Jastak, & Bijou, 1965) and the California Achievement Test (Tiegs & Clark, 1970) are available for assessing children's academic performance in key educational areas such as reading, arithmetic, and language arts. Typically, the child's performance on the achievement test is compared to performance on a standardized intelligence test. In this way, assessment is made about the relationship of a student's potential for learning and actual achievement level. If a discrepancy is noted in a particular academic domain, special diagnostic tests in arithmetic, spelling, spoken language, and written expression can be administered.

Some typical diagnostic tests are Key Math Diagnostic Arithmetic Test (Connolly, Nachtman, & Pritchett, 1973), Houston Test for Language Development (Crabtree, 1963), Gates–Russell Spelling Diagnostic Test (Gates & Russell, 1962), Lincoln Diagnostic Spelling Tests (Lincoln, 1955), and The Picture Story Language Test (Myklebust, 1965). These tests help define remedial education programs. Remediation is based upon the specific interlocking of the child's academic strengths and deficits. For example, Johnny achieved a superior IQ score and high reading and arithmetic proficiency. However, his spelling skill is extremely low. On the WISC-III, the coding subtest showed a significant number of reversals. Johnny seems to possess superior analytic ability and skill in reading and comprehending material in context. The Lincoln Diagnostic Spelling Tests (Lincoln, 1955) might be administered to pinpoint his specific spelling deficits. Results of the spelling diagnostic test might suggest, for example, that Johnny needs extra training in left-right sequencing and figure-ground discrimination. In contrast, another child, Sally, has a WISC-Ill score that is one standard deviation below the mean with no significant subtest scatter. Oral reading tests and spelling achievement reveal consistent performance about one year below expected grade level. Sally's remediation will be more broadly based. Most likely, she will profit from special instruction in reading and will need texts aimed at the instructional reading level indicated by a reading test.

Early Childhood

Several tests are available for screening children's school readiness. Two such tests are the Boehm Test of Basic Concepts—Revised (Boehm, 1971) and the Denver Development Screening Test (Frankenburg & Dodds, 1970). The early childhood screening tests may be administered individually or in groups and generally do not require extensive training. These tests attempt to measure children's performance in affective, language, and motor domains in hopes of identifying children with significant developmental lags that may prevent their successful adaptation to school. Of course, the early identification needs to be followed by special preschool training. Many of these tests provide limited standardization data. Moreover, most of the preschool training programs are too recent for a reliable measure of their effectiveness. Current research suggests that these preschool programs are most effective when parents are taught to stimulate speaking and behavior in identified deficit areas. The stimulation needs to be specific to measured deficits, and the remediation pursued within the child's primary environment, the home (Hunt, 1975).

Learning Disability Assessment

In discussing achievement tests, we noted that educational researchers have been particularly concerned about children for whom there is a large disparity between measured intellectual potential and academic achievement. We mentioned that emotional problems have been posited as preventing full academic growth for some of these children. Sociological factors, such as lack of stimulation in the home or poor and inconsistent educational experiences, also have been proposed to explain this discrepancy among children.

A group of educational researchers (Frostig, Lefever, & Whittlesey, 1964; Kirk, McCarthy, & Kirk, 1968; Minskoff, 1975) have suggested that some of these children may be experiencing deficits in sensory or motor integration. Although the visual and auditory acuity and the musculature of these children are intact, they may not be efficient in processing information. Thus, a child may have 20/20 vision but not be able to discriminate significant forms from background, or may experience difficulty orienting objects in space. Another child may have no hearing loss but still be unable to concentrate in a room with background noise. Other children with normal reflexes may be inefficient learning fine motor tasks, such as writing. Clearly, children with problems of processing sensory and motor stimuli may experience difficulty completing typical school tasks. The term "learning disability" is used to describe these children and is broadly defined as a learning difficulty characterized by a significant disparity between measured achievement and intellectual ability with no associated organic pathology or loss of acuity.

Perceptual motor, auditory discrimination, and psycholinguistic tests have been designed to identify learning disabilities among children. Commonly used tests include the Frostig Developmental Test of Visual Perception (Frostig, Lefever, & Whittlesey, 1964), Auditory Discrimination Test (Wepman, 1958), and the Illinois Test Of Psycholinguistic Abilities (Kirk, McCarthy, & Kirk, 1968).

These tests offer extensive reliability and validity data and are normed to a broad range of children of different ages and ethnic groups. Materials also have been developed for school personnel to teach processing skills once deficits have been identified.

However, there is much controversy among educators about whether mastery of the processing skills improves academic performance. Hammill and Larsen (1974) argue that task analysis is more effective than perceptual motor testing and remediation material in measuring and teaching to process deficits. In task analysis, the academic difficulty is operationally analyzed into discreet subtasks. Children are taught the discreet subskills that are requisite to the target learning deficit through the sensory modalities with which the child is most adept, under systematic reinforcement conditions.

Others argue that testing of perceptual motor deficits and teaching of process skills are helpful for some children with specific disabilities. They state that learning disability testing and remediation is effective under specific conditions, but that research findings are yet too limited to predict which children will profit most from the training (Minskoff, 1975).

Summary of Academic Assessment

The field of academic testing is becoming increasingly complex. A number of sophisticated instruments have emerged and concomitantly a number of controversies have arisen pertaining to the usefulness of testing and the devising of remediation programs to correct academic deficits. The child welfare worker may find it useful to gain an in-depth understanding or the findings of one or two academic tests of each of the major types. Again, the social worker needs to be aware of the range and possible uses of academic assessment instruments so that clients can be referred for appropriate educational diagnosis when necessary.

Social and Personality Assessment

A number of instruments used for assessing children's affective reactions and behaviors are adaptations of adult scales, while others have been developed specifically for children. In either case, administrative procedures must be built upon developmental levels and different responses can be expected according to the child's cognitive and social sophistication. In general, the younger the child, the fewer and more concrete the responses will be. Moreover, with young clients, the examiner must typically assume an active role. Thus, there are few self-administered, standardized personality tests for children. In general, the childhood personality assessment devices can be divided into measures of overt behavior versus underlying psychological dynamics.

Measures of Overt Behavior

These tests attempt to assess children's individual and/or social behavior and do so with varying degrees of objectivity and standardization. Although not a formally standardized test, behavioral assessment is a very important systematic means of recording children's overt reactions. In behavioral assessment, several target behaviors are operationally defined. The examiner decides upon the target behavior after interviewing parents and the child. When interviewing all parties, the examiner keeps in mind that their perception may be distorted by their experiences. Thus, the examiner encourages each person to be as specific as possible in describing the problem that led to the referral. The environment in which the difficulty occurs is delineated. By talking with the child, the examiner attempts to gain a picture of reinforcers and punishing agents associated with the target behavior. Then, the examiner observes the child's target behavior in the problem-ridden environment. The duration and frequency of the behavior for whole periods of time or systematic intervals is recorded. The behavior is observed under baseline conditions and under hypothesized reinforcing and punishing conditions. Of course, observer reliability must be considered. It often is helpful to chart other children's behavior in the environment in order to gain a comparison measure (Erickson, 1978). The behavioral assessment helps the social worker determine the conditions prompting the problematic behavior and more appropriate behavior and thus provides a very objective guideline for therapy.

Sociometry can be used as a measure of children's social behavior. This approach is useful if the problem behavior appears at school or in some other social situation. The client and peers are asked to name children they prefer to participate with in various activities, such as working on school tasks, playing a game, leading an activity on the playground, or sitting next to on the bus. In this way, a measure can be gained of how other children relate to the client. Sociometric measures can offer an alternative view to the child's perception of his or her problem. For example, a child may report that he or she has no friends. Yet, classmates may state that they like to play with the child. Therapy might then focus upon helping the client gain a more realistic appraisal of his or her interpersonal skills. Sociometric measures also are a useful index for assessing therapy gains (Keat, 1974).

A number of questionnaires are available for assessing children's interpersonal skills. Generally, these scales are completed by important adults in the child's life. Perhaps the most renowned social questionnaire for children is the Vineland Adaptive Behaviors Scales (Doll, 1965). This instrument is administered orally to parents. Questions concern the child's self-help skills (eating, dressing, walking), ways of occupying time, communication skills, and socialization with adults and peers. Answers are scored according to whether the child demonstrates the behavior at home and for the examiner, only at home, or not at all. The overall score is computed by comparing the child's tested social maturity age to chronological age. Other scales such as the Burks' Behavior Rating Scale (Burks, 1969) are completed by teachers. The difficulty with most of these scales, as with the Vineland, is their limited objectivity. The informant (usually one of the parents) is not asked to keep a systematic record of target behaviors as in behavioral assessment.

Informants may define target behaviors differently. Thus, what one teacher considers "angry outbursts" may not be congruent with another's perception. In a study by Erickson (1978), parents were asked to respond on a questionnaire about how counseling related to their child's attendance at school. The parents reported that attendance increased with counseling, while actual review of school records revealed that attendance had decreased. Overall, results of behavioral and social questionnaires tend to have low interrater reliability as well as low reliability for a single rater over time. In addition, the validity of such measures also is open to question.

Some scales have been developed in which behaviors are operationally defined and informants are asked to systematically observe children's responses to the various criterion questions (Erickson, 1978). Yet, these scales are generally research instruments that are cumbersome to administer and are not widely available or employed.

Measures of Psychological Dynamics

These tests attempt to assess the child's intrapsychic functioning. Each relies upon a set of theoretical constructs about how personality develops and what constitutes adjustment and maladjustment.

Apperception Tests. The Thematic Apperception Test (Murray, 1943) and Children's Apperception Test (Bellak & Bellak, 1971) are comprised of a series of cards portraying people (TAT) or animals (CAT) in ambiguous social situations. The child is asked to tell a story to each card. Interpretation is based upon the notion that subjects will reveal much about their perception of social relationships and their needs as they create stories to the ambiguous stimuli.

The TAT is widely used with adults. Bellak and Bellak (1965) developed the CAT because they felt children would find it easier to compose stories about animals than about people. In practice, most therapists agree that some children prefer the human figures and others the animals (Chess & Hassibi, 1978). Thus, the examiner may need to experiment with a card from each set to determine which is more appropriate for a particular child.

Elaborate schemes for scoring motivation and attitudes about parents, peers, and siblings are available. The CAT cards are further scored to determine the child's attitudes about heroes, concepts of the environment, significant conflicts, nature of anxiety, defenses versus fears and conflicts, adequacy of superego, and integration of ego. Reliability of the scoring system is low, barely above zero in most studies (Palmer, 1970). Many practitioners prefer to view the test results in a more casual fashion, looking for common themes that run throughout the stories. The results are used for clinical hunches that must be confirmed with further interviewing and assessment

Figure Drawing Tests. The Human Figure Drawing Test was originally developed as a measure of intelligence (Goodenough, 1926). However, a revision by Machover (1949) frequently is employed in personality assessment. First, the child is asked to draw a few human figures under very open-ended directions. Then, specific inquiry is made: "What is the child or person in the picture doing?" "What is the best (worst) part of the boy?" "Does he have any friends?" "How much does he enjoy his family?" "How much does he like school?" According to Machover (1949), stylization of drawings and response to inquiry questions hold symbolic significance. Thus, lack of arms or hands might reflect feelings of guilt about actions or an inability to act. Drawing a person of the opposite sex may represent confused sexual identity (Machover, 1953).

Research has not consistently supported Machover's thesis. The child's experience and drawing skill greatly affect results. Koppitz (1968) compared human figure drawings of normal and disturbed children on 30 dimensions suggested as most significant in the literature on human figure drawing. Only four were shown to be significant:

1. poor integration of body parts in girls above 6 and boys above 7

2. shading of body parts and limbs for girls above 7 and boys above 9

3. slanting by 15 degrees or more

4. drawing a tiny picture

Koppitz (1964) noted further that omission of major body parts and grotesque figures were so rare that statistical analysis was not possible. Thus, despite wide use, the human figure drawing does not seem to be a reliable measure for discriminating types of emotional disturbance among children before age 6. Moreover, among older children, caution must be exercised in attaching particular symbolic significance to small distortions.

Also commonly used is the House-Tree-Person Test (Buck, 1950). Extensive guidelines for scoring results are offered, but caution, as suggested with the Human Figure Drawing, needs to be exercised in interpretation. As a whole, the drawings should be employed to offer clinical hunches, not definitive statements, about children's attitudes and behavior.

The Rorschach.   Of course, it is not possible to relate the major constructs of Rorschach testing in this brief review. Nor can we begin to elucidate the pros and cons and reliability of the Rorschach protocol. The Rorschach is aimed at assessing the child's preconscious and subconscious experiences. Whether or not the reader accepts this tenet or finds such results valuable depends of course upon his or her theoretical approach to counseling and therapy. We will attempt to show through some brief examples of scoring issues how the content of responses to the Rorschach cards and perceptual modes are viewed as indicators of the child's emotional dynamics. The same underlying rules of Rorschach assessment are applicable to children as with adults. However, in the children's Rorschach, developmental trends are emphasized. Thus, for young children, magical thinking is not as diagnostically significant as with adults. Color responses are common and are believed to reflect the more spontaneous emotional character of children. Fewer texture responses are expected since children's experience of anxiety is more diffuse and less introspective. The average number of responses for children ranges between 10 and 20, considerably less than for adults. Inquiry and testing the limit responses to the last card are considered diagnostically significant about how the child deals with separation (Halpern, 1953).

Sentence Completion Test.   Sentence completion tests tend to be used with older children because the young child's limited linguistic development circumscribes his or her repertoire of responses. Rotter's Incomplete Sentence Blank (Rotter, Rafferty, & Schachtitz, 1965) offers a systematic way of scoring responses for degree of resistance and degree and nature of conflicts for children 13 years and older. Although linguistically simpler sentences can also be constructed for the younger clients, if the examiner administers the sentences orally, the test is more appropriate for the young child. Although many such forms are available, a difficulty is that most incomplete sentence blanks are not built upon a consistent rationale (Palmer, 1970). The range of responses is limited by the nature of the incomplete sentences presented. Unless the responses are carefully interpreted, it is easy for the test creator's bias to appear as the child's primary concern.

A semi-projective test that is quite appealing to young children is the Rosenzweig Picture Frustration Study Form for Children (Rosenzweig, 1950) which can be used with children between the ages of four and 13 years. In this test, children look at cartoon figures which are portrayed in difficult social situations. One cartoon figure is portrayed as making a comment (e.g., "I'm not going to ask you to my birthday party.") The style is akin to that in a comic book. The child is asked to complete the comment for the other figure in the space provided. The results can be scored on one primary personality dimension of aggression—extrapunitiveness or intrapunitiveness. Extrapunitive is aggression turned outward toward the environment, while intrapunitive is aggression turned inward on the subject.

Standardized Personality Instruments.   Compared to the many standardized personality instruments available to assess adults, there are very few comparable instruments for children. For the most part, children lack the cognitive ability to answer the kinds of questions upon which standardized personality profiles are drawn. For example, the California Psychological Inventory (Gough, 1969) is one of the most widely used standardized personality instruments employed with youth, and its youngest norms are for children 13 years and older. The CPI consists of 480 items answered as either true or false and yields scores in 18 scales. The scales provide scores in such personality dimensions as Dominance, Sociability, Self-acceptance, Responsibility, Socialization, Self-control, Femininity, Achievement-via-independence, etc. The overall test reliability is relatively high, as are intercorrelations among scales. The CPI has been used to predict delinquency, high school grades, and high school dropout (Anastasi, 1976).

A good overview of a number of other standardized psychological tests and rating scales that can be used with children can be found in Harrington (1984), and Rutter, Tuma, and Lann (1988).

Tests of self-concept are rather widely used. The Piers–Harris Self-Concept Scale (Piers & Harris, 1969) can be administered individually to children under grade three and group-administered for older children. Coopersmith's (1967) Self-Esteem Questionnaire, which attempts to measure the child's feelings about self in relation to parents, school, peers, and personal interests, also has been used widely with children in grades 5 and above. These questionnaires tend to report moderate reliability coefficients, but their validity is limited by questions about the underlying constructs they are measuring.

Summary of Social and Personality Assessment.   As a whole, the reliability and validity coefficients of the personality instruments employed with children have been relatively low because of the children's developmental limitations. In some cases, the instruments have not been subject to close empirical scrutiny. Most likely, validity increases when a test battery rather than a single instrument is employed in the assessment of a child. The efficacy of the tests is certainly increased when the social worker employs good standards of practice; that is, any reports or conclusions based upon test results should be reported accurately, in a manner that can be understood by the audience and in a way that explains the limits of reliability and validity of the test. The test instruments should not be employed if the individual therapist has not been trained to administer and interpret them as recommended in the test manual. The testing should not be done without the consent of the child's parents or legal guardian. Upon proper written consent, the social worker should share relevant data with the other mental health professionals working with the child (Koocher & Keith–Spiegel, 1990). In contrast, behavioral assessment techniques appear to be highly reliable and valid. It is not surprising that this approach is gaining wide use by practitioners of various theoretical persuasions. The sensitive practitioner probably can make good use of information obtained from personality assessment instruments; however, it is important to also obtain and use more objective information about the child's behavior prior to attempting a diagnosis.

Summary

Usually therapy with children begins with assessment so that the therapeutic process can take a meaningful, specifiable direction. Interviews and tests can be useful in obtaining needed information about the child. The reliability of interviews is limited by the subjective perceptions of the clients and informants and the practitioner's biases and limits of understanding. The reliability of the information obtained on a test is limited by the boundaries of standardization as well as by the practitioner's skill in administration and interpretation. There is much room for error. Referral for specialized testing (e.g., for suspected organic interference or learning deficit, or because the test administration requires extensive training) should be considered, keeping the child's best interests in mind. If we search for clues to a child's maladjusted behavior through the accumulation of test results, employing a variety of carefully chosen assessment techniques, the chances of discovering the breadth of the child's problem increase. If we look at assessment as an ongoing process and continually reevaluate the client's progress as well as the therapeutic goals with the client, assessment becomes an integral part of therapy.

We have discussed theories of child adjustment and therapy and looked at a variety of ways of assessing for the presence of those problems in the individual client. We will now consider ways of assessing the family dynamics and determining the relationship of the child's problems to the family's overall functioning.

Chapter 10
Family Assessment and Case Management

Knowledge about patterns of behavior within a family is critical to alleviating many children's problems. Understanding how this information is gathered and implemented necessitates a grounding in family theory and research. Family practice has long been associated with social work, one illustration being Mary Richmond's landmark text *Social Diagnosis,* published in 1917.The first professional journal was named, *The Family,* but under the influence of psychology and psychiatry, social work shifted to a case work approach (Proctor,Davis & Vosler, 1995). Then in the early 1980's as represented by the publication of *Family-Centered Social Work Practice* (Hartman & Laird, 1983) a new focus on family work began. Family Preservation programs also brought a renewed emphasis on the family unit in the 1970's.

Growing out of child welfare's permanency planning efforts, and mental health's need to avoid institutionalization, and developmental disabilities case management; Family Preservation services refined many family therapy techniques and moved family assessment into the home (Hooper–Briar, Broussard, Ronnau & Sallee, 1995). Guided by a set of principles and values, the outcome criteria for Family Preservation can be defined as a high quality assessment which informs a permanent plan (Lloyd & Sallee, 1994). One of the rather unique principles of Family Preservation is the family is viewed as an expert and thus the assessment becomes a collaborative process. Family preservation is discussed in more detail in Chapter 13.

In this chapter we discuss key issues pertinent to successful family assessments. Identifying the present phase of functioning in a family's overall development provides important clues for a successful assessment and treatment

.Various theories attempt to explain how families function, and each offers guides to the selection of techniques for assessment. This chapter identifies critical assessment points in a family with examples based upon three theoretical perspectives: Behavioral, Adlerian, and Bowenian. The Chapter concludes with an overview of the process of case management, which may be critical for child welfare practitioners in order to effectively interact with agencies that the family may also need.

Family Assessment

Theory Guides Assessment

An examination of child welfare practice raises the following questions:

> Do theories explain why an assessment technique works? or

> Do practitioners develop family theories first and then develop assessment techniques?

Very often it appears practitioners select assessment points and devices in a somewhat idiosyncratic or arbitrary fashion. Then theory is employed to justify their approach. If family theory is an explanation of the interrelationships of variables in family interaction, then it is important to understand the specifics of the theory as a framework before we can analyze the dynamics of a given family. On the issue of inference, Richmond (1917) writes, "Inference, then, a passing from known to unknown facts is the reasoning process most familiar when it takes the form of drawing a conclusion from the relation existing between a general truth and particular incident" (p. 81).

The problem-solving process or scientific process assures a close application of theory to practice. The problem-solving process includes gathering information, assessing that information, planning for change, and evaluation. Some suggest that these steps are interrelated and continue concomitantly (Hoffman & Sallee, 1994). Others believe you must take these steps one at a time before beginning intervention.

A theory of family functioning is the way we give a logical explanation of how variables or facts are related; the theories of family therapy were presented in detail in Chapter 7. Assessment, information gathering, and analysis are critical steps that must take place in applying a theory of family dynamics to clinical assessment of the family framework. Analysis or assessment then becomes a way to make sense of the data we have collected. Treatment techniques and intervention strategies should be based upon a logical connection with family theory.

Assessment Considerations

What is the composition of a particular family? Who will participate in the family and under what conditions? Culture, the locus of the identified issues and the interaction between family members usually drives who will participate in a family assessment far more than what the practitioner might plan. Engaging all members of the family may not be necessary, yet the lack of a quality engagement is one of the major reasons for failure in family therapy (Carr, 1990).

Another assessment consideration is the concept of intergenerational family systems. The family a child welfare worker assesses today has been shaped by powerful influences, often from several generations back. As explained later in this chapter, Genograms are a useful tool for helping the worker and the family to understand the range or this influences and their power (Hartman, 1995).

The current functioning of a family is yet another consideration. The context in which the family lives and grows is often critical to understand and will aid the selection or application of the appropriate theory base for assessment. This is one reason why assessments completed in the family's home are so much more accurate and illicit much better communication from the family.

A gender blind process is a critical aspect to a family assessment, given that most of the family theories have conventional patriarchal views of the balance of power in a family and portray the roles men and women play as being equal. Unfortunately, the family theory literature and some major training video tapes often define women and their roles in negative terms, such as being overly involved in a child's life (Hartman, 1995). Thus, in family assessment we must guard against stereo typing and remember families come in all types, sizes and culture. For example the following section on the family life cycle may not apply to all families, and should be used in the assessment phase with the above considerations in mind.

Family Life Cycle

As the family develops, it grows through distinct developmental phases, and particular developmental tasks must be completed (Solomon, 1973). For example, the birth of the first child thrusts a family into a new developmental stage. A couple must readjust from the partner role to the parent role. Another example is the grieving process at the departure of the oldest child from the family to college or the military. Identifying the stage of a given family in the family life cycle offers clues for assessment and intervention planning. Identification helps to focus attention on presenting problems within the family and the resulting problems for a child. Further, the stage of family development can provide a focus to begin assessment. The importance of each stage will vary with every family and culture; however, the following events commonly prompt significant changes in most families' development (Bloom, 1984).

Stages of Family Development

1. *Courtship.* This period is sometimes called the unattached young adult stage. The young adult is dating, exploring sexual and moral behavior with the opposite sex. The adult begins to examine relationships with partners for their long-term potential. Friendships are established which may lead to more permanent relationships.

2. *Marriage and Couplehood.* Marriage publicly identifies the young unattached adult as a member of a couple. Young adults experience separation from their families and begin to invest in each other. The couple begins to explore living with another person and adjusting to a partnership role. Alternative family forms such as gay units may emerge at this stage (Harry & Devall, 1978). There is a shift from the idealized wish for a perfect partner to compromising and relating intimately with a realistic view of the spouse. Also during this time, adjustments are made within the extended family, as in-laws accommodate to the new marital relationship.

   Conflicts that typically arise during this stage are associated with the couple's relating intimately as the increased close contact may expose incompatibilities. These conflicts can cause breaks in the relationship or push the dyad to deeper levels of intimacy.

3. *First Child.* The transition to parent includes accepting the childbearing role. Preparation for childbirth provides a new definition to the role as spouse. Further, sexual behavior is altered or in interrupted during pregnancy. The birth or adoption of the first child impacts the extended family as well. In many cultures, the role of parent increases one's status.

   Bonding and attachment hold important consequences for the child in later life. Effective parents are sensitive to the crucial importance of bonding and to the developmental phases of the child and adjust their lives accordingly. The parents must establish a home environment that will accommodate both the roles of spouse and parent. New limitations to privacy and mobility imposed by the child's needs present areas for adjustment. The marital dyad has now become a triad with all the complications and issues involved in group dynamics.

4. *Growth of Children.* In this phase, additional children are born into the family. Older children are introduced to community institutions, such as school, church, and social development groups. Children seek their own roles and pass through developmental phases. Many of the individualized roles, however, are not based upon the family responsibility but upon community and social needs. The child looks at the parents' actions even more than words for guidance of the child's moral behaviors, so that it becomes important for parents to carefully monitor their responses. The issue of discipline becomes an important topic of parental discussion and parental joint efforts. The sharing of affection between child and parent may become important gratification for parents. During time, family financial resources may be stretched, placing further stress and responsibility upon the parents.

5. *Departure of Oldest Child.* In adolescence, peer groups become important and are powerful competitors to the parents for the youth's allegiance. Erratic behavior by adolescents at home and in peer relations may be spurred by lack of knowledge and experience about their emerging sexuality. Child rivalry may become intense as children enter the teenage years and begin to assert their independence to parents and siblings. When the family begins to release young adults, optimally they maintain supportive relations

(DuVall, 1971). The family is particularly prone to stress at this stage since it is more likely to face problems such as illness and career change.

6. *Aging Family or Retirement.* This stage is reached when all children have left home, and the couple returns to a dyad. This is a time for renewing the marital relationship. The couple's relationship may be strained if either or both are distressed over the loss or work. Feelings of isolation may increase if the couple experiences fewer social systems available to them. Dealing with leisure time may require adjustment in the marriage roles. Earlier retirement may result in mid-life crisis for career persons and has been associated with higher divorce rate among this group. Adult children may continue to visit, and the extended family may now include grandchildren and younger generations. Parents grieve the departure of children and establish new relationships during this final stage. Parents may need to accept their roles as elders and transfer business and central social responsibilities to adult children. Although the drastic changes and losses pose much stress for the couple, their relationship can be deepened by the lifetime of shared experiences and the problems resolved. The death of one partner later in this stage marks the end of the family cycle.

Evaluation of Family Life Cycle.   The above discussion of family life development can be helpful in focusing thinking about the stresses family members incur but may reflect the myth about the American family. Few American families complete this total life cycle today. About 60 percent of all children born now can expect to live with only one parent sometime during their lives (Kamerman, 1965). The traditional dyad of leadership in a family is rapidly becoming nonexistent.

The life cycle paradigm does have some utility in understanding traditional families where conflicts or serious child-related problems exist. For example, it points to the concept that the more children in a family, the more complex the dynamics of that family. However, it is inappropriate for a practitioner to consider families that fail outside this paradigm as abnormal.

The family life cycle is of little utility to some theorists. Behaviorists have a limited need to examine the family life stages, as they consider family behavior at the present time to be most crucial.

Critical Assessment Points

A number of factors determine which information the family social worker attempts to collect in the assessment process. These factors can be considered along the dimensions of a longitudinal development versus present functioning, internal forces in the family versus external factors affecting the functioning, and factors promoting health versus factors prompting illness in the family. In the sections that follow, we will explore the points of interaction that would be the focus if one were to adopt extreme positions at each end of the continuum. In reality, the social worker does not need to make a choice of techniques at either extreme, but may choose a point along the continuum (Reiss, 1980).

Development Versus Present Situation. In determining critical assessment points in the family, some consider the longitudinal development of an individual family (Bowen, 1960). The longitudinal assessment examines the family history and is the least used approach in family diagnosis.

Others focus upon the current family functional level. In this second approach, current patterns of behavior that cut across the developmental stages of a family are analyzed. The examination of the stage of the family in the family life cycle is considered of little functional utility (Reiss, 1980).

Assessment techniques used for assessing the family's functioning differ widely if one ascribes to a developmental rather than a present situation orientation. The following brief discussion of the psychoanalytic and behavioral processes of family assessment illustrates the types of data one would obtain from the developmental and present situational orientations, respectively.

In assessing a given family dilemma, the psychoanalytic approach assumes surface phenomena or variables only hint at the underlying experiences and motives of the family. These underlying phenomena are inaccessible to the client system and can only be discovered through the help of a clinician. Treatment encourages family practitioners to search for causes that are not apparent to the family. Assessment is only the beginning in identifying solutions for the family problem.

Behavioral assessment consists of determining the events just prior to or just after an incident that influences the frequency and force of a behavior. Patterson (1971) studied the frequencies of certain classes of behavior and then measured these behaviors by using trained observers or the spouses themselves. Baseline information was gathered. A precise program was developed to reduce the force and frequency of the behavior.

Intra Versus External Family Factors. According to one's orientation, one may focus upon internal family functioning or the sociological or external world in which the family grows and copes. In the intra-family assessment, the family/community interaction is considered subtle, primarily directed by strong intra-family functioning patterns. The family is united against the world.

The sociological approach gives more consideration to the environmental impacts upon the family and is more a traditional social work approach. As an example of research conducted from the sociological approach, Bott (1971) examined family networks. She noted that families which rely upon only one set of friends may be more subject to familial problems and are more likely to follow traditional sex roles. Families with different sets of friends are more egalitarian in their power system. The setting for the collection of information is dictated by the weight practitioners place upon the environmental impact. If the practitioner adopts a more sociological perspective, he or she may suggest a meeting with the family in its home and community.

Strength versus Deficit. The traditional mental health approach to assessing children and their families has been to primarily identify deficits or problems of families. Social Workers employing a strengths approach put energy into finding the child's and family's talents, resources, and abilities. The application of a strengths approach does not imply a denial of real problems that may exist in the family; in fact, risk assessment and the strengths approach are seen as being compatible (Ronnau, 1990).

Identifying strengths is more than simply "restating the problem in a positive light," although this is a beginning. Observing the family and recording positive aspects, asking the family members what strengths they see, and asking other professionals for strengths they have viewed are three methods to identify strengths (Ronnau, 1991). The strengths perspective can be applied to the assessment frameworks we have presented, including the family life cycle, family resources, interaction and functions of institutions. For example, a teacher walks a child part way home each day even though the school has complained about the child's behavior. The teacher's interest and caring are a strength of the school system.

Illness Versus Heath. Practitioners often are polarized around the dimension of viewing the family from an illness or a health perspective. According to the illness or medical model, the practitioner should focus upon a disorder and symptoms within individuals. This approach is employed extensively in the literature.

The health orientation involves examining the competence of the family to meet problems. The competence or health model addresses family resources, including economic, emotional, social (Howells, 1971), and cognitive (Reiss, 1980) supports. For example, a study of returning World War II husbands (Hill, 1949) determined that how a family dealt with crisis, and what experience the wife had outside the home influenced the adjustment of postwar families.

The health perspective also points to the importance of considering the adaptive style of the family in understanding how families tend to cope with crises. For example, a study of Puerto Rican versus Anglo middle-class persons (Spiegel, 1981) found that Puerto Rican families tended to stress loyalty to the family and a present time orientation. Anglo families, on the other hand, stressed individualism and delayed gratification. Puerto Rican families considered themselves subject to nature, while the American families felt capable of mastering nature. Cultural styles are important in assessing a family. For example, according to the research by Spiegel, one might expect a Puerto Rican family to rely more upon extended family members in times of crisis than an Anglo family.

According to the health orientation, the following characteristics determine healthy family systems:

1. Power balance is understood and accepted by all family members.

2. Each member has rights and autonomy is encouraged.

3. Each member can tolerate separation, and members support one another through losses.

4. Members perceive reality in compatible ways.

5. All members are free to express their feelings.

Based upon these characteristics, Lewis developed a scaling procedure to help determine the potential of a family to deal with a crisis (Lewis, Beavers, & Gossett, 1976).

Some Technical Measurement Decisions.   Three measurement decisions must be made before initiating the family assessment. First of all, one will glean different information if the assessment is totally completed before intervention is begun if assessment continues at the same time as intervention. If a behavioral approach is used, the assessment must be completed before any intervention is introduced. On the other hand, psychoanalytic practitioners begin intervention during the information gathering stage.

The selection of the site of the assessment is a critical issue that is often not carefully considered. Most psychologists, counselors, and psychiatrists assess families within clinical settings, while social workers may use home visits. O'Rourke (1963) found the office was seen as men's turf and might introduce more conflict between father and son. The home was seen as the woman's turf, which exposes more mother–daughter conflicts. Informality versus formality of the assessment, time of day (for example, as soon as Dad gets home from work), and the environment are all critical aspects to consider in family assessment.

The choice of measurement techniques in assessing the family is a critical determinant of what one will learn. The practitioner must decide whether to conduct an individualized or a standardized assessment of the family. A fully individualized assessment will not provide the practitioner with any comparative data and is subject to a lack of objectivity. On the other extreme, an assessment which relies completely upon standardized measurement fails to note some uniqueness in the family and might set the stage for unsuccessful intervention.

An example of measurement that relies upon some individualized approaches and some standardized techniques is Goal Attainment Scaling (Compton & Galaway, 1984). Goal Attainment Scaling is an individual, quantitative process that is used to assess family process. Individual objectives for each family member are ranked on a five-point weighted scale. Goal Attainment Scaling helps clinicians to be sensitive to clinical change within each family member. The importance of the goal to the family is not evaluated with Goal Attainment Scaling.

Standardized tests may also be used with families. An excellent example is the Parent Attachment Structured Interview (P.A.S.I.) (Roll, Lockwood, & Roll, 1980). The P.A.S.I. is used to gain a better understanding of how closely the child is bonded to each parent and other significant adults by assessing dimensions of (R) responsiveness, (S) security, © confidence, and (H) hostility to each significant adult. The child is asked 50 basic questions regarding daily interactions with each parent and other attachment figures. Some examples are

> Who likes to put you to bed?
>
> Who is too tired to play?
>
> Who helps with your homework?
>
> Who breaks promises?

The answers show the range and degree of positive and negative attachments.

Clinical research has advanced to the point where theoretical and technical family assessments can be tested for reliability and validity. A cross-sectional rather than developmental clinical tool used by Costell and Reiss (Reiss, 1980) in their research laboratory has individual family members sort cards. Although family members cannot see each other (they are in separate booths), by using earphones and microphones they can communicate during performance of the task. How do they work as a group or as individuals? Do they see the task as solvable? The answers to these questions can be measured objectively. Then a classification system of families can help predict the usefulness of clinical treatment (Straus & Tallman, 1971).

One of the difficulties of employing standardized tests in family assessment is the ability of the social worker to provide feedback to the family in a useful manner. Another difficulty is the general problem of classifying complex social units such as the family. You as a practitioner must balance the need for standardization with an understanding of the unique factors of every family.

Outline For Family Assessment

Based upon the previous discussion, we find information regarding the family life stage, patterns of behavior, and the environment important variables in making an assessment of family functioning. The following outline can serve as a guide for gathering information of significance for clinical intervention.

I. Family life cycle stage

In this assessment, the social worker determines the family life cycle phase, critical points of conflict, and potential growth within this phase.

A. Relationship of the couple within the phase

1. sexual

2. emotional

3. role definitions

4. power balance

5. division of labor

B. Children's interaction with the community

   1. academic issues

   2. peer group

   3. extracurricular activities

   4. learning disabilities or other physical problems

C. Family constellation

   1. children's roles

   2. children's and parents' responsibilities

   3. intensity of bonding and mutuality of attachments

   4. use of resources (economic, social, societal)

II. Family patterns of interaction

A. Family structure

   1. How are decisions made?

   2. Is parenting democratic?

   3. What is the family history?

   4. Is this a "blended" family (children and parents joined from previous marriages)?

B. Individualism

   1. Can children and parents express themselves safely?

   2. Is everything done as a family or can individuals act independently?

   3. Do children have a sense of self-identity?

   4. How is affection shared?

   5. Are children allowed to mature and grow at appropriate developmental stages?

C. Interaction and communication

   1. How do families resolve conflicts?

   2. Who starts the conflict resolution?

   3. Are conflicts addressed or ignored?

   4. Are certain conflicts left to brew?

   5. Do family members clearly understand each other?

D. Crisis intervention
   1. When faced with a problem, is the family adaptive?
   2. How does the family restore equilibrium after a crisis?
   3. What resources can be brought to bear upon a crisis?
   4. What process does the family use in coping with a crisis?

III. Family environment
   A. How is the home arranged?
      1. shared or own bedrooms?
      2. arrangement of bathrooms
      3. privacy
      4. parents' view of neighborhood
   B. What resources does the community provide?
      1. upwardly mobile job
      2. school
      3. fire protection
      4. recreation
      5. Boy Scouts, Girl Scouts
   C. Family social status
      1. additional career activities
      2. child care
      3. friends
         a. father's
         b. mother's
         c. children's
      4. activities
      5. extended family

This outline elucidates broad data to be gleaned in each family assessment. These data will help identify the areas which may require a more in-depth assessment for an individual family.

Assessment Process According to Family Theory

The family assessment approach employed by a child welfare worker is greatly dictated by the theoretical basis for treatment. Spiegal (1981) lists three common assumptions held, to some degree, by the majority of family practitioners. First, the family system is critical to working with an individual client. Second, observed behavior is considered as a presenting problem, which is only symbolic of deeper structures and patterns of behavior. Third, effective family treatment depends upon interdisciplinary orientation. The openness to outside professional influence is characteristic of family therapy.

Despite these commonalities, a closer examination of family therapy highlights a divergence among family theories and assessment. To gain a better insight to different approaches to family assessment, we present three specific (of more than 43 recognized models of family therapy) approaches to family assessment based upon Behavioral, Adlerian, and Bowen ideological analyses of family functioning.

Behavioral. The assessment of a family according to a behavioral theory is based upon the relationship between a stimulus and a behavior in the environment of a family. The assessment focuses upon identifying specific outcome behaviors, the clients' capabilities, and the impact of behaviors upon individuals within the family. Direct observations of behaviors and related antecedents are made when feasible. Behavioral assessment is an ongoing endeavor that continues to correct the intervention while evaluating progress. The assessment in behavior modification is a process that answers the following questions:

1. What aspects of the problem are due to specific behaviors of the individuals involved?

2. What specific behaviors are to be changed.?

3. What factors maintain the dysfunctional behaviors or prevent the occurrence of functional behaviors?

4. What resources in the client's environment are available for changing the behavior?

5. What intervention is most likely to have a positive effect on the target behaviors? (Fisher & Gochros, 1975)

Although these questions may be rather simplistic, the method of obtaining precise information on a client's behavior at a specific time is a complicated task. Multiple sources of information are needed to obtain an accurate picture of the relevant behavior. Parental accounts of a child's behavior may be quite inaccurate (Evans & Nelson, 1977). Many variables may produce a behavior. The behavioral basis for assessment is that a behavior may be understood only by breaking down a general behavior to very specific parts. This information may be gathered through:

1. check lists

2. inventories, such as marriage inventories

3. schedules, such as sexual survey and reinforcement schedules

Blackham & Silberman (1971) developed a short schedule for identifying potential reinforcers for children with school problems:

1. What games would they buy, if they could.?

2. What three things do they like to do in their classroom?

3. What three jobs do they most like in their classroom?

4. What would they most like to buy with 25 cents?

5. What other kinds of things do they enjoy doing in school? (pp. 173–174)

The behavioral family practitioner attempts to change observable behaviors; therefore, behaviorists do not focus upon the history of a family. A distinction is made between the description of a behavior and the functional analysis of a behavior. A parent may describe a five-year-old as hyperactive. The mother is asked exactly what these hyperactive behaviors are, when they occur, and how intense they are. In functional analysis, the social worker must identify the events that influence and maintain the behavior. The assessment focuses on identifying the relationship between the behavior and its reinforcement. Because most behavior is affected by the environment, the behavior therefore can be changed by modifying elements in the present environment. This orientation does not preclude the assumption that patterns of behavior develop over a period of time, but emphasizes that by examining current problems in detail, a planned intervention is incorporated into the current environment.

Fisher and Gochros (1975) list 12 basic steps in behavioral assessment:

1. an evaluation of the presenting problem
2. a survey of the patterns of the client's behavior in an environmental context
3. discussions with the family
4. identification of specific behaviors for targeting for change
5. collection and analysis of base line information on the target behavior
6. identification of behavior just prior to the target behavior and the resulting experience
7. development of terminal goals and intervention objectives
8. selection of an intervention plan by the family and the social worker
9. specification of modification techniques
10. evaluation of potential reinforcers for the intervention
11. selection of potential reinforcers for the intervention
12. collection and analysis of data on the changes in behavior after the intervention

Behavioral assessment also considers cognitive, cultural, physical capabilities, or emotional factors that may facilitate or limit the outcome behaviors (Gambrill, 1981).

If some criteria are not established for the collection of behavioral information, the social worker may spend all of his or her time in the assessment phases. A helpful filter is to determine whether targeting the behavior will address the following questions:

1. Will it help decide which problems are of concern?
2. Is intervention about this behavior necessary?
3. What specific behaviors should be pursued?
4. How should they be pursued?
5. How will progress be monitored?
6. How can positive change be maintained? (Gambrill, 1981, p. 77)

Adlerian Family Education.   As explained in Chapter 7 on the socially oriented perspective to child counseling, the Adlerian/Dreikursian family education model is a form of family counseling based on the premise that behavior is purposeful. If a family can identify the causes or goals of a child's misbehavior and the parents' reaction to it, then appropriate interventions can be identified. A primary task of Adlerian/Dreikursian assessment is identifying the goal of a child's misbehavior. These goals revolve around four principles: (1) attention-getting behavior, (2) power struggle with the parent, (3) revenge, and (4) displays of total inadequacy (Dreikurs & Soltz, 1964).

During the Initial steps of assessment, the social worker may ask the family to recount the previous day beginning with a specific description of getting up. The child's behavior, what went wrong, and the feelings of the parents are discussed. Many times the child's nonverbal answers are keys to assessing the goals of misbehavior under this model.

Jimmy, aged 12, cannot be awakened by his mother, who continually goes to his room while cooking breakfast to beg, plead, and then scream at him to get up. Jimmy and his parents are questioned alone by the practitioner to identify the goal of misbehavior. Jimmy's eyes widen and he smiles when the practitioner asks if he wants to show Mom he is the boss. The mother confirms a power struggle by stating she feels "powerless when it comes to getting Jimmy up."

Adlerian therapists can often identify the child who is responsible for the unpopular task of taking out the garbage after a brief discussion with the family. This may be the oldest child or the youngest depending upon the family interaction. By guessing the child who takes out the trash, the therapist has a validation of his or her assessment and gains legitimacy with the family. This assessment is possible through careful attention to the family consultation. Comments about the children indicate the child or parent who is most unpopular in the family.

Bowen Family Systems.   Assessment is a major undertaking for a client and practitioner using the Bowen Family Systems approach discussed in Chapter 7. The client does most of the work with the practitioner serving as a coach by providing guidance and making suggestions (Hartman, 1981). The assessment process covers two major dimensions. One is the study of the intergenerational family over four to six generations. The second dimension is the current family emotional system. Hartman has added a mapping process to the intergenerational family, the Eco-Map. The Eco-Map is a combination of the genogram, which maps the family's resources and emotional strengths and weaknesses (Hartman, 1978).

The family history provides an opportunity for the client to learn about current family functioning by understanding family history. The family history

1. organizes facts

2. clarifies distortions

3. demystifies mysteries

4. identifies major events in the family

5. identifies issues and themes that continue to be addressed by the current generation

Examples are the family's attitudes toward work, sex, parenting, religion, and handling crises. Most individuals in the family comply completely with the family tradition or rebel and do the exact opposite.

Genogram.   The genogram is a precise family tree which includes important social data. This allows the therapist to record in a shorthand manner information regarding family members and their relationships over several generations. The therapist can build hypotheses about the child's problem from a rich gestalt of complex family patterns which have evolved over several generations (McGoldrick & Gerson, 1985). As demonstrated in Figure 10.1, a male, indicated by a square, and a female, by a circle, are connected by a line during marriage with *m* and the date of the marriage. Offspring are shown beneath the marriage with the date of birth. An x through a circle with a *d* and a date denotes the death of a female. A dotted line is drawn around family members who comprise a household. The generations are portrayed in a linear fashion. The reconstruction of the family tree is complex and time-consuming. A genogram may be up to 30 feet long with small type. Figure 10.1 depicts six generations of a family as a small example of this process.

The impact of world history and major world events is readily apparent. The family's responses to these crises provide insight into the type of family.

Occupational patterns also may be useful. An example is a workaholic husband. A genogram reveals four or five generations of high achieving males who moved West and worked night and day to achieve their dreams.

The genogram may become rather complex. It may contain a great deal of information and therefore be difficult to read. To structure the investigation, Hartman (1979) suggests an examination of the inner generational identification and "transmission" of values to the child. How do individuals identify with other individuals in the family? For example, a child is born at the same time another person in the family dies, becomes a replacement for that person, and carries the emotional burdens and expectations of the deceased person. Transmission takes place when parents identify their children with others who occupy the same birth order in the parents' generation (Hartman, 1981).

Another way of making the genogram relevant is to explore its personal relevance to the current generation. What are the family themes? For example, is there continual Western movement or do the women marry husbands who then move them from their family's homes?

As another example, a professional woman's husband may leave her after the children are grown. Her daughter, another professional woman, sets the stage for her husband to leave after the children are grown. Such patterns may be transmitted through several generations. Overall, the assessment under the Bowen Family System is to step outside of the family and help them become aware of the interlocking relationships through the generations (Figure 10.1).

FIGURE 10.1

Genogram

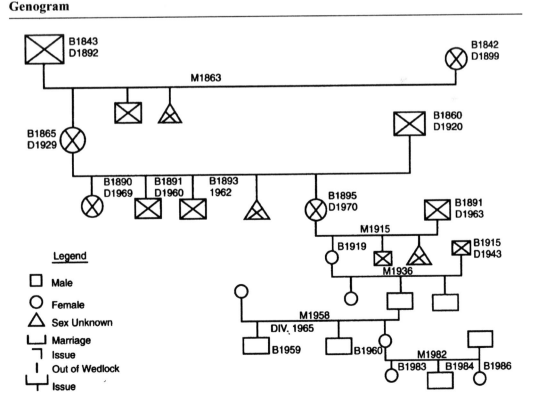

Eco-Mapping. Ann Hartman has built upon Bowen's family systems theory and developed the family Eco-Map (Hartman & Laird, 1983). Eco-Mapping is a paper and pencil assessment process completed with a family. Social distance, importance, and the flow of positive and negative energy are coded and recorded on the paper. The discussion of the Eco-Map begins the assessment process. Eco-Mapping has been found helpful with a wide range of "problems" with children and their families, including adoptive children, abused children, special needs children, and children in new blended families.

An example of an Eco-Map is shown in Figure 10.2.

FIGURE 10.2

Eco-Map

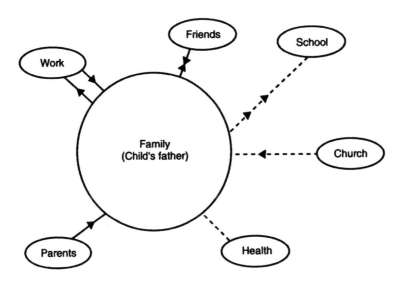

Code

1. Distance from family indicates importance to the family: the farther away, the less critical in the family's view.
2. Types of lines:
   _____ solid for strong positive relationship
   - - - - - - - tenuous relationship
   .... stressful relationship
3. Arrows indicate the direction of the flow of energy.
4. Ovals are drawn around significant people, institutions, and issues.

In this example, the father of a 10-year-old boy experiencing academic problems in school completes an Eco-Map. Notice how important the father's work and friends are and the strong positive flow of energy for each. The rest of the relationships are tenuous or stressful. This allows the therapist to begin the assessment by identifying the strengths (strong ties to friends and work) and the concerns (health, school, church, and parents).

Case Management

Definitions

While not critical to clinical treatment for all children, the process of case management may prove extremely helpful to child welfare workers as they communicate with third parties, including agencies, insurance companies, professional groups, and human service agencies. Case management provides support to children when family support is unavailable or insufficient. Society must act as the parent in these cases. The case manager articulates the needs of the family, coordinates services to them, and advocates on their behalf (Johnson, 1990). Case management emphasizes decision-making, coordination, and service. Rose (1992) identifies three objectives from a systems perspective for case management practice: (1) continuity of care; (2) accessibility and accountability of service systems; and (3) service system efficiency.

The knowledge, skills, and roles of a case manager include

1. Knowing the resources available

2. Holding expertise in the particular area of practice such as child abuse, incest, neglect, mental health, or developmental disability

3. Employing the interpersonal and group skills to interact as a colleague with other professionals

4. Being able to coordinate services to the client and provide an overall service plan

5. Educating the community on needs for additional resources and services or duplication of services (Mayhall & Norgard, 1983)

The major components of case management identified by the Joint Commission on Accreditation for Hospitals are

1. assessment

2. developing an individualized plan

3. linking and coordinating

4. monitoring

5. advocacy (Johnson, 1985)

Historical Roots of Case Management

Casework.   Case management has evolved from social casework, group work, and community organization. Social casework's early roots are found in the pioneer work of Mary Richmond's *Social Diagnosis* (Richmond, 1917). During the 1930s, the functional approach, first developed at the School of Social Work at the University of Pennsylvania, viewed change as coming from the client, not the caseworker. The purpose was to give focus, direction, and content to the social worker's practice. Casework was seen as a way of providing social services with a psychological understanding and skill in helping the individual client. Social caseworkers were agency-based (Smalley, 1971). In the late 1950s, Helen Harris Perlman, at the University of Chicago, introduced the problem-solving approach to social casework. This approach taught the client how to solve problems he or she faced throughout life. The client's ability to perceive, grasp, remember, control impulses, judge, and perform other skills generally associated with ego functioning are critical to the problem-solving process (Perlman, 1957).

Thomas (1977) stated that the behavior modification approach is a valid approach to casework because social caseworkers frequently are involved in altering or stabilizing a client's behavior. The behavioral approach is a highly specific conceptualization of human behavior with specific techniques for assessment and modification. Evaluation of practice also is critical to this approach.

Group Work and Community Organization.   The roots of case management also are tied to social group work, family theory, and community organization. Environmental impacts on children, such as poverty, racism, or lack of services, may be outside the power of their parents to control. Therefore, a case manager may be required to mobilize change at a macro level, in the legislature, a school system, or a professional group. The impact of policy on child welfare workers is discussed in Chapter 15.

Settings

Case management has evolved in a number of settings as a highly desirable approach to working with clients. The child welfare worker will no doubt be involved with case management services at some point in time. Case management is being used in the child welfare, mental health systems, systems for the developmentally disabled, and in institutional structures for the elderly. We will address the first three of these.

Child Welfare.   Protective services to children across the country are adopting the case management system as a method of involving many support services to keep children in their own homes. A number of studies (Fanshel & Shinn, 1978) have shown the detrimental effect of long-term foster care upon children.

One model for avoiding foster care is Family Preservation, also known as home-based services (Hutchinson & Nelson, 1985). A key to this model is early identification of abuse and neglect, provision of relevant treatment, and societal services. In order to provide these services, a case management model is necessary as we shall see in greater detail in Chapter 13. The role of the case manager in protective services is to develop a service agreement with the parents which is approved by the court. This agreement is time-limited and notifies the parents that failure to comply with the service agreement might result in termination of their parental rights and placement of their children for adoption. A child welfare worker may be called to provide an evaluation and therapy to the child during this stressful period of change.

Model Format for Case Management.   A format for case presentations developed for student interns is presented below. The case is a military family who has recently relocated.

1. Demographic Data and Source of Referral.

    Example: This is the case of Mrs. W, a 21-year-old Catholic Caucasian woman and her four children: Elizabeth, age 5; twins Tony and Larry, age 3; and Marianne, age 2. Mrs. W is newly separated from her husband, a 23-year-old PV3 in the Military Police unit at Ft. Bliss. Mrs. W was referred to Social Work Services hospital OB-Gyn Clinic after her first visit for prenatal care in the fifth month of this pregnancy.

2. Presenting Problem(s).

Example : Mrs. W is in the second trimester of a complicated pregnancy and is expected to have her second set of twins. She has a history of spontaneous abortions (two). Upon initial examination, the referring M.D. noted old bruises on her abdomen, and upper forearms. Client admitted to a marital problem but stated her husband is a "good man" who "sometimes" becomes violent when he drinks too much. Their recent separation occurred after a quarrel about his drinking during which he "beat her up." When she reported this to her husband's CO, he confined the man to the barracks "until he sees a social worker." Mrs. W says "they can make him go but nothing will change." She is afraid he will be released and harm her again. The W family is about to be evicted from their three-room apartment for failure to pay the rent.

3. Brief Family History.

Example: The W's met in high school and have been married seven years. Mrs. W and the children came to El Paso from Boston against Mr. W's wishes three months ago. Although he is a high school graduate, until Mr. W joined the Army, the family was on and off welfare as he could not hold a job for long "because of his bad temper."

Both Mr. and Mrs. W are the youngest children of large working-class Catholic families. Most members of their respective families of orientation reside in the Boston metropolitan area. Just prior to their coming here, Mrs. W and the children had been living with her oldest sister and her husband. This couple financed their plane fare to El Paso. Several of Mr. W's siblings are said to be alcoholics. Mrs. W blames their strained relationships with her family on her husband saying, "They think he's no good, just like his brothers."

Mrs. W has a pretty face but is somewhat obese and needs dental work. She was a high school dropout at 15 and has never held a job outside her home. She is proud of the fact that she is "very good with kids" and has done a lot of babysitting to earn extra money. She draws well and "always wanted to go back to school and study art."

4. Psychosocial Evaluation.

Example: These young, overwhelmed, multi problem parents who are geographically distant and emotionally alienated from family and friends now face compounded interpersonal, social, and financial problems in accordance with previously established patterns.

5. Case Management Goals/Objectives.

Example:

   a. Strengthen family relationships.

   b. Build community support system.

   c. Assist family with basic human needs.

   d. Coordinate agency services.

   e. Enable parents to assess strengths, evaluate current situation, and establish future goals and objectives

6. Psycho-Social Treatment Plan.

Example:

   a. Explore military and civilian community resources.

   b. 1 x 1 counseling support to Mrs. W.

   c. Coordinate with social worker responsible for family violence cases; offer conjoint/marital counseling to the W's.

   d. On-going consultation with referring M.D. and with Mr. W's CO.

   e. Refer W children to Pediatric Clinic for health assessment.

7. Progress Evaluation (for update and future discussion).

Example:

    a. Strengths assessment.

    b. Problem areas/resolutions.

    c. Case management issues.

    d. Revised/ongoing treatment plan. (Gloria Shipley, TCSW, ACSW, TXCSW-ACP, N.M. LISW, with permission)

Mental Health and Developmental Disabilities. Public Law 95-602 of 1978, the Developmental Disabilities Training Act, and Public Law 96-398 of 1980, the Mental Health System Act, have incorporated case management requirements (Johnson, 1985). Case managers must coordinate services, provide support, and advocate for disabled clients. New York, Minnesota, Georgia, and Utah already have created case management systems, and other states, such as Florida and New Mexico, are giving it serious consideration.

Many of these services are modeled after the Fountain House in New York City. There are now 180 programs in the United States that resemble the 19th century settlement houses in Britain and the United States (Johnson, 1985). The settlement house workers' philosophy of reform, democracy, and working through existing social structures is key.

Case managers rarely should conduct the child psychotherapy (Austin & Caragonne, 1981). At times, case managers are referred to as social brokers. As such, they are aware of the resources in a community that can be matched to the client in a customized fashion. An example of how a case manger successfully organized a range of services for a family is Case 10.1 of the Salazar Family.

Case 10.1   The Case of the Salazar Family

A Hispanic family from a very rural area, was referred to the Social Services Division because their children, both of which had mild mental retardation, were found on several occasions by the police outside, poorly clothed for climatic conditions, and begging food from the neighbors. Mrs. Salazar, age 21, and Mr. Salazar, age 24, frequently smoked marijuana. They were absent from their home for a period of two or three days every other week. The child welfare worker, using the case manager model, gained legal custody of the children through a court hearing as a first step toward protecting the children. The case manager worked with the district attorney to prepare the case.

Mr. Salazar was unable to hold a job because of his drug habit, although he expressed interest in returning to work as an auto mechanic. The case manager contacted the local mental health center to provide drug abuse treatment. Then she contacted the employment office and enrolled Mr. Salazar in a training program to update his skills. After four weeks, he received on-the-job training.

Mrs. and Mr. Salazar began attending parent education classes for parents of children with mild retardation through an outreach service. The children were evaluated by a physician and a psychologist for physical and psychological functional levels and any potential problems. No physical problems were found; however, the psychologist found signs of detachment and began reattachment therapy. The Salazars expressed some marital problems and were referred to a clinical psychologist for marriage counseling.

After a period of six months, Mr. Salazar was employed as a mechanic. The couple had completed the parent education program and were more effective as parents. Attachment became apparent between the children and the parents as role functions were restored. The clinical psychologist continued to work with the Salazars concerning their marital problems. The child welfare worker with the approval of the court relinquish legal custody of the children's cases. The case manager assumed the role of monitor and continued to check on the Salazars for the next six months. At the end of one year, the case was closed with the approval of the district judge.

Conclusion. On a typical day, a case manager may perform an assessment of a new case, monitor a number of other cases, work with a self-help group in the afternoon, and present testimony before a legislative committee in the evening. This "switching of hats" makes the job of the case manager very interesting but also makes it extremely difficult for most social workers. A case manager must have a broad knowledge base and be well versed in legal, social, psychological, and economic theories. He or she must be aware of the interaction necessary to work with a system of agencies and other professional groups.

The largest profession performing case management is social work. Often, job descriptions require social work education for classified positions (Johnson, 1985). Nevertheless, it is important for all helping professionals to be aware of the case management system and its importance in working with children.

Public and private funds may continue to decline for direct human services. Continued interest in deinstitutionalization will require a case management approach in communities. A case management system will use available resources more efficiently (Rose & Moore, 1995).

Summary

A good family assessment provides the child welfare worker with critical insights regarding the internal and external functioning levels of a family. The framework for understanding the family is based upon the theoretical perspective used. Since family practitioners work with the family as the basic unit of intervention, understanding the family dynamics, patterns of behavior, and life cycle stage enables the child practitioner to be more effective.

We have stressed the importance of a theory-based assessment; through examples, we have applied three different theoretical assessments to cases. Critical assessment points help guide us to a consistent, objective method of collecting information. The information obtained during the assessment determines the intervention or treatment plan. A well-planned and well-executed assessment clearly states the family's and the child's problem. A well-stated problem is half the solution.

Case management is a comprehensive process to link and coordinate all involved parties working with a child or family. Steeped in the tradition of casework, group work, and community organization, the process is being used as a center function with programs for children with developmental disabilities, mental health, and child welfare services. A child welfare worker may serve as a case manager or more likely as a member of the team working with the family.

Chapter 11
Selection of Child Treatment Modalities

The selection of child treatment modalities refers to the structure and attitudes adopted by the child welfare worker or therapist to facilitate communication with the child and to preclude behavior that is counterproductive to the treatment goals. At this level of intervention usually only very experienced child welfare workers holding the Master of Social Work also serve as the therapist. The therapist is often a MSW, or a Ph.D. psychologist or counselor. In most cases the child welfare worker collaborates with the therapist and other agencies as a case manager, as discussed in the last chapter. The treatment modalities include; how the therapist initiates and terminates the session, sets limits, selects styles of therapy (play therapy, group, etc.) and when the child welfare worker seeks adjunct services or refers the client. These activities are all part of the treatment plan. The treatment plan must be consonant with the worker's theoretical position, but a number of treatment issues cut across sessions regardless of the therapist's theoretical persuasion. The treatment plan must be adjusted to individual child's needs and vulnerabilities. The plan will be unique to each client and change with progress in treatment.

In this chapter, we will discuss issues of treatment modalities in broad terms as guidelines for integration in your approach to therapy. First, we will consider issues about the child's development that help the worker or therapist to select treatment modalities (whether play therapy, bibliotherapy, etc.). Then, we will overview the various stances the worker may adopt when working with parents. Next, we will analyze the stages of the helping relationship. A number of specific approaches (such as art therapy, play therapy, storytelling, bibliotherapy) that are appropriate at the various stages will be over viewed. Part of the treatment plan involves the worker's decision about whether the child will profit more from individual or group therapy; therefore, the purposes and structures of group therapy will be discussed. Effective treatment requires the worker to carefully monitor and manage his or her own reactions to the child and the child's family, for the worker's effectiveness is limited by the level of his or her own adjustment. In a section titled Professional Issues, we will identify key factors that may alert the worker of personal concerns that are interfering with the clinical progress. Finally, the issues concerning referral are reviewed. The last section of this chapter overviews reasons for and sources of referral.

Developmental Factors that Determine the Plan

As emphasized in Chapter 3, the child welfare worker must be knowledgeable of developmental processes in the social, cognitive, affective, and motor domains. A good understanding of developmental psychology will assist the practitioner in making important decisions concerning the course of treatment.

The worker must first consider the child's social developmental level. The young child is highly dependent upon the parents. Typically, the parents or teachers choose therapy for the child. The child may not feel he or she has any problem. If the child is aware of difficulties, most likely he or she externalizes the cause, stating, for example, "School is hard"; "My parents yell a lot"; or "They did it first." Thus, consideration of the child's social developmental level helps the child practitioner judge the child's commitment to the therapeutic process (Freedman, Kaplan, & Sadock, 1976). A prime goal of the treatment plan with a child client is to create motivation for therapy, and we will look at ways of instilling motivation in the following section.

The child's social development must be considered in order to assess whether there are issues concerning the child's separation from parents. For example, if a child of three or four is brought to therapy and is too frightened to leave a parent, this is not unusual. The social worker may want to begin by seeing parent and child together. If, on the other hand, a school-phobic child of 11 is unwilling to come into the worker's office alone, although the child has shown social independence in a variety of other ways (e.g., joining the Boy Scouts or going to the store alone), a very different approach may be used. In the latter case, the worker may want to insist upon the child coming in alone. The worker may want to then work with the child in the child's home. Or, the worker may enact a behavioral shaping procedure, rewarding the child for entering the therapist's room alone for progressively longer periods of time.

The method and extent to which the child welfare worker includes parents and other significant adults in the treatment plan depends in part upon the child's social development and of course the parents ability to do so. If the child's difficulties involve developmental and/or social events such as eating, going to bed, or relating with teachers, effective intervention may necessitate the worker's working closely with significant adults in the child's environment. On the other hand, sometimes children are overly dependent upon parents, as in the case of the 11-year-old school-phobic child mentioned previously. In these cases, the worker may choose to focus most intervention upon the child as a way of building the child's self-reliance. The interaction of the child's social developmental level with the quality of the social influences in his or her life must be assessed and used to therapeutic advantage. The worker's relationship with the parents can vary not only in the amount of contact, but also in the purpose of the contact.

In the next section of this chapter, we will overview the stances a child welfare worker or therapist can assume when working with parents. At this point, we want to emphasize that the way the child welfare worker decides to manage time with the parents and child depends in part on the child's developmental capacities and liabilities.

An important facet of the treatment plan with children is to incorporate ways of dealing with the clients' developmental capacity to conceptualize. Because of children's limited conceptual ability, they may not be able to fully understand the purpose of therapy. Their initial willingness to attend sessions may not be built upon hope for change, as is typically true of adult clients, but rather upon secondary factors such as liking the worker, enjoying the special attention, or being reinforced by parents for meeting with the worker. The worker and therapist must find some way of enlisting the child client's interest in therapy, and great skill and sensitivity often is required for this feat.

Evaluation of the child's level of conceptualization also will affect the type of counseling employed. For children under four years of age, interpretations may not be meaningful because the child may not completely comprehend certain relationships that are beyond his or her symbolic ability. A young client most likely can understand and name certain feelings. Thus, help in labeling feelings or identifying a wish or fantasy which serves as the stimuli for emotions may help a young child sort out diffuse feelings and contribute to the child's adjustment. The worker working with a very young client will want to create a therapeutic medium such as play therapy that is conducive to the clinician's identifying and helping the client identify feelings and behaviors.

As children reach school age, their ability to understand and to sit and talk with the therapist increases. However, they also recognize the asymmetry of talking with an adult and often become much less conversant than if talking with a child of similar age. For these children, techniques such as role playing, tape recording, and storytelling are useful (Lester, 1975).

The child's level of affective development must be carefully considered in the treatment style. The young child tends to act spontaneously upon feelings. Feeling and behavior are not perceived as distinct until conceptual ability to introspect about oneself has developed (Chess & Houseboy, 1978). The more limited the developmental ability to conceptualize about feelings, the more action-oriented therapy must be. At the earlier affective developmental levels, the therapist learns much about the child's feelings from the child's behavior. However, the therapist must decide just how much acting to encourage. It is counter therapeutic for traumatic feelings and events to be re-enacted so globally that diffuse distress is expressed (Freedman, Kaplan, & Sadock, 1976). Thus, the therapist must create a treatment plan in which enough action is encouraged to provide understanding of the child's problems. Then, the child welfare worker can identify these for the child and develop programs for change. However, the therapist must provide enough structure and limits to activity that self-destructive behavior or pervasive anguish is not elicited. In fact, if ego functioning is significantly impaired, the therapist may want to use the sessions to help the child distinguish play and reality. In such cases, the therapist may terminate activities if the child seems to-perceive the acting as reality.

Finally, the therapist needs to assess the child's level of motoric development in evolving the treatment plan. At earlier developmental levels, much diffuse motor activity is observed, and attention span is short. Sessions need to be shorter for younger children. The preschooler may be seen for several weekly sessions of 20-30 minutes' duration, while most children of age 10 and older can handle a 45-minute or an hour session. Less goal-directed activity also should be expected for younger children. As we have discussed previously, from infancy, children differ in motor activity. Generally, this difference in activity level between children continues through to adulthood. Thus, in addition to assessing the child's motoric development, the therapist will want to plan treatment strategies in relationship to the child's motoric temperament. For the extremely nonreactive child, a medium will be picked that encourages activity so that behavior and feelings are expressed and can be identified for therapeutic purposes. For the highly active child, activities should be chosen that increase control while reducing total activity so that introspection and insight can be achieved.

In general, when aspects of the child's development are carefully considered, the client will feel and act more positively about the sessions, and the potential for establishing a positive relationship between therapist and client increases. Moreover, when the structure of therapy takes into consideration the child's development in the cognitive, affective, social, and motor domains, the child's developmental strengths can be maximized while opportunity is provided for the child to develop skills that are immature or blocked. Of course, the child's development should not and will not remain static over time. Thus, the treatment issues will change as therapy continues, and the treatment structure should reflect these changing needs.

Role of Parents in the Treatment Process

As you read in detail in the unit on theories of childhood, child theorists prescribe vastly different recommendations concerning how much and in which ways parents should be engaged in the treatment process. On the one hand, strict classical analysts believe that treatment should focus upon the child and that parents should be excluded from the therapy process. The classical analysts maintain that this focus upon the child is necessary to maintain confidentiality and the child's trust. Further, the analysts believe that the parents' emotional problems have contributed greatly to the child's distress and that the parents are unable to be therapeutic until they complete extensive personal therapy. As a consequence of this stand, some classical analysts such as Bruno Bettelheim (1967) suggest that preferred treatment often involves removing the child from the home and placing the client in residential treatment. Other theorists, especially some of behavioral persuasion, maintain that effective intervention can be completed by working primarily with the parents. Some behaviorists work exclusively with the child client's significant adults such as teachers and parents to set up elaborate behavioral modification schemes to change the child's socially maladaptive behaviors.

Each of these extreme positions is subject to certain limitations. Those who work almost exclusively with the child and very little with the parents seem to be ignoring the reality that the parents spend many hours with the child and will continue to exercise tremendous influence over the child. Furthermore, as we have stated, the parents are generally responsible for initiating and bringing the child to the sessions. If the child welfare worker does not engage the parents into the treatment process, they may withdraw their support and may withdraw the child from therapy. Most parents, (even those who have abused) who have their child to therapy are open to feedback and can be helpful therapeutic allies. Their perception of the child's problem is significant, even if distorted by their own problems and needs, because their perception of the child is clearly affecting their interaction with the child and the child's life. The social worker can best understand the child's total milieu by gaining knowledge about parents and their perceptions of the relationship. Moreover, if parents are unaware of the worker's goals with the child, they may unwittingly sabotage therapeutic efforts.

On the other hand, those who work almost exclusively with significant adults and not the child may err by not recognizing the child's needs, feelings, and rights. As you read in the chapter on the humanistic and the psychosocial perspectives to child therapy, most child theorists agree that when a child is treated with positive regard and respect during the therapeutic process, the child is more likely to become motivated to change and may have many answers to his or her own dilemmas. Furthermore, severely limiting the child's role in the therapeutic process ignores the child's right to privacy in his or her interactions with the parents.

It is not surprising, then, that most therapists adopt a moderate position in which they work with both the child and parents. Yet, even within this moderate orientation, theorists and practitioners differ greatly in how approach parents. Some child practitioners of the humanistic persuasion recommend that the practitioner should adopt a supportive, clinical role with parents. The parents are viewed as distressed about their child and their relationship with the child and needing support to work through their feelings about the child and their own parenting skills (Axline, 1969; Ginott, 1961).

Many theorists and practitioners see their roles with parents as advisors and consultants. For example, Dreikurs and Soltz (1964), Moustakes (1973), Keat (1979), and others adopt a problem solving strategy with the parents in which they help the parents plan more appropriate ways of interaction with the child. Models of child therapy have developed in which parents are trained in therapeutic techniques so that they respond as "paraprofessional" practitioners to their own children (Guerney, 1964; Ack, Beale, & Ware, 1975). We will discuss these approaches in detail in the chapter on preventive mental health. Those theorists and practitioners ascribing to a family system viewpoint assist the "identified patient" by working with the family as a unit. As one more example of the variety of orientations for working with parents, Gardner (1975) recommends seeing the parents and child together for the first session in order to foster a sense of openness about the child's problems and to communicate to the child that the social worker will attempt to adopt an objective position concerning family issues. Following this initial contact, Gardner may meet parents separately in order to gain a systematic history about the child's difficulties. Then, Gardner conducts somewhat traditional individual therapy while the parents remain in the room. The parents' roles vary from passive observers to active participants during the sessions.

Given the wide range of orientations proposed by child theorists, it is difficult to draw definitive conclusions about how the social worker can best interact with the child's significant adults. Empirical data about the relative efficacy of these approaches are lacking. At the minimum, it is advisable to talk to parents about the goals and process of therapy. The parents will be interested in learning about the therapist's strategies (such as play therapy and storytelling), about changes they might expect during the therapy, and about how long the therapy is likely to continue. Clearly, the therapist's orientation with the parents should be congruent with his or her overall theory of treatment. The theorists and practitioners agree that parents can be valuable allies or formidable blocks to the change process. Within the framework of his or her theory, the worker should give careful consideration to the best way of engaging particular parents into the counseling process. The child welfare worker and therapist should review in their thinking the variety of stances that can be adopted when working with parents and select an approach that seems most likely to foster the child's movement toward their goals.

Stages of Child Therapy

As we have stated, the therapy sessions should be characterized by change as the child uses the sessions to further growth and development. The exact changes will depend upon the child's personality and specific personal difficulties. Nevertheless, certain issues are characteristic at the initial, middle, and final stages of child therapy and should be considered in the treatment plan.

The Initial Sessions

Several treatment issues are critical at the initiation of therapy. The worker needs to establish him- or herself as a person who can be trusted by the child, parents, and other significant adults. Child welfare workers must help their child clients understand why they are receiving this special intervention. Importantly, the treatment must enlist the child's commitment to the therapy. Frey, Heckel, Salzburg, and Wackwitz (1976) correlated a number of dimensions of children's personalities with therapist's views of gain in psychotherapy as indicated by reduction in target symptoms. The child's motivation for psychotherapy correlated most highly with therapist's perceived change in symptoms. Yet, we have said few children choose therapy voluntarily. Thus, stimulating a child's interest in and motivation for therapy is a major goal of the initial sessions.

To begin with, the worker must set a tone of neutrality. When meeting the child and parents, the worker communicates to everyone that he or she will try to understand all viewpoints. Even when expressing an opinion in controversial issues between the child client and parents, the worker attempts to communicate a respect for all parties. The practitioner quickly sets the tone that he or she will not offer quick advice or get angry, but rather will try to understand the child's behavior. It is important to remember that the child is seldom the initiator of the treatment. The initial clinical task is to win the child's cooperation for the therapy process. In his classic text on psychotherapeutic approaches to the resistant child, Gardner (1975) offers many helpful and creative suggestions to enjoin the child's cooperation. In the initial contact with parents and child, Gardner explains that he employs "seductive reasoning;" that is, he attempts to make the sessions seem appealing and fun to the child. He begins by asking the child relatively innocuous questions ("Where do you go to school?" or "What is your favorite game?") He shows the child his "clinical wares" (games, videotapes, music, magic tricks). He gradually moves into a discussion of problematic concerns while monitoring that the child's resistance is not increasing. If resistance does build, Gardner (1975) resorts to other "seductive" strategies.

Once the child's willingness to participate is gained, the child welfare worker must help the client understand about the process and goals of therapy. The practitioner communicates that the practitioner and child will be working together, that they will be actively engaged in a joint discovery about the child. Statements such as the following may be made:

"This is your time to do and say whatever you would like to."

"You seem like a child who has a lot to say. This is a place where you can do that."

"I'd like to ask you some things about yourself because I'd like for us to know each other better."

Early in the sessions, the therapist helps the child identify a reason for coming. The therapist may begin by posing a question to the client: "Do you know why your parents brought you here?" Yet, the worker must be cautious about telling the child that he or she is coming because of others' complaints. The child may not know he or she is considered a problem. Most likely, the child feels some discomfort and wishes the worker would do something about those things and people that are perceived as the cause of the problem. Thus, the presenting symptom as labeled by others may not be the child's concern. For example, it may be counter therapeutic to tell a child, "Your parents brought you here because they can no longer tolerate the many fights you have with your sister." It is generally more productive to determine if the child is concerned about any aspect of his or her life. Almost always, the worker can gain the child's interest by treating the sessions as a way of helping a child with concerns about growing up. The offer of aid for the difficult task of development is almost always enticing to the child (Freud, 1965).

McConville (1976) coined terms for three opening styles to aid different children in their growing up concerns:

1. "What's In It For You"—To be used with children who are aggressive or experiencing difficulty dealing with authority. The worker emphasizes what the child may personally gain in therapy. For example, "In therapy, we can help you not get thrown out of school and then you can stay in the club with the guys. Think you might be able to get an office in that club?"

2. "How Can I Help You—Or Take 'Good Enough' Care of You?"—To be used with children who are very anxious and pursue very destructive patterns. The worker may adopt a stance communicating, "I will help you grow up less painfully." For example, the worker might say, "As you tell me about how those kids pick on you and what you do about it, I will help you find ways of dealing with them. We will help you learn to protect yourself."

3. "What's It Like Being You?"—Works best with a very withdrawn child where the worker may need only offer counseling as a place where the child can begin more open and spontaneous expression. Here, the therapist may say, "The point of this time is for you to have a place where whatever you want to do or not do is okay."

The child also will profit from an explanation of how therapy works. Imagine children's puzzlement when they are told that therapy will make them feel better, make friends, etc., without any explanation of how it works. No doubt many children wonder if they will be taking medicine, if they will be asleep, or if therapy is some kind of magic. Practitioners have tended to minimize explanations about the child therapy process to their clients because they feel the children would not understand or would not be interested. Yet, several classic studies indicate that children prepared for the process of therapy through "training sessions" are perceived more positively by their therapist (Jennings & Davis, 1977) and are more able to report information about therapy, show more reduction in target symptoms, and drop out of counseling at community mental health centers less frequently (Urie, 1975). The practitioner should explain to the child that in therapy:

- Play and fantasy will be considered communications about him- or herself. This explanation minimizes the child's feeling that clinical interventions are an intrusive attack.

- Talking and/or playing together increases the child's awareness about him- or herself.

- Through increased awareness, the child's ability to grow and mature can be nurtured.

- Through some specific activities that worker and child plan together, the child's problems can be decreased.

During the initial sessions, the child welfare worker should talk about confidentiality. Most young clients will not mind if their parents know about their activities or conversations in the therapy sessions, but a few clients do. The worker should be honest about issues of confidentiality. Total confidence should not be promised if it cannot be delivered. In many cases of referral to child practitioners (for example, with child abuse, or if the child is highly disruptive at school or in determining child custody cases), total confidentiality is practically impossible and/or not in the child's best interests. Generally, the social worker can make a commitment to not disclose information about the sessions without first informing the child. If the child remains upset about the possibility of disclosure, the worker might recommend that the child be present if critical issues must be discussed with the parents.

Structural limitations of the sessions should be set early and maintained consistently. Most social workers agree that causing physical harm to self, the worker, or other clients is not permitted. However, therapists in social work and other fields differ greatly in how much nondestructive activity they allow. The important point seems to be to distinguish wild behavior which serves no therapeutic purpose from activity in which the child can be assessed, understood, and assisted. In the first case, the behavior is labeled "acting out," because the child acts upon his concerns and frustrations with little conscious awareness of the emotions or the stimuli precipitating them. In the latter case, activity may be very active or highly charged, but sufficient control is maintained that the child is helped to understand the behavior. Generally, if the worker is very responsive to the client, acting out behavior is short-lived, and arbitrary controls will not have to be established frequently.

Ornstein (1976) explains that if acting out cannot be controlled by the therapist and significant adults through support and sensitive interpretation, then limits must be set as a palliative measure. The limit setting may not in itself stop the client's problem, but is necessary for the client and others to look at and resolve the child's concerns.

If issues of establishing rapport, identifying goals, and setting limits are given careful attention within the initial sessions, the therapeutic process is greatly enhanced. The worker and client work together to accomplish these goals. Thus, the initial treatment tasks well completed build a "therapeutic alliance."

The Middle Phases

Once a therapeutic alliance is established, the therapy moves into a "work phase." With adult clients, Carkhuff and Berensen (1977) have identified this therapeutic work phase as: (1) helping a client understand the nature of his or her conflicts and (2) aiding a client in developing action plans that will change maladaptive patterns. Applying the Carkhuff and Berensen (1977) scheme to child therapy, it can be seen that child practitioners employ a variety of activities to help their clients move through the understanding and action phases of therapy.

Numerous activities for child therapy have been described in the child literature, and almost all writings are expository in which an activity is described and
applied to a clinical case. Each activity seems to offer advantages for helping
specific children express their difficulties directly or symbolically. Some activities, such as art therapy, seem particularly helpful in understanding a child's
dilemmas Other activities, such as role playing, are particularly effective in stimulating a child to act in new ways. Of course, the activities will be helpful only to
the extent that the therapist competently uses the findings that emerge in those
sessions. It would be impossible to review all the techniques employed with
children in this text, but in this section, we will attempt to describe the major
ones.

Play Therapy.   Almost all child therapists use play as a technique in their treatment approach. The medium of play provides a very practical way of forming an
alliance and learning about a child. Play, as compared to the recreation of adults,
serves a practical function for children. Erikson (1963) explains that the play of
children is preparatory for life. Through play, the child attempts "to synchronize
the body and social processes within the self" (p. 211). The child practices
mastery of himself or herself and of the world through this "internal reality
between fantasy and actuality" (p. 212).

Play was first introduced into therapy by Hug-Hellmuth in 1913. She stated
that the analyst paves the way for analysis by sharing in the play activities (Kanner,
1962a). As we have discussed in detail in an earlier chapter, Melanie Klein and
Anna Freud employed systematic play therapy techniques in the 1930s. Erikson
was the first therapist to systematically observe differences in children's play
throughout their development and to identify differences in play between males
and females. He noted that the toddlers play is mainly "autocosmic," a way of
bringing material to the child. The preschoolers play is "microspheric," in that the
child begins to move toys to replicate the child's view of the world. Erikson
reported that male preschoolers' play often deals with themes of "high" and "low."
He builds towers and rockets as he works out his Oedipal concerns. Erikson noted
that girls' play often deals with themes of "open" and "closed," for example,
building and designing interiors of houses. Erikson believed girls were working
through their Electra concerns, practicing for the female roles they will assume.
He believed that if a disturbed child were allowed to express these themes with
an accepting adult therapist, the child would gain "play peace" (Erikson, 1963).
Today, most social workers do not accept the premise that play activity is aimed
at the child's working through oral, anal, and phallic conflicts. However, most do

hold to Erikson's concept that the child begins to experience subjective comfort when play activity is watched and responded to by an accepting adult.

A number of other purposes of play therapy have been posited. Kanner (1962a) sees the primary advantages as catharsis, to drain off excess energy, and self-expression, as a means of satisfying needs before the child is skilled enough to directly impact the world. Ginott (1961) and others see added advantages of play therapy in helping the child learn new life skills, providing means for interpreting a child's behavior, and for evaluating gains in therapy. Dimick and Huff (1970) emphasized that play provides a very effective way of facilitating the therapeutic alliance. While the child is playing, he or she tests limits with the worker and in doing so learns more appropriate ways of relating to the worker and others. Therefore, play therapy is an activity that can facilitate movement through all major phases of therapy from acceptance and forming a therapeutic alliance, to understanding of the problem, then action and practice, and finally to termination.

Clinicians are surprisingly consistent about the materials they recommend for effective play therapy. A room about 10' by 15' is preferred. This size allows activity and yet is small enough to provide some natural control to acting out and to keep the therapist and child in relatively close proximity (Dimick & Huff, 1970; Keat, 1974). Generally, toys should be picked that allow a child to create, to project his typical behaviors and thoughts. Thus, structured games are generally not as effective as dolls, puppets, paints, trucks, and animals.

A problem that often arises in play therapy is that children may want to borrow some material and take it home with them. Again, on this matter, most practitioners agree. The child should be allowed to take home his own creations, such as paintings and clay models, but not to take toys home. As a whole, keeping material in play therapy is considered an important structural limit for teaching children about the role of therapy within their lives.

There is much more controversy on how the therapist should respond in play therapy than there is in how to set up the play therapy environment. The practitioner's theoretical orientation affects how active he or she is in the play therapy session. As discussed earlier, Axline (1969) popularized a nondirective approach to play therapy. The play therapy atmosphere is very permissive. Only acts injurious to the child or worker are limited. The worker conveys understanding without interpretation. Axline (1969) maintains that first unrealistically negative, then unrealistically positive, then appropriately mixed emotions about the child's significant adults and self will be expressed in this permissive atmosphere.

Other practitioners are more interpretive or active in play therapy according to their theoretical underpinnings. For example, Moustakes (1973), identifying himself as existential therapist, actively responds to the child in play therapy in order to remediate the child's previous experiences and to form a close, constructive relationship.

The research about the efficacy of play therapy is controversial and limited. Sabatani (1976) compared the effects of participating in individual play therapy to watching films about social interactions for a random group of elementary school age children. Play therapy facilitated more popularity (according to sociometric choice) than the systematic watching of films. In contrast, when 26 children were divided into an experimental play therapy group which received 15 weeks of 45 minute individual play therapy sessions and a waiting list control group, no differences were found on six primary dimensions of adjustment (Barrett, 1976). With the paucity of research findings, it is clearly too early to try to evaluate which approach to play therapy is most effective. The somewhat bleak findings clearly suggest that a social worker should not assume he or she is doing therapy with the child; that is, helping the child, simply because they are playing together. With the lack of empirical guidelines, it becomes even more important for the child welfare worker to carefully delineate the purpose of the play therapy, to develop a directive or nondirective approach consistent with theory and treatment goals and to assess progress toward those goals.

Art Techniques.   A great range of art techniques can be employed. Some therapists encourage free drawing sessions. Others like to have children draw pictures of their families, 'themselves, their neighborhood, etc. An approach developed by Winnicott (1971), the "Squiggle Technique," in which the client and worker draw lines alternately and discuss them, became quite popular. Stein (1976) has found it useful to have her clients make "funny books" of their drawings and discuss them.

In her highly creative text, *Windows to Our Children*, Oaklander (1978) offers a wide range of drawing techniques that she implements from a gestalt perspective. She assists children to become more aware of their sensory experiences and, through sensory enrichment more cognizant of their feelings. For example, she asks children to complete individual or group paintings on large poster boards with car paint. "The flow of the paint and the sensuous feel of I as well as the sheer enjoyment of the activity, open the child up to sharing some deep feelings and this leads to his talking about some problems in his life which in turn leads to a discussion of his options in resolving that problem" (pp. 60–61). Employing finger paints or clay, she may direct her child clients to become aware of the sensation of pulling, tugging, and smoothing the milieu to increase their sense of control and mastery. "Bunch it up. Tear it. Tear little pieces and tear big pieces. . . . Bunch it up. Pick it up and throw it down. You may have to peek for this. . . . Do it again. Do it harder. Make a loud noise with it. Don't be afraid to hit HARD" (p. 70). She then encourages the children to move from a discussion of their sensory experiencing to their overall personal experiences.

Almost always, the drawing is seen as an adjunct to therapy that aids understanding of thoughts and feelings. The therapist offers commentary about the drawings and encourages the child to talk about them. The drawing techniques are particularly useful in the middle phases of therapy. Most therapists do not look for universal symbolism to the drawings since the child's developmental level, culture, and experience all affect artwork. Rather, comments are usually intended to lead children to talk more about the drawing and thus to tell what it means to them. For example, statements about firmness of footing, size of body parts, and color preferences, as well as questions about what a certain part of the painting is, may facilitate further verbal therapeutic exchange (LeRoy & Derdeyn, 1976).

Oaklander (1978) offers a number of guidelines by which the worker can employ art media as a backdrop to clinical intervention:

- Ask the child to share the experience of drawing, his or her feelings about doing the task, how he or she decided to approach it.

- Ask the child to discuss the drawing itself, giving it a title, etc.

- Ask the child to elaborate upon parts of the picture, describing shapes, forms, colors, people, and objects in it.

- In accord with gestalt principles, encourage the child to describe the picture as if the picture were the child; for example, "I am this picture. I have curvy soft lines. I have hard lines. I am mostly blue."

- Pick specific parts of the picture and ask the child to identify with it. For example, "Be that lion in the picture. Describe yourself. What do you look like? What are you doing?" Then ask the child to elaborate further about that part. For example, "Where would the lion rather be?"

- Prompt the child to dialogue between two parts of the picture. "What does the mouse say to the lion?"

- Encourage the child to pay attention to the colors. "What does blue mean to you?"

- Watch for missing parts or empty spaces in the drawing and ask about them; for example, "I wonder why the mother has no hands."

The use of *drawings* as an adjunct to verbal therapy requires a sensitive response to nuances of the child's creation while avoiding over interpretation. In the Case of the Ill-Tempered Artist that follows, the therapist used drawings to move through the first several stages of treatment (Caron, 1980). By allowing the client to draw quietly, without forcing verbalization through the first few sessions, a therapeutic alliance with this guarded youth was established. Using the drawings as a topic of conversation, a dialogue between the therapist and client emerged gradually, leading to a discussion of the referral issues.

Case 11.1   The Case of the Ill-Tempered Artist

Reason for Referral: This 12-year-old client was referred for psychotherapy primarily due to problems in controlling his temper. He reportedly was breaking school windows, lying, writing obscene notes, and refused to accept responsibility for his actions. Although previous intelligence test results indicated low average intelligence, the school diagnosticians determined that he was five or six grade levels behind his peels. Additionally, he was thought to be oppositional, guarded, and inaccessible to contact from the outside world.

Intervention Strategy: This client was guarded, quiet, and inactive during initial sessions. The utilization of art therapy provided him with a safe way to begin to communicate in a monologue fashion. Art provided a method of developing a therapeutic relationship. Eventually a therapeutic dialogue emerged. Within the therapeutic dialogue, the client talked about the meaning of some of the pictures and eventually discussed his school problems.

Therapy Progress: The client drew a series of 10 drawings over the initial two months of therapy (see Figure 11.1). The first four pictures were of birds, two of which looked quite aggressive. Picture five was a stylized desk, and picture six was once again a bird, but not as aggressive. The bird's reflection resembled the lower part of a naked man. For the seventh picture, he drew a ram with a human mask-like face. This is the first sign of a person in any drawing. Next, a van with a C.B. radio was drawn. Through the front window, one can see the obscured face of a person. Lines around the antenna indicate communication. Next, he drew the first clear person. He chose to reproduce a picture hanging on the wall. This was seen as a good prognostic sign as it indicated the youth's sense of connection to therapy and to the therapist. The tenth picture was probably the most unusual of all the pictures. The client stated that it was the skeleton of an animal in a casket. This fictitious animal lived in the forest and chased people. The people were afraid of it because they didn't know what it was. Then one day while crossing the road, the animal was run over and killed by a truck. The people placed its body in a casket. For the next picture, he drew a somewhat aggressive cartoon character. He chose not to draw in future sessions, but rather played air hockey and even brought a friend to participate. It seemed as if he had symbolically buried a wild aspect of himself and was reaching out to peers and the therapist. A month later he brought five additional pictures to a session consisting of three birds, one walrus, and a man's face (see Figure 11.2). The pictures were seen as less aggressive. The man's face showed distress but displayed an adaptive movement toward understanding his and others' emotions.

Behavioral Progress: When therapy began, the client was being disciplined in the school office almost daily. After about one month of therapy, he quit having to go to the office. He continued to write an occasional obscene note, but was now usually willing to admit his guilt when caught. He was somewhat more verbal and spontaneous.

Six-Month Follow-up: In a six-month follow-up interview with his mother, she stated that he had maintained the behavioral gains in school and with his peers. She felt that temper control was no longer a problem.

FIGURE 11.1

Client Drawings

FIGURE 11.1

Client Drawings *(continued)*

FIGURE 11.2

Client Drawings

Writing Approaches. Some child clients respond well to invitations to write about their life circumstances and feelings. Children can be encouraged to write stories about themselves, others, or fictional characters. The stories about others and fictional characters are seen generally as a child's projection of his or her own life views. According to the social worker's theoretical persuasion, these stories can be responded to in a variety of fashions. The child may be asked to talk about her or his feelings about the story, to expound upon various characters' responses, etc. The social worker may offer explanations or interpretations about the characters' actions.

Oaklander (1978) encourages her child clients to write poetry. She devised a modified version of Japanese haiku which she has found most of her children are able to enjoy writing. The modified haiku consists of five lines. The first and fifth line are the same single topic word. Line two is a two-line descriptor of the topic word. Lines three and four are three- and four-word descriptors, correspondingly. For example, a child might write:

Mothers

Very Nice

You Love Them

Make You Feel Safe

Mothers

School

Very Hard

Not Enough Play

Summer, Please Come Soon

School

Again, the therapist can use the children's poetry in a variety of clinical fashions.

Structured Interpersonal Approaches. Naturally, all child therapy involves stimulating intimate interaction between the therapist and child. In traditional play therapy, the interactions grow in depth through a relatively unstructured format. Several practitioners, with Richard Gardner as a leading proponent, have created structured strategies for engaging children and deepening the therapeutic relationship. Gardner (1971) originated a storytelling technique involving several steps. First, the child is encouraged to tell a story and give it a moral. Gardner videotapes the child's story. He may create a fantasy situation about the tape recording, for example, telling the child to pretend that he or she is a famous storyteller and is about to broadcast a story through a national television circuit. Gardner then introduces the child storyteller to the "listening public" with a flamboyant, complimentary opening: "Today, ladies and gentlemen, we have for your enjoyment Bobby, who will be telling us a story on our show. Bobby, tell the folks a little bit about yourself." If the child is hesitant to begin a story, Gardner offers nondirective verbal leads. He tells the child that he will begin the sentences and the child should finish them. Gardner's leads are open prompts such as:

"Once upon a time, a _____."

"Then the animal _____."

"Afterwards he felt _____."

"And lo and behold, right then _____."

Gardner consistently requests the child to end the story with a moral. It is Gardner's thesis that the child will reveal frustrations and conflicts through the dynamics of the tale.

On the assumption that the child's story is really about the child, the practitioner listens, asks for clarification, and tries to understand the psychodynamic meaning. Then the practitioner makes up a story selecting one or two of the same themes, but providing an ending moral that represents a higher level of adjustment. In Case 11.2, The Case of the Unsure, Angry Eight-Year-old that follows, the storytelling technique is exemplified (Furgeson, 1981).

Case 11.2   The Case of the Unsure, Angry Eight-Year-Old

Eight-year-old Sandy lives with her mother, father, older sister and brother, and a younger brother. Her school problems go back to being suspended from her four-year-old preschool class for hitting and biting. Currently, her third-grade teacher finds her behavior unacceptable. She does not complete her independent work and disturbs others. Sandy has a poor self-concept, accepts herself as a problem child, and does not feel that she can change her school behavior.

At home, her parents find her temper tantrums very difficult. Sandy erupts with uncontrolled anger, screaming and yelling, at what seems to be the slightest provocation. These tantrums are often unexpected, and her parents have not been successful at either preventing or stopping them. They feel that Sandy knows her tantrums are unacceptable, but that she feels unable to change her behavior. Her family considers her their difficult member, and Sandy seems to feel trapped in that role.

At her third session, Sandy told her therapist, Julie, the following story about their visit together.

Sandy's Story

Once there was a girl named Sandy. She was a cheerleader. One Sunday afternoon, she went to her brother's soccer game. He was only five, and the team was called the Super Jets. Sandy's sister Lynn who is 11 always calls it Blue Jets. Then Sandy says, "No, it's Super Jets." While Sandy was cheering, she saw a lady named Julie. Sandy got very embarrassed because she thought Julie would get mad at her because she wasn't very good. After the soccer game, Julie and Sandy went to Swensen's where Sandy had a Chocolate Ring-a-ding. It was in a really high glass, a Parfait glass. And after that, Sandy said she was freezing. And Julie said, "Do you want to go wait out?" and Sandy said, "No." And then Sandy got her shirt dirty from cheerleading, and she's going to get in trouble, don't worry. She's going to have to clean it herself, by hand. Sandy wondered if Julie knew any ladies who got in trouble when she was a girl. Sandy and Julie went riding in the car. Sandy knows a boy in her class who gets in lots of trouble. Then they went through a green light. Then they went over a big hill into the telephone wires and b-o-I-n-g the storyteller's brain stopped again, and nobody would talk to her. The moral of this story is, "Nobody likes a storyteller."

The therapist decided to focus on Sandy's poor self-concept as represented by Sandy's cheerleading, her dirty shirt, and the boy who got in trouble in school. In the story, the therapist suggests to Sandy that she accept her behavior and herself as a likable person and consider that as she grows, she will change. The therapist's additions to Sandy's story are underlined.

Therapist's Story

Once there was a girl named Sandy. She was a cheerleader. One Sunday afternoon she went to her brother's soccer game. He was only five and the team was called the Super Jets. Sandy's sister Lynn who is 11 always calls it the Blue Jets. Sandy says, "No, it's Super Jets." <u>Sandy felt pleased to be right, to get noticed for being right</u>. While Sandy was cheering, she saw a lady named Julie. Sandy got very embarrassed because she thought Julie would get mad at her because she wasn't very good. <u>What she didn't know or maybe she'd forgotten, was that Julie would still like her even If she wasn't very good. She'd still take her to Swensen's</u>. After the soccer game, Julie and Sandy went to Swensen's where Sandy had a Chocolate Ring-a-Ding. It was in a really high glass. And after that Sandy said she was freezing. And Julie said, "Do you want to go wait out?" Sandy said "No." And then Sandy got her shirt dirty from cheerleading, <u>but she knows how to clean it herself</u>. Sandy and Julie went riding in the car. Sandy wondered if Julie was like her. <u>Sandy was afraid Julie wouldn't like her if she knew how much trouble she got into. But Julie knew girls like her and as they grew up, they changed and didn't get into trouble</u>. Then they went through a green light. Then they went up a big hill over the telephone wires and <u>landed on the top eating ice cream. The moral of the story is, "It's more fun to watch yourself as you grow and change than to be mad at yourself."</u>

The case of the Unsure, Angry Eight year-Old demonstrates how a child at the concrete operational level can be helped to rethink her approach to life. It probably would not have worked to offer this eight-year-old interpretations about her tendency to repress feelings and cover her efforts, but she learned about her ways of defending against anxiety and her personal dynamics in the storytelling technique.

An infinite variety of modifications to the storytelling approach are possible. For example, the social worker can create an open-ended story representing a conflictive area for the child, and have the child finish the story. Words can be written for favorite songs. The child's needs often prescribe the exact storytelling approach.

Related to the structured storytelling technique is the use of bibliotherapy in child counseling. Published books on relevant themes can be read together. Stories can be useful discussion guides in group counseling sessions or can be given to the child to read at home. If the practitioner wishes to conduct a relatively unstructured verbal or play therapy session, it may be unwise to keep the bibliotherapeutic material in the therapy room. Some resistant child clients may begin reading as a way of avoiding interaction with the clinicians. Table 11.1 lists a number of bibliotherapeutic references and games that the child therapist may wish to employ.

The therapist may want to use structured games with some child clients. Gardner (1975) has devised a number of games that foster intervention. Very well known is his "Talking, Feeling, and Doing Game" (Creative Therapeutics, 155 County Road, Cresskill, NJ 07626). In this board game, the clinician and client compete to reach the end point by throwing dice and moving on a pathway. The players land on squares which signal them to pick up either talking, feeling, or doing cards. The cards request players to describe or act out ideas of potential clinical relevance (for example, "What is the worst thing a child can say to a mother?" "Say something that tells about a feeling." "Pretend you are having a temper tantrum." "Why are you so angry?"). If the player responds at all to the request on the card, he or she receives a chip. The player reaching the end point first receives five extra chips. The winner of the most chips can select a trinket from the prize jar. Gardner (1975) reports that highly resistant and reticent clients are quite responsive to this structured approach. Through these relatively non-threatening activities, the children reveal their attitudes and feelings, which allows the clinician to prompt for further explanations and to offer interpretations.

With N. L. Kritzberg, Gardner (1975) devised a game, "Board of Objects," which the clinician can set up with inexpensive play material. Small figurines are placed upon each square of a 64- or 100-square game board. One face of each of two dice is painted red. Players throw the dice. If a red face lands up, the player selects an object from the board. If the player can say anything about the object, he gets one chip. If he can make up a story about the object, he receives two chips. This game allows the clinician to gain insight and offer feedback about very young clients.

TABLE 11.1

Bibliotherapeutic Material and Games for Children

Books on Resiliency In Children & Adolescents

Title	Author	Price
Adolescent Suicide: Assessment & Intervention	Berman	$26.50
Boundaries: Where You End & I Begin	Katherine	10.00
Bringing Up Kids Without Tearing Them Down	Leman	10.99
Counseling The Defiant Child	Mordock	12.95
Delinquent Gangs	Goldstein	24.95
Drug Abuse Prevention With Multi-Ethnic Youth	Botvin	59.95
Eight Steps Ton Conflict Resolution	Weeks	13.95
Growing Up Adopted	Benson	19.95
High Risk Children Without A Conscience	Magid	12.95
How To Reach & Teach ADD/ADHD Children	Rief	27.95
How To Talk So Kids Can Learn At Home & In School	Faber	22.00
In Search Of Values: 31 Strategies For Finding Out What Really Matters To You	Simon	8.99
Making The Most Of Today: Daily Readings For Young People On Self-Awareness, Creativity & Self-Esteem	Espeland	19.95
Parents, Teens, & Boundaries	Bluestein	8.95
Peter The Puppy Talks About Chemical Dependence In The Family (Grades K–6)	Johnson	59.95
Raising Peaceful Children In A Violent World	Cecil	16.95
Relaxation: Comprehensive Manual For Adults, Children, & Children With Special Needs	Cautela	19.95
Resilient Self	Wolin	21.00
Skills For Living—Adolescent	Morganett	31.00
Skills For Living—Elementary	Morganett	31.00
Skillstreaming The Adolescent	Goldstein	18.50
Skillstreaming The Elementary School Child	Goldstein	18.50
Thinking, Feeling, Behaving Grades 7–12	Vernon	32.50
When Kids Are Mad, Not Bad	Paul	5.99
When Someone Very Special Dies Workbook	Heegaard	6.95
When Someone Has A Very Serious Illness Workbook	Heegaard	6.95

TABLE 11.1

Bibliotherapeutic Material and Games for Children *(continued)*

Videos On Resiliency In Children & Adolescents

Title	Author	Price
Bonding Years	Burns	$39.50
Early Childhood: Discovering Delight In Challenge	Burns	39.50
Moving Youth From Risk To Resilience	Burns	19.00
Resilient Child	Burns	39.50

Games For Resiliency In Children & Adolescents

Title	Author	Price
Adoption Story Cards	Gardner	$16.95
Classroom Behavior Game (Ages 4–12)	Childswork	41.95
Good Behavior Game (Ages 4–10)	Childswork	39.95
Pocket Ungame: All Ages	Talicor	9.95
Talking, Feeling, & Doing Game (Spanish)	Gardner	36.95

Books For Children

Title	Author	Price
10th Good Thing About Barney	Viorst	$3.95
12 Steps & 12 Traditions Of Overeaters Anonymous: A Kids View	OA 1	1.75
Alone Together; Single Parent Activity Book	Boulden	4.95
Annie & The New Kid	Carlson	3.99
At Daddy's On Saturdays	Girard	5.95
Bully On The Bus: The Decision Is Yours Series	Bosch	4.95
Carl Goes To Daycare	Day	12.95
Clouds & Clocks: A Story For Children Who Soil	Galvin	6.95
Dinosaurs Divorce	Brown	5.95
Divorce Workbook: A Guide For Kids & Families	Ives	12.95
Don't Make Me Go Back, Mommy: A Story About Ritualistic Abuse		7.99

TABLE 11.1

Bibliotherapeutic Material and Games for Children *(continued)*

Books For Children *(continued)*

Title		
Double Dip Feelings: Stories To Help Children Understand Emotions	Cain	8.95
Drawing With Children	Brooks	12.95
Forever Family: A Child's Story About Adoption	Banish	4.95
Gentle Willow: Story For Children About Dying	Mills	8.95
Helping Children Grieve	Huntley	6.95
I Can Talk About What Hurts: A Book For Kids In Homes Where There's Chemical Dependency	Hazelden	7.95
I Have Diabetes	Althea	7.00
I Have Epilepsy	Althea	7.00
Ignatius Finds Help: A Story About Psychotherapy For Children	Galvin	6.95
It's My Body: A Book To Teach Young Children How To Resist Uncomfortable Touch	Freeman	4.95
Liking Myself: Assertiveness & Self Esteem Building For Children Ages 5 to 9	Palmer	6.95
Little Tree: Serious Medical Problems	Mills	6.95
My Body Is Private	Girard	11.95
My Name Is Brain, Brian (Dyslexia)	Betancour	13.95
My Real Family	McCully	13.95
My Secret	Boulden	4.95
On The Road Of Stars: Native American Night Poems	Bierhorst	15.95
Otto Learns About His Medicine: A Story About Medication For Hyperactive Children	Galvin	6.95
Russell Is Extra Special (Autism)	Amenta	6.95
Scary Night Visitors: A Story For Children With Bedtime Fears	Marcus	6.95
Spike & Ben: A Story About Sad Feelings	Thaut	4.95
Tell Me A Story, Paint Me A Sun: When A Girl Feels Ignored By Her Father	Chaplan	7.95

TABLE 11.1

Bibliotherapeutic Material and Games for Children *(concluded)*

Books For Children *(concluded)*

Title		
Trouble With Secrets	Johnsen	4.95
What Kind Of Family Do You Have?	Super	4.95
Why Did It Happen? Helping Children Cope In A Violent World	Cohn	15.00
Why Was I Adopted?	Livingston	8.95
Zachary's New Home: A Story About Foster & Adopted Children	Blomquist	6.95

These books, videos, and games are offered through:

The Serenity Shop Booklist
3401 San Mateo NE
Albuquerque, NM 87110
(505)889-0885
1-800-892-0885

Many social workers employ with great success a variety of role-playing techniques with children. The basis for and theory behind developing such techniques was discussed fully in Chapter 5 on cognitive behavioral approaches in child counseling. Lazarus (1976) has written avidly about the approach and reported that behavioral rehearsal was twice as effective as direct advice and nondirective treatment. His research has been criticized because he personally administered all three treatments while clearly holding a bias in favor of the behavioral approach. However, Lazarus' findings have been replicated in a variety of closely related studies (Smith, 1976). The role-playing may be casual in which the clinician and client play out a conflict situation. Roles may be reversed so that the child learns how significant others are feeling. Role-playing may involve watching stimulus films or acting out roles in structured plays or unstructured psychodrama. The role-playing may be employed in group sessions to practice a particular personal/social issue, such as learning to be more assertive or learning to talk with divorced parents. Role-playing techniques can be particularly effective in later phases of counting because they facilitate action, adoption of new beliefs, and practicing of new behaviors.

A variety of other structured techniques can be incorporated into the treatment plan. The social worker and child can act out open-ended plays, respond to film vignettes, produce puppet shows, etc. Some child practitioners employ relaxation training fairly regularly during sessions to help the children feel more comfortable about themselves and about discussing their concerns. The structured techniques can be particularly effective in the middle and later phases of therapy. They can facilitate understanding of the client's and significant others' values, ideas, and problems. These techniques also provide a means for integrating new cognitive understanding and practicing new verbal behaviors, thereby helping to move clients through the action phase of counseling.

Summary of Activity Therapy.   As we look at the variety of activity therapies, several points emerge. The activity is a means to therapy, not therapy itself. Although the therapist may recommend an activity for a child, the activity will not help facilitate a therapeutic alliance unless the child finds the activity of interest. Children differ in the degree to which they like to be active or talk with the social worker. The practitioner must use the strategy to accomplish specific clinical aims. Therefore, some degree of clinical verbal communication between the worker and child should occur during or after the activity in order for counseling to progress.

The beginning practitioner often wonders which approach to use with a particular client. Although there is no single answer to this question, several guidelines can be offered. The nature of the child's development and presenting complaints guide the choice of technique. For example, a withdrawn child might respond well to a low-threat game. An overly active child might respond well to acting out a play. The high action in this case would help delimit nontherapeutic movement. Building upon Lazarus' (1976) Theory of Multimodal Therapy, Keat (1979) follows the acronym BASIC ID to select techniques that will strengthen the child's adaptive functioning within each of the following modes:

Behavior

Affect

Sensation

Imagery

Cognition

Interpersonal Relationships

Drugs and Eating Habits

Keat (1979) completes an analysis of the child's functioning in each sphere and then selects relevant techniques to strengthen the child's functioning. An example of such a multimodal profile is presented in Table 11.2.

We suggest that the various techniques tend to be appropriate for different phases of the therapeutic relationship. Some techniques serve broad purposes and may be employed through several stages, while others are particularly useful at discreet phases to help resolve particular problems. The phases overlap since movement through those therapeutic stages may be uneven. Overall, the worker's selection of treatment techniques should reflect the child's particular needs and movement through the therapeutic process.

TABLE 11.2

An Example of Mufti-Modal Profile for Johnny

Multi-Modal Scheme from the Basic Acronym	*Johnny's Problems*	*Treatment*
Behavior	difficulties relating to father after divorce	Bibliotherapy, read books on children of divorce
Affect	anger, fears of abandonment	relaxation training role-playing, talking with father
Sensation	has interest in art	draw family pictures then and now and discuss
Imagery	hesitant to reveal feelings about self	Talking, Feeling, Doing games
Cognition	has stopped completing schoolwork since parents' divorce	family conference, conference, behavioral contracting
Interpersonal relations	area of strength, no apparent difficulties	not applicable
Drugs and eating habits	erratic eating times since divorce	nutritional discussion and bibliotherapy

Terminating Therapy

The timing and method of termination is at least as important as the initial meeting procedure in affecting clinical gain. Much therapeutic benefit can be lost if a child feels rejected by the therapist or if separation from the social worker causes great anxiety.

Of course, no simple guidelines can be given about when to terminate. A growing body of literature suggests that short-term therapy of eight weeks' or so duration is often as effective as long-term therapy that lasts a year or more. Thus, it is likely that in some instances, practitioners are keeping children in therapy longer than parents and children believe necessary or beneficial. The more clearly the therapy goals are defined, the more this situation can be avoided.

Of course, child practitioners of different theoretical persuasions suggest very different criteria for deciding when to terminate. Humanistically oriented practitioners speak of terminating when children feel good about themselves and when they talk more positively about themselves. They maintain that the child client generally tells the social worker when he or she is ready to terminate. Such broad goals usually require four months or longer to accomplish. The behavioristically oriented therapies on the other hand, looks for extinction of symptomatic behavior which often is accomplished in fewer than a dozen sessions. The analytically oriented practitioner is concerned about children's ability to interpret their own play and to play less stereotypically and defensively. Again, such goals require relatively long-term treatment. In interviewing 1200 clinicians, Weissman (1975) reported that the primary factor listed for termination was development of effective coping mechanisms and problem-solving strategies. Along these lines, we believe that the decision for termination should involve evaluation of the child's developmental progress. Termination is appropriate if the child's cognitive, affective, social, and motoric development is moving forward in a systematic fashion. The developmental sequence laid down in earlier chapters offers a systematic way of evaluating the appropriate point for termination. The worker and therapist should not assess development only within the sessions. The new personal skills learned with the practitioner should have transferred to the child's normal environment.

Once the child practitioner believes termination is appropriate, it should be discussed with the child. Most likely, the child and family will need several sessions to fully deal with their attitudes about termination. These final sessions should be employed to determine whether new skills are firmly established in the child's everyday life, not reduced once the therapist begins to discuss termination. It is the therapist's responsibility to raise the termination issue over a number of sessions. After all, even constructive parting can be difficult to handle. Learning to deal with the parting constructively becomes an integral part of the therapeutic process. The child may need assistance is talking about feelings about leaving. In most cases, new reinforcement systems may need to be established in the child's everyday environment. The practitioner must also be very closely attuned to his or her feeling of loss. Some children want to know that the practitioner will remember them, that their relation had an impact upon the worker. Whereas most clinicians will not take or give presents or toys during the therapy process, some do exchange gifts at termination. As the child and practitioner work out a constructive approach to termination, child clients will learn effective ways of parting that will help them in many later life experiences.

With termination, the treatment plan has almost ended. Whenever possible, the worker should include follow-up sessions to the overall treatment plan to ascertain that gains are maintained. Direct contact visits are advisable at three to six months following treatment. Many renowned practitioners attempt to follow their clients' progress for several years (Axline, 1969; Moustakes, 1959). Klein (1960) has stated that the real test of treatment success cannot be evaluated until puberty, when the client's full identity unfolds.

Group Therapy

So far we have discussed primarily individual approaches to child therapy, but group counseling often is employed and preferred (Schopler & Galinsky, 1995). In reviewing outcome studies of group therapy, Abramowitz (1976) reported that a variety of techniques (activity, play, and verbal therapy and behavior modification) and outcome measures (self-concept academic performance) have been employed. About one-third yield positive results, one-third negative, and one-third mixed findings. On a comparative basis, the most positive results were obtained through behavioral approaches.

Among practitioners there is relative consensus about the children who will profit most from a group therapy experience. Weissman (1975) sampled 1200 clinicians with a 20-item questionnaire and found that group therapy was preferred for children who need to address themselves to social inhibitions or to impulsive acting out behavior. Thus, group therapy provides an excellent medium for children with interpersonal difficulties who need to learn to identify their mistaken interpersonal goals.

Group therapy also has been shown to be useful with developing social skills (Hepler, 1991), and socially withdrawn children (Axline, 1969). When sociometric choice was used as a criterion of change, those students who were judged by their peers to be of low social acceptance and who received a model reinforcement counseling program made significantly more gain in social acceptance than similar students who received counseling without models or a control group that did not receive counseling (Hansen, Niland, & Zani, 1969). Models in this study were students who had been accorded high social acceptance by peers. The high and low social acceptance students met together and workers merely reinforced ideas, insights, and suggestions relevant to acceptable social behavior put forth by both groups of students.

Group work also may be preferred for dealing with children who have all experienced a similar situational stressor. Thus, groups for children of divorced parents or for children experiencing the stress of having to move are recommended (Weissman, 1975).

Practitioners recommend that children's groups be carefully structured. A group of four to six members is usually cited as the appropriate size to maximize constructive social interaction. However, dual group therapy also has been used, in which two children are placed together because it is believed that their personal or interpersonal difficulties are compatible yet different enough that they may be of assistance to each other. For example, one of the authors worked with two children in dual therapy who both were grappling with the knowledge that they had been adopted. Each child had learned about the adoption in a disturbing way (in one case by a peer and in the other by a sibling). Both felt inferior to their siblings. One had responded by withdrawing from family and peers. The second child seemed to mask her concerns by constant activity; but her activity was so frenzied that she too had few friends. The children reached each other on common issues. The second child, feeling befriended, became more controlled, and the first one began to model the second's gregariousness.

In group therapy, the length of the session should vary with the children's ages. Children between five and eight years should generally meet for no more than about 40 to 60 minutes. For children from nine to 12, groups may last longer, from one to one-and-a-half hours. As for the frequency of sessions, younger children may need to meet more than once a week to maintain changes, while older children can usually assimilate ideas from weekly sessions.

Attention also must be paid to group composition. In the early days of child counseling, therapists recommended single sex groups (Dimick & Huff, 1970). This idea has not been supported by most current writers unless the children comprising the groups are particularly conflicted about issues of sex roles and sex identification. It also is important that children be at about the same cognitive and social developmental level. Developmental homogeneity is more important than absolute age.

As a whole, more communication rules need to be set with groups than in individual therapy with children. Dimick and Huff (1970) recommend telling the children that the groups are an opportunity to really listen to one another and to look at problems and find solutions. Keat (1974) tells his child group members that they will be expected to cooperate with one another. Additionally, he insists that children listen to one another and not interrupt, that only one person may talk at a time, and that the group will stay on one topic until all agree that they have finished talking about it. The practitioner also should spend considerable time making certain that the children realize the importance of keeping group activity confidential and that they know what the concept of confidentiality means.

Again the workers' theoretical approach will guide the leadership style (Shulman, 1992). Group therapists and therapists differ in how much they interpret conflict or how much they allow children to "work through" conflicts for themselves. According to Abramowitz's (1976) review, although the behavior modification approach resulted in more positive outcomes than the other approaches, it is impossible to conclude that this approach is significantly more effective in all cases. Regardless of how directive and/or interpretive the worker is, it is generally perceived to be the leader's responsibility to define and set group goals, help the children move towards those goals, and maintain the group's limits. Since most children's defensive structures are not well-developed, the leader also may need to actively stop or prevent a member from being rejected or verbally attacked.

A variety of activities may be used in conjunction with the group discussion. The leader may direct group work with art, writing, reading, or structured interpersonal activities. A number of group games may facilitate interchange. For example, the children may be told to look in a mirror and describe what they see, what they like and dislike. Children may be told that they can go to a "magic store" and purchase anything they want. Group discussion follows about each member's choice. Recorded music can be used to establish a mood or provoke discussions about the ideas of a song. For a group of inhibited children, creating music with bells and drums, etc., can facilitate interaction. Open-ended play therapy may be employed. Highly unstructured groups such as open-ended play therapy groups usually are comprised of fewer members, about three or four, and highly aggressive children are generally excluded. As a rule, the more disturbed the members of the group, the more structured the group should be.

Research about group effectiveness with children is relatively encouraging. Yet, the variety of approaches makes the task of empirical investigation quite overpowering. The groups differ in all combinations of size, composition, age, activities, and leadership style. Ultimately, research needs to focus upon specific techniques appropriate for specific children.

Professional Issues

We have talked about plans to facilitate client expression of affect and constructive activity. The effective child welfare worker also must monitor his or her own attitudes and behavior. As we discussed in Chapter 6, the humanistic theorists have written adamantly and prolifically about how important the practitioner's overall adjustment is in determining the clinical progress. Their research about the importance of the core conditions now is broadly accepted as a necessary (though not always a sufficient) condition for effective therapy. Gardner (1975) summarizes characteristics about effective child practitioners. They like children; they can project themselves into the child's situation; they can react and use insights from their own memories about growing up; they have the capacity to express warmth and excitement; they are nurturing and can express strong parental impulses; they are flexible and creative; they tolerate frustration and can accept failures. On top of projecting these overall qualities, effective child practitioners consistently monitor their feelings and behavior to assure that they are not responding to particular clients in counter-therapeutic ways. As another way of conceptualizing this issue, the child practitioner checks that he or she is not falling into a countertransference mode where actions and statements reflect the worker's needs, not the child's. Child therapy places special stress that may elicit countertransference. It is very easy to respond to a child client as a parent, especially if these needs have been thwarted or frustrated in the practitioner's private life. The worker may find himself or herself responding like an angry or critical parent. The worker may become over-solicitous, similar to a smothering or overprotective parent. Another signal of countertransference may be the practitioner's feeling frequently bored during the sessions. The boredom may indicate that the practitioner is expecting his or her own needs to be met in the sessions.

It also is very easy for a child welfare worker to regress along with the child. The younger the child, the more likely is countertransference regression to occur. In these cases, the child welfare worker begins playing with the child instead of responding therapeutically to the child's play. One signal of regression spurred by countertransference may be the worker's making childlike reflections or interpretations. Or, practitioners may realize that they am feeling very defensive. Many children are initially negative or hesitant about counseling. The worker should be able to analyze these responses in the context of the child's total adaptation. For example, the child may feel anxious about the practitioner's stance of neutrality if the child is used to being told what to do. Other children may feel uncomfortable about the lack of structure in therapy. If the worker finds himself or herself responding defensively to the child's hesitancy, possibly the practitioner's own childlike needs for security and acceptance have been provoked.

When a child specialist recognizes signs of countertransference, he or she should include professional consultation in the case treatment plan. If these reactions cannot be successfully resolved, referral of the child client to another practitioner may be in order.

Referrals

A critical aspect of a treatment plan is knowing when and to whom to refer. Child welfare workers may refer a client to another worker or to a qualified therapist, as exemplified in the previous section on countertransference. The worker also may refer when psychophysiological intervention may be helpful and when milieu therapy seems needed. There are a variety of psychophysiological and milieu approaches, and we shall summarize the major aspects of each.

Psychophysiological Approaches

The psychophysiological approaches assume that at least part of maladjustment is organically based and that once pathology is expressed, psychosocial stresses exacerbate the symptomatology. The psychophysiologically oriented child practitioner probably accepts one or more of several basic assumptions: (1) psychological and physiologic treatments are not mutually exclusive and often are additive; (2) relief of a child's suffering (from depression or anxiety, for example) is a worthwhile goal, even if "the cause" of the problem remains unknown and unknowable; and (3) a child cannot achieve optimal functioning if the possibility of dysfunction is ignored (LeVine, 1985). The healthy child prompts less negative reactions from others. As others become warmer and more accepting to the child, symptomatology decreases further. Reduction of the physiological disturbance curbs the child's destructive cycle of interaction with others. Most psychophysiological approaches can be included under the rubric of shock therapy, psychosurgery, or psychoactive drugs.

The psychophysiological approach of shock therapy in child treatment was pioneered by Loretta Bender (1955). As early as 1940, she employed electroshock therapy with schizophrenic children. She theorized that shock stimulated maturing and patterning of undeveloped nervous systems. She claimed many gains and that 25% of her treated children demonstrated higher long-term adjustment than the nonshock control group. Nevertheless, a high percentage of her experimental group was schizophrenic on follow-up so that many believe her use of shock therapy to be unsupported and of questionable ethical value. Today, electrical shock therapy is not used to treat schizophrenics. No authorities advocate its use in children (LeVine, 1985).

Psychosurgical approaches with children were initiated by Narabayashi (1972). Severing a part of the amygdala or posterior hypothalamus, Narabayashi (1972) reported calming effects on some uncontrollably aggressive children. No doubt the reader can quickly generate the sharp ethical issues psychosurgery has aroused. Can there be an appropriate reason for permanently severing nervous tissue in a child's brain? Moreover, how can the relative effectiveness of these approaches be assessed since it would be unethical to conduct sham surgery with control children?

Psychotropic medication is basic to treatment for a number of organically based disorders, such as epilepsy and some forms of hyperactivity. In treating many syndromes, psychiatrists who specialize in psychopharmacology have not developed a systematic theory about what medication and quantities to employ. In fact, the mechanism by which many of the drugs affect children's behavior is little understood. If the medicine ameliorates symptoms, it may be that physiological imbalances are being corrected. So far as is known, psychotropic drugs ameliorate symptoms, just as aspirin relieves the pain of a toothache. The relief may be of value for its own sake, but the diseased tooth has not been corrected. Increasingly, the drug effects are providing clues about psychologic mechanisms involved in mental symptoms and behavioral disturbance (LeVine, 1985).

The psychophysiologically oriented practitioners offer several guidelines for employing psychopharmacological treatment with children. First, they point out the importance of teaching parents about the uses and limitations of the drugs. Thorough parent education helps to ensure that parents will administer the appropriate dosage to children. Parents have been known to alter dosages given to children because of their own needs. The dosage of a tranquilizer may be increased, for example, when a parent "is having a difficult day." Parents also are educated to watch for possible side effects of particular medications. In this way, the parents help the practitioner decide upon the best type and dosage of medication (Chess & Hassibi, 1978). Psychotherapists who specialize in psychopharmacology explain to parents and others that the amount of medication must be measured carefully when treating the child. Children tend to vary more in sensitivity and reactions to the drugs than adults. Recommended dosages must be uniquely determined, beginning with small amounts and gradually increasing dosage until the desired effect is achieved. Feedback about the effect of the increasing dosages should be systematically sought from parents, teachers, and others closely involved with the child. Most specialists recommend that children be given "drug holidays." Every few months, preferably when the child is out of school and his or her quality performance need not be demanded, all medication should be terminated for several days. The drug holiday seems to help prevent the development of side effects and to assure whether or not the psychopharmacological treatment needs to be continued (Freedman, Kaplan, & Sadock, 1976).

Although nonmedical child therapists cannot prescribe psychotropic drugs, all child clinicians need familiarity with the types of drugs and their effects so that they can communicate intelligently with other professionals and clients' parents about the efficacy of psychopharmacological treatment with a given child. With some understanding of the possible uses and limitations of these drugs, the child practitioner or therapist can make wise decisions about when to refer a child to a physician for possible drug intervention.

Milieu Therapy

In the milieu approaches, the daily environment is ordered as a partial or complete psychotherapeutic program. The social worker refers a child to programs when the child and/or family is too disturbed to be assisted by short-term outpatient interventions. Types include residential living centers, special education classes, and therapeutic summer camps.

Residential Treatment

One poignantly difficult decision that a child practitioner periodically faces is, "Should this child be institutionalized?" The child specialist may encounter this question when parents or teachers no longer feel able to cope with the child or when the specialist's interventions have created little noticeable impact. Unfortunately, the decision to institutionalize is usually based upon negative rather than positive reasons. The child is institutionalized because all else has failed.

Before the child welfare worker and family decide to institutionalize the child, they should consider several factors. First, the child needs contact with nurturing parents. In residential treatment, adult figures hopefully will respond positively to the child, but they cannot provide the ongoing interaction of natural parents. If the child is separated from parents, feelings of loss and depression about separation from parents generally emerge, and these emotional problems must be dealt with as well as the previous emotional problems. It also should be kept in mind that in residential treatment, a child's interactions with peers usually is limited to his or her own age group. The child is separated from experiences of dealing with older and younger siblings. For this and other reasons, Freedman, Kaplan, and Sadock (1976) write, "Cure, whatever that may mean, is rarely an attainable goal for children in residential treatment" (P. 1138). In one study, Lovaas, et al. (1973) reported that even among autistic children, those raised at home improved more than those raised in institutional settings.

Ideally, the residential center should include specific programs for the child that foster development in the cognitive, affective, personal, and social domains. Unfortunately, many centers are merely custodial, while others offer no more than hospital maintenance and a regular visit to a therapist. Given the above limitations, are there any possible reasons for institutionalizing a child? The answer is a cautious "yes." If the family system is very pathological and the family members indicate an unwillingness or inability to change, it may be preferable to live away from the home. Even so, foster care placement, which maintains the sense of a family unit, may be preferable to institutionalization. If the family can afford a highly specialized program offering much individual attention, residential treatment may facilitate a child's working through critical traumas and developing socially appropriate skills. Redl (1972) states that a good residential treatment center is characterized by:

- staff roles that are clearly delineated to the children
- daily routines that are a part of the therapeutic goals
- placing children in living groups so that their problems will not be exacerbated by one another, but instead so that they will be able to assist one another
- positive morale among staff
- lots of space and a variety of activities

As a whole, the child should be managed within the home as long as the family is able and willing to cooperate in treatment. Residential treatment is best viewed as a stopgap measure for breaking destructive family patterns. Once new adaptive patterns can be established, plans should be enacted to return the child to the home.

Summer Camps

Knopf (1979) recommends that therapeutic summer camps can offer a compromise in which a child lives in a structured therapeutic environment for part of the time while not being removed entirely from the family. The camps may be day treatment or residential. Ideally, they offer opportunity for children to develop social, personal, and physical skills, thereby increasing their sense of independence. They may be beneficial in helping some children learn to get along with peers without added academic stress of the school setting.

Special Education Classes

It seems logical that children may profit from help in special education classes if their problems lead to difficulties in getting along with peers, learning disabilities, attention problems, or academic lag. The difficulty is that we do not yet know which emotionally disturbed children are best served in what kinds of special education classrooms. For example, there is a high correlation between hyperactivity and learning difficulties so that hyperactive children are often referred to special education classes with highly individualized instruction. However, it is not well documented that these children learn more in such environments. Apparently, they seem less different in individualized classrooms (probably because other children are as active in these open environments as hyperactive children). The academic accomplishments of hyperactive children are less than other children in both environments (Routh, 1979).

Before recommending a maladjusted child to be placed in a special education class, Knopf (1979) asks workers to consider the following questions. Does the child feel a significant social stigma by being isolated from peers? Will the child's social development suffer because of a lack of healthy, adjusted peers to model? Is the special education classroom structured to allow gradual mainstreaming back into the traditional classroom so that the "hothouse" effect of a child losing gains once returned to the traditional setting, can be controlled? With the answers to these questions in mind, referral may be appropriate if the child's adjustment is so impaired that he or she is abused by or abuses peers or if the maladjustment is so significant that the child's ability to learn academic and social skills is largely blocked.

Summary

In developing a treatment plan, a variety of information must be synthesized. The child welfare worker will consider various facets of the child's development that have been gleaned through observation, formal interviews, and informal assessment of the child and parents. The child's and parents' values and their goals for treatment must be clarified. Once the worker has accumulated extensive background information, he or she selects therapeutic structures that offer most promise toward working through the child's dilemmas. A great variety of therapeutic structures are available: individual versus group therapy, play therapy, art therapy; and a number of specific techniques such as role-playing, storytelling, art therapy, and music therapy are possible. The goals of therapy and the stage of the therapeutic process help the worker and therapist select the appropriate technique. The child specialist considers the role of significant others in the child's dilemmas and brings them into the treatment plan for consultation for group therapy, or for support to the child whenever appropriate. In many cases, the child can be assisted best by seeking consultation or services from other professionals. It is the child welfare worker's ethical responsibility to know when to refer to physicians, special educators, and other professionals. Moreover, the worker must know him- or herself well to be certain that all proposed treatment procedures are designed to meet the child's best interests, not for the practitioner's or significant other's convenience.

Although each child is unique, therapy tends to follow broad stages from acceptance and forming a therapeutic alliance, to uncovering and understanding a client's problem, to changing maladaptive patterns and practicing new behaviors, and finally termination. Varied therapeutic structures and techniques will be helpful as the therapy progresses through the stages. For example, supportive techniques such as nondirective play therapy may be particularly helpful in building a therapeutic alliance. Storytelling techniques can help uncover and restructure maladaptive thinking. Role playing, behavioral rehearsal, and group therapy can help move the client to new appropriate stages.

The varied structures and techniques that comprise the treatment plan are the strategies that seem most likely to promote working through personal problems with a given client. The strategies provide an environment for but do not themselves create change in the client. Playing with a child, telling stories, and drawing can model good relating, but do not assure that significant conflicts are worked through or that new adaptive behaviors are learned. The amelioration of significant distress requires the systematic application of theoretical principles of human behavior within the strategic therapy setting. The child specialist needs to implement specific verbal and behavioral approaches that are a part of his or her theory of child therapy. In the next chapter, we demonstrate through an extended case analysis how various treatment strategies and a theoretical approach to child practice can be combined.

Part IV
Vulnerable Children

At this point, you are well aware that our sensitivity in listening to our children and in selecting the appropriate intervention strategies depends upon a number of factors, such as the extent of our knowledge about counseling theories, one's comfort in applying particular approaches, and our expertise in identifying the problem and outlining treatment steps. In addition, our sensitivity and effectiveness are enhanced by our knowledge about particular types of childhood needs. We are more likely to identify a child's problem if we are fully cognizant of the broad spectrum of children's special concerns. Moreover, certain clinical approaches are particularly applicable to particular kinds of issues.

However, attempting to overview the various special concerns of children is a difficult task. Hundreds of attempts have been made to classify childhood disorders, and none has been completely adequate. What we have chosen to do in this unit of the text is to provide an overview of the types of psychosocial stresses that can leave a child vulnerable to maladjustment. Thus, Chapters 12 through 14 identify the special concerns of children that are largely perpetuated by the children's interface with disturbed or adequate familial and broader social environments. These chapters will be of prime importance to social workers and other child practitioners who serve as child advocates. The causes as well as effective modes of intervention in child abuse and neglect are described in Chapter 12. The emotional difficulties for parents and impediments for aligning services for special needs children are discussed in Chapter 13. Chapter 14 identifies situations where children have new families. Major topics include children of divorce, adopted children, and children in foster care. We will see that in many cases, the child's problems will abate dramatically if we correct the familial and social disruption.

Throughout Part IV, we will attempt to apply principles presented earlier in the text. We suggest means for setting up treatment plans that are appropriate to the special needs of a given child.

Chapter 12
Physical Abuse, Sexual Abuse, and Neglect

Scope of Problem

Numerous investigators have tried to estimate the magnitude of the problem of child abuse and neglect in the United States. Since the early 1960s, with the identification of the battered child syndrome (Kempe, 1962), numerous studies have estimated the number of incidences of child abuse. These estimates vary widely and are based upon different definitions of abuse, different designs to the studies, and varied sources of data. In addition, problems involved in trying to accurately estimate the magnitude of this social problem have to do with differences in the statutory definitions of abuse and neglect, in the ages of children covered by the laws, and in the types of cases.

Most studies and estimates show child abuse incidences on the increase. In 1992 state and private child protective service agencies received almost 2 million referrals on almost 3 million children (National Center on Child Abuse and Neglect, 1994). Reports more than doubled from 1980 to 1992. With the passage of the Child Abuse Prevention and Treatment Act (CAPTA) in 1974, states were required to have mandatory reporting of child abuse and neglect (Wells, 1995).

A unique epidemiological study was conducted by Nagi (1977). Using incidence rates for the state of Florida, Nagi extrapolated the reported cases of suspected abuse and neglect to cover the entire U.S. population. In arriving at a national incidence rate, Nagi computed three estimates: low, medium, and high.

Nagi (1977) estimates the national frequency of child abuse from approximately 600,000 (low estimate) to 1,000,000 (medium estimate) to 1,400,000 (high estimate). In his analysis of the demographics of child abuse, Nagi (1977) reports that children under the age of 5 years are the most vulnerable (38.1%) to abuse and neglect, while the sex of the child does not appear to be a significant variable. There is little difference in the incidence of abuse and neglect by the sex of the child. As for ethnicity, the highest incidence rates per 1,000 children are associated with Anglos, but the incidence rate for Blacks is close behind.

Nagi's statistics from Florida and corresponding population for the United States indicate that allegations in reported cases would place mothers as the most frequent abusers, followed by both parents and then fathers. A sizable proportion of stepfathers also are reported.

Statistics from the U.S. Department of Health and Human Services delineate the categories of child maltreatment as follows; neglect 53%, physical abuse 26%, sexual abuse 14%, emotional abuse 5%, and all other forms 22% (DHHS, 1994). Nagi (1977) also compiled data concerning the type of abuse and neglect. (Beatings (16.0%) are the most common form of child abuse. Neglect falls into the major categories of disorganized family life (31.0%), left unattended (21.6%), medical neglect (16.0%), and lack of food, clothing, or shelter (12.5%).

Sexual abuse is perhaps the least discussed and form of child abuse, yet victims of child sexual abuse are found in almost every practice setting (Conte, 1995). Experts usually concede that the unreported incidence of sexual abuse among children is considerably higher than the reported incidence. An in-depth study of 930 San Francisco women identified a history of child sexual abuse (including rape) in 38% of the women before age 18 (Russell, 1983). A number of other studies establish that sexual abuse affects a sizable number of children (Finkelhor, 1984). Further, the usual victim in sexual abuse is a female child; however, the reported incidence of sexual abuse of male children is on the increase.

In addition, the statistics pale when confronted with a single abused, neglected, or sexually abused child (Chambers, 1980). Few children suffer more emotional and physical pain than abused children. Although there is public concern about this pain children suffer, almost all resources have been directed to treatment of parents (Cohen, 1979). A review of the literature on abuse reveals a large number of articles addressing family and parental therapy but far fewer on specific treatment for the child (Kinard, 1980). An approach for children, Reattachment Therapy (LeVine & Frazier, 1983), is presented in this chapter.

Definitions

Definitions of abuse and neglect vary somewhat from state to state. The Federal definition taken from the CAPTA definition states in part: child abuse and neglect "means the physical or mental injury, sexual abuse or exploitation, negligent treatment, or maltreatment of a child by a person who is responsible for the child's welfare..." (42 Sec. 510g, 1992). Chase's (1975) classic summary of what is usually meant by these terms can be a useful guide. According to Chase,

> Child abuse is the deliberate and willful injury of a child by a caretaker—hitting, beating with a belt, cord, or other implement, slamming against the wall, burning with cigarettes, scalding with hot water, locking in a dungeon, hogtying, torturing, even killing. It involves active, hostile, aggressive physical treatment. Child neglect is more passive negative treatment characterized by a parent or custodian's lack of care and interest, and includes not feeding, not clothing, not looking after, not nurturing. The legal definitions vary in different states; so does the degree of harm done to the child (p. 1).

While this is a good definition of abuse and neglect, it does not encompass an explanation of sexual abuse. The identification of sexual abuse is relatively recent and few treatment approaches are empirically tested. Definition of sexual abuse includes behavior ranging from exhibitionism to forcible rape. For example, one researcher defined as a sexual attack the exposure of genitals by a male to a child. Another definition required some form of physical contact (Elwell, 1979). In addressing such a complex issue as human sexually, there is a wide range of acts which children are exposed, from fondling to intercourse (Conte, 1995).

To encompass all forms of abuse and exploitation within its mandate, the National Center on Child Abuse and Neglect adopted the following tentative definition of child sexual abuse:

> Contacts or interactions between a child and an adult when the child is being used for the sexual stimulation of that adult or another person. Sexual abuse also may be committed by a person under the age of 18 when that person is either significantly older than the victim or when the abuser is in a position of power or control over another child.

> (Child Sexual Abuse, 1981)

An area of sexual abuse which appears to be on the increase is the use of children in pornography (O'Brien, 1983). The amended, Child Abuse Prevention and Treatment Act (CAPTA) of 1974 defines sexual abuse to include the obscene filming of children as follows:

> the obscene or pornographic photographing, filming, or depiction of children for commercial purposes, or the rape, molestation, incest, prostitution, or other such forms of sexual exploitation of children under circumstances which indicate that the child's health or welfare is harmed or threatened thereby . . .(subsection 5(3), 1992)

Causes

Social and behavioral scientists have looked for the "cause" of child abuse so that it can be eradicated. We now recognize that the types and causes of child maltreatment are multiple (Wells, 1995) Eradication will require extensive societal changes and intervention in family patterns that are deeply entrenched in our society. "Spare the rod and spoil the child" is a maxim that appears to be practiced still in the United States despite our advanced knowledge about parenting and effective ways of modifying behavior through the use of positive reinforcement.

The authors' clinical experience with abusive families reveals that an older sibling may carry out the abuse of a younger child through either overt or subtle orders from the parents. These attacks are severe and may include attempted drowning, poisoning, and setting fire to clothing. Parents refuse to see these attacks as serious and may shrug them off (Tooley, 1977).

Generally, child maltreatment is spurred by a combination of parents' personalities, children's temperaments, and stresses (e.g., poverty (Wells, 1995)), which overload the family system. There is little consensus about the characteristics of the abusing parent (National Research Council, 1993). Parents have been reported as disturbed, immature, narcissistic, egocentric, or aggressive (Freedman, Kaplan, & Sadock, 1976). However, most abusive parents are not very different from average parents. They love their children and want the best for them. They also get angry at their children and do things they later regret. While child abuse cuts across nearly all social categories, it is especially likely to occur among young and uneducated parents, for their self-esteem is often low and their need for social support is usually high. In their immaturity, they expect too much from their babies. When the infant cries, they interpret the crying as deliberate mis-behavior, intended to upset and anger them.

Many abusive parents were themselves victim of neglect or abuse as children (Egeland, 1988). Parents with poor interpersonal skills, without family and friends as resources, are ill-prepared to raise children.

> When a parent is asked to describe the child in detail, a worker may find that the description focuses on how well the child meets the parent's needs. The child is perceived as a "good child" if he is capable of meeting these expectations and as a "bad child" if he does not. In asking for the parents' ideas of appropriate behavior for a child of a given age, one discovers that their perception has little relationship to normal child development. An abusive parent states, with ap-proval, that a four-year-old little girl is good because she has helped to toilet train her two-year-old brother, clean up the living room every morning, and is always watching out for her two younger siblings, playing with them and show-ing concern for their safety. Of course, she also is expected to take major respon-sibility for her own care.

(Kemper & Kemper, 1976, p. 122)

When the child fails to successfully complete these parental tasks, the parent strikes out at the child, perhaps even in a systematic form of torture. Child abuse is not usually premeditated, nor is it a rational act. Most abusive parents are sorry and display deep guilt after the abuse (Kempe & Kempe, 1976).

The general public finds it inconsistent that such a loving parent can inflict so much pain on the child. Related health professionals see these parents as being extremely solicitous. Parental low self-esteem, a high need for nurturing, use of alcohol, and isolation are identified as common characteristics of abusive parents (Justice & Justice, 1976).

According to Anderson and Lauderdale (1982), approximately 10% of the abusive parent population is considered psychotic or aggressively psychopathic. Those that are extremely abusive to newborns are especially prone to psychopa-thology. Resnick (1969) studied the personalities of parents who killed their infants within 24 hours of life. He reported that were severely disturbed, often suicidal. They overvalued their children and believed that they killed them as "acts of mercy," or that they had been ordered by God to kill their children.

In some cases, one parent observes and tolerates the abuse by the other parent. In such cases, one wonders whether both parents are psychologically disturbed or whether the primary pathology leading to child abuse comes about only when both parents are together. A persistent trait that appears in a number of studies is that the parents are intolerant of the children they abuse. They spend less time in auditory and tactile stimulation of these children. They are frustrated with their hyperactivity or slow development. Along these lines, Wolkenstein (1977) worked extensively with parents who had a disproportionate fear of abusing their children. He reported that most wanted these children, but began feeling anger toward them even before their birth.

For more discussion of family dynamics, please refer to Chapters 7 and 10. We now will examine the physical, psychological, and developmental impacts child abuse may have on children.

Impacts

A backdrop to understanding the impact of abuse and neglect upon the individual child is evaluating the impact of abuse and neglect on societal institutions in a community. Of course, child abuse affects the family, but it also impacts on economics (through foster care payments, loss of work, etc.), health care, education, government agencies, and the media. Somehow child abuse touches everyone in a community (Brissett–Chapman, 1995).

Physical Impacts

Physical injuries to children range from subdural hematomas (bleeding in the skull), spinal fractures, burns, and scalding to more bizarre injuries. Less obvious injuries now are being identified and reported. Although bruises, welts, and lacerations may quickly heal, the trauma which produced them may permanently affect the central nervous system. Physical blows, shaking, neglect of infections, malnutrition, and water deprivation can cause brain damage or abnormal development. These may result in seizures, mental retardation, hearing and vision loss, cerebral palsy, and learning disabilities (Martin, 1980).

The mistreated child may suffer secondary physical problems because of poorer health care. When abused children are compared to children who have accidental trauma, Gregg & Elmer (1969) noted abused children are seven times more likely to have serious lapses in child care, such as lack of immunizations and proper hygiene. Studying infants in Australia, Oates, Davis, Ryan, and Stewart (1978) reported that abused infants had a five times greater chance for significant illness than the control group.

The lack of proper nutrition, particularly with neglected children, may result in anemia. Neglected infants are given bottles with water, Kool-Aid, or juice, which contain low levels of iron. The resulting behavior is a shorter attention span, poor learning ability, and apathy (Martin, 1980). Hearing loss from lack of medical attention for ear infections, below-average height, and poor weight gain are more common in abused children (Mayhall & Norgard, 1983). Recent research is documenting increasing links between abuse and subtle physical impairments.

Psychological Impacts

The psychological effects of maltreatment can be devastating. The clinical history of abused children shows failure to thrive, reduced height and weight, poor hygiene, irritability, and repressed personality (Freedman, Kaplan, & Sadock, 1976). The aggressive tendencies of abused children have been widely documented. Analytically oriented specialists speak of the child's tendency to identify with the aggressor. The analytically oriented specialists state that these children develop rudimentary superegos filled with violence. This violent superego formed through identification with the aggressor is redoubled by the child's frustration in not getting his or her own needs met. Since expression of the aggression would prompt more battering, the child suppresses it and becomes strongly passive and masochistic. As the child matures, he or she is likely to express this rage with his or her own children, and thus the pattern of violence is passed through families (Bender, 1974). Behaviorally oriented specialists also point to the child's identification with the abusing parent, but in this approach, the explanation is based on the modeling role of the parent. The parent models aggressive behavior, and even though the child is the target of the aggression, the child displays aggressive behavior against objects and other children. Years later, the formerly abused child becomes a parent who abuses his or her own children. Much research suggests that child abuse can lead to lifelong patterns of severe social maladjustment characterized by hostility, alcoholism, drug addiction, sexual difficulties, and inadequate parenting ability (Wells, 1995).

While many abused children become very aggressive, others are withdrawn, reclusive, or obsequious to others. The child feels alone and must use all of his or her energy to survive day to day. Living a confused, violent life, he or she may retreat to a fetal position and withdraw totally from others. Or the child may become the perfect child always eager to please the teacher as a way of avoiding abuse. This low self-esteem correlates with a higher self-abusive behavior. Green (1978) found that 8.3% of abused children with a mean age of 8.5 had attempted suicide. A total of 20% of them demonstrated self-mutilative behavior.

Abused children's emotional development is likely to be delayed in several areas. Kinard (1980) established differences between abused and nonabused children on psychological tests measuring self-concept, aggression, socialization with peers, establishment of trust, and separation from the mother. The test battery included the Piers–Harris Children's Self-Concept Scale, the Rosenzweig Picture-Frustration Study, and the Tasks of Emotional Development (TED) Test.

To summarize, the psychological impact of abuse or neglect is a list of numerous traits and characteristics that stalk a child into adulthood. The child faces parents with unrealistic expectations who do not meet his or her of basic needs, and the child attempts to survive in an environment of fear. The family may be under tremendous economic, social, and psychological stress. In this environment, many children can do little more than survive day to day, leaving little energy or time for normal child development.

Developmental Impacts

Abused and neglected children also may suffer developmental delays in areas such as IQ, learning ability, and language development (Martin, 1980). Often abused children have lower verbal abilities and more likely to be distracted than other children (Friedrich, Einbender, & Luecke, 1983). Developmental delay and deviation have been consistently correlated with abuse, although the exact developmental impact varies from study to study (Mayhall & Norgard, 1983). Martin (1980) reviewed the studies investigating the impact of abuse on intelligence development. While he found a variation of degree of impact, he concluded that abused children have lower IQs, use poorer language, and show less academic progress than nonabused children.

One study of abused children suggests that neglected children have a higher risk of mental retardation, 39%, than abused children, 24% (Kent 1976).

Research on developmental delay is complicated by compounding factors in experimental design as many of the children are receiving education and psychological intervention. Yet, even given clinical intervention, development of these children is delayed. An evaluation of children in three treatment programs reported abused children functioned poorly on motor, language, and cognitive skills (one standard deviation below the mean), but did not have serious delays (Cohen, 1979). Evaluation of Child Abuse and Neglect Demonstration Projects (1977) states that over 50% of abused children were behind (one or more standard deviations below the mean) on cognitive, language, and motor abilities. A number of research studies from around the world attest to the impaired cognition in abused and neglected children even as young as five months old (Martin, 1980).

Treatments can help children overcome delays to some degree. For example, one study (McKay, Sinisterra, McKay, Gomez, & Lloreda, 1978) suggests that cognitive delays can be overcome through intensive medical and nutritional treatment. Direct, specific therapies for individual children have provided some, but not complete, success (Martin, 1976).

In working with abused and neglected children, a good developmental assessment is necessary to alert the therapist to possible developmental delays. Treatment for these delays may necessitate medical, nutritional, educational, and social services.

Treatment of Abuse and Neglect

The first and foremost step in treatment to ensure the child's physical and emotional safety is to stop the abuse in the family. A discussion of family interventions is presented in Chapter 7, so here we will address treatments for the child.

Establishing a Relationship

An abused child comes from an environment in which he or she feels isolated and untrusting of adults. This world view tends to create the impression during clinical assessment that the abused child is less capable than he or she really is. Thus, in establishing contact with the child, the practitioner needs to be sensitive to and learn to work around these presenting behaviors.

Martin (1976) identified seven behaviors displayed by abused children which may present difficulty in assessment and in establishing contact:

1. *Hypervigilance*

   The child may feel threatened by the intense scrutiny inherent in the assessment for therapy. A preoccupation with every move, facial expressions, or other habits of the social worker is common for an abused child until he or she feels comfortable interpreting the social worker's nonverbal behavior. The child is easily distracted by anything that is unfamiliar.

2. *Fear of Failure*

   The abused child's efforts to avoid failure are tested during any evaluation session. Assessment should begin with simple, easily achievable tasks which progress to more difficult tasks. The child may be overcome with anxiety. The fear of failure may have been imprinted so strongly by parents with unrealistic expectations that the child has failed to internalize any positive feelings about his or her successes. If the child is assured he or she will not suffer punishment for a mistake or for sharing thoughts, then a basis for a relationship can be established.

3. *Difficulty Attending to Instructions*

   When faced with an evaluation task, most abused children react in one of two extremes. The child may grab materials and become aggressive in an attempt to control his or her environment. The other extreme is the child who withdraws and shuts out instructions. Inability of the child to focus on the task makes following instructions almost impossible.

4. *Touching objects*

   Abused children have over learned the lesson not to touch in many cases. This may result in grabbing toys or test materials in order to possess them. The child may continually glance at the social worker while reaching for a toy trying to read any dissatisfaction or disapproval. Permission to touch at will is usually not permitted by abusive parents who have unrealistic expectations of the children.

5. *Verbal Inhibition*

As we have explained, language development may be delayed in abused and neglected children. As a result, assessments which require verbal responses may require the social worker to prompt the child, and pictures often are helpful in eliciting meaningful answers from the child. The child's home environment may have taught him or her that it is dangerous to speak.

6. *Failure to Scan*

Many abused children impulsively select the first answer they come to, not realizing that a better solution may be found later. Instant direct feedback to a child's correct or incorrect responses may help the child to look for other alternatives.

7. *Passive-Aggressiveness and Resistance*

Abused children rarely will confront an examiner by refusing to attempt a task. As the tasks become more difficult and the threat of failure increases, the responses may be weak and may be shrugged off. The child may say "yes" but then do "no." The child may do things he or she wants to do, such as play with a toy when he or she just said "yes" to completing a paper/pencil evaluation. This is clearly a coping mechanism developed at home to do as the child wishes with minimal threat of abuse by the parent. At this point, the practitioner may begin to feel the frustration the parent faces every day.

Child welfare workers and therapists should convey new attitudes to the child such as

1. The therapist likes the child whether or not the child can do things.

2. The therapist wants to help the child with the problems he or she faces.

3. The therapist will not reject the child.

4. The therapist will not be surprised by what the child says, including detailed discussions of the abuses. (Martin, 1976)

In order to convey these attitudes, the practitioner must possess a good self-understanding of his or her own feelings and abilities to work with abused children. We now will explore these issues.

Professional Self Issues

Some studies raise the subject of the practitioner's values and personal abilities and gender to work with abused children and the parents who abuse them (Deblinger, Lippmann, Stauffer, & Finkelhor, 1994, Jackson & Nuttall, 1994). Mayhall and Norgard (1983) list a number of excellent questions the practitioner should honestly assess before working with these clients.

1. Can I use authority appropriately in the treatment process?

2. Do I have a strong support system in my personal life and long-term relationships?

3. Can I find a silver lining in every cloud? Am I optimistic?

4. Can I be objective in assessing situations by identifying pluses and minuses?

5. Can I handle myself in a crisis and in unfamiliar situations?

6. Basically, do I think people are good and want what is best?

7. Can I be accepting of different cultures, values, and child-rearing practices?

8. Can I plan ahead and stay on a course for a year or more and be able to anticipate the results?

9. Can I meet my personal needs away from the job so I do not depend on satisfaction from a child or his or her parents?

If the child welfare practitioner cannot answer yes to these questions, then serious consideration should be given to not working with abused children. The population of abused children and their parents can be very difficult to work with, and the reinforcements for the practitioner's efforts may be few and very delayed.

The practitioner's frustration can foster more distress to this vulnerable population. As well-meaning as a social worker may be, if one's professional self is not
suited to meeting the above criteria, then other client groups should be served.

Child's and Family's Resources

What strengths and competencies exist within a child and the family in overcoming the abuse cycle? With clients' developmental delays and possible physical
and emotional problems, the strengths on which to focus may not be apparent.
However, a very negative assessment may be a product of the social worker's
reaction to a painful situation and may not be fully objective. The parents' sincere
statements of love and caring for their child should not be ignored. Rebuilding
parental self-esteem can be facilitated by the understanding that the parent probably lacked loving, nurturing parenting (Helfer, 1987). The specialist may need
to look for strengths from the child's personality, from the extended family, and
from the community. Treatment goals are based upon an understanding of dys-
functions in the family, the child's maladjustment, and possible strengths.

Reattachment Therapy

We believe the primary unit for intervention for child abuse is the family; however, as cited above, the family often has been viewed as the only point of treatment. The victim, the child, may require not only emotional support and
understanding but also assistance in learning coping behaviors. A review of abuse
and neglect literature suggests that the child plays a larger role in abuse than
previously believed (Friedrich & Borinskin, 1976). Special needs children may
develop maladaptive interaction patterns with parents, such as being the scapegoat for family stress or creating strong feelings of guilt in the parents who are
resentful or feel responsible for their exceptionalities.

We need to recognize that the children may not change just because their
environment changes. Thus, the abused child who harbors much hostility and
clings in a passive-aggressive fashion to a parent may continue to provoke hostile
behavior from a parent who is attempting to curb an abusive pattern.

We also should keep in mind the tenets of family system theory that teach us
that if any member of a family changes, changes in the overall system may occur.
Thus, if an abused child changes and learns appropriate ways of assertiveness,

he or she may modify the violence in the family. A practitioner may serve a vital role in helping abused children to modify their own behavior so that they do not provoke and instead avoid abuse.

A model, "Reattachment Therapy" (Frazier & LeVine, 1983), has been developed for ameliorating the developmental disturbances associated with early abuse in young victims, as well as enhancing the ability of the child to actively reestablish a more healthy bond with the primary caretaker. Reattachment Therapy is accomplished through the use of two overlapping phases of intervention. The first, Attachment Substitution, involves the systematic formation of a substitutive attachment bond between the child practitioner and child so that the youngster can experience relief from symptoms prompted by the lack of a consistent and benign attachment figure. The second, Parental Attachment Inducement, is geared toward aiding the child to comport him- or herself in order to elicit attachment behavior from others, particularly the original caretaker.

In the attachment substitution phase, the practitioner employs the following steps:

1. The worker creates a benign, permissive, and warm atmosphere. Severely battered children rarely respond immediately to such social overtures. Their experiences have taught them that adults are frequently violent, punitive, and unpredictable. As such, they justifiably have little desire to readily entrust yet another strange adult with their affection. Thus, the establishment of an accepting, warm, and nonpunitive climate is essential to the facilitation of a substitutive attachment bond, and failure to create such an atmosphere jeopardizes further attempts to bring the victims into therapeutic relationships. Refusal to scold, punish, or conditionally accept the young child, especially during this initial phase of treatment, is a basic factor in establishing such a climate.

2. The practitioner stimulates attachment bonding from the child by actively gratifying various development needs. The exact attaching behaviors to be elicited from the child depend, among other things, upon the child's given level of psychosocial development (Schaffer & Emerson, 1964). From birth to 2 months of age, the child learns to be responsive to adults as opposed to other objects in the environment. Then, the child begins to discriminate among adults, a skill which normally appears from 3 to 7 months of age. Next, the child learns to approach the caretaker when wanting physical or

psychological nurturance, and the selectivity of this major step is apparent in the appearance of separation or stranger anxiety about this time. Finally, by age 1 to 3 years, the child and caretaker enter into a goal-directed relationship in which they actively accommodate their behaviors to each other.

The unique parameters of Reattachment Therapy dictate that the ministrations of basic needs be used so that the child learns that the practitioner and other adults can be helpful in meeting the child's needs. Feedings, treating accidental cuts or scratches, occasionally facilitating sleep, and changing soiled clothes (with a same-sex aide available) are just a few of the ways in which the social worker can facilitate a reparative bond.

The second phase of Reattachment Therapy is a systematic changing of the abused child's behavior so that he or she is a more attractive child, more actively inducing affectionate responses from the primary caretaker. If the abused child is removed from the permanent care of the abusing parent, then the attachment inducement techniques to be described are aimed at teaching the child how to exhibit attaching behaviors toward the new caretakers. The guiding parameters for affecting attachment inducement are

1. The therapist focuses upon improving the child's physical appearance. The typically unattractive or unusual appearance of the young abuse victim makes him or her a likely target for displaced aggression. Though there are inherent limitations in those dimensions of the child's physical appearance which can be affected in psychotherapy, treatment interventions can be focused toward improving those aspects of the victim's physical appearance which are susceptible to intervention, such as personal hygiene, bizarre body movements, or treatable physical anomalies. For example, one mother, Mrs. B., reported that she often became "disgusted" at her daughter's crossed eyes and stuttering, inaudible speech. The practitioner referred the child for appropriate speech and ophthalmic care, as well as reinforcing gains in these behaviors during treatment. As the child's speech and, wandering eye improved, her mother commented that she was finding Linda much more "attractive and lovable." Additionally, during most sessions, the practitioner washed the child's face and combed her unkempt hair. Occasionally, her hair was even worked into various styles. Linda's mother seemed to have noted and appreciated these appearance improvements, for after

several months of this, she began to bring her daughter to treatment clean, with new clothes.

2. The practitioner reinforces aggression neutralizing behaviors. Certain attachment-eliciting behaviors, such as looking, smiling, laughing, cooing, and reaching tend to neutralize aggression. Actively rewarded in treatment, these behaviors will serve to retard the overt discharge of the caretaker's violence. For example, Linda's eye contact was systematically reinforced and increased, and this behavior positively transferred to interactions with her mother. Mrs. B. mentioned that Linda didn't seem to be "hanging her head so much lately" at one point in treatment. Further, the child's mother reported that after spanking Linda on one occasion, she "looked into my daughter's eyes and just felt sick. . . ." Thus, increased eye contact and other aggression-inhibiting behaviors can help to minimize future abusive episodes.

3. The practitioner focuses upon decreasing clinging behavior. Clinging behaviors are characterized by desperately holding the caretaker, acting helpless, and crying and throwing fits when the caretaker leaves, even momentarily. To the extent that trust can be reestablished during the substitutive phase of therapy, the clinging behavior will subside, since the roots of this difficulty lie with the desperate need for bonding. Once the major task of establishing trust between the child and practitioner is accomplished, shaping of the child's behaviors toward psychological individuation (Mahler, Pine, & Bergman, 1975) from the attachment relationship can proceed. The practitioner encourages the child to attempt novel activities, and points out and reinforces the youngster's autonomous behaviors with praise. For example, the therapist once commented to Linda, "Today I am sitting farther away from you, and you are doing just fine." On another occasion, the therapist pointed out, "Today I had to leave the room for a moment and you were such a big girl and stayed by yourself—you knew I would be back!" Even attempting a novel puzzle was responded to with such individuation oriented remarks as, "Look how fast you have figured out that new puzzle—and you'd never even seen it before. It was new, and you weren't even afraid of it!"

The practitioner focuses upon eliminating behaviors in the child which frequently preceded the abusing parent's attacks. These behaviors are typically described by the abusing parents with such phrases as, "When he does that, I could just knock his head off," or "It's almost as if he were just begging for it, so I gave it to him!"

For example, Linda's self-mutilation and refusal to go to sleep at night without an emotional outburst greatly provoked her mother, and the removal of these behaviors relieved this pressure, decreasing the probability of further abusive episodes. The removal of her stuttering verbal style had a similar effect. As another example, the child's mother described to her therapist that, "I always lose it when Linda wets her pants—she's just a big baby." Linda reenacted these traumatic episodes in play therapy. When the social worker suggested that the baby doll had wet her pants, Linda began to yell, "Bad girl" at the toy and hit it with a larger doll. At this point, the practitioner took the large doll from the child and began to "point out" to it that the baby doll had simply gone a very long time without being able to go to the toilet and that severe punishment is uncalled for. The child hesitated momentarily, then moved away from the toys. A few moments later, however, she walked over to the mother doll, picked it up, and said to it, "Mommy, it's okay if baby wets her pants, it's not so bad." Now Linda could view her own wetting in a realistic manner, and thus could openly talk about the topic, making appropriate toilet-training more possible. Omission training, as well as nonpunitive ministration of the situation when "mistakes" occasionally occurred in therapy, gradually led to a decrease in the amount of times that the young girl urinated in her clothes, thereby decreasing the overall possibility of an attack being incurred by this situation.

4. The practitioner terminates when the child has become reattached to his or her caretaker and normal developmental processes have been restored. The final phase of attachment inducement involves the practitioner's gradually fading the intensity and frequency of contacts with the child, while encouraging the child to establish bonding with the original caretaker. This termination must be accomplished very gradually, so that trust and affectionate bonds formed with the treating person are not disrupted prematurely, restimulating original feelings of rejection. The child needs time to talk about the upcoming separation and to work through emotions prompted by it.

In Reattachment Therapy, as in any collateral treatment, the counseling of family members should be coordinated. For example, at one point in treatment of Linda's mother, her therapist noted that Linda was displaying signs of potential depression. The child was seen for daily therapy sessions until the crisis period had ended. The termination of treatment for Linda was planned, to some extent, to coincide with the resolution of Mrs. B's own issues in treatment.

Play Therapy

It has often been said that play is children's work. Children use play as a natural method of expressing their feelings and problems; therefore, play may be a useful assessment and treatment modality. The practitioner may provide guidance and interpretation of play for the child, or the child may direct play in a nondirective approach. If abused children with low self-esteem are difficult to manage in therapy sessions, depressed, or aggressive, they may greatly benefit from instituting play therapy. Children frustrated by limitations imposed by special handicapping conditions can use play therapy to vent their feelings without danger to themselves or other children. As a caution, the behavior of a severely disturbed abused child may become very volatile in a totally unstructured play environment. Thus, the practitioner needs to balance the creation of a free and supportive environment with the structure required because of the child's temperament and problems.

Sexual Abuse and Incest

Sexual abuse and incest are now considered separate from other forms of child abuse and neglect. The sexual abuse literature has matured from personal and case descriptions to theory development and research. Reports of sexual maltreatment have dramatically increased from 1,975 in 1976 to 71,961 in 1983 (American Humane Association, 1985). Because of the societal taboo against adult/child sex and the limitations child victims have in exposing the crime, the number of incidences reported is probably a small percentage of the actual cases. Three major studies suggest that 16 percent of all men and 27 percent of all women have sexual contact with an adult before age 16 (Finkelhor, Hotaling, Lewis & Smith, 1990). Much sexual abuse is perpetrated by close family members over the period between ages of 3 and 5 (Sanford, 1980). Most victims are unable to tell anyone of the sexual abuse and may suffer substantial and long-lasting emotional scars (Finkelhor, et al., 1990).

Affects of Sexual Abuse

The use of children for adult sexual stimulation, whether through child pornography, abuse, or incest, damages the child in seven basic ways (O'Brien, 1983).

1. *Psychological*

   The introduction of sexual activity too early in a person's development strips part of the childhood. Children are not prepared for strong emotional feelings associated with sex (Helfer, 1987).

2. *Low Self-esteem*

   Sexual abuse produces withdrawal from friends and depression, and is personally degrading and destructive. The child's attempts to gain self-respect are confused by the continued love/hate relationship with the parent.

3. *Exploitation*

   By the very definition of sexual abuse, the child is being used by an adult to meet the adult's own needs. Some perpetrators may try to blame the child for their actions, but should hold no more weight than blaming a child for any crime an adult may commit.

4. *Creates Vulnerability*

   Children are dependent upon adults, so children are vulnerable. The use of the child sexually creates more pressure, and anxiety, so that the child begins to interpret dependency as dangerous.

5. *Distorted View of Sexuality*

   Although some children do not realize it until they mature, sexual abuse creates an abnormal view of the sexual relationship. Victims of child pornography may relate to a later sexual relationship strictly in terms of sexual performance.

6. *Violates Child's Privacy*

   Pornography violates a child's privacy every time a magazine or film is viewed. If an incestuous relationship is discovered, the child's privacy must be invaded by police and child practitioners.

7. *Distorts Moral Development*

As a child's knowledge of right and wrong develops during the time he or she may be a victim of sexual abuse (age 9–11), inappropriate moral development may occur. Many cases of incest occur in churchgoing, disciplined, rigid families (Sanford, 1980), creating a sense of hypocrisy and confusion among the victims about what constitutes morality.

Few persons fail to recognize that sexual use of children affects their normal, healthy development. Children are not prepared to cope physically, emotionally, socially, or intellectually with an adult sexual relationship regardless of how the children may feel about the experience.

Factors Affecting the Impact of Abuse

Several variables affect the intensity of the impact of sexual abuse upon children. Boys who have been sexually abused usually have greater problems adjusting than girls (Kemper & Helfer, 1980) as many theorists believe it is culturally more acceptable for girls to have sexual experiences with adults than for boys (Mayhall & Norgard, 1983). The longer the duration of the sexual abuse, the greater the likelihood for severe damage. About 70 percent of sexual abuse victims are abused more than one time and over a long period of time (Conte, 1995). The age of the child at the time of discovery of the sexual abuse in part determines the psychological effects. Kemper & Helfer (1980) argue that younger children do not understand the mores of society, and therefore, sexual abuse may create fewer problems for a young child than for a sexually abused adolescent. Sexual abuse ranges from violent physical attacks upon the child to caressing and hugging. Thus, the amount of force or violence used by the perpetrator may greatly affect the prognosis for the child. The manner in which the perpetrator encouraged silence and cooperation may determine whether or not the child assimilates the experiences as highly destructive and permanent. How professionals and significant others react to the situation once the sexual abuse is revealed greatly affects how the child will react.

Clearly, the effects of sexual abuse can vary according to a number of intrapsyche and extrapsyche factors. In a very extensive review of the sexual abuse literature to that time, Browne and Finkelhor (1986) report that at least some proportion of the victim population have significant initial affects of fear,

anxiety, depression, anger, hostility, aggression, and sexually inappropriate behavior. Frequently reported long-term effects include depression, self-destructive behavior, anxiety, feelings of isolation and stigmatization, poor self-esteem,
difficulty in trusting others, a tendency towards revictimization, substance abuse,
and sexual maladjustment. The variables that appear to be most damaging are
sexual experiences involving father figures, genital contact, and force.

The literature differs about the degree of psychological trauma suffered by
the child, depending on whether the perpetrator is a significant other or a stranger
(Mayhall & Norgard, 1983). There is agreement, however, that the closer the child
and the perpetrator, the greater the chance of a continued incestuous relationship.
Children may have a better chance of recovery if the perpetrator is a stranger
rather than a family member (Finkelhor, 1979).

Causal Theories

Four major theses about the causes of sexual abuse have dominated the public
literature:

1. The popular public image is that the abuser is a sexual degenerate
   who must be punished for his or her crimes. Current research does
   not support this explanation.

2. The classical Freudian model postulates that the sexual abuser has
   suffered impairment in his or her sexual development during the
   Oedipal phase. Very little research substantiates this theoretical
   perspective.

3. Other theorists maintain that early learnings of sexual abusers
   reinforced their fixating on sexuality. They reach adulthood with no
   prohibitions against having sex, even with children. Some research
   from the social learning perspective supports this thesis.

4. A final viewpoint sees sexual abuse as part of a larger maladaptive
   lifestyle. The adult may be influenced by a number of problems,
   including alcoholism, marital problems, sexual problems, and lack of
   close friends. The adult's sexual relationship with a child is promoted
   more as a need for closeness than sexual gratification. Social system
   and family theorists subscribe to this thesis of the cause of sexual
   abuse.

These four assume the child is in a biological family; however, national reports (Child Sexual Abuse, 1981) indicate biological parents are far less involved than stepparents and other adults (such as boyfriends).

Research from a family and social psychological perspective is adding valuable information about etiological factors that contribute to sexual abuse (Cohen, 1983). A mother's new live-in boyfriend or step-family usually creates strong sexual undertones in a family. Teenage children may not feel secure with the new adult and may use seductive behavior to ensure affection. Sexual acting-out may occur because of the weakened incest taboo (Visher & Visher, 1979).

Generally, the family ambience contributes to the conditions under which incest or sexual abuse occurs. Often, the nonsexually abusing parent contributes to the pattern by ignoring it or remaining silent to signals of the abuse, being absent, subtly encouraging the abuse, or not assuring the child's safety. A child may be at risk of sexual abuse in a family with a strained marriage in which divorce is not seen as an option. The father turns to the daughter for sexual gratification, many times with the willingness or complacency of the mother. A family where one parent is often left alone with the child while the other parent is at work or pursuing a hobby may set up a situation for incest. Role reversal may take place where the mother tells a 12-year-old girl, "Be sure and take care of Daddy tonight." An overly protected child, whom the parent tries to isolate from other contacts within the family and community, may indicate an incestuous parent fearing the child will tell or will take another partner.

A family with potential for sexual abuse may do everything together and have very little outside contact. The father is seen as all-knowing. The family can totally depend on him. Such symbiotic family ties, especially in conjunction with the factors discussed above, can create fertile ground for an incestuous relationship between the parent and child (Sanford, 1980).

High stress levels created by loss of work, death of a significant other, moving from one town to another, serious personal illness, or other stressors may rob the family of the energy to invest in meaningful relationships in the community. Therefore, the father or mother may turn to the daughter or son for affection and, eventually, for sexual gratification.

Accurate Assessment of Child Sexual Abuse

Since it is now widely recognized that sexual abuse of children is highly prevalent and that the psychological effects can be debilitating, early detection of sexual abuse, termination of the abusive relationship, and psychotherapy for the abuse victims are essential. The law enforcement and judiciary systems have turned increasingly to child specialists to provide assessment of the probability of sexual abuse, and practitioners are becoming aware that the determination of the likelihood of sexual abuse, particularly among children under 12 years of age, creates some particular difficulties.

Until relatively recently, the indicators of sexual abuse in children were considered to be uncomplicated and direct. Basically, believed that if the child claimed sexual abuse, the abuse did happen. The general clinical wisdom of the time said no child would think about, let alone talk about, this taboo subject unless it had really occurred. Today, we realize the naivete of this assumption. Some children who have been sexually abused are so frightened of the consequences of revelation that they will not speak about it directly. They may have been threatened that if they disclose information, they will be severely punished. They may have conflicting feelings about the abuser and may not want that person to leave them or for that person to be in trouble.

A further complication is that with the removal of the taboo against disclosure, many false claims of sexual abuse are emerging (Mantell, 1988). False allegations of sexual abuse, particularly in child custody cases and cases against child care center workers, are dramatically on the rise. Therefore, the psychologist's task of identifying the likelihood of sexual abuse is a complex and ominous one. The cost of an error, that a child who has been sexually abused does not receive help or that an adult who is innocent has been accused of a heinous crime, is particularly high.

Current standards developed by child practitioners indicate that the effects of child sexual abuse are diagnosable in the same sense that other psychological and medical conditions can be diagnosed—on the basis of history, physical exam and judicious use of various psychological tests. The standards developed by the Council of the American Academy of Child and Adolescent Psychiatry (1988) serve as the backbone to the following guidelines for conducting interviews with children who may have been sexually abused.

1. Persons completing evaluations of child sexual abuse must be professionals with special skills and experience in the area of child and adolescent sexual abuse. Specialists performing these evaluations should possess sound knowledge of child development, family dynamics related to sexual abuse, effects of abuse on the child, and the means of assessing children, adolescents, and families.

2. The child should be seen for a minimum number of times necessary and interviewed by the fewest people necessary. The development of teams which integrate local police and report agencies is the preferred approach for minimizing evaluation trauma to the child.

3. The interview should take place in a relaxed and neutral environment, preferably not in the emergency ward or a place where there are trappings of authority such as a police department.

4. Gathering history on a child and parents or other care givers is a very important part of the evaluation and should include developmental history, cognitive assessment, history of abuse, relevant medical history, behavioral changes, history of the parents' abuse as children, and the family's attitudes toward sex and modesty. Prior psychiatric disorders in the child and parents are, of course, also important.

5. The use of psychological testing does not alone diagnose sexual abuse. It is helpful as part of the evaluation of the alleged offender. In cases of possible false allegations, it may be helpful to have testing of both parents.

6. It may be helpful to obtain a history from the perspective of each parent. Sufficient time should be spent with each alone involving a psychological evaluation.

7. If custody is an issue, a guardian ad litum for the child should be appointed to represent the child's best interest.

8. The possibility of false allegations needs to be considered, particularly if allegations are coming from one parent rather than the child and/or if the parents are engaged in a dispute over custody or visitation. False allegations also may arise when the child's statements are misinterpreted by the relatives or caretakers. Children who have experienced sexual abuse sometimes may misinterpret actions of a parent or accuse the wrong parent of abuse.

9. Because of the magnitude of charges involved in alleged child sexual abuse, evaluations must be done very thoroughly and carefully. The specialist must maintain emotional neutrality. Great care must be taken to avoid leading questions and coercive techniques. The child must be allowed to tell the story in his or her own words. More effort needs to be invested in obtaining corroborating information from other sources.

10. Factors enhancing the child's credibility include a detailed description in the child's own language and from the child's viewpoint, spontaneity, an appropriate degree of anxiety, consistency of allegations over time, behavioral changes consistent with abuse, absence of motivation, or undue influence for fabrication.

11. Anatomical dolls may be useful for eliciting the child's terminology for anatomical parts and for allowing the child who cannot tell or draw what happened to demonstrate the alleged abuse. However, the research concerning anatomical dolls indicates that they may bias some children toward discussing sexual information. Thus, it is clearly not necessary to use anatomically correct dolls and care should be taken not to use these dolls in a way to instruct or lead the child.

12. Children's drawings can be helpful in assessing the likelihood of child sexual abuse. These may include spontaneous drawings, kinetic family drawings, self-portraits, asking the child to draw a male or female, or the House/Tree/Person drawings. The primary usefulness of these drawings lies in the affect and information they elicit when the drawings are discussed.

13. Videotaping should be attempted whenever possible because it serves several useful purposes, including preserving the child's initial statements and avoiding duplication of efforts.

14. The sexual abuse must be reported within the ethical and legal requirements of each state. Therefore, persons should be very aware of the state requirements and must not place themselves in position of judge by trying to determine complicity of the act before reporting.

15. Every child who may have been sexually abused should have a physical examination, preferably performed by a pediatrician or family physician known to the child and family.

16. The specialist's recommendations should be based on thorough history, evaluation of child and parents, and a review of corroborating evidence. The conclusions should be carefully documented in a written report. It must be recognized that in some cases, the evaluator may not be able to determine whether sexual abuse has occurred. This dilemma may occur when the data are contaminated by too many evaluations, a child is too young to verbalize what has occurred, or too much time has passed since the incident for the child to remember.

These guidelines and others emphasize the importance of obtaining extensive collaborative data about any child who may have been sexually abused. The broad understanding of the child's history can serve as a backdrop for determining the impact of specific events, statements, and behaviors. For example, one of the writers of this text was recently involved in a case in which she was appointed by the court to complete an evaluation of a child whose mother said the child was sexually abused by the father. A pediatrician had reported that the child most likely was sexually abused because "there were soft signs of sexual abuse." By that, the pediatrician meant the child did not indicate any resistance to a gynecological exam. The pediatrician commented that the typical child is uncomfortable about such exams. It would have been helpful if the pediatrician had taken into consideration that this child had very extensive physical handicaps and at the age of five had undergone several serious operations for those handicaps. Thus, this was a child who was very used to being physically examined. Clearly, she had learned that her survival was potentiated by being compliant with medical professionals.

Figure 12.1 includes some of the Sentence Completion items completed by the young girl. Her answers certainly indicate this six-year-old's confusion and that she had learned to state that she had been sexually abused by her father even though this didn't seem correct to her. The background information on the father indicated that he had a sterling reputation at work that he had maintained for 15 years. In contrast, the mother had lost several jobs. Her most recent employer in her position as an aide in the schools reported that she had some serious problems in relating to children.

Extensive collaborated data also is important in that it can help substantiate a number of findings. No matter how effective a child welfare worker is, that worker cannot read minds. In another case in which the writer was involved, the mother was accused of being an alcoholic by the father, by the stepsister, and by

FIGURE 12.1

Incomplete Sentences

1. I am afraid _____ of Daddy _____
2. My father never _____ touches my private parts _____
3. I know I can _____ live with my mom _____
4. 1 worry about _____ Daddy _____
5. I wish I could stop _____ and spend the night _____
6. There is nothing _____ wrong, that he'll do something bad _____
7. Father and I _____ love each other _____
8. I just _____ can't believe it _____
9. When I got mad _____ I don't want to go to my dad's house _____
10. I want to know that _____ I want to stay home with my mother _____
11. I never _____ get to do anything in the house _____
12. 1 love _____ my mother _____
13. My father _____ mean to me _____
14. My mother _____ is very nice _____

the family physician. In talking with the family physician, the evaluator learned that the physician had based his conclusions about the mother's alcoholism upon his belief that the mother had been admitted to the hospital several times in the last year with medical problems and relatedly high alcohol levels in the blood. Apparently, this physician had gleaned most of that information from a secondary source, namely the father. When the evaluator spent several hours in the hospital attempting to gain collaborative data about this finding, there was simply no evidence that the mother had been in the hospital for several years.

The writer was involved in another case in which an 11-year-old boy had accused his father of sexually molesting him. The father had had custody of this boy and two younger siblings for over a year following the parents' divorce. The father had not wanted the divorce and had conceded that he had threatened his wife in a number of ways if she were to leave him. The wife had left in the middle of the night for her safety; and when she returned two months later, filing for divorce, he would not give her the children. In fact, the father won primary physical and legal custody of the children on basis of abandonment by the mother. Around the time of the sexual abuse evaluation, the mother had reinstated a court case because she said the three children had been telling her that they wanted to live with her. The son, who was the suspected sexual abuse victim, was well aware of the custody struggle between the parents. At one time he had commented to his mother, "You're the adult, why can't you handle it?" He was angry that his mother had not been able to be more effective in gaining custody of him. Also implied in his statement was that the client seemed to think that he would have to figure out for himself how to be able to live with his mother. The reader will notice in perusing Sentence Completion data presented in Figure 12.2 that the client seemed very concerned about lying. Especially significant is his response, "I'm afraid of not telling the truth." I am sure the reader also will be aware of the closer attachment to the mother, the anger toward the father as well as a kind of diffuse frustration, worry about lying and suggestions of wanting to act out.

It was very easy to glean information from the client about the alleged sexual abuse events. In fact, he was quite anxious to sit down and talk about them. He talked about his father making him take too hot a bath and insisting that he masturbate while his father was masturbating during a pornographic movie. The client talked quite freely about his family. He said that he wanted to live with his mother, that she understood him more. He said his father was fighting with him and his little sister all the time and that the fighting bothered him. He also indicated that he felt his father was never happy with him and always thought he was doing something wrong. When asked his three wishes, he said, "I wish for world peace, every book I want, and to live with my mother." Figure 12.3 includes his house and figure from the House/Tree/Person Test. The client described the House as his father's house and said it was ugly and he did not like it. The barring of the gate and windows gives a suggestion of being locked in. The shading of an area on the left which he referred to as a large bush may indicate some anxiety. The subject's human drawing was really quite good although very small and on the upper side of the page. This may suggest some lowered self-esteem and limited sense of attachment in his world.

FIGURE 12.2

Incomplete Sentences

1. I am afraid _____ of not telling the truth

2. My father never _____ understands me

3. People are always ___ wrong

4. I know I can _____ get what I want

5. I hate _____ being criticized

6. My family _____ doesn't

7. I worry about _____ getting to do what I want

8. My mother won't ___ tell me what to do

9. I wish I could stop ___ being mad

10. Father and I _____ are men

11. I wish _____ I were alone

12. I just can't _____ concentrate at school

13. Mother and I _____ get along

14. When I grow up ___ I'm going to be a lawyer

15. A brother should ___ be nice to his little brother, but who cares

16. I love _____ my mom and sister and brother (long pause) the most

FIGURE 12.3

Subject's Drawings

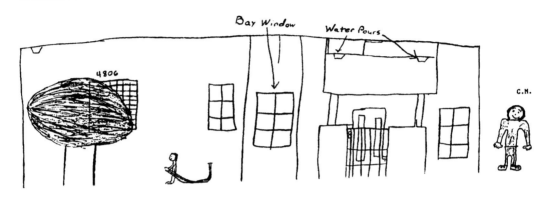

No evidence in the testing collaborated the thesis that this youngster had been sexually abused, nor was there evidence of extreme psychopathology in either parent. The client's description of the sexual abuse in some ways bordered on the bizarre, suggesting that it might be the fantasy created by a young person. In other ways, it seemed to lack details in specificity as well as the emotional constructs generally seen in cases of sexual abuse. In contrast, there was clear motivation for this child to create some allegations of sexual abuse. He did not feel free to live with his mother, and he clearly wanted to live with her. Although the data and history-taking do not definitively prove or disprove the allegations of sexual abuse, the collaborative data do indicate that in the absence of more concrete findings, the allegations of sexual abuse in this case should clearly be viewed with extreme caution.

Collaborative data also is important because it can help elucidate areas of vagueness. Several years ago, the writer was involved in a case in which the child had spontaneously spoken of sexual abuse by her father and then recanted her story. The clinical evaluator had a number of reasons to believe the child had been coached to deny sexual abuse, but was not able to substantiate these clinical hunches with concrete data in interviews. Because the child had recanted, the judge ordered supervised visitation with the father. The supervisor of the visitation was the father's new wife.

During an interview with this psychologist immediately following a visit with the father, the child was asked how she felt about the visit. The child said, "It went all right except when we went to go see the dogs." She continued, "my father didn't do it or nothing."

These were clearly strange comments, and the evaluator tried to follow up on them, but the child would not talk about them further. In attempts to obtain more extensive collaborative data, the evaluator did talk with the new wife of the father and among other questions asked the wife if there were any chance of the father being alone with this child during the last several visitations. The wife Said, "No," that she had been there at all times with the father except for one time when she dropped the child off at a gasoline station in town which was run by a friend of the father's. The new wife explained that the man who owned the gasoline station also was the town dogcatcher and that the little girl had always enjoyed going with him on his route. The plan was for the wife to drop the child off and for the father to meet the friend at the gasoline station so the three, father, friend, and daughter, could go on the dog catching route.

With this piece of information from the new wife, the evaluator had a way to further communicate with the child. In a subsequent interview, the evaluator asked the child if anything had happened when she had been waiting for her father to arrive to go catch the dogs. At this point, the little girl began to discuss more openly that the father had pressured her while waiting at the gas station for the friend to complete his work. The father had tried to convince her that he had not done anything bad to her and that someone else had hurt her.

Interestingly, while the child was talking about this coercion, she drew the pictures in Figure 12.4. She stated she had drawn a silly-looking girl who was five years old. When asked who the sun might be if it were a person, she said her mother. The reader will notice the poor body image presented in this drawing. There is a fierce look on the face as well as a shadow around the face. There is a pronounced black mark around the abdominal area. The client identified the House as her father's house. She said it was a rainy day with tornadoes. When asked to draw a sun in this picture, she commented, "No, I can't. I will put a black spot for the sun and say it is nighttime."

The more information the evaluator gleans from various sources in cases of potential sexual abuse, the greater the likelihood of obtaining reliable findings. In assessment of child sexual abuse, there is seldom a finding that is singularly conclusive. If a child has a venereal disease, he or she has most likely been sexually abused. However, for the most part, the data relied upon are much more

FIGURE 12.4

Girl's Drawings

vague and interpretive. The reliability of our findings and, therefore, the validity of our conclusions are greatly increased if much data point in the same direction.

In summarizing the suggestions for successful evaluation of potential child sexual abuse victims, it is important to keep in mind the indicators of sexual abuse, to know the limitations of each kind and method of evaluation, and to look for collaborative, unfolding data across indicators. Hopefully, future standards for assessment will include more systematic ways of integrating the various bits of information that are gleaned.

Treatment

Much attention and research are being completed on the treatment of perpetrators, although we find little substantial research on the effect and treatment of the victims. Some research has suggested that it is not the sexual assault upon a child that creates the most profound trauma, but rather the other adults' and professionals' reactions that foster severe psychological distress. Conte (1984) refers to this phenomenon as system-induced trauma. He states that medical, legal, mental health, and social work professionals are aware of the possibility of creating system-induced trauma. However, many children am subject to insensitive interviewing by professionals who do not understand the dynamics of sexual abuse. The physical examination, which may be necessary, may create additional trauma to the child. To further intensify the trauma, parents may create a crisis atmosphere (Elwell, 1979).

Often, the child is blamed for the abuse. Appropriate crisis intervention is necessary to work with victims of sexual abuse. As long as the sexual abuse is stopped immediately upon discovery, therapy can take place with less crisis orientation. The "normal" panic response of parents and professionals may be unwarranted, as the child may not see this as a crisis.

Hoorwitz (1983) points out several general steps to take in the treatment of victims of child abuse. The first step is to clarify the specialist's role with the other involved professionals, including the court so the specialist can present him- or herself accurately to the family. As in the treatment of child abuse, it is important to ensure that the child is adequately protected. A choice of last resort is removing the child from the family home. A preferred approach is to remove the perpetrator if necessary.

Research has shown that children rarely make up serious allegations of sexual abuse, and even if they do, some type of dysfunction exists within the family (Giarretto, 1976; Finkelhor, 1984). However, the denial of the abuse is of upmost concern to most perpetrators and their spouses. The specialist needs to ensure that the question of the veracity of the allegations of sexual abuse does not dominate the communication to the point that the child's needs are not addressed. Often, it is helpful for the practitioner to emphasize that the child who claims sexual abuse is in serious distress and that family problems are evident. This distress must be addressed. The specialist needs to ensure that there is a commitment to treatment. Several hours with the child may be necessary to build a lasting and trusting relationship. O'Brien (1983) outlines important messages a victimized child needs to hear from the specialist.

1. It is all right to talk about the abuse with the worker. The child may feel guilty for "turning in" the offender because he or she liked the adult or was told he or she would be severely harmed if "our little

secret" was ever told. The therapist should try not to focus upon the actual acts which occurred but rather upon the child's feelings. The child may not view him- or herself as a victim and may be puzzled about questions on the subject.

2. The child must understand that the specialist believes him or her. Even though the child may not be able to give specific information such as dates, times, and other details, through the use of anatomically correct dolls and descriptions, he or she may be able to give a very clear description of the sexual abuse.

3. The worker must assure the child that he or she is safe with the worker. Although the child may not have experienced fear during an incestuous relationship, discovery may create anxiety. Children need assurances that no matter what has happened in the past, they are now safe. The end of abuse through the efforts of the police or the child welfare worker will begin to build trust in the child. The child must feel that it is all right for him or her to feel any suppressed guilt, hurt, anger, and confusion. The opportunity to express these feelings honestly, in an atmosphere of trust, begins a sense of security.

4. The child needs to be assured that under no circumstances is he or she responsible for the abuse. Children may or may not know that they have been abused, but regardless, it is important that they understand the abuse was not their fault as a way of relieving present or future guilt feelings. An explanation of adult's problem deflects blame from the child. An example is explaining to a child that sometimes adults don't have adult friends so they make friends with children. What they do to the children is unfair. The adult needs help so that he or she won't do this again to anyone else.

Many times children have a distorted view of why the sexual abuse took place, linking it with some minor misbehavior on their part. To address this concern, the specialist should let children know that bad things happen to everyone at some point in time. The example of Cinderella as cited by O'Brien (1983) is a story of how someone who lived a good life was mistreated by her stepmother. It wasn't Cinderella's fault that her stepmother treated her badly.

The specialist needs to be very empathic, to express deep concern about the abuse. The specialist may tell the child that he or she wishes this had not happened to the child. The child welfare worker communicates that while he or she regrets what happened, it is important to continue to move on in one's life. The specialist, through words and behavior, emphasizes that the child can count on the specialist as long as the child needs help. Hoorwitz (1983) suggests eliciting a family member as an ally for the abused child.

During the therapy, a number of special topics need to be addressed. The child's feelings about the parents must be explored. Very often, the parent/child roles have been distorted as the child plays a surrogate spouse role. Clarification of role may require extensive therapy. The child may feel a lack of support from the nonabusing parent, so very negative attitudes about each parent may surface. The issue of trust and the child's sense of well-being also are subjects for treatment. After years of sexual abuse, the child may begin to blackmail the parents by extracting bribes and privileges. This distorted method of relating to adults must now be addressed and corrected if present. Treatment of long-term effects of sexual abuse includes understanding the child's sexuality and how comfortable the child is in his or her sexuality. Future sexual relations may produce anxiety, deep fears, and images of the sexual abuse, unless negative feelings about one's sexuality are discussed.

Adult victims of child sexual abuse report that they are confused about their sexuality and feel sexually stigmatized (Meiselman, 1978). Finkelhor (1984), in his study of possible effects of sexual abuse on sexual feelings and behavior, found a statistically significant difference between victimized women and nonvictimized women in his sample of university students. Victimized women stated they felt awkward in sexual situations. Men who were sexually abused as children stated they were very dissatisfied after sexual experiences. Some research about the long-term effect of child sexual abuse indicates that the victim is likely to become involved in homosexual activity. The premise is that boys who are molested by men will become homosexual. Women who were sexually abused by men will turn to women for sex, because sex with men brings back terrible images (Finkelhor, 1984). Finkelhor did find a connection between childhood sexual abuse and adult homosexual behavior for boys. However, he did not establish this relationship for girls. Boys who were sexually used by older men are four times more likely to be homosexually active as adults than nonvictims.

The clinical treatment of sexual abuse victims only recently developed a theoretical and research base to guide practice. Child practitioners can help children deal with emotional trauma of discovery and prosecution by developing an attitude in the children that they are believed and now safe. Individual child therapy should be conducted in conjunction with family therapy that addresses the immediate family, sometimes the extended family, and factors that may have led to a high-risk situation. The institutional approach to treatment of the perpetrator is a heterogeneity of therapy and criminal prosecution which makes it difficult to integrate child and family treatment. The number of children reported as sexually abused likely will climb as the general population becomes aware of the problem. Determination of appropriate treatment for the perpetrator, victim, and family is critical.

Summary

The first and foremost aim of treatment is to stop the abuse within the family. So far, the most success has been achieved by group therapy for parents combined with social case management in which parents are taught new ways to handle family stress. Among the most successful groups seem to be the self-help groups sponsored by Parents Anonymous. Many communities have established telephone hotlines for parents to call when they find themselves losing control as well as around-the-clock crisis nurseries where parents in need of a few hours' peace can drop off their children. Experts agree that most child abuse and neglect can be prevented if

- parents can reach out for the help they need to cope with the stresses in their lives.

- professionals and agencies that provide services to families can be attentive to families having particular difficulties in the demanding task of raising their children.

- communities can support preventive programs to help families in stress, such as Parents Anonymous, family stress centers, parental stress hotlines, and crisis nurseries.

A combination of volunteer groups, hotlines, crisis nurseries, and social case management has led to some alleviation of this problem. Unfortunately, we still have no good base rate of remission to compare with these treatment gains. Evaluation of treatment modalities is as difficult as determining the many causes of abuse. Studies that report high success rates often have biased subject selection processes. None of the studies thus far has been conclusive. Many of the findings appear contradictory.

Prevention of child abuse has taken several directions. Broad educational programs are helpful in making parents cognizant of their violence to their children and of places where they may receive help. Some screening instruments attempt to identify the potential for violence in parents, but these tests produce many false positives (that is, they do identify a large percentage of the potentially abusive parents, but they also include a significant number of parents who are not violent). Even if the tests were more reliable, it would be nearly impossible to force the potentially abusing parents into treatment. Some social scientists believe that we need to eradicate all types of corporal punishment. As long as corporal punishment is accepted in the school, many parents will continue to believe it is all right to beat their children. Prevention of child maltreatment rests on major social reforms. Only to the extent that we are able to alleviate the causes of child abuse, e.g., poverty, inadequate parenting behavior, mental illness of a parent, etc., will this significant social problem decrease. Until we reach this ideal goal, child welfare workers must work closely and intimately with both perpetrators and victims of abuse so that the cycle can be interrupted as swiftly as possible, and healthy family functioning can be restored.

In terms of the treatment of sexual abuse, the last 20 years have brought striking progress in public willingness to deal openly with this subject and legal sanctions regarding reporting, treatment, and prosecution. We are increasingly recognizing that when family members are willing to cooperate, sexual abuse problems can be viewed as a product of family dysfunction and can be treated from a family perspective. When this is possible, it is the preferred mode since the disruption of the family is a secondary trauma to the child who has already been traumatized. Treatment for the sexually abused child follows in accord with many of tenentes for treating other traumatic disorders; that is, allowing catharsis and employing techniques that neutralize affect.

Chapter 13

Special Needs Children

In this chapter, we will review the emotional development of "special needs children," those with limiting conditions imposed by their biology and/or social experiences. We will discuss the stresses and needs of children with retardation, those who are gifted, those with physical illness, and those who are deaf. Many physical problems are precipitated by conditions associated with being poor, such as malnutrition, poor housing, and limited prenatal care. Because of these predisposing conditions and the unusual stresses of being raised in a low socioeconomic environment, these also are considered special needs children. Although more types of special needs children could be discussed, we have limited our review to those conditions that are most frequently manifested in child welfare. We hope the reader will find that many of the ideas presented are applicable to other special needs children.

Children with Mental Retardation

The term mental retardation has been employed to describe a wide range of intellectual abilities ranging from minor deviations from the norm in tested IQ to limited functional ability that requires the individual to be totally dependent on others for basic care. Within the past decade, the term developmentally disabled has increased in usage to describe persons with mental retardation, autistic, brain or central nervous system damaged, epileptic, or cerebral palsied, or who have a learning disorder such as dyslexia. Although a number of treatment modalities described below apply to children with developmental disabilities, our discussion in this section will focus on mental retardation.

Definition

The 1990 Developmental Disabilities Assistance and Bill of Rights Act, (P.L. 101-496) defines Developmental Disability as a severe, chronic disability of a person 5 years or older that is 1) attributable to a mental or physical impairment, or combination; 2) manifested before age 22; 3) will continue; 4) results in functioning limitations in three or more life activities; 5) needed for treatments except for children from birth to age 5 (DeWeaver, 1995). Young children are again left out.

Though definitions of Developmental Disabilities are still evolving, there are five major conditions:

- mental retardation
- cerebral palsy
- epilepsy
- autism (Baroff, 1991).

The prevalence of mental retardation has been estimated as ranging from 3% (American Psychiatric Association, 1980) to 20% of prepubertal children (Robinson & Robinson, 1970). Rapid industrialization may be catalyzing a higher reported incidence as people with borderline IQ scores and adaptive skills find it increasingly difficult to cope with the demands of a technological society such as that in the United States.

Historically, mental retardation was considered a unitary deficiency in some genetic component of intelligence, and it was assessed by the unitary score of an intelligence test. In 1959, the American Association of Mental Deficiency (Heber, 1959) laid down the more expansive criteria used today. The criteria place less stress on the IQ score per se and more emphasis on functional skills. Mental retardation is diagnosed if three factors are present:

1. Significant subaverage intellectual functioning as measured by a score of 70 or below on an individually administered IQ test

2. Concurrent deficits in adaptive functioning

3. The developmental period is between ages 1 and 19 (Grossman, 1977)

As clear as this definition sounds, determination of mental retardation in practice is complex. It is often difficult to ascertain whether the measure of IQ represents the subject's maximum performance (or whether instead performance was limited by experience and adjustment). Similarly, it can be difficult to assess the subject's competency especially if she or he has been abused or neglected or is experiencing concomitant emotional problems. Below, we review some of the complications in assessing the three factors associated with retardation. An in-depth discussion of measurement is found in Chapter 9.

IQ Assessment.   Dickerson (1981) lists the three psychometric instruments that are most frequently used when assessing IQ.

1. Cattel Infant Intelligence Scale (1940): This test is used primarily with children between the ages of 3 months and 30 months. It assesses imitative behavior, motor skills, language, and perceptual development.

2. Stanford–Binet Intelligence Scale: This test of IQ can be used with children of 2 years through adulthood. The global assessment of IQ is made through subtests requiring verbal and psychomotor reactions.

3. Wechsler Intelligence Scale for Children III (Wechsler, 1991): This test is designed for children between the ages of 5 and 15 years. In addition to the global assessment of IQ, discreet analysis of verbal and performance (psychomotor) skills is provided.

Although the standardized tests are helpful to the practitioner to determine general intellectual functioning, without an assessment of cultural and social skills and adaptive behaviors, dangerous conclusions may be drawn, as in the case of José below. Case 13.1 is drawn from actual case material brought to the attention of the second author of this text.

Case 13.1   The Case of José

José, a Yaqui Indian, lived on a reservation in rural southern Arizona until age 9. In the 1950s, he was brought to an institution for the mentally retarded. Speaking in Spanish (a second language for Yaquis, José's mother explained that he "was difficult to care for." The staff administered the Stanford–Binet test in English, José's third language. José scored 57 on the verbal scale and 71 on the performance scale. The

State of Arizona considered scores below 80 officially within the range of mental retardation, so José was institutionalized. When José was 13 years old, he tore some ligaments in his knee while working on the institution's ranch. A doctor in the nearby town of 2000 operated on the knee and, unfortunately, permanently damaged the ligaments. José, who grew to 6'3" and 235 pounds, could not do physical labor from then on.

At age 22, José was moved to a new community residential facility in Tucson. Every new resident received a totally new assessment, including adaptive behavior and IQ tests. José was retested (for the first time since age 9) with the Stanford–Binet, this time in Spanish, his second language. He scored 91 on the verbal and 82 on performance. Because of the years of sheltered living with few expectations or assistance in developing social skills, José's adaptive tests showed he needed to live in a highly supervised group situation.

The State of Arizona was faced with the problem of institutionalizing a young adult who was, according to the standardized IQ testing, not retarded, yet after a life of institutionalization, could not function outside a residential setting. Some staff spoke of a lawsuit against the first hospital for institutionalizing José as retarded.

The next week, José hit his girlfriend in the face several times. Quickly and quietly, he was transferred to the state hospital with the diagnosis of mental illness.

Assessment of Adaptive Functioning.   Because mental retardation describes the functional status and adaptive behavior of an individual child, a person may meet the criteria of retardation at one point in his or her life and not at another (Mandelbaum, 1977). In 1983, the American Association on Mental Deficiency (AAMD) continued to refine the definition of mental retardation as, "Mental retardation refers to significantly subaverage, general intellectual functioning existing concurrently with defects in adaptive behaviors and manifested in the developmental period" (p. 56). In 1987, AAMD changed its name to the American association on Mental Retardation (AAMR) and in 1992 defined mental retardation as:

Mental retardation refers to substantial limitations in present functioning. It is characterized by significantly subaverage intellectual functioning, existing concurrently with related limitations in two or more of the following applicable adaptive skill areas: communication, self-care, home living, social skills, community use, self-direction, health and safety, functional academics, leisure, and work. Mental retardation manifests before age 18. (AAMR, 1992, p. 1)

Subaverage general intellectual functioning means the child's score on an IQ test is two or more standard deviations below those of other children of the same age. The term adaptive behaviors refers to age-appropriate behaviors necessary to function in a family and as a social being within the community. It also incorporates an assessment of the sensory motor skills, communication skills, and developing vocational skills (Grossman, 1977).

The measurement of adaptive behavior is difficult and often subjective. Therefore they have evolved over time. The 1974 revision of the adaptive behavior scale published by the American Association of Mental Deficiency (Nihira, Foster, Shellinas, & Wand, 1974) was most frequently employed. Based upon interviews with persons knowing the child well, the adaptive behavior scale (Nihira, et al., 1974) attempts to quantify behavioral development in varied domains (independent functioning, economic activity, memory of time, domestic activity, responsibility, and socialization) as well as tabulating maladaptive behaviors and use of medication. Unfortunately, the adaptive behavior scale was normed only to the institutionalized retarded children and thus is not adequate for assessing the behavior of the retarded children who live at home.

The Vineland Social Maturity Scale (Doll, 1965) assesses infants or young children's motor, cognitive, and social skills. The scale assesses the ability of an older child to function autonomously regardless of her or his physical handicaps, language usage, verbal comprehension, or social skills. The skill level of the person interviewing the suspected retarded child has been shown to affect results of adaptive skill assessment. Thus, questions of appropriateness of the test instrument, relationship of scores of varied instruments, skill of the assessor, developmental changes over time, and compounding psychological and social factors make it difficult to reliably assess adaptive behavior.

Development During Childhood. The third criterion for classification of the mentally retarded (MR) is that this functioning be manifested in childhood. If a low IQ score and minimal adaptive behavior are not apparent until adulthood, the symptoms are labeled an organic brain syndrome.

Classifications. Based upon the assessments mentioned above, children with retardation abilities were usually classified as follows:

> Mild. Commonly referred to as educable, children with mild retardation represent the IQ range between 51 and 70. This child can grow to be fairly independent and maintain a job.

Moderate. Commonly referred to as trainable, this group's IQs are between 36 and 51. Through specific training, these children can live in group homes or live semi-independent lifestyles. They experience delayed development.

Severe. These children will fall into an IQ range of 20 to 35 with delays in speech and motor skills and will require a supervised, protective workshop environment. These children may acquire some self-care skills and minimal independent behaviors.

Profound. These children have an IQ of less than 20 and are totally dependent upon others throughout their lives. They are highly impaired in sensory and motor skills and have no language skills.

The profound category represents approximately 1.5% of the MR population. The severe category represents approximately 3.5% of the total MR population. The moderate range includes 6% of the retarded. The largest percentage, 89%, of retarded persons are classified in the mild range (Dickerson, 1981).

In 1992 the AAMR replaced the adaptive behaviors with 10 adaptive skill areas, which focus on the person's ability to function with in their environment. The four levels of retardation listed above were replaced with a description of patterns of support systems and how intense the service need is. These are; intermittent, limited, extensive, and pervasive. During the development of services and treatments for the D. D. population there has been a movement away from labels, the medical model, and a focus on IQ, toward a strengths perspective and an understanding of the child's environment (DeWeaver, 1995).

Etiology

The view of the etiology of mental retardation employed in hospitals, clinics, and other medically oriented facilities associate the various causes of retardation (Grossman, 1977) with:

1. infection

2. disease or intoxication

3. trauma or physical agent

4. disorders of metabolism

5. new growth

6. prenatal conditions

7. unknown disease but with structural reaction manifested

8. unknown disease with functional reaction manifested

The etiology of mental retardation is complex. In fact while a wide range of disorders are associated with retardation, the etiology of up to 50 percent of the cases is unknown (McLaren & Bryson, 1987). Prenatal factors are causes about twice as often as postnatal factors. Some symptoms of retardation arise from dissimilar causes, while similar causes have disparate effects. Thus, rubella in a pregnant mother, especially in the first trimester of pregnancy, may result in retardation and deafness in some infants, only deafness in others, and no ill effects in a few (Robinson & Robinson, 1970).

Infection from such diseases as rubella or syphilis may cause retardation by attacking the central nervous system. Drugs, including alcohol and prescribed medications, may seriously damage the fetus, causing retardation. A type of mental retardation receiving increasing attention is fetal alcohol syndrome (FAS), a pattern of physical malformation observed in offspring of women who drink alcohol during pregnancy. Current estimates show that 1 to 2 children per 1,000 are born with FAS. Both prospective and retrospective studies indicate that children born to alcohol-treated mothers perform poorly on tests of cognitive ability. Since alcohol consumption is increasing among women, FAS is expected to increase also.

Meningitis and whooping cough also may cause damage to the central nervous system. Metabolic defects (phenylketonuria, cretinism, galactosemia) may now be detected through diagnostic surveys while the child is in utero. Phenylketonuria (PKU) is a metabolic disorder transmitted by a recessive gene. This creates an excessive amount of phenylpyruvic acid in the urine. Approximately 1 of every 10,000 live births results in a PKU disorder (Dickerson, 1981). With detection within the first 2 years of life, PKU can be treated with dietary supplements which may prevent excessive cerebral damage.

A common type of retardation associated with new growth is hypothyroidism or cretinism, which is caused by insufficient secretion of the thyroid hormone. The physical development may be arrested creating mental retardation. A child suffering from cretinism may have obvious, unusual physical characteristics such as a large head, round face, no forehead, flat broad nose, thick protruding tongue, short neck, or eyes set far apart (Dickerson, 1981).

Maternal malnutrition, particularly during the first trimester, may result in fewer brain cells developing in the fetus. This may produce mild retardation in the newborn child. Other abnormalities may be prompted by the carbohydrates or proteins consumed by the mother during pregnancy.

Blood type incapability may result from a mother with a Rh-negative blood carrying a baby with Rh-positive blood. During the term of the pregnancy, the mother's body will produce anti-Rh antibodies destroying many of the baby's red blood cells by releasing bilirubin into the baby's bloodstream. Excessive amounts of bilirubin may cause damage to the brain of the fetus. This condition now can be diagnosed easily and treated with blood transfusions at birth (Mandelbaum, 1977).

Chromosomal abnormalities cause approximately 10% of the retardation of children who reside in institutions for the retarded (Mandelbaum, 1977). Down's syndrome (trisomy 21) is the most pervasive type of mental retardation resulting from a chromosomal aberration. The probability of its occurrence increases dramatically with the mother's age so that among expectant mothers 45 and older, the probability is 1 in 65 live births. Other trisomies of the autosomes usually lead to death of the fetus. An abnormal arrangement of the chromosomes that transmit sexual characteristics creates Klinefelter's syndrome (an extra sex chromosome, XXY, arrangement in males) affecting 1 in 450 births. Turner's syndrome, a chromosomal abnormality marked by a single X chromosome arrangement in females is recognized by the short stature, short neck, low set ears, broad nose, and retardation. Both Klinefelter's and Turner's syndromes cause very serious developmental delays and retardation. Because of the serious developmental problems associated with these syndromes, many of these children die before or at birth or at a young age.

Microcephalus and hydrocephalus are caused by the premature closure of sutures in the skull. Microcephalus is characterized by a small head, while hydrocephalus is characterized by a very large head created by an accumulation of fluid within the brain. Since hydrocephalus develops in infancy when the skull is soft, the head may become extremely large. Hydrocephalic children may be very quiet and passive in their behavior with blindness, deafness, and seizures commonly present.

Severe injuries to the head caused by accidents or child abuse also may, as mentioned earlier, cause damage to the central nervous system resulting in retardation. Low birth weight, prematurity, and lack of oxygen during birth increase the probability of retardation of the infant.

The majority of mentally retarded children in the United States are found in the lowest socioeconomic groups. Of importance to child welfare workers is that epidemiological findings from a number of studies demonstrate high correlation between mental retardation, particularly in its milder forms, and low social, economic, and cultural status of the retarded (Mandelbaum, 1977). The lack of proper prenatal care, maternal and fetal malnutrition, and a variety of correlates of premature birth (such as alcohol and drug use) that are more common among low socioeconomic status parents create many risk factors for children to be born mentally retarded. As a general rule, mild retardation is more likely to be fostered by environmental deprivation, while more serious retardation is generally genetic or organic in nature.

Psychological disorders are sometimes associated with mental retardation. The emotional disturbance may damage a child's intelligence. Psychological features such as tantrums, stereotypical movement, or aggressiveness may be caused by the same organic factors responsible for retardation. Or the psychological factors may be a result of frustration in trying to cope with and adapt to a world created for people with more sophisticated conceptual ability. Those children with mental retardation are particularly vulnerable to social stress because of deficiencies in judgment and because they learn to anticipate frustration and failure.

A study of 133 children classified as educable and trainable mentally retarded indicated that they were significantly more likely than matched control children who were not retarded to express a number of fears. Most of the fear shown by the retarded children is realistic and learned and relates to their difficulties coping with environmental stresses (Derevensky, 1979). They are more dependent on their families and thus disturbance in the families affects them greatly. In addition, those children with problems in impulse control often find themselves in difficulty with their parents or other caretakers. Discrepancy of developmental growth rates may be greater for the retarded than the non retarded, leading to asymmetry of motivation and increased pressures by self and others. Retarded children may be inappropriately subject to demands that while appropriate for their age are inappropriate for their developmental stage. The inappropriate demands may create frustration and tension. The classic Chess & Hassibi (1970) study reported that children with limited intellectual abilities may become anxious and restless and engage in repetitive aimless activity when confronted with social or academic tests they are unable to complete. It is not surprising that the possibility of a psychiatric disorder is 3 to 4 times greater among the retarded than the rest of the population (American Psychiatric Association, 1980).

Over half the children diagnosed as psychotic have tested IQs that are well below the average score of 100. The cause and effect are not always clear. Generally, the thinking disorder seen in psychotic children creates the functional retardation. The child may demonstrate a failure to learn caused by severe anxiety. This anxiety may be provoked through childhood trauma, including the death of a parent, severe child abuse, or other early experiences. These early traumas make it difficult for the child to discriminate between internal and external signals. The lack of differentiation of self, others, and the external world may make these disturbed children function as retarded (Mengeot, 1982). If the thinking disorder is primary, the retardation may clear when the psychotic disorder is ameliorated (Robinson & Robinson, 1970). Upon early assessment, this child may be identified as an irreversible mental retardate. However, through psychiatric treatment, the retardation may be remediated to some degree. However, normal intellectual functioning is seldom restored if emotional problems are present through much of the early childhood.

Therapy with Children with Mental Retardation

Much of the clinical work with mental retardation has focused on the parents' and family's interaction with the child. Family treatment has helped parents understand and accept their children's limited behavior through education and therapy. Also, the use of groups for socialization building and basic living skills has helped ease the frustration many children with mild retardation feel (Proctor, 1983; Laterza, 1983; McBroom, 1976). Our discussion will examine treatment suggestions for social workers working with an children who are emotionally disturbed and with retardation.

Until the 1950s, mental retardation was seldom treated with psychotherapy. It was felt that intervention with this population was not possible since these children lacked the motivation and verbal ability necessary for psychological change. Today, we recognize that the children with retardation feel personal pain as much as those who are not retarded. We know that many of the psychological problems are an emotional overlay of their frustration and can be eased with therapy.

Newcomer and Morrison (1974) reported a study in which children with mild to moderate retardation were treated in individual and group play therapy. Both play therapy treatments resulted in adaptive gains as measured by a developmental screening test in comparison to non treated controls. Morrison & Newcomer (1975) then demonstrated that the children with retardation improved equally with non directed and directed play therapy. Erickson (1978) concludes that although few studies have measured the effectiveness of play therapy with mental retardation, the results are no less encouraging than those studies of therapy with children without mental retardation.

Several factors should be considered when conducting therapy with these children. First, they are subject to the same laws of behavior as other children. Behavior modification works, as does nondirective counseling. Extinction of inappropriate behavior is likely to take longer with retarded than non retarded children (Robinson & Robinson, 1970). In the past, children with mental retardation have been viewed as fundamentally different with odd ideas and perceptions of reality. Today, therapists see them as developmentally delayed. The essential issue is to plan therapy according to the child's developmental level. Many children with mental retardation have difficulty concentrating. Their distractibility may be related to inability to filter external stimulation or to internal causes. Thus, they do not necessarily need to be worked with in an environment devoid of stimulation. They will, however, probably require extra effort and patience since their attention is limited, and they have difficulty in transferring learning from one environment to another.

A powerful therapeutic approach with this population is modeling. A therapist can model behaviors that provide a child with retardation clear, concrete examples of how to influence the environment. The use of role-playing in difficult situations allows the child to assimilate the new knowledge (Proctor, 1983).

Various medications often are used in the treatment of youngsters with retardation. Medication is helpful for controlling seizures and impulsive behavior among some retarded. However, the danger of over medication should not be overlooked. In a classic study, Lipman (1970) surveyed 100 institutions for the mentally retarded and demonstrated many cases of over medication. Approximately 37% of the children were taking large doses of tranquilizers—probably to ease the work of the staff, not to aid the children. While this treatment is limited, it is an important area for the child welfare worker to monitor. Modification of diet also may be helpful in some cases. As in children with phenylketonuria, a diet free of phenylalanine, although not reversing the retardation, does lead to a cessation of brain damage and to a reduction of behavioral problems. It usually is advisable for a child welfare worker to consult with a physician prior to treating a child with mental retardation. In this way, the worker can know something about the medication that the child is taking and what its behavioral effects should be as well as helping determine whether the child should or should not be on medication.

Gifted Children

The child who is gifted is often overlooked in our society, especially among the child welfare population. This topic does not even appear in the Encyclopedia of Social Work and is rarely found in Child Welfare texts. Gifted children are a little acknowledged minority group and a relatively untapped natural resource. Gifted children are an under served minority population that is neglected because of societal acceptance of myths and stereotypes (Freundlich, 1987). A significant number of gifted children do not reach their potential, either intellectually or creatively and are at high risk for underachievement and psychosocial maladaptation (Grenier, Dawson & Gray, 1989). Discriminating the concept of giftedness from high IQ and superior academic performance, Marland (1972) identified various types of gifted children as those displaying one or more of the following: general intellectual ability, special academic aptitude, creative thinking, leadership ability, ability in the visual and performing arts, and psychomotor ability. The focus upon the special talents of gifted children has been followed by some statutory recognition of their special needs under P. L. 94-142, which mandates education for all handicapped children. Most states now hold statutory provisions for education of children who are exceptional "by virtue of giftedness."

Nevertheless, identification of types of giftedness remains imprecise. Feldman (1979) writes, "Giftedness is as varied as the fields in which humans produce excellence" (p. 662). Although it is relatively well established that a high IQ and/or superior academic performance do not assure giftedness, it is not clear whether a certain level of intellectual aptitude is a prerequisite for giftedness. Some operational definitions have been offered to discriminate the types of giftedness, but still unknown is the degree to which the varied types of giftedness draw upon similar cognitive abilities. New educational procedures for teaching the gifted are being explored, but many are embryonic and others lack empirical documentation. A yet incomplete area is the personal needs of gifted children. Do gifted children have special attitudes, personality traits, and emotional problems associated with their special talents?

Psychological Adjustment

The psychological adjustment of the gifted is surrounded by folklore. The idiom "genius is next to insanity" is highly accepted by the general populace. Terman's (Terman & Oden, 1959) classic study was instrumental in dispelling this myth among social scientists. Following the development of a group of gifted children over 30 years, Terman reported that as children, this group tended to be taller, heavier, and healthier, and to reach sexual maturity before other children. They did better in school and were advanced in reading, arithmetic, and other academic indices. Terman and his students reported that gifted adults were more successful and better adjusted than the general population. They also were much more likely than the general population to rate their lives as "deeply satisfying."

Nevertheless, we need to recognize that gifted children are not a homogeneous group. Although the development of some gifted children is relatively uneventful, others do experience personal and social stresses because of their giftedness and are vulnerable to psychological problems and maladjustment.

Some of their vulnerability to psychological problems may be prompted by inappropriate responses of parents to their giftedness. Some parents exploit their gifted children, treating them like showpieces. Other parents may be very responsive to the child's analytic abilities, but do not take into account their physical and emotional immaturity. Still others may be angry at the child's differences and thus respond to the child as a nuisance and scapegoat them (Cornell, 1983). Some parents have ambivalent relationships with their gifted children. They are proud of the child, but tend to be uncomfortable with the child's differences and to denigrate them (Whitmore, 1980).

Educational Adjustment

Many gifted children are reacted to adversely by teachers and are thereby vulnerable to adjustment difficulties. What often is noted about gifted children in school settings is their atypical behavior rather than their productive or unusual creations. A number of studies imply a pattern of learning preferences exist for many gifted children (Griggs, 1984). Gifted children are generally independent in attitude, internally controlled, persistent, perceptually strong, nonconforming, highly motivated, and quality judgment (Griggs, 1984; Roe, 1976; Toffance, 1972). They tend to be introverted and unconcerned with social norms, and often reject external constraints (Taylor & Holland, 1964; Walsh, 1975). Although they can demonstrate social presence and poise, they appear to be relatively unconcerned with societal expectations. A low level of sociability may be portrayed, and an asocial attitude may be presented (Guilford, 1968; MacKinnon, 1962; Torrance, 1975; Walsh, 1975). They seem to be more interested in reflective than concrete thinking and more preoccupied with ideas and things than with people

(Guilford, 1975; Roe, 1976; Toffance, 1962). Therefore, teachers and child welfare workers may find it difficult to become close to the gifted child. Even more distressing, the worker and teacher may hold limited means of modifying the creative child's behavior. Because these children strive for an internal focus of control, they often are unresponsive to shaping techniques and operant disciplinary approaches. Several authors (Griggs, 1984: Roe, 1976; Taylor & Holland, 1964; Torrance, 1975) have suggested that gifted children may have difficulties with their teachers and workers because they resist the teacher's exercise of power. The gifted child may internalize aversive reactions of teachers and the worker, thereby feeling emotionally isolated and disturbed. Further, they may be ridiculed or ignored by their classmates so that they begin to retreat as social isolates or become antagonistic to their peers.

Personality and Social Interaction

In addition to emotional distress spurred by the aversive reactions of a parent, teacher or worker to the gifted child's temperament and behavior, preliminary research suggests that gifted children may be predisposed toward certain emotional problems. Some of these children tend to be perfectionistic, especially if their achievement is highly valued by their parents (Cornell, 1983). They may set unrealistic goals for themselves, leading to chronic feelings of inferiority and inadequacy (Whitmore, 1980). The heightened intelligence and social awareness that often are characteristic of gifted children may at times spur emotional concern. An early study (Hitchfield, 1973) demonstrated that gifted children tend to worry more and respond more seriously to competition than their non gifted peers. These children may be hypervigilant to events and others' responses.

If others are critical of their creations or behavior or if they are unsuccessful, some hypervigilant gifted children experience an exaggerated sense of isolation or rejection (Kams & Wherry, 1981; Whitmore, 1980). At times, gifted children become frustrated with their discontinuities in development and their inability to complete tasks that they can conceptualize but lack the psychomotor skills to complete. Many gifted children lack peers with whom they can communicate. Some accept this difficulty and look for friendships with older children. The difficulty in finding friends often means that gifted children have problems in learning to socialize. The problem often is exacerbated if these children associate with older children since their lack of social skills is even more apparent. On occasion, the gifted child may attempt to dominate relationships with peers and experience much strife (Chess & Hassibi, 1978). Still others try to disguise their ability and may in time fully block the expression of their giftedness.

As a whole, the gifted are under represented in child guidance clinics and other mental health agencies that provide services to children (Freundlich, 1987). It is fallacious to assume that all gifted children experience an unusual degree of psychosocial stress. It also is wrong to assume that gifted children are somehow different or invulnerable to stress and would not profit from mental health intervention. If the gifted child's behavior or affect suggests that he or she is vulnerable to maladjustment because of difficulties associated with accepting and experiencing his or her giftedness, counseling is clearly appropriate. The gifted appear to be particularly good candidates for therapy because of their conceptual ability.

Therapy with Gifted Children

The gifted child is quite a challenge to the child practitioner. Within this as any group there are similarities as well as differences which suggest child welfare workers provide for individual preferences in such areas as design, mobility, and cerebral dominance (Griggs, 1984). The social worker must be very astute in order to identify the child's giftedness. What the practitioner is likely to perceive initially is the child's nonconformity and unwillingness to cooperate. The sophisticated child practitioner will be alert to indirect or subtle signs of giftedness, such as the child's production of unusual ideas or generation of a variety of ways of employing play objects in the play therapy room. In general, the child practitioner identifies the child's giftedness through a combined assessment of the child's divergent thinking and productive ideas when talking, playing, and/or responding to standardized tests.

Once a child practitioner identifies a child client as highly gifted, new challenges emerge. Many of the emotional problems are a social overlay from receiving negative responses for the child's divergency. The practitioner must determine means of helping the gifted child adjust to society sufficiently so that he or she does not continue to provoke others' aversive reactions. Yet, the practitioner must guard against negating the child's constructive divergency, thereby further inhibiting his or her giftedness.

A challenge emerges also in defining appropriate therapeutic techniques with gifted child clients. Gifted children often are quite resistant to typical clinical approaches. The ineffectiveness of these approaches seems tied to the child's preference for internal control and motivation by inspiration rather than pleasing others. Torrance (1975) writes that gifted children are less likely than other children to desire to emulate significant adults. Therefore, therapeutic procedures such as modeling and social reinforcement may be less effectual with gifted children. Moreover, since motivation to identify with others is limited, transference and consequent interpretation of transference may be of limited relevance. Since these children strive for maximal self-control, they often react adversely to behavioral modification techniques. Cognitive restructuring techniques may be relatively ineffective. As mentioned previously, their high giftedness presupposes complex analytical skills. As masters of abstraction, gifted children are capable of presenting complex rationalizations that may block logical, concrete discussions about their problem. Ironically, the very divergency and autonomy of the gifted child that the practitioner wishes to nurture may stand in the way of building a therapeutic alliance!

There is a lack of empirical data about effective therapeutic techniques when working with gifted children. LeVine (1984) has identified nine strategies for conducting counseling with gifted children based upon LeVine's extensive clinical work with this population and the theoretical writings on giftedness. The principles underlying these nine strategies are to support the child's giftedness through the therapeutic discussion and to implement the child's wisdom when selecting techniques. Therefore, the first four strategies for assisting these children involve the identification of issues of relevance to gifted children, and helping them learn what it means to be gifted and how one can be gifted and still adapt to society. The next five strategies involve using the child's creative and bright ideas to design techniques that will capture his or her imagination, thereby maximizing the clinical alliance so that the child can successfully work through identified themes and issues.

1. The client needs counseling assistance to learn to identify that he or she possesses special talents. Because this child most likely has experienced criticism from those not identifying or understanding the nature of his or her giftedness, he or she may have internalized very unrealistic or negative self-attributes. A beginning goal of treatment is to help the child learn to identify and to prize his or her uniqueness. During discussions and activities, it is critical therefore for the child practitioner to point out to this child that "you are a person with many good and many unusual ideas."

2. Once the child has learned to appreciate his or her giftedness, the practitioner helps the child understand that a degree of social marginality may be associated with the giftedness. In essence, the practitioner communicates, "Your creativity is a very special gift. As is true of most gifts, there is a certain cost. The cost of creativity is that you perceive events and objects in new ways that most others will not understand. Because they do not understand, you may sometimes feel different and sometimes feel alone."

3. As treatment progresses, an important theme to be discussed is the responsibility associated with the "gift" of giftedness. Many gifted children, especially those referred to therapy, have introjected such negative feelings about their unique views and products that they become very passive, refusing to produce anything and thereby defaulting upon their creativity. The reader may have noted that the second of the themes of typical relevance to gifted children discussed above rings familiarly of existential psychology in that the child is encouraged to analyze his or her feeling about being alone in the world. A further extrapolation from existential writings leads to this third theme to be discussed. The existentialists inform clients that because they are basically alone, they must assume responsibility for their own attitudes and actions in order to give their lives some meaning (Frankl, 1963). In working with gifted child clients, the practitioner encourages the child to view his or her creativity as a gift that should not be ignored. The therapist states in various ways, "It is not alright to always give up. You have a very special gift. It may be hard to carry that gift but you will feel better if you use it rather than hide it. In fact, you have a responsibility to share your gift with those who are less endowed."

4. A final theme that emerges when conducting therapy with gifted children is that they may need to learn to compromise. The issue surfaces because of their inner-directedness and independence. The practitioner should help the client recognize that a certain degree of social marginality is quite adaptive and probably a necessary result of the child's giftedness. Yet, extreme inner-directedness and consequent loneliness can be debilitating. The child needs to learn to identify when he or she feels so alone that anxiety ensues and overall functioning is impeded. At that point, the child must compromise and adapt to society sufficiently so that his or her overall development is not impaired.

No doubt these themes and issues will emerge at various times in various forms through treatment. The following techniques have been found most helpful for allowing the emergence of these critical issues.

5. An essential technique for working with gifted children is to guard against power struggles. This is important because creative children tend to be very independent and to value internal control. If the practitioner becomes engaged in a power struggle with the client, the child is likely to perceive the practitioner as another adult who doesn't understand and doesn't value him or her. Thus, the practitioner should support the child's present sense of autonomy and encourage further self-control.

6. An effective means for fostering the child's sense of autonomy is to allow the client to exercise maximum control over the sessions. The therapist does not surrender responsibility for the ultimate therapeutic orientation of the sessions but whenever possible does encourage the child to select topics of conversation and play material to be employed. When this principle is implemented, gifted children are likely to invent unusual ways of using play objects and novel activities in which they wish the therapist to participate.

7. The practitioner then employs the child's choice of novel activities and creative ways of using toys to emulate critical events in the child's life. The gifted child's tendency to reject concrete, rational discussion of problems has been discussed. However, through the activity of play that the child selects, life's dilemmas can be paralleled. The therapist then can stimulate the child to try out alterative behaviors for coping with the dilemma. The child is encouraged to develop his or her own answers to the existential dilemma of being creative with its inherent joy and marginality. Furthermore, this technique exploits the child's desire for increased autonomy and increased control.

8. Another helpful technique in treating gifted children is to appeal to their highly sophisticated, abstract sense of logic when discussing moral and social issues. Kohlberg (1966) writes that for most elementary age children, moral value resides in performing "good" or "right" roles and maintaining conventional order and die expectancy of others. Most children's analysis of morality is "conventional," circumscribed by their tendency to think concretely.

Because of their keen analytic skills, gifted children are likely to exhibit a higher-level conceptualization about morality. For example, when fourth- through seventh-graders were asked to fantasize about the three wishes they would most like to actualize, gifted children selected highly altruistic wishes (Karnes & Wherry, 1981). The morality of gifted children is a morality of "self-accepted principles" (Kohlberg, 1966). They recognize that moral value is not an absolute but resides in a conscious decision to adopt standards that protect both the individual and society.

The gifted child is stimulated by discussions that consider existential questions and relative truths and may be unaffected or respond adversely to discussions which focus upon the sanctions rendered by society for specific attitudes and behaviors. In treatment, gifted children may respond poorly to actions which center upon their directly modifying their behavior, and they are more incited to change by ions in which they are prompted to analyze the relative effects of their behavior upon their personal goals and those of others.

9. Whenever possible, the practitioner employs metaphoric communication to point out self-defeating patterns and teach socially appropriate behaviors. Because of gifted children's fine abilities at abstraction, they can easily manipulate discussions into supra rational arguments that avoid the underlying dynamic issues. The use of metaphor in therapy is well established as an effective therapeutic technique in working with a wide range of clients because metaphor allows clinicians to suggest changes at a subconscious level by circumventing typical defenses. The therapeutic metaphor is particularly helpful with children because it captures their imagination and attitudes while paralleling life events in a language that children understand. By virtue of their appreciation for divergency, gifted children often delight in fantasy and metaphoric communication. A therapeutic metaphor can be particularly helpful with creative children because it bypasses their tendency toward rationalization while holding their attention.

In sum, the nine strategies outlined for working with gifted children are designed to exploit the child's creative processes towards achievement of the treatment goals. Identification and discussion with the child of themes and issues typically associated with being gifted can help these children adapt to society without stifling their special talents.

Child practitioners can also play a vital role in preventive mental health for gifted children. Working as a consultant with educators, the worker can conduct sessions for gifted children and their families so that all better understand and appreciate the children's special talents.

Children with Physical Liabilities and Illness

When children suffer severe illnesses or catastrophic injuries, both parents and children experience traumatic grief reactions. Each may not know how to deal with the other's feelings. If the parents' and the child's concerns are consistently ignored or repressed, long-term psychological effects may ensue. A child practitioner may be vital in fostering the overall recovery of the child by helping the parent and child understand the psychological states of recovery from a traumatic illness and helping the family deal with the child's pain and/or handicap.

Neely (1982) describes four issues that commonly arise in counseling handicapped children. These issues are other relations, self-conflict, maladaptive behavior, and a need for vocational counseling. Donovan and McIntyre (1990) add in *Healing the Hurt Child* the handicapped child is particularly prone to feeling that his or her life is out of control, even the body and consciousness may be out of the child's felt control. Many of the emotional problems of the handicapped, for example, manipulating and controlling others, may reflect an underlying desire for self-control.

Coping Phases

A child generally passes through several phases in learning to cope with a chronically disabling disease or permanent physical impairment. First, the child displays reactive effects. Behavior may regress to an earlier developmental level. The child may become depressed (as exhibited by an unwillingness to talk about the physical impairment), cry without warning, show a lack of energy, and demonstrate increased dependency. Belligerence and withdrawal are normal initial reactions to severe physical disability. The child may even misinterpret his or her illness as punishment by parents. Gradually, the child moves into a recoil phase.

He or she begins to talk about the physical disability but demands increase and depression continues. Finally, the child enters a restitution phase in which he or she attempts to adjust to the impairment, reenter society, and master the environment. Even if a child seems to have reached a restitution phase, she or he may regress in acceptance of the disability as she or he reaches pubescence. Increasing peer rejection may lead to depression and withdrawal. The child may need to be supported through a reenactment of the reactive and recoil phases until he or she develops a new, realistic view of how to relate to others.

Work With Parents

A child practitioner can aid parents in understanding that a child with severe physical disability will initially experience withdrawal and regression and may react belligerently to others. The practitioner can further aid parents in learning that it is important to allow the child to express the negative feelings and attitudes, that movement from a reactive to restitution phase necessitates the child's expression of his or her frustration. Naturally, the parents want to alleviate the child's psychological and physical pain as much as possible. They may need to be taught how to allow the child to express his or her personal despair. Communication training workshops such as parent effectiveness training (Gordon, 1970) and filial therapy (Guemey, 1964) have been helpful in this regard. A practitioner can also be helpful in identifying when the child's expression of personal anguish is not promoting his or her recovery. For example, it is not healthy for a child to begin adopting in "invalid" identity in which the child sees all of his or her reinforcers tied to the illness. In contrast, it is a good clinical sign that the child needs assistance directly after surgery. However, if the child does not begin to express some hopefulness and desire toward mastery after basic recovery from the physical trauma, intervention with the family and child may be helpful.

The practitioner also can be of aid in alerting the parents to possible psychological consequences of certain handicaps. Literature is rapidly expanding concerning the psychological effects of particularly physical handicapping conditions. In the paragraphs that follow, we will outline a few of the behavioral and psychological effects the child practitioner will want to keep in mind and share with parents when working with hearing impaired, visually impaired, disfigured, or psychosomatic children.

Deaf Children

Many deaf children do not trust hearing persons, believing that they cannot understand their problem (Portner, 1981). Deaf children with deaf parents show better ratings on maturity, responsibility, and independence than do deaf children with hearing parents (Meadow, 1976). This may be because hearing parents have limited communication with their deaf child early in development. Because the psychosocial development of a child is closely tied to language, a deaf child has little choice but to act out what he or she is feeling or thinking (Portner, 1981). Acting-out behavior in a deaf child may be inappropriately classified as impulsive behavior. For example, a number of researchers have documented motor restlessness, impulsivity, and doubt coexisting with rigidity and obstinacy as psychological concomitants of deafness among children (Lesser & Easser, 1972). Therapy with a deaf child requires far more time and specialized skill if communication must be translated with sign language. Deaf children need practitioners with signing skills and an understanding of the unique developmental dynamics of a deaf child (Portner, 1981).

Blind Children

Blind children may develop tendencies to touch others and some have short attention spans coupled with intense fear of their environment (Chess & Hassibi, 1978). If parents are aware of possible psychological and behavioral effects of certain handicaps, they will be less likely to blame the child or themselves for these unavoidable problems. For instance, visually impaired children may break rules without meaning to. If the child then is disciplined for disobeying an order that he or she did not understand, the child will feel angry toward the parent or teacher.

Disfigured Children

Body image is closely associated with development of a positive self-image. Children may be disfigured by bums, cancer treatments, operations, amputations, and disease. For a disfigured child to gain a better self-image, he or she must have a narcissistic investment in his or her body and have positive reflections in significant others and in the community. Treatment usually includes helping the child learn that the disfigurement is limited to a body deficiency, not a personality or a social deficiency. There is mourning and then acceptance with compensatory actions, such as wigs, prostheses, and plastic surgery (Woods, 1975). With the increased survival of children with cancer have come new adjustment problems. These children have poorer total self-concepts, and more depressive symptoms (Greenberg, 1989). Denial is the most frequent coping mechanism to moderate the emotional impact of the cancer experience. Increasing social contacts help the child's long-term adjustment.

The goals of therapy for the handicapped child may vary considerably depending upon the type of problem and the competency of the family. The goals can include pain control, social skills training, facilitating family functioning, serving as advocate for family with the medical or social security establishment, management of grief, fostering new senses of control, and helping to establish some hope and reasons for optimism (Barden, 1990).

Children of Poverty

With the advent of welfare reform, child welfare workers will be faced with working with an increased number of low income children and the issue of neglect. We know poverty is associated with a wide range of psychosocial problems among adults. Mental illness, alcohol and drug abuse, suicide, and child abuse all are correlated positively with poverty. It also is known that there is an increase in these psychosocial problems during periods of economic recession as individuals lose their employment and consequent economic security. Psychological stress due to poverty and economic uncertainty is the most important link that has been identified in explanations of why the poor experience higher rates of psychological maladjustment.

Risk Factors

Children are not immune to the same pressures that their parents experience because of poverty and economic uncertainty. First of all, they may be the recipients of their parent's discontent. Chess and Hassibi (1978) write that if parents are satisfied, they

> impart a sense of pride and satisfaction and they create family legends that are
> congruent with their own pride . . . they find heroes and retell their history in
> a manner that nurtures hope and optimism in their children. By the same token,
> parents' hopelessness, their inability to change what they do not accept, and

their shame about their own past and present status within the culture adversely affects their children's outlook on life and creates the conditions for their future failure (pp. 118–119).

Furthermore, children raised in poverty are more subject to certain developmental risks. The elevated risks begin before the children are born. Children who grow up in poverty are usually born of poor mothers. As we discussed in an earlier chapter on normal developmental processes, the mothers medical and nutritional history can have dramatic effects upon the child's physical and cognitive well-being. The mothers poor nutrition correlates positively with difficulties during pregnancy and prematurity, which in turn correlate with neurological difficulties of the newborn. The effects of the mother's poor nutrition may be compounded by her inability to receive and pay for good medical care.

After birth, the organic risks remain higher for poor children. They are more likely to experience malnutrition, which can retard physical and intellectual growth, and are less likely to receive needed medical care.

Children raised in poverty are likely to experience a number of psychosocial stresses. There is often only one parent in the home, who must work. These parents cannot afford excellent day care. The children may be left for extended with minimal supervision. In many cases, they lack appropriate sensory and educational stimulation (Achenbach, 1974).

When the poor children attend school, their sense of vulnerability is further exacerbated. In the 1960s and early 1970s, poor children often were considered "disadvantaged" and "culturally deprived"—implying that they lack any sense of social structure and culture. Most social scientists and practitioners now recognize that these children are "culturally different" from traditional middle-class norms, but not culturally deficient. Nevertheless, our school systems generally do not take into account these children's cultures. Instead, the poor children are expected to adapt swiftly to the middle-class norms. Yet, these children may be unfamiliar with the materials and ideas of the typical classroom. Moreover, the children often speak a different language or special English dialect in their homes. The linguistic differences pose some difficulties in comprehending the teacher, but the inability to speak standard English is an even larger detriment as it may lead to the poor children's being evaluated negatively. Even if the children speak standard English, many experience prejudice and ridicule at school. They may be teased for their shabby dress. They may feel left out if they lack the money to participate in activities joined by most of their peers. Teachers also may be biased against poor children and come to (a) expect less of them academically, (b) instill in them a sense of failure, (c) reinforce their acting out behavior, and (d) impose on them feelings of being less than adequate socially. Thus, children in poverty often must not only undergo psychologically harmful stresses at home, but must endure stress in their social sphere.

Invulnerable Children

It is important to point out that although the poor can be considered a high-risk group to develop psychological maladjustments, there is great variability in the psychological consequences of growing up in poverty. Many poor children are no more maladjusted than affluent children. In fact, some forms of childhood pathology such as autism may be more common in the middle and upper classes. One could posit that a great number of poor children actually are more psychologically healthy than their affluent counterparts precisely because they have not become severely maladjusted under highly stressful situations. It is important not to characterize children who grow up in poverty as less emotionally stable but instead focus upon their vulnerability and the constant stress they must endure. Garmezy (1981) has coined the term "invulnerables" to characterize youths that are raised in very aversive and poor environments who excel in personal development. According to Garmezy, these individuals complete their education, do not have an arrest record, gain meaningful employment, and lead constructive, happy lives. Support for Garmezy's position can be found in an epidemiological survey of psychological disorders in children (Langner, Herson, Greene, Jameson, & Goff, 1970), which found higher proportions of welfare children as compared to a cross-section sample in both the "well" and "impaired" tails of the distribution. Some suggest that poor children from two-parent homes and with older siblings experience the negative effects of stress less than do children from single parent homes and from homes without older siblings. If we can identify the factors contributing to these "invulnerable" children's success, perhaps we will be better able to assist other children in shedding the shackles of poverty.

Mental Health Services

On top of identifying and supporting the "invulnerables," workers need to reach out to the many poor children who are highly vulnerable to psychological stress. In this regard, well established mental health records are quite alarming. Lower socioeconomic parents are less likely to bring their children to mental health services unless pressured by schools or law enforcement agencies. Psychotherapy is less likely to be offered to lower-class children. When counseling and psychotherapy are offered to lower-class children, they are more likely to be conducted by trainees. Poor children are more likely to miss counseling appointments. Very often, social workers and poor clients feel a mutual misfit and distrust.

Just as therapists have described the "preferred" or "attractive" psychotherapy adult client as "Mr. or Ms. Yavis," that is young, attractive, verbal, intelligent, and successful, we can speak of "Yavis, junior." In other words, child practitioners prefer and acknowledge that they are most successful with children from middle class backgrounds. When a lower socioeconomic emotionally disturbed child is referred for professional help, the referral is made to a middle class teacher, social worker, psychologist, or psychiatrist to whom the child is a "non-Yavis junior." These children may receive only minimal assistance from middle-class practitioners because the children lack verbal "good client" skills that make them attractive clients. Thus, the lower-class emotionally disturbed child ultimately finds himself or herself hospitalized in a state mental hospital, while his or her middle-class counterparts receive extensive outpatient therapy. In one study, Jennings and Davis (1977) showed that hospitalized lower-class children and adolescents could be taught verbal skills that would enhance their effectiveness to communicate when being interviewed. Further, as their ability to communicate effectively increased, so too did their "attractiveness" to the interviewer.

It also is likely that the poor clients find many of the services provided to be inadequate or irrelevant to their needs. Whatever the exact reason, many lower class children experience marked psychological stress because of their poverty and are frequently not given adequate social services.

Even when adequate mental health services are provided to vulnerable children in poverty, the clinical sessions are clearly not adequate leverage against the organic, social, and educational stressors these children experience. In working with children in poverty, the child practitioner often needs to break out of the traditional clinical role and assume an advocate position for the children, helping them receive the various medical and remediational services they need.

Prevention Services

Achenback (1974) also identifies a number of primary prevention strategies that are most important if we are to meet the needs of vulnerable poor children:

- direct provision of nutritional and medical care to low socioeconomic status pregnant women

- improved obstetrical care for this population of women

- after birth parent training programs for the poor

- provision of adequate food to poor children

- mass screening for lead poisoning and strict building code enforcement to eliminate peeling lead paint and other hazards

- routine preventive inoculations for the poor

- provision of adequate day-care centers offering sensory and educational stimulation

- increased use of the media for children's education

- public school programs geared to mesh with preschool programs provided for the poor

- school-based educational and recreational activities after school hours and during vacations

- graduated series of mental health services offered through the educational system so that the problems are detected early and dealt with: first, by consultation between educators, parents, and mental health workers; second, by special educational planning; and lastly, by individual and group counselors who work with the child and family

Achenback's (1974) guidelines are quite constructive. Most require tremendous social effort not yet present. On the individual basis, many practitioners experience significant barriers from society, schools, and parents when they attempt to implement these strategies. Prevention, consultation, and policy formulation for child practitioners are explained in more detail in Chapter 15.

Additional studies are necessary pertaining to techniques, strategies, and guidelines for working more effectively with children from poverty backgrounds. It is important to emphasize that the child practitioner must be ever mindful of the cultural background of the child client from a poor socioeconomic status. Only when both the practitioner and the child understand each other's values is there a good probability of a successful clinical intervention.

The Culturally Different Child

From a cross-cultural perspective, mental health and good human relations occur concomitantly. Although norms for psychological functioning are difficult to determine, it can be said that the mentally healthy child maintains open communication and feels respected and responded to by people from all walks of life.

Mental Health Services Cross-Culturally

According to the cross-cultural perspective, the parameters of mental health are determined by a particular culture. For example, in some African cultures, it is mentally healthy to exhibit a ceremonial neurosis characterized by frenzied activity, laughing, and crying. This state is voluntary and reversible and serves a socially sanctioned purpose of designating a leader to the tribe (Wallace, 1970). In the United States, it is considered mentally healthy to lament over the death of a significant other. Bereavement serves a personal purpose of catharsis and a social purpose of gaining solace from others. In other cultures, stoicism and rejoicing are the mentally healthy responses to another person's death. The death is a signal for reaffirmation of life among the survivors. Thus, to the extent that an individual's creativity, spontaneity, and happiness fulfill social expectations, he or she will be viewed as mentally healthy within the culture. Examples of major differences in what is considered adjustment to Native Americans and the dominant culture include:

- others before self versus putting self first
- honoring one's elders versus valuing youth
- children belong to all versus children are the parents' property
- few rules are best versus having rules for everything
- simplifying problems versus making nothing simple (Richardson, 1981)

Of course, social roles and personal aspirations are not always congruent. This is especially true in large, complex societies in which individuals may find themselves caught between conflicting social roles. Such conflict has two general and mutually exclusive results: it may be the impetus for positive personal growth and enhancement, or it may result in emotional and behavioral problems that are no longer appropriate to the culture and the time (Burger, 1974). The first of these is usually ignored or not given serious attention. An individual who turns a conflict situation into a growth experience is considered well adjusted and mentally healthy. It is the maladjusted response to conflict that is of concern.

The personal problems, like adjustment, serve cultural functions. The child in need of services can admit social wrongdoing, receive help, and minimize punishment The suspension of logic and the emphasis on emotion that are characteristic of many children with problems provides a feeling of escape from intolerable situations (Burger, 1974). Symptoms provide some personal organization while the individual attempts to develop more efficient ways of thinking and behaving. Finally, the symptoms may motivate others to help the child reenter society.

Children need services in all cultures; however, the pattern of symptoms varies across cultures, and what constitutes maladjustment is culturally determined A few classic syndromes investigated by anthropologists illustrate this point. The Algonkin Indians of Canada suffer *windingo*, which is characterized by cannibalistic impulses. In Southeast Asia and Indonesia the maladjusted may show symptoms labeled *latch*, involving a startle reaction followed by obsessive/compulsive behavior. In northern Japan, women in particular are susceptible to *emu*, an obsessive/compulsive syndrome. A disturbance in a certain Kenyan tribe is *saka*, a convulsive attack associated with hysteria. The Eskimo of Greenland suffer *pibloktog,* in which excitement is followed by convulsions, heavy sleep, and amnesia (Bamouw, 1963). Hispanics speak of *susto,* which is marked by restlessness during sleep and by listlessness, loss of appetite, disinterest in dress and personal hygiene, loss of strength, depression, and introversion during waking hours (Rubel, 1964).

On one level of abstraction, children's problems are the same cross-culturally. For example, 'across cultures the maladjusted are unable to function effectively within their group, and a common symptom of severe maladjustment is hallucinations. On another level of abstraction, symptoms are culturally specific. For example, the specific content of hallucinations varies across cultures. Some experiences, such as hearing voices, may be indicative of maladjustment in one culture and common and accepted in another (Torrey, 1972).

The differentiation between normality and abnormality also is culturally determined. Critical cues to this discrimination include nonconformity to appropriate social patterns, exaggeration of norms, and unusual behavior (LeVine, 1973; Wallace, 1970). In the United States, treatment and hospitalization are considered indices of maladjustment. Only a few societies have followed this

Western pattern of hospitalization for mental illness. In the Western world, therapists have become moral legislators, and social engineers. In the United States, for example, the American Psychiatric Association wields enormous power in defining the parameters of normal and abnormal behavior. A good example of how this power is used, positively as well as negatively, can be seen in the APA's decision to drop homosexuality as a diagnostic category, declaring in doing so that homosexuality was no longer a disease or mental illness.

Classification of emotional problems varies by culture, and a culture's conception of causation fixes its system of classification. In the Western world, those problems are attributed to biological and psychosocial factors and are thus categorized as either organic or functional in origin. Many other cultures believe that there are three causes of maladjustment: biological, psychosocial, and metaphysical. Maladjusted behaviors then may be classified as due to organic or functional causes, to witchcraft or other supernatural forces (Torrey, 1972).

Even though the definition of children's problems is culturally specific, members of one culture cannot be considered more or less adjusted than members of another culture. Wallace (1970) states that it is a contradiction in terms to consider an entire culture as maladjusted, although one culture may be more proficient than another in its control over the environment. Maladjustment is the inability to function within a group. If a culture survives over time, then it is adaptive and healthy. Only those individuals who cannot cope within the culture can be considered disturbed. Labeling a culture as having neurotic or psychotic tendencies can be a political maneuver for sanctioning discrimination. For example, the effort of Black slaves in the United States to run away to gain freedom was considered a serious symptom of basic pathology by their slave masters (Wallace, 1970). In similar fashion, the patriarchal structure of Mexican culture has been reported to instill serious neurosis in Mexican women, fostering the concept that the Mexican woman is inferior to the man (Diaz–Guerrero, 1975). Descriptions of culturally specific syndromes of emotional disturbance do not imply that a group itself is ineffective but rather that, when an individual experiences stress, it is likely to be expressed in culturally specific ways.

In general, mental health involves a realistic acceptance of self, a clear perception of the world, open relationships with others, and the ability to handle stress and crisis. The overall processes of mental health and maladjustment are universal attributes of culture. The specific events creating stress and the behavior manifestations of disturbances are culturally defined (LeVine & Padilla, 1980).

Therapy with the Ethnic Minority Child

A critical question then emerges. Are there any therapeutic conditions that are relatively universal and equally valid when working with children from ethnic minority cultures?

One condition that facilitates therapeutic gain is that there must be a significant engagement between the therapist and child. *Engagement is* defined, albeit abstractly, as the commitment by therapist and client to work on mutually defined goals. Since Freud's early writings, it has been well accepted in therapeutic literature that resistance must be worked through before effective therapy will occur. Empirical research has shown that, regardless of the therapist's theoretical persuasion, clients attribute much success in therapy to their feelings about the therapist's personality. Simply stated, the therapist needs to be a person who is encouraging and understanding of the client (Sloane, Staples, Cristol, Yorkston, & Whipple, 1975).

A number of factors may be necessary for high engagement, and the therapist must be very sensitive to cultural nuances to incorporate these factors into the therapeutic interaction. A congruence of therapist and client expectations about the therapeutic process fosters engagement (Garfield, 1978; Heine & Trosman, 1960). The higher the client's motivation for therapy, the more likely there will be a positive engagement (Garfield, 1980). Finally, if a client likes the therapist's personality, engagement is facilitated (Sloane, et al., 1975).

A second factor posited as a universal condition for effective cross-cultural therapy is that the therapist helps the child label his or her problem in constructs that are meaningful to the child. The child enters therapy after attempting many approaches to resolve his or her dilemmas and personal discomfort. He or she feels unsuccessful and confused. A critical and universal dimension of therapy is to help the child develop a sense of what factors are contributing to the problem. According to Toffey (1972), Garfield (1980), and others, the exact label for the problem can vary greatly as long as the child accepts the label as a logical explanation for his or her difficulties. Labeling the problem in culturally relevant constructs is aimed at helping the client gain a sense of causality about the nature of his or her difficulties. The culturally relevant label for the problem reduces the client's feeling of confusion, and in doing so, helps instill a sense of hope that he or she can overcome the crisis.

Appropriate labeling means that whenever possible, therapy is conducted in the client's primary language. Research by Marcos (1976) demonstrated that bilingual Hispanic clients are diagnosed differently and often are perceived as more disturbed when they speak in English than in Spanish. Clearly, many nuances of a client's problems will be lost if the client is not allowed to speak in his or her native tongue. Effective labeling also involves discriminating intra- and extrapsychic sources of stress. This discrimination is necessary so that clients learn which factors they can and cannot control and whether it is more appropriate to change the system or change themselves (Ruiz, 1977).

A third factor posited to cut across all effective therapy is that the therapist helps mobilize the child to change. In other words, the learning of the therapeutic interaction must be transferred to the client's everyday life (Carkhuff & Berense 1977). As a result of the positive relationship with the therapist, the child feels more hopeful about dealing with his or her problems. With renewed hope, the child is able to surmount intra and interpersonal barriers and can change.

Change may be one of cognition in which clients learn to think new ideas about themselves or to accept others in new ways. Usually, change is manifest as extinction of inappropriate or learning of new appropriate behavior. Action-oriented therapy approaches such as behavior modification, gestalt techniques, and psychodrama can be beneficial in prompting movement through the third universal dimension of the therapeutic relationship. However, when working with ethnic minority clients, it is essential that the client's goals to be fostered by these active approaches are established with the client during the second state of effective labeling of the problem so that the changes are congruent with the clients life view and sense of causality.

Many of the processes considered universal concomitants of therapy seem loaded with Anglo conceptions of adjustment and may not foster improvement in ethnic minority child clients. In Chapter 15, we outline the main competencies a child welfare worker will need to work with clients from ethnic minority groups (LeVine & Ruiz, 1984).

Family Preservation

An emerging perspective in child welfare is that children can best be served by keeping them with their own parents, with their brothers and sisters, with their peer group, and with their school. Services are usually delivered in the home often in a very intensive manner. Family preservation is a new movement in working with children built on the best traditions of child welfare practice and the latest technologies of social change (Hooper–Briar, Broussard, Ronnau, & Sallee, 1995). Family preservation also is known as family-centered practice, home-based services, or in-home services. Family Preservation takes many forms yet shares common principles and values. Marian Wright Edelman of the Children's Defense Fund states, "Millions of children at risk need child care, not foster care; a check-up, not an intensive care bed; a tutor, not a guardian; a head start, not 12 years of special education" (Edelman, 1990).

Principles and Values of Family Preservation

1. Children need their families. This approach supports the belief that children can best develop and be protected, with few exceptions, by remaining with their biological families. Parents want to parent. However, for emotional reasons or lack of education or modeling, they are unable to do so. If the biological family is unable to raise the child, then adoption is examined as an important alternative.

2. Family preservation values families' culture and heritage. It is important to identify the family's cultural and ethnic background and employ intervention strategies that build on and reinforce these strengths. A family's cultural strengths include rituals and traditions.

3. Family preservation focuses on family strengths. This approach places an emphasis on assessing and using the family's strengths as the basis for growth. Family preservation workers look at what is right with this family rather than looking just at the problems and deficiencies.

4. Respect is a belief in the dignity of the individual family. Family preservation workers demonstrate behavioral confirmation of the dignity of the family. The worker's confirmation can range from how they dress, to how they enter a home as a guest, to addressing the family with respect.

5. Family integrity is a belief that families have the potential to change and that most troubled families will do so with help that meets them where they are. Families do not want to live in pain or dysfunction. Workers meet families where they are—in their homes, at school, in jail, and are ready to teach, clean, and work with clients as partners.

6. Family preservation uses family-focused theory and policies of helping. Therapists regard the troubled family as the group to be served rather than focus on the "troubled child" or "sick parent," and offer to help within the context of the family's total environment.

7. Respect is shown for each family's strengths, potential, natural striving toward growth, and capacity for change. Each family is individualized, and its unique strengths and capacities are identified. Therapists recognize and expect a family's growth and capacity for change.

8. Family preservation emphasizes the therapist's role in teaching or helping family members develop coping and mastery skills, rather than just "treating" them. Family Preservation social workers work *with* families, rather than *treat* families, to ensure a partnership role.

9. Family preservation assumes a health/growth orientation in understanding and working with the family. Problems or areas of concern are reframed as strengths.

10. Family preservation workers attempt to instill hope and enhance motivation in family members and regard the clients as colleagues or partners in the helping process. They provide pep talks to families and encourage them as they make their way along the path of reunification or preservation.

11. Therapists empower families to "do" for themselves and avoid dependence upon the social service system (Ronnau & Sallee, 1991).

Family Preservation Service Components

How are these principles and values put into practice? The therapy or service is as complete, comprehensive, and intensive as necessary to effect problem resolution (Lloyd, 1984). Operationalized, this means very small caseloads (two to seven families at once), staff being available on a 24-hour basis, and creative staff who believe in exploring all possible options. The following components are characteristic of many family preservation services:

- *Basic needs:* Provisions to meet the family's basic needs (food, shelter, clothing, medical care, etc.).

- *Ongoing risk assessment:* Ongoing family assessment and counseling (working with the family in the home provides the best assessment of risk and the family's capacity to provide safety).

- *Flexibility in meeting unique needs:* Parenting, household management, life skills training and education services (homemakers, day care, parent support groups).

- *Ongoing support:* Finding and/or creating formal or informal support groups for isolated, lonely families.

- *Service Partnerships*: Family Preservation services coordinate all the services which the family receives through stronger partnerships and integrated strategies.

- *Advocacy:* A strong commitment to advocate on the local and federal levels for program and policies that respond to the needs of troubled families (Mannes, Ronnau, Lloyd , Sallee & Shannon, 1990).

Family Preservation Worker Competencies

What do competent family preservation social workers look like? What can they do and how? What knowledge, skills, and values should a person possess to practice family preservation? These questions are answered to some degree in the following eight competencies. Notice cultural competence, a strengths perspective, and empowerment as principles that underlie the competencies. A competent family preservation worker:

1. Frames problems in solvable, acceptable ways and employs techniques and skills that build on each family's unique strengths and motivate families to attain self-sufficiency.

2. Engages family, agencies, and community systems in genuine partnership and teaches skills necessary to attain the family's goals.

3. Understands, respects, and practices within the family's cultural context, experience, and history as the framework for family preservation practice.

4. Is knowledgeable, respectful, sensitive, and responsive to issues of human diversity in the course of working with families.

5. Applies knowledge of human growth and behavior, systems theory, and multiple change strategies to develop systematic options for each unique family system.

6. Integrates and applies the values and techniques of family preservation (services and practices) based upon a commitment to the core belief in the importance of the family system.

7. Joins in partnership with the family to facilitate empowerment of the family while supporting family preservation values and using the family preservation change process to enable the family to meet its goals by whatever means necessary (Family Preservation Institute, New Mexico State University, 1991).

Implication for Traditional Children's Practice

What implications does family preservation have for traditional children's practice?

1. *Accept clients as partners*: Therapists become team members with families and, as such, recognize the fact that they must share as they expect families to share. Most therapists are not educated to see the client as an expert, yet clients are experts in many ways. They are experts in how the problem affects them, their family history, etc. Family preservation therapists do not hesitate to use self-disclosure when appropriate.

2. *Do what is necessary:* Family preservation workers are as comfortable with "cockroach" therapy in the home as they are with "couch" therapy. They recognize that cleaning yards to provide safe play areas for children may be as critical to families as therapy. Family preservation therapists have overcome the fear of clients becoming dependent on them and build empowerment strategies into their work with clients.

   As therapists, they are flexible and meet the family's time frame. They focus on assessment, not diagnosis, and they learn to work comfortably in families' homes rather than in their own offices.

3. *Use natural systems:* Family Preservation makes use of informal natural support systems in work with families. Agencies do not have all the answers and solutions. The families' friends and community can become helpful allies.

A Successful Family Preservation Case

Family preservation may be the best opportunity to successfully address a multitude of issues raised concerning a child. Through the following case illustration, let us see how family preservation is practiced at the direct service level. Our special thanks to June C. Lloyd, a family preservation expert who supplied this case.

Case 13.2   Jerry

Jerry is a 13-year-old boy who refused to attend school or comply with his parents' house rules. His father, having grown up in a strict home as a child, became frustrated and beat Jerry with a belt on several occasions, raising welts on his neck and shoulders. At the time of the referral, Jerry had run away to a friend's house. He and his friend were arrested and jailed for breaking and entering. Jerry had been in contact with the law and was referred to as "a child in need of supervision." His behavior had resulted in several psychological evaluations, one of which raised the possibility of schizophrenia.

The family preservation social worker's goal was to give the family maximum support and help the parents learn to parent this type of child. The social worker immediately introduced behavioral programming to interrupt the chaos and provide the structure necessary before traditional therapy could occur. In this family, that meant supporting the parents in providing clear and simple limits and expectations. Introduction of this intervention can be very stressful, which meant that the social worker had to be consistently available to coach the family through the crisis.

Jerry is typical of bright, angry adolescents in that he had much experience in manipulating adult systems. Thus, the social worker spent extensive time preparing and coaching other systems to unify and support the intervention. This included the family, the schools, the juvenile probation officer, and other social service staff.

Because the parents and the other systems held firm, Jerry was able to experience a protected world. In fewer than three weeks of intensive services, he was attending school, living at home, and abiding by his parents' rules with only minimal conflict. The mother and father attended family education classes that helped direct them toward alternatives to physical discipline with Jerry. The father verbalized that with this support, he no longer felt he was entirely responsible for Jerry's behavior, but that the community was helping the family.

Summary

Certain biological characteristics and social or physical limitations make children vulnerable to psychological stress. In this chapter, we have reviewed some of the more common handicapping conditions (sensory impairments and illnesses), genetic traits (giftedness and mental retardation), and social conditions (poverty) that increase children's vulnerability. We have attempted to explain that knowledge about the psychosocial stresses these children incur will aid the child practitioner in several ways. First, the practitioner will be alert to subtle ways that a particular child is struggling with issues related to the social or physical condition. Secondly, the practitioner can alert parents to the issues with which their child must wrestle. By working closely with the parents of special needs children, psychological disorders prompted by the unique stresses that special needs children experience can be attenuated. The family preservation approach provides intensive services to the child and family through the application of family-focused principles and values.

Chapter 14

Children with New Families

There is no greater social impact on children than their families. As we have stressed throughout this text, familial factors can cause or help resolve many of the emotional stresses children experience. In this chapter, we examine the research and dynamics of children of divorce, children in substitute care, and adopted children. Naturally, new families do not necessarily create maladjustment, but we will see that the added stress makes these children vulnerable to problems. Treatment considerations are presented for each type of new family, but it is clear that primary and secondary prevention strategies can better minimize children's vulnerability to the change of families.

Children of Divorce

Few social issues provoke as much emotion and debate as divorce. Divorce changes the most significant system of social and psychological influence in a child's life. Numerous relationships are effected; with parents, siblings, school friends, church, neighbors, new adults, and even basic needs such as living arrangements. Each of these issues may have a major influence on child development stages such as self-esteem and identity formation.

> I remember it was near my birthday when I was going to be 6 that Dad said at lunch he was leaving. I tried to say "No, Dad, don't do it," but I couldn't get my voice out. I was too much shocked. All the fun things we had done flashed right out of my head and all the bad things came in, like when he had to go to the

hospital with his bad back, and when he got mad at me. The bad thoughts just stuck there. My life sort of changed at that moment. Like I used to be always happy and suddenly I was sad.

> An 8-year-old girl. *Newsweek,*
> February 11, 1980

Much of an editorial nature has been written that children of divorce are vulnerable to stress. Until the 1970s, many of the empirical findings were incomplete or contradictory. In this section, a review of recent research and a background on the frequency of divorce is offered. Then, a synthesis of the complex social and psychological affects of divorce upon children is discussed.

The Difficulties of Research About Children of Divorce

Levitin (1979) points out major flaws of many of the studies of the effects of divorce conducted during the 1950s and 1960s:

- conceptualization of the single-parent family as deviant
- perception of single-parent families as a homogeneous group, a fact that mutes differences such as ethnic and social class
- single global variables such as single-parent status with little or no attention to mediating factors such as parental adjustment, economic status, and age and sex of child

Nevertheless, the results of two classic studies (Nye, 1957; Burchinal, 1964) have been consistently upheld by more recent investigation. Wallerstein (1989) in a 10 longitudinal study reported children are adversely affected by the divorce of their parents. Nye conducted a retrospective study of 780 adolescent boys and girls from three high schools. He hypothesized that the adjustment of children is related to family functioning whether or not it is legally or physically broken. His comparison of adjustment (delinquent behavior, psychosomatic illness, relationships to parents and peers) of adolescents in broken and happy or unhappy unbroken homes revealed that children of single-parent or reconstituted families were significantly better adjusted than children in unhappy (conflicted) two-parent families. Burchinal (1964), in another retrospective study, compared 1,566 adolescents in selected areas of personal and social adjustment from unbroken,

broken, and reconstituted families. He concluded that divorce itself was not the overwhelming influential factor, rather, family functioning was a much more important variable. More recent research has taken issue with this position given the age of the child, social economic class, and gender (Wallerstein, 1989; Wallerstein & Lewis, 1997).

In contrast to these large-scale studies, most of the clinical studies of individual children of divorce ". . . depict children as *highly* though often *temporarily distressed*" (Levitin, 1979, p. 5). Levitin (1979) maintains that these findings cannot be generalized to large populations of children of divorce but do offer poignant portraits of children for whom divorce is so traumatic and painful that they required treatment.

Intervening Variables.   The sex of the child is important in identifying the psychological effects of divorce. Boys may be affected more negatively and intensely than are girls (Heatherington, 1966; Heatherington & Deur, 1971; Heatherington, Cox, & Cox, 1976, 1979, 1985; Lang, Papenfuhs, & Walters, 1976; McDermott, 1970; Wallerstein & Kelly, 1975, 1976, 1980; Wallerstein & Lewis, 1997). For instance, in research examining matched pairs of children of divorce and children from intact families, one study (Hetherington, Cox & Cox, 1985) reported that boys separated from fathers before age 5 displayed more negative and less masculine self-concepts (as evidenced by playing with dolls with nurturing intent despite taunting by peers), and older boys displayed more compensatory masculine behavior (such as aggression against peers, stealing, and gang behavior) than did boys from intact families. In the same study, few significant differences between girls from divorced homes and matched girls from intact families were noted. In another study the only major difference was that mothers reported their daughters were ill more often (Stewart, Copeland, Chester, Malley, & Barenbaum, 1997). Santrock (1976) corroborated the findings that boys from divorced families were more impulsive, less self-controlled, and less able to delay gratification.

While most researchers agree that the younger the child at the time of onset of disruption and divorce, the greater the potential for the child to be detrimentally affected (Heatherington & Deur, 1971; Lang, Papenfuhs, & Walters, 1976; Santrock, 1977; Wallerstein & Kelly, 1975, 1976, 1980) a 25 year longitudinal study found children reacted especially poorly to divorce in middle to late childhood. Preschoolers were somewhat less affected that teenagers (Wallerstein, 1989). Santrock (1976) states that most detrimental to a child is a divorce within the child's first two years of life. Santrock (1977) employed doll play interviews and teachers' ratings of 45 father-present boys and 45 father-absent boys and reported that early loss of a father through divorce was more highly correlated with aggressive and disobedient behaviors by the child than if the father were lost through death.

An alternative hypothesis concerning the relationship of the child's age and the effects of divorce has been proposed. Warshak and Santrock (1980) theorize that the period of separation in the child's life determines the focus rather than the intensity of the detrimental effects. For example, a child whose parents separated during the child's conceptual developmental stage where egocentrism is foremost are likely to perceive the divorce as something that the child controlled and thus blame him- or herself for the separation. Thus, the child's adjustment problems focus upon self-blame, primarily because of his or her limited conceptual ability at that age. However, if parents separate during the child's adolescence, the child may be more likely to experience problems in his or her own love relationships. The effects of divorce may be felt most in the post divorce stage from toddlerhood through college (Wallerstein & Lewis, 1997).

A final intervening child variable reported to correlate with increased difficulties of adjustment following divorce is the child's previous psychological history. Generally, the divorce has more profound consequences upon the "temperamentally difficult child," those children defined by Chess and Hassibi (1978) as highly reactive to stimuli, changeable, and moody. Each child's psychological history needs to be considered when developing a prognosis of his or her adjustment to divorce (Gardner, 1977).

A number of variables about the divorcing parents also contribute to the child's vulnerability to psychological stress. The sex of the custodial parent may be important in the continued development of the child (Wallerstein & Lewis, 1997). Boys living with divorced mothers showed clinically significant signs of social maladaptation, including, impulsivity, aggressiveness, and hyperactivity (Hetherington, Cox & Cox, 1985).

The nature of the parents' relationship following divorce can affect a child's adjustment. In about a third of divorces, a turbulent relationship continues between the parents. These effects can be very destructive. If a child hears one parent frequently demeaned by the other, the child begins to view the parents ambivalently. The child may experience guilt about his or her ambivalence, and the child's ability to identify with the same-sex parent may be hampered.

At least as important as the child's reaction to the divorce is the child's adaptation to a single-parent home. Current research suggests that the traumatic effects of the divorce are vastly ameliorated if the custodial parent copes well with single parenting. If the custodial parent does not experience tremendous post-divorce depression, if that custodial parent continues to present the other parent in a positive light, and if the single parent does not sexualize or otherwise distort the relationship with the children, the children's response to the divorce is greatly eased (Chess & Hassibi, 1978).

However, some negative effects of single parenting are difficult to avoid. The single parent often must be provider and cannot be around the children as much as preferable. Until recently, almost all children remained with the mother. The degree of the father's availability is important in determining the intensity and duration of the effects of divorce (Daniel, 1977). The loss of a significant adult can prompt great mourning but can be minimized through relationships with in-laws, relatives of the custodial (or noncustodial) parent, and friends.

Often divorce leads to low socioeconomic status because of the following:

1. loss of "economics of scale"

2. inadequate child support and alimony payments

3. probability of welfare dependence because of fewer work opportunities and lower wages for women than men (Espenshade, 1979)

Divorce is more prevalent among poor families. Thus, divorce may lead to lower socioeconomic status, which, in turn, may lead to less positive child-rearing practices.

Range of Effects. Several studies shed light on the initial impact of divorce on children (Wallerstein & Lewis, 1997; McDermott, 1970; Ahrons, 1980; Bernard, 1978; Jacobson, 1979; Hess & Camara, 1979; Brown, 1983; Gardner, 1976; Westman, Swift, & Kramer, 1970) and concluded that the short-range effect is painful and profound. A study of the short-range impact of divorce on children revealed that important differences in reactions occurred among children at different developmental stages initially and one year after the separation/divorce. A five-year follow-up of 58 of the original 60 families revealed several important findings on all the age groups. Thirty-four percent of the children maintained a sense of well-being and self-confidence. Thirty-seven percent were judged to be suffering from moderately severe depression, which was manifested in a variety of behaviors including drug abuse, stealing, and pronounced unhappiness. The remaining 29% had resumed normal developmental progress, but experienced intermittent feelings of sadness about the divorce and resentment toward one or both of their parents (Wallerstein, 1989).

Long-range effects of experiencing divorce while growing up are extremely difficult to measure because of intervening variables such as parents' personal, social, and economic adjustment and personal characteristics of the child.

Findings from a ten-year follow-up of 38 youngsters now 16 to 18 years old, whose parents divorced during the children's early latency, suggest that separation from families and the transition into young adulthood are burdened by fear of disappointment in love relationships, lowered expectations, and a sense of powerlessness. A need for the father, especially among boys, appears to burgeon at middle and late adolescence (Wallerstein, 1987).

Much of the research of long-range effects (Nye, 1957; Burchinal, 1964; Hetherington, Cox, & Cox, 1976; Kulka & Weingarten, 1979) seems to indicate that most children of divorce eventually adjust as well as other children and that other variables such as parental conflict are more important predictors of a child's eventual adjustment than the divorce per se. Yet, the results of a 25 year study on 60 families indicates that divorce is a cumulative experience that may shape the behavior, emotions and relationships of children into adulthood (Wallerstein &Lewis, 1997). Beyond these generalizations, the limitations of the research cause much confusion. Few studies have succeeded in controlling for such confounding variables as socioeconomic status and racial background. Divorce is too often conceptualized as a static event, not a process.

A model proposed by Bohannan (1970) helped clarify the nonstatic nature of divorce. Bohannan (1970) viewed divorce as comprised of six overlapping phases that vary in intensity and sequence for specific families. In the phase of "emotional divorce," spouses attend to emotional issues that are causing the disruption of the marriage and the resolution of those interpersonal conflicts. Children's feelings and adjustments may be greatly affected during this phase, although many parents believe that they are hiding their discord from the children. Younger children are given more responsibilities around the house and more decision-making power (Luepnitz, 1982). The "legal divorce" phase is the sanction-seeking phase in which the couple receive the right to remarry. Children often view the court hearing as a last chance for a fantasized reunion of their parents, and stress often ensues. The "economic divorce" is the phase in which money and property are divided. The actual as well as the perceived fairness of the distribution of the couple's assets often directly (sufficiency of financial support) and indirectly (perceptions of the child of the blame for lack of financial support) affect the child. Certainly, one of the most volatile phases is the "co-parental divorce," which lasts until one of the parents or children dies. This phase includes the potential conflict areas of custody, visitation, and the ongoing child-parent relationship. The "community divorce" phase is the evolution the divorced individual experiences with his/her friends leading to subjective sense of less community. Lastly, the "psychic divorce" concerns the parents regaining a sense of autonomy.

A developmental vulnerability model (Kalter, 1990) identifies three major concerns; handling anger and aggression, the issue of separation-individuation, and gender equity. Another process model advanced by Stolberg and Bloom (1992) explains how the phases of divorce impact children in each stage. These include; predecision period, final separation, adjustment to separation, and the recovery-redefinition (Stolberg &Bloom, 1992).

Often, divorced parents overlook how important their movement through these phases is for the child. If a parent models insecurity or dependent behaviors and attitudes (for example, encouraging the child to become a surrogate partner, so that the child experiences stress when separating from the parent), the child may learn faulty means of achieving his or her needs. Models aid in conceptualizing divorce as a series of overlapping phases of development that create a multiplicity of experiences and pose varied threats to a child's previous conceptions of family.

Detrimental Psychological Effects of Divorce Upon Children

The detrimental psychological and social effects of divorce upon children fall into three primary areas: academic and school performance; delinquency; and intrapersonal concerns. The ability of the divorcing parents to minimize conflict during and after the divorce has a great impact on the duration and insensitivity of these effects (Stewart, Copeland, Chester, Malley, & Barenbaum, 1997).

School Performance. A popular assumption concerning children of divorce is that their academic performance is hindered by the trauma of the family disruption; yet, empirical evidence is equivocal. In their longitudinal study of 131 children whose parents divorced in the children's infancy, early childhood, and latency, Wallerstein and Kelly (1975, 1976, 1980) noted that not only did school-peer relationships deteriorate, but also half of the children declined noticeably in their academic performance. The children displayed decreased ability to concentrate, and their playground behavior became more aggressive than previous to the divorce (Wallerstein & Kelly, 1975; Wallerstein, 1984). In the one-year follow-up, slightly more than 25% of those who had suffered lowered academic performance returned to their previous education and social achievement levels. In contrast, a study investigating the effects of divorce upon the children's school behavior reported nominal detrimental effects. Acting-out behaviors as well as withdrawal were more pronounced for children of divorce, but the children's school behavior improved to predivorce levels 3 to 4 months following their parents' divorces (Gonso, 1977).

Two studies comparing IQ scores of children in families with and without fathers report that prolonged separation (especially early separation) from the father is correlated with lower IQ scores (Deutsch & Brown, 1964; Kreisburg, 1967). Edwards and Thompson (1971) examined the differences of scores on a picture intelligence test administered to 2,500 seven-year-olds of divorced and intact families. No significant differences were found in their scores.

In general, the school performance of many children of divorce is impaired for a short time period following the disruption of the family unit. Well-controlled studies indicate spontaneous resolution of many detrimental effects shortly (3 months to 1 year) after the onset of divorce. More research is needed to identify which children of divorce are vulnerable to school difficulties.

Delinquency.   Some studies have correlated divorce and especially father absence with a propensity for children to become juvenile or child delinquents. In the Wallerstein and Lewis study (1997), half of the children in the 60 family study became involved in drugs and alcohol and many became sexually active early in adolescence. However, lack of systematic variance of familial and psychological factors and lack of use of control groups has led to confusing conclusions. Many studies linked father absence to child outcomes such as juvenile delinquency, mental illness, and lower intellectual and psychosocial functioning. Most of the studies neglected to distinguish (1) the cause of the father's absence, (2) the duration or degree of the father's absence, (3) the child's age when the separation occurred, (4) the differences between the effects of the father's absence and poverty, and (5) the difference between the consequences of poverty and ethnicity.

Shinn (1978) concluded that the variable of father absence is less important than other less emphasized variables such as (1) the cause, onset, and duration of father absence; (2) the family's socioeconomic status; (3) the nature of the relationship between the child and the absent parent; and (4) parental conflict before and after divorce.

Determination of the relationship between parental divorce and child delinquency is complicated by the potential bias in police records. About one-third of the delinquency hearings result in dismissal or warning. The most common basis for dismissal is the personal conception of the police officer or judge as to "the stability of the child's family" based on whether the parent was divorced or married.

Yet, some studies do suggest that divorce and father absence can be associated with minor infringements of the law or moral code (Santrock, 1976; Wasserstein & Kelly, 1976). Following divorced children's development over a number of years through observation and questionnaire, they reported only slight differences in acting out between children of divorce and those of intact families. Children of divorce were slightly more likely to engage in petty lying and stealing.

Intrapersonal Concerns. Within the last decade, a rather large body of literature is developing about how divorce may lead to interpersonal difficulties for children so that they are vulnerable to more profound maladjustment. Several studies (Wallerstein & Lewis, 1997; Stewart, Copeland, Chester, Malley, & Barenbaum, 1997) reported that father-absent children are more aggressive, disobedient, and independent than those children with a father present. Further, Santrock (1977) noted that father-absent children are more aggressive in their doll play and more likely to display disobedience the earlier the onset of father absence in the child's development. In another study, Santrock (1976) observed the father-absent boys were less morally advanced as evidenced by Kohlberg's scale (1968) of moral development.

A well-designed study controlling for father absence identified many similarities and few differences between children with and without fathers in their homes. No significant differences were noted in self-concept attitudes toward family, and peer relationships (Thomas, 1968). However, significantly higher levels of anxiety were displayed by children without fathers present, and these children also perceived themselves as receiving less recognition for their accomplishments. As stated previously, children from one-parent homes may have less opportunity for receiving attention. Increased anxiety levels have been observed in other studies conducted with children of divorce. Anxiety can be manifested in many different behaviors and psychological symptoms. Grollman (1975), in his assessment of children of divorce from his clinical experience, noticed that bodily stress might be expressed as trembling, restlessness, headaches, appetite loss, stomach aches, diarrhea, fitful sleep, frequent urination, or increased pulse and respiration rates.

Anger toward self or parent and issues of allegiance and loyalty often are exacerbated by custody battles. Children may feel that they are hurting a parent's feelings by a preference for custody, and thus confusion and anxiety may be expressed through bodily or behavioral symptomology. As cited earlier, most symptoms diminish 1 or 2 years following divorce, but some do not. In Wallerstein and Kelly's (1975, 1976, 1980) extensive longitudinal studies, more than 3 months after divorce, some children continued to experience depression, to report low self-concept scores, and to display difficulties with their peer relationships. In a one-year follow-up (Wallerstein & Kelly, 1976), data indicated that in 25% of the cases the following occurred:

1. Phobic reactions spread and generalized

2. Thievery and truancy increased

3. Those who were isolated became more withdrawn

Many children of divorce blame themselves for a parent leaving or for causing a divorce (Gardner, 1976; Heatherington, Cox, & Cox, 1977, 1978; Heatherington & Deur, 1971; Kelly & Berg, 1978; Wallerstein & Kelly, 1975, 1976, 1980). Consequently, they feel guilty for causing the family disruption. Frequently, the guilt is manifested somatically as well as emotionally through clinical signs of depression and grief (Grollman, 1975).

As previously described, children of divorce may be more aggressive in their play than children of intact families. Many researchers have posited that one cause of the hostility and anger might be the child's blaming a parent for the divorce that has disrupted his or her world (Daniel, 1977; Gardner, 1976; Heatherington, Cox, & Cox, 1979; Heatherington & Deur, 1971; Kelly & Berg, 1978; Wallerstein & Kelly, 1975, 1976, 1980). For example, divorced children may feel betrayed by their noncustody parents, believing that noncustodial parents have abandoned them. These children may seek revenge through hostile acts toward the noncustodial parents as well as the custodial parents and others (Gardner, 1976; Wallerstein & Kelly, 1975, 1976, 1980, 1984).

During the most intense conflicts of an impending divorce, the child may be left out of conversations and activities of the parents, and the child may feel alienated and lonely (Gardner, 1976). Then, following divorce, some children fear that they will be abandoned by their remaining custodial parent They may worry intensely about the remaining custodial parent's health and fear being left alone to fend for themselves. For example, some children will fear being left alone in a car or at home even for short periods of time. In some cases, the child may run away from home to avoid the feared rejection (Gardner, 1976; Heatherington & Deur, 1971; Kelly & Berg, 1978; Wallerstein & Kelly, 1975, 1976, 1980).

Children of divorce may experience conflicts of loyalty and allegiance when asked to take sides by either parent over custody or ongoing issues of blame, finances, visitation, etc. Children may become so aligned with one parent that they reject the other and form a surrogate partnership (a fantasized relationship by the child of being the single parent's marriage partner) with the remaining parent. Some children, especially those of latency age, become hypermature, displaying characteristics of the absent parent to compensate for their custodial parent's loss (Gardner, 1976; Wallerstein & Kelly, 1976). Children may become distressed over loyalty and confidentiality if parents ask them information concerning the other parent and may feel like they are tattling and breaking an allegiance or confidence. Children of divorce may develop fantasies to defend against the personal distress they are experiencing. A common fantasy noted by researchers is that the parents will remarry and all will "live happily ever after" as a reunited family unit. Occasionally, the fantasy may be acted out in plots attempting to bring the family back together.

Summary of the Research About the Effects of Divorce. As divorce has become increasingly prominent in our society, social scientists have begun systematic investigation of its effects upon children when young and as maturing occurs. Research consistently documents that divorce spurs behavioral disorders and psychological stress for a great number of children; however, most children from divorced families recover from the negative effects 3 months to a year following the dissolution of the marriage. Yet, a significant minority of children from divorced homes seem particularly vulnerable to the psychosocial stresses associated with the dissolution of their intact families, and these vulnerable children may express emotional concerns about the divorce (such as feeling guilty, yearning for the reunion of the family, anger at a parent), exhibit behavior disorders (such as poor school performance or delinquency), or act out emotional concerns (promiscuous sexual behavior) into their adulthood. We do not know exactly which children are most vulnerable to divorce stress. A combination of factors about the parents (their overall adjustment age, nature, and how well they adjust to the divorce) and variables about the child (his or her temperament, age, and attachment to the parents and to other supportive adults) interact to determine the child's sense of vulnerability. It will be helpful when we can predict which children are most vulnerable to stress from divorce so that we can provide the psychosocial support they need to prevent their experiencing significant personal problems. In the meantime, several treatment strategies have emerged that can be helpful to a broad range of children.

Clinical Intervention for Children of Divorce.

While each child reacts individually to the divorce process, some common observations include the following for children involved in divorce:

1. *Denial.* Children often try to convince themselves and others that the divorce is not really happening and that the pain will go away.

2. *Grief.* The loss of the day to day interaction with significant persons in their life and the security of the daily routine create a grieving process.

3. *Anger.* Grief moves to anger against the parents and other significant persons for perceived betrayal and for not keeping the family together. The child may be angry at themselves, taking blame for the divorce.

4. *Bargaining.* The child tries to be a better child to make things easier on the parents.

5. *Depression.* When the child realizes the divorce will occur despite their efforts they may become depressed with changes in behavior, emotional swings, eating and sleeping habits.

   (*Families First,* 1994)

Clearly, prevention is important and is aimed at teaching all children how to adjust to potential losses in their lives through death of a parent or family member, divorce, or moving away from friends. The greatest prevention must begin with the parents behavior throughout the divorce process. The parents should be educated early as to the potential harmful effects of divorce on children. Both parents should speak to the children together, so they hear the same message at the same time from both parents (Stolberg & Bloom, 1992).

The remedial approaches emphasize assisting the child and/or the family in adjusting to the divorce of the parents. Some child practitioners prefer mandatory participation of all family members, including the noncustodial parent (Goldman & Coane, 1977; Hozman & Froiland, 1976). Still other child practitioners, while not negating the importance of parental adjustment, favor treating the child either individually or in small groups.

Some practitioners believe it is helpful to assist children of divorce in expressing their grief about the loss of the intact family. They aid family members in coping with the dissolution of the family, redefine the family, and accept new relationships. Another family systems approach is built upon a four-part model that emphasizes redefining the family to include all members regardless of the divorce. Boundaries of family relationships are reset. Under the family therapist's guidance, members recall the history of the marriage to gain insight into the conflicts leading to the disruption. An expression of grief is catalyzed, and finally, new supportive relationships are fostered (Goldman & Coane, 1977).

Others recommend working with children individually or in groups to identify and correct interpersonal concerns, such as self-blaming, blaming a parent, and fantasies of a reunion. In addition, Gardner (1970) has written a text for children to help them understand the divorce process and to correct inappropriate perceptions.

Therapy for divorced parents has been helpful in increasing the speed of litigation and decreasing custodial fights (Stolberg & Bloom, 1992).

Also needed are corrective personal and social intervention programs to aid the single parent so that the ongoing environmental circumstance is conducive to the child's growth. However, much more research is needed to explicate the effects of being raised in a single-parent home. This research must address the interactions of the child's sex and custodial parent's sex. Day-care centers that provide a truly nurturing environment and are reasonably priced could greatly ease the load of the single parent and thus facilitate the child's and parent's adaptation. Continued opportunity for the child to relate to the noncustodial parent and other opposite-sex relatives of the custodial parent is important.

In sum, widespread supportive experiences are needed for a very large number of children who experience stress associated with divorce and single-parent homes. Therapy can help family members refocus upon the beneficial aspects of divorce for both parents and children. The presence of both parents in a household is not sufficient condition for psychological stability. In many cases, psychological equilibrium returns only after the parents separate. Until recently, this was not a popular topic when discussing child-rearing practices. Today, we recognize that in some cases, a single parent is better than two parents where there is no love. Much can be done to assure a nurturing family environment for children of divorce.

Substitute Care (Foster Care)

Foster care is the temporary (maximum 1 year) placement of children outside their biological family with a family foster home. This is a new but temporary family for the child and therein lie many complicated issues. This drastic change is necessary when the child's basic survival is threatened. Inadequate social and emotional care is provided in the child's primary home. During the temporary placement, there is total separation from the primary family except for occasional visits from the child's family. The child experiences a change of school, peer group, sibling group, and sometimes community. The pervasiveness of change is so drastic, foster care is considered a last resort to protect the child.

Substitute care involves a number of professional groups, because legal and physical custody must be granted to a state or temporary caretaker. Expert testimony from psychiatrists and psychologists and case management by social workers may be necessary. Because of the complexity of the foster care system, some long-term foster care placements have become permanent, so that child is not shuffled from one home to another.

Statistics

In 1960, there were 256,000 children placed in out-of-home placements. By 1992 there were over 442,000 children living in foster care, an increase of 5 percent from the previous year(Everett, 1995). There are many other children living in institutions who are not included in this number.

Each child has his or her own individual story of pain, neglect, illness, physical injury, or other condition that required his or her removal from home. The authors' experience with more than 1,500 foster care cases has shown that children without homes are a heterogeneous group. They range in age from infancy to 18 years. The age of foster care children is becoming younger. From 1982 to 1990, the average age dropped from 12.6 to 8.6. The number of infants jumped from 7,100 in 1982 to almost 20,000 in 1990 (Everett, 1995). There are three major problems which required out-of-home placement, including: parent related, child disability, and delinquency. The parent-related problems involve parental illness, mental health condition, abuse and neglect of children, sexual abuse, and incest. Parent-related problems accounted for about 75 percent of all children placed outside their own homes. Child-related problems, the condition of the child, such as mental retardation, emotional disturbance, or delinquent behavior, accounted for between 15 percent and 20 percent of out-of-home placements. Environmental circumstances, including poverty, accounted for between 3 per cent and 5 percent of children placed (Shyne & Schroeder, 1978). The one common denominator is that the children come from stressful family situations that make them vulnerable to additional stress.

Departments of human services are generally overloaded and understaffed. Moreover, technical constraints often prevent older children from being legally adoptable until several court hearings. As a consequence, many older children spend years in temporary foster homes before they can be and are adopted. Reports from state agencies indicates that the length of care increased in duration from 1982 to 1990 (Everett, 1995). Goldstein, Freud, and Solnit (1979) present a powerful rationale about why older children in extended foster placements are particularly vulnerable to emotional stress. Both the child and the parents know that the placement is temporary and that the social service agency reserves the right to remove the child at any time. For the foster parents, this legal structure is a warning against becoming deeply emotionally involved with the child. For the child, the feelings of impermanence clash with the developmental needs for emotional constancy. If, on the other hand, the foster parents and child do not heed the admonitions of the social service agencies and do become deeply involved with one another, then the child is likely to experience significant trauma when taken from the foster home for placement in a permanent setting. Goldstein, et al. (1979) have coined the term "common law adoptive parent–child relationship" to characterize extended-term foster placements in which the parents and child have bonded firmly.

Foster care has become an easy course of action for social workers. Hubbell (1981) wrote,

> Yet, the system scars those it ensnares; it is often emotionally debilitating and humiliating. Perhaps, the saddest aspect of foster care in the United States is that it was originally designed to reunite families after providing them with temporary respite from child care—a respite that would be beneficial to both parents and children. Yet, too often the nation's foster care system fragments families and sabotages their eventual reconstruction into functioning units again (p. 5).

Of the 442,000 children living in foster care or group homes, 26 percent remain in care for over 3 years. Most children live in foster care for at least 2 and years. Of the children in foster homes, 54 percent have lived in two or more foster homes (Everett, 1995).

Research about the care of children outside their own home between 1933 and 1984 demonstrates some interesting trends. The number of children in care per 1,000 has stayed fairly consistent from a low in 1960 of 3.5 to approximately 6 per 1,000 today. A shift has taken place from the use of institutions to foster family homes. In 1933, 2.5 per 1,000 children were placed in family homes, compared to 3.4 in institutions. In 1972, this trend had clearly been reversed with 3.6 per 1,000 children in family foster homes and 1.3 children in institutions (Kadushin, 1980).

A major classic longitudinal study by Fanshel and Shinn (1978) of 8,600 children in New York City led to the conclusion that, as a whole, biological parents are more effective in facilitating long-term adjustment of a child than are out-of-home caretakers. This study examined the impact of foster care on children. Children were rated over five years according to the results of psychological tests and by parents, teachers, and social workers. Fifty-two percent of the children were rated "normal" by psychologists, while 25% were rated "abnormal" or "suspect" after five years of tracking. Twelve percent of the children were always rated as "abnormal" or "suspect." At the end of the study, approximately 25% of the children were viewed as emotionally impaired. Social workers rated children at the end of five years by the degree of difficulty experienced in foster care. Thirty percent of the children had no difficulty, 40% had slight difficulty, 17% had moderate difficulty, and 12% were rated as showing substantial difficulty. Approximately 30% of the children in care experienced difficulty in their lives. Teachers rated the children on overall emotional adjustment According to their ratings, 9% were very well adjusted, 27% were well adjusted, 33% were adequately adjusted, and 24% of the children were rated poorly and very poorly adjusted. The last two categories were considered pathological, and again 31% of the children experienced major adjustment problems. Although Fanshel and Shinn's (1978) study did not contain a control group, based upon careful analysis of the children over five years, psychologists, parents, teachers, and social workers portrayed 25–33% of the children as showing signs of emotional impairment.

The placement of minority youths in foster and substitute care is much higher than for white youths when compared by percentage of the population (Stehno, 1982). African–American children comprised approximately 15% of the total population of youths under age 18 in 1970, yet they made up between 22% and 32% of the institutionalized population (Shyne & Schroeder, 1978; Children's Defense Fund, 1978). In 1990, African–American youth made up 40.4 percent of the foster care population (Tatara, 1993). Native American children who represent less than 1% of the total population of youth under 18 are placed in out-of-home placements at a higher rate than any group of children. Twenty-five percent of all Native American children are placed in foster, group, and adoptive homes. An additional 25,000 Native American youths are in boarding schools which are more similar to residential than educational facilities (Stehno, 1982). Hispanic youths comprise approximately 7% of the total population of youths under 18. Almost 12 percent of Hispanic children are in foster care placements (Tatara, 1993), and another 6% are in juvenile delinquency placements (Children's Defense Fund, 1978). Approximately three-fourths of the children studied in the Fanshel and Shinn study (1978) were Black or Puerto Rican.

Economics play a major role in the placement of children. With a higher percentage of minority children living at or below the poverty level, we see more of them placed in foster care where they remain for a longer period of time (Fanshel & Shinn, 1978).

When children are removed from dysfunctional families and placed in foster care, they bring with them certain defensive behaviors. Mayfield and Neil (1983) have identified four roles that children may assume upon removal from their homes.

1. The lost child. This child is quiet and well-behaved, appearing comfortable with minimal care and supervision. The lost child may be a high risk for severe depression or suicide during adolescence or

adulthood because of a low sense of self-worth and an inability to create and maintain emotional attachments. The lost child may have been the victim of sexual abuse and learned the hard lesson that noninvolvement is the best course to pursue for protection from further abuse. The quiet shyness of the lost child may be a wall behind which loneliness, inadequacy, fear, and doubts of self-worth lie.

2. The clown. Clowns hide their true feelings by joking around and being cute and charming. The clown will do anything to attract attention, is highly energetic and verbal, and appears hyperactive. The affects of abuse and trauma may appear to be minimal or nonexistent. The child in this category will probably deny any pain and quickly change the subject. The child refuses to admit even to him- or herself that he or she has been abused and hides fear, insecurity, and extreme confusion.

3. The troublemaker. This child is rambunctious and presents severe behavior problems. Troublemakers are low achievers in school, have few friends, and often are involved in petty delinquent activities. They have few close relationships, and foster parents may find caring for them extremely difficult. Troublemakers may experience multiple placements, eventually ending up in residential treatment. This child may have been the scapegoat in his or her own home and may have been blamed for the family's problems. The troublemaker is a high-risk child for substance abuse, using drugs to mask anger, fear, rejection, guilt, and loneliness.

4. The achiever. This child is the foster parents' ideal child. Achievers are well-behaved and pleasant and show little reaction to being moved. They have many friends and do average or better work in school. The achiever may appear unaffected by placement and may hide feelings of inadequacy, confusion, and anger behind independence and responsibility in a facade of maturity. These children may achieve at the cost of developing a rigid ego structure. If so, they are high risks for emotional disturbance in adulthood.

All of children have the feeling that they are helpless and moved against their will through a series of new environments by adults.

Treatment

To help children cope with the psychological trauma of separation and reattachment, with the tension between biological parents, foster parents, and child welfare workers, and with learning a new social system, the practitioner must address basic security issues and the precipitating factors which necessitated placement. Clearly, this is not an easy task. The child welfare worker should:

1. Attempt to build self-esteem by helping children become aware of their own individual strengths and special attributes.

2. Teach children basic coping and communication skills to enable them to reach out and establish relationships.

3. Help children assert themselves so their needs are clearly stated to the caretakers.

4. Build trust.

5. Alleviate the children's guilt by helping them realize they are not responsible for their family's dysfunction (Mayfield & Neil, 1983).

Examining the process of development of a child in substitute care is a useful tool for analyzing disruption in the child's life. The child may have difficulty developing stable, meaningful relationships with other people. He or she may lack control of destructive behaviors and fantasies. Self-esteem and the development of ego functions, including adaptation through reality testing and cognition, may be impaired. The foster child may lack the intense symbiotic dialogue with the parent, as his or her needs have not been met. The detachment from the mother may result in an emotionally withdrawn, apathetic child who will proclaim "love" for any adult who will pay any attention. Children who grow up in foster care can be as abused by the system of care as they may have been in their own families.

To an abused or special needs child, the added stress of a new environment may increase the vulnerability to maladjustment. The influence of separation from the biological family may undermine the child's overall development (Steinhauer, 1991). The treatment approach needs to focus on development of self-esteem and attachment to the biological family and significant others. Other interventions should relate to the family, such as increasing the number of in-home services available to children while the dysfunctional family is attempting to retain homeostasis. Frazier and LeVine's (1983) Reattachment Therapy, described in the previous chapter, can be a treatment strategy for children returning to their biological families. Close contact through visits is critical to a successful reunion.

Fanshel and Shinn (1978) identified a strong negative correlation between the length of out-of-home placement and the visitation with biological parents; that is, the longer the child is out-of-home, the fewer the visits. Although clear difficulties are inherent in the visitation of parents with children, these visits are critical for several reasons (Kadushin, 1980).

1. Children identify with their parents, even if they have been victims of severe abuse and see foster care placement as rejection by their parents. This may create low self-esteem within the children.

2. Children may develop fantasies of the "ideal" parent if they do not occasionally see their parents. This may affect children's ego functioning in relation to reality testing.

3. Children will miss their parents and mourn their absence, resulting in at least mild depression.

4. Effective visits with the biological parents can help children adjust to the reality of separation and to remember that they are safe in their present environments.

Longitudinal studies on foster care show that biological family centered activities facilitated the return home of the child (Prasad, 1988). A number of studies (Steinhauer, 1991; Kadushin, 1980; Littner, 1971) and our experience show that visits between the biological parents and the child can be extremely disruptive to the foster family. Visits may be at inconvenient times, and the child may return from the visits and act out his or her anger and frustration. Foster parents may be threatened by the biological parents. Despite these difficulties, it is important for the child welfare worker to maintain the relationship between the biological parents and the child if a return to the home is the permanent plan.

Some strides are being made for more in-home services so fewer children will need to be removed. However, few alternatives to out-of-home placement exist, given the lack of homemakers, specialized day treatment, day care, public housing, and other social services. The Adoption Assistance and Child Welfare Act of 1980 (Public Law 96-272 and its amendments) attempted, at the policy level, to stem the placement of children in foster homes and has met limited success (Cahn & Johnson, 1993). Children with special needs including; physical, emotional, social and cognitive; improve their functioning when they are placed in a family on a permanent basis (Cohen & Westhues, 1990). Although a great amount has been written on the foster care system, research on substitute care's long-term and short-term impact on children's emotional, social, and physical development has been limited.

Adoption

By the very definition of adoption, children enter a new legal family. Adoptions in the United States are approximately evenly divided between relative and nonrelative adoptions (Kadushin, 1980). We will address primarily nonrelative adoptions.

Relative adoptions account for about 100,000 children per year and another 119,000 are freed for nonrelative adoptive placements each year (Flango & Flango, 1993). In 1982, approximately 14,400 of these were older children (Maximus, 1984).

Eighty-five percent of the children available for nonrelative adoptions are born out of wedlock. Another group of children comes from abusive homes, where parental rights have been terminated. The majority of the abused children freed for adoption are older, with their own unique problems of entering a new family. A number of problems may plague adopted children. The lack of knowledge of biological parents and the adoptive parents' acceptance of their role as nonbiological parents may create special problems. The lack of knowledge about their biological parents, their roots, may prompt outbursts with teachers, parents, and other significant adults. Frisk (1964) theorized that the adoptee's genetic ego is replaced by an hereditary ghost. In the case of transcultural adoptions, the cultural ghost also may complicate healthy development of an identity. Young adolescents see themselves as a link in their biological family's genealogical chain. Lack of health information and multiple foster home placements also may create insecurity and emotional detachment of older children.

In their classic stimulating text, *Beyond the Best Interest of the Child*, Goldstein, Freud, and Solnit (1979) write, "Blood . . . carries no weight with children who are emotionally unaware of the events leading to their birth . . . What registers in minds are day-to-day interchanges with adults who take care of them and who, on the strength of these, become the parent figures to whom they are attached" (pp. 12–13). Given that the process of parent–child bonding, rather than the biological birth, is critical to healthy development it may seem surprising that many theorists and child practitioners view adopted children as particularly prone to stress. Child welfare workers report adopted children often are preoccupied with fantasies about their natural parents. They may express feelings of being unwanted or different from other children. Norvell and Guy (1977) concluded that adoption status alone cannot produce a negative self-concept. Adoption status can make children vulnerable to stress. Kadushin (1980) writes, "The adopted child faces all the general problems of development encountered by his nonadopted peers. In this sense, he is a child among other children. But in addition, like the adopted parent, he faces some special problems that are related to the fact that he is an adopted child" (p. 487).

Adjustment

The literature on the adjustment needs of adopted children and their families is not extensive, yet available data indicate adjustment to adoption is highly taxing both emotionally and behaviorally for the child and family (LeVine & Sallee, 1990; Barth & Barry, 1988). A study of youth adopted as adolescents showed a disruption rate of about 24 percent—twice as high as for other special needs children (Berry & Barth, 1990). The adoptive child's adjustment is dependant on a number of factors including; age, preadoption preparation, match with the adoptive parents, culture, and length of time in care. Can there be a greater adjustment for a child than totally changing families?

Perhaps our best insight on adjustment problems of adopted children comes from adoptees themselves. *The Adoption Triangle*, by Sorosky, Baran, and Pannor (1978), lists a number of letters by adoptees on their feelings and problems. "As a child I can remember how strongly my need was to know more about my birth parents. For all the love and attention I got as a child, I still knew deep inside that my uncles and aunts and cousins and grandparents were never really mine. I never really felt like I was part of the family" (p. 92). An adolescent states, "During my adolescence, I became very concerned with my own identity, and its relationship to my past and future. What will I look like has always been a question of great importance to me" (p. 110).

Research.   In a review of the adjustment patterns of adopted children, Lawton and Gross (1964) reported such inconsistency in methodology and results between studies that conclusions about adjustment among adopted children cannot be reached. Although the feelings of adopted children toward their adoption have not been systematically investigated, some studies have compared the adjustment of adopted to nonadopted children. Some of these studies speak to the success of adoptive placements and define outcomes ranging from capable and satisfactory to removed and experiencing adjustment problems.

Kadushin (1980) cites 20 major agency and nonagency adoption outcome studies from 1924 through 1980. Based upon the referral of adoptive children to mental health services, 72% of the placements were successful, 16% of the children were labeled as having intermediate success, and 12% had very poor adjustments and were unsuccessful. These studies address family characteristics that create stress for adopted children. There appears to be more stress if the adoptive parents are older, if marital interaction is characterized by much strife, and if the adopted child is an only child. The acceptance of the adoption also impacts upon the effectiveness.

Adopted children always are faced with the possibility of a disruption (removal of the adopted child from the home) in their new family. Based upon his analysis of nine major studies related to failed adoptive placements, Kadushin (1980) concludes that, for all adoptions, the disruption rate is 3.1%. These studies were conducted between 1955 and 1970, a period when most placements were made for infants and not for special needs children. With the signing of Public Law 96-272, the Adoption Assistance and Child Welfare Act of 1980, states and agencies are placing more older and handicapped children in adoptive homes. These children are more likely to encounter a disruption. Spalding for Children, a highly publicized placement agency of special needs children, completed a study between 1968 and 1976 of 199 older and handicapped children. The disruption rate was 10.6% (Unger, Dwarshuis, & Johnson, 1977). Many agencies expect disruption rates for special needs children to run approximately 12%. A United States and Canada study of the placement success of 735 developmentally disabled children discovered an overall disruption rate of only 8.7%. If the child was adopted by foster parents, the disruption rate dropped to 4.4%, and the new family adoption rate was 10.4%. Age is an important variable for disruption rates as well. Developmentally disabled children under 7 years of age had a low, 3.3%, disruption rate, but children 8 and over showed a very high rate, 17.7% (Coyne & Brown, 1985).

It is estimated that only about one to two percent of all children are nonrelative adoptions (McRoy, Grotevant, & Zurcher, 1988); however, research data indicate that 4.6% of the children in psychiatric facilities are adoptees (Kadushin, 1980).

These data are particularly interesting in light of Schechter's (1964) study, which examined the tendency of adoptive parents to use pediatric clinics and concluded that adoptive parents did not frequent pediatric clinics more than biological parents. Therefore, if adoptive parents use agencies at the same level as biological parents, the 4.6% usage of psychiatric facilities may reflect a high frequency of adjustment problems among adopted children.

Several classic well-designed studies point to greater maladjustment of adopted than nonadopted children. Bohman (1972) systematically sampled 168 adopted children in Stockholm, Sweden. He studied the children's school records, interviewed all parents, and talked with all but five of the teachers. No difference was reported in academic performance between adopted and nonadopted boys and girls. However, 22% of the adopted boys versus 12% of the nonadopted boys were reported to display significant behavioral problem. A similar, nonsignificant statistical trend was noted between the adopted and nonadopted girls. Another study identified apparent differences between adopted girls' and boys' temperaments (Maurer, Cadoret, & Cain, 1980).

A study by Weiss (1984) compared the parent–child relationship of adoptive adolescents with those living with biological parents who were receiving treatment in a Philadelphia psychiatric hospital. Data were collected through a review of medical records of 140 youths between the years of 1970 and 1979. Statistical analysis demonstrated that adoptive parents were more restricted in their visits with their adopted children and that adoptive parents were more likely to have serious problems relating to the adolescents.

McRoy, Grotevant, and Zurcher (1988) addressed the complex and multidimensional process of adoption, as it emerges during adolescent in an in-depth study of emotional disturbance in adopted adolescents. The findings from their study, based upon an extensive exploratory study of adopted adolescents in Texas and Minnesota living in residential treatment programs as compared to adopted adolescents living at home, indicated all of these children are at risk.

Approximately one-third of the adopted children are at risk before placement due to genetics, drug or alcohol abuse, poor prenatal care, or multiple placements. Children with schizophrenic and alcoholic birth parents are at a greater risk. Thus, preimposed placement services should prepare adoptive parents for these potential problems and help them to identify the early signs of schizophrenia and alcohol addiction. Information on genetics and prenatal care were limited by the information the social worker obtained from the birth mother. Early multiple rejections (multiple placements) created rejecting and distrusting behavior.

This study also addressed early childhood and parent–child compatibility, or bonding. Hyperactivity was reported in almost all cases. The term "elbow babies" was developed by the authors to refer to avoidance behavior by the child. Incompatibility appeared to be more prevalent in families that exaggerate positive or negative aspects of the birth parents.

The context of the family relationships was explored theoretically in the research project. Divorce and death affected each children's group the same. Stress in the child's life was an important factor, but more critical was how the stress was dealt with by the family. Military families experience some unique problems as adoptive families. While some of these problems may be attributed to "warrior fathers," clearly most military personnel are now technicians and bureaucrats. Contributing factors were hypothesized as frequent moves, and strict order and obedience rather than democratic discipline and parenting styles (McRoy, Grotevant, & Zurcher, 1988).

Identity issues are central to adoptive children's problems. Interracially adopted children reported in 44% of the cases that they had trouble adjusting to adoption. Adopted children experienced rejection and anger at the birth parents, and a number of these children in residential care transferred their anger to adoptive parents and feared rejection by them (McRoy, Grotevan & Zurcher, 1988).

Adoption Phases for Children.   The adopted child and the family pass through predictable phases in the adoption process that usually coincide with individual and family development. These phases are depicted in Table 14.1. An understanding of these phases helps child welfare workers determine the focus of therapy over time.

Phase I addresses the period before children turn 3 years of age or are aware of their adoptive status. Adjustment is necessary as the typical adoptee is moved two-and-a-half times before final placement (Grabe, 1990).

In Phase II, the child's first insights about the adoption seem to center upon his or her recognition that somehow he or she is different from other children. Adopted children know they are not living with their biological parents, yet they have not begun to grapple with the implications of adoption.

Phase III denotes a time, approximately between eight and 11 years of age, for children adopted at birth to learn about their distinctiveness in being raised by parents who are not biologically their own. In this phase, children may express curiosity about their biological parents.

The personal and identity crisis occurs in Phase IV during adolescence. Teens may become very concerned about their adoptive status and their biological roots. Some adoptees may be vulnerable to narcissistic disorders as we discuss in the treatment section.

Phase V, acceptance of the biological and adoptive family, can begin at any time after the child and family identify and accept differences. In some families, the transition is smooth, while in others, full acceptance may not occur until adulthood (LeVine & Sallee, 1990).

Certain personal and emotional issues seem to be characteristic of adoptees in each phase of their development.

TABLE 14.1

Phases of Adoption Adjustment

Phase	Typical Psychological Issues	Signs of Severe Maladjustment
I. Preawareness	Over activity, withdrawal, acting out	Severe delays in development
II. Dim awareness	Talk about feeling different Confusion of past and present home	Poor object relations
III. Cognitive integration of biological and social differences	Opposition to adoptive parents Increased questioning about family of origin	Desperate search and desire to be reunited with family of origin
IV. Identity crisis of the adopted adolescent	Active search for family of origin and biological roots	Severe narcissistic and borderline disorders
V. Concomitant acceptance of the biological and adoptive families	Adoptive issues reconciled	Feelings about early abuse, neglect, and loss not reconciled and manifested as various personal, relationship, and social issues in the adult

Telling the Child He or She is Adopted.   A parent may be secretive about the child's adoption. The child then may feel he or she is an embarrassment to the family. A classic study shows that telling the child as early as he or she is developmentally capable of understanding about the adoption minimizes this risk (Mech, 1973). While, some theorists believe the move to open adoptions may be detrimental to the child because the biological parent may then have an impact on the child's environment (Kraft, Palombo, Mitchell, Woods, Schmid & Tucker, 1985), others believe the adoptive parents control over the child's contact with biological parents is critical to the success of the placement (Barth & Barry, 1988), and the parents' comfort with the placement (Berry, 1991).

Parents may overestimate the child's ability to understand the adoption process and confuse the child with early discussions of adoption (Brodzinsky, Pappas, Singer, & Braff, 1981; Brodzinsky, Singer, & Braff, 1984). Brodzinsky's study used open-ended interviews with adoptive and nonadoptive children in grades 1, 3, 5, 7, 9, and 11. The children were interviewed about their knowledge of adoption. Responses were organized into "levels" of understanding the complex adoption process. Children in the first grade usually could differentiate between birth and adoption but had only a vague awareness of a third party that served as an intermediary in the process. Not until children reached the upper elementary years did a majority recognize the role an agency played in the adoption process to assure the mutual rights, needs, and welfare of children and their parents (Brodzinsky, Singer, & Braff, 1981).

In another study on the child's understanding of adoption, Brodzinsky, Singer, and Braff (1984) examined 200 adopted and biological children, ages 4 to 13. The results from this study indicate a clear developmental trend in the child's knowledge of adoption and its implications for families. Between the ages of 8 and 11, Brodzinsky sees a general increase in adoption knowledge, resulting for some adoptive children in a tenuous family relationship. Therefore, early telling may be important to diminish anxiety and mystique concerning adoption, but the discussion must be tailored to the child's cognitive development.

The research demonstrates the complexity of adoption and the difficulty of assessing the impact the adoption process has on a given child. Adopted boys and special needs children are subject to more adjustment problems than adopted girls or their nonadopted peers. In addition to this finding, the research is inconclusive on the impact of other variables such as age of parent, socioeconomic status, and income on the success of the adoption. Yet, the question of importance from our perspective is success at what emotional and developmental cost to the child. Besides the fact that adopted children have a much higher representation as clients in mental health services, we have little research to guide treatment.

Treatment

The configuration of the child's presenting problem, developmental stage, previous experiences, number of placements, and the adoptive family's dynamics determine the therapeutic strategy. A case management approach can facilitate assisting the adopted child so he or she is less vulnerable to maladjustment. Enlistment of significant adults in the child's life, with an understanding of the special issues of adoption, creates an environment for the children where they feel secure. Group therapy for adoptive children, which explores at an appropriate developmental level grief, separation, and myths regarding adoption, can be very helpful.

Based upon their extensive study of adoption disruptions, Barth and Berry (1988) conclude that the skills required of a clinician working with families on adoption disruptions need to center on "serious academic, behavioral, and interpersonal shortcomings" (p. 143). Treatment usually must address children who run away, lie, steal, set fires, horde food, and have great difficulty in reciprocal interpersonal relationships, particularly related to attachment (Barth & Berry, 1988).

A common issue in adoption concerns disclosure. How much information should be shared of the child's history and biological parents? Until the 1950s, this information was rarely concealed from an adopted child. The usual practice is to conceal records with the belief that knowledge of the child's history prevents the child's adaptation to his or her present environment. Nothing in our present understanding of child development verifies this assumption. To the contrary, the knowledge of the child's past demystifies the adoption process, prevents the child from creating false fantasies about his or her parents, and lessens the adopted child's fears of being different or bad. Also, the family's ability to deal openly with the child's adoption keeps adoption from becoming a covert issue used in family interactions.

The age of the child at the time of the adoption is a key determining factor in how much to discuss the biological parents with the child. If the child was adopted as a newborn, the adoptive parents may unfortunately know little of the biological parents. If the child is older, he or she will remember the biological parents, raising a variety of issues. Child welfare workers may need to deal with the child's feelings of rejection by the biological patents or of hostility toward the adoptive parents for taking him or her away. In both cases, the adoptive parents may be confronted with intense feelings which are difficult to handle.

A nonadopted child accepts the fact that his parents may be both loving and rejecting, but an adopted child has two sets of parents. Adopted children may separate these sets of parents along the lines of loving and rejecting. One set of parents assumes all the attributes of the negative parent, while the other assumes those of the positive parent. Adopted children, of course, usually idealize the absent biological parent. On the other hand, the children understand that these are the same parents who gave them up for adoption. Thus, a dilemma in the adopted child's development of a positive self-image emerges.

Adoptive parents may interpret a child's resistance as a test of their love. A maladaptive pattern may emerge where parent and child question their commitment to each other. The parent may compare the adopted child to nonadopted children, making the adopted child feel inferior. Parents may attribute the child's negative traits or behaviors to his or her biological parents, rather than to faulty child-rearing practices. This child becomes the "identified patient" as described in the chapter on Family Therapy. Both parents and the child in question may come to regard the child as intrinsically bad, rather than examining the problem of family interaction.

Child welfare workers report that parents who have adopted a child may experience stress about the child's adoption and transmit concern to the child. Adoptive parents may experience marital crises because of their need to have a child. This stress affects how they interact with the adopted child. Other parents are overprotective of their adopted child, setting in motion psychologically unhealthy situations for all. On the other hand, some adoptive parents communicate verbally or nonverbally to children that, although they love them, they are different. This love-rejection relationship ultimately proves disastrous to the child and parents, especially during the early teenage years.

The onset of adolescence creates many concerns for adoptees and their families. Physical concerns become an issue. An adopted girl's sexual development can threaten an infertile mother through seductive actions toward the father. In adoption, the incest taboo may be weakened as well. As an adopted son's sexuality emerges, a sterile adoptive father may be threatened.

A theory on the unique identity crisis faced by an adopted teenager (Sallee & LeVine, 1990) is illustrated by the Greek myth of Narcissus. As a youth, Narcissus fell in love with his own image in a pool of water. He never could touch the image in the pool, yet he could not leave. He learned the lesson that energy invested totally in oneself does not lead to a more enduring meaning. As we discussed in the developmental chapter, all teenagers tend to be very narcissistic. A teenager must harness dramatic physical, social, and psychological changes that will enhance his or her personal development. The changes in teenagers may preoccupy them as they spend many hours before a mirror, preening or grooming themselves. The adolescent faces many societal changes. Few meaningful contributions to society are required of today's teenagers, driving their efforts inward. Teenagers will speak for hours on the phone on rather trivial matters; however, to them, this is part of their identity. Other activities such as chores around the house pale in comparison to this powerful personal search for identity. As these needs are met, newborns quickly learn to reciprocate. They share coos, smiles, and cuddles. So begins a shift from total narcissism to individualism as a social being who enjoys mutuality with the parent. Giving and taking continues through the developmental stages until the beginning of adolescence.

In young adopted children, we may see selfishness, unreasonable demands, and other behaviors which are soundly criticized by adults. The child develops a negative self-concept which emerges during the identity crises. Even if removal from the biological mother was within the first few weeks of life, a normal attachment may fail to occur. Based upon this theory, attachment therapy, as discussed in Chapter 12, can be quite effective in working with these adoptive children.

If the process of bonding, attachment, and gradual separation is disrupted, the movement from total narcissism to mutuality is blocked. Thus, adopted children who suffered early bonding difficulties may be particularly prone to narcissistic behavior.

Family therapy can help parents and children air their mutual worries, thereby fostering bonding. Most critical is the prevention strategy of placing children in permanent adoptive homes as soon as possible. Adopted children do not necessarily experience extreme emotional problems. However, there remains a large number of adopted children who are highly vulnerable, particularly children who in their teenage years experience troublesome identity crises, older children who have been separated from their biological parents, and children of cross-cultural adoptions. An understanding of the possible developmental interruption of bonding with the parent and the ensuing social problems will enable the therapist to work with the child, the family, and the social service system to diminish the stresses placed upon the adopted child experiencing a new family.

Summary

We stressed in our earlier chapters that not all disturbed children grow up to be disturbed adults, and many disturbed adults were not overly disturbed when young. Yet, many of the maladjusted adults who were not disturbed as youths were vulnerable children. Over and over again, clinic records of adult patients reveal a childhood of new families.

Vulnerable children are in personal and social pain, but often have enough ego strength that they are not referred to treatment. Rather than losing ego control and exhibiting encopresis, acting out, and other behaviors that would lead to clinical referral, they withdraw and fail to thrive. They are "no problem" to most until later. As an adult, the adopted or foster child may become asocial or antisocial, feeling alienated from his roots and society. As an adult, the child of divorced parents and from a single-parent home may be confused about relationships with the opposite sex. If the practitioner is alert to these issues among children experiencing new families, later emotional problems can be prevented.

Part V

Looking Forward

When we listen to our children, we realize that:

Too many are suffering tremendous personal pain.

Too many lack the personal skills to change adverse social situations.

Too many are not receiving the assistance they need.

For many, the disturbance is very profound by the time they receive assistance.

For many, amelioration of their distress will require extended intervention in the family system.

For many, intense, individual counseling will be required before they can again begin to grow toward their personal potential.

It is obvious that we best help and protect our children by, whenever possible, preventing the need for child welfare intervention. Child practitioners can use their skills in many ways to help create a nourishing environment for children. This unit reviews some of those means. If every child practitioner would consider it a part of his or her professional responsibility to participate in some preventive strategy, we could indeed look forward to a world in which children have an opportunity to grow up without despair and to meet their potential. A world of such healthy children is probably the only way of creating a different world ambience. For, healthy children once grown up would be better prepared to deal with the critical problems of our technological age. The responsibility of child welfare workers is tremendous, but also great is the practitioners' potential for impact, if they are actively involved in preventive services.

Chapter 15
Emerging Roles for Child Welfare Practitioners

Our review of the child practice literature has focused almost entirely on discussion of psychosocial stresses and on treatment approaches for working with children. This review is not complete without a discussion of prevention strategies and policy implications for clinical practice. Clearly, efforts to prevent problems before they occur are a necessary ingredient of a systematic approach to promoting healthy childhoods. Similarly, understanding the impact of clinical decisions upon the community facilitates the long-range emotional and social health of children. Understanding the roles and functions of consultation enables the child welfare worker to effectively link and mobilize community services to meet the needs of the child.

Prevention

Primary prevention services began in the settlement house era (late 1800s) to respond to the profound need for changing the environmental and family conditions that lead to low quality of life. The 1915 National Conference on Social Welfare presented six papers on prevention (Bowker, 1983). By the 1930s, ideology shifted to preventing death, disabilities, and illness for mothers and infants through the U.S. Children's Bureau grant-in-aid programs (Costin, 1979). Efforts in the late 1970s to promote federal interest and funding were prompted largely by a monograph, *Primary Prevention: An Idea Whose Time Has Come* (Klein &

Goldston, 1977). In 1993, with the passage of the Family Preservation and Support Act and its reauthorization in 1997, federal funding for creative community based prevention services is in place. Yet, the technology for collaboration and interdisciplinary work has not been developed (Lloyd & Sallee, 1994). For almost a century of concern, a clear, commonly accepted interdisciplinary model for primary prevention has yet to emerge. After we present three types of prevention, we will examine family crisis prevention.

In this chapter, we will explore various ways in which child welfare workers can fulfill their obligation to serve as prevention specialists. It is important to recognize that the area of prevention constitutes a major challenge, and it is exceedingly difficult for one individual alone to be instrumental in effecting changes that result in marked reductions in childhood psychosocial problems. None-the-less, it is our hope that child welfare workers in collaboration with one another can serve as effective advocates and change agents for children.

Types of Prevention

Prevention strategies in child welfare draw heavily from mental and physical health models. Community organization strategies used to empower and support health programs (Bracht, 1995) have been adapted in the new approach to child welfare. Three types of prevention have been identified by helping professionals (Lorin & Lounsbury, 1982). We will define each type and provide several examples of how it applies to children.

Primary Prevention.   Primary prevention refers to a group of approaches that share the common objectives of (1) lowering the incidence of a child welfare issue (i.e., the rate at which new cases occur) and (2) promoting conditions that reinforce positive child development and psychosocial health. Primary prevention is concerned with populations not yet affected by individual problems, especially with groups at high risk. This approach is proactive in that it seeks to build adaptive strengths through education and reduce causes of children's harm through social engineering.

We can differentiate at least four distinct types of primary prevention programs (Goldston, 1978). The first type involves preventing vulnerable populations from succumbing to emotional problems. High-risk target groups might include children having one or two schizophrenic parents, children of alcoholics and drug addicts, youngsters experiencing the death of a parent, and children with physical handicaps.

A second type of primary prevention program focuses on preventing the onset of carefully defined target disorders. Programs attempting to prevent poisonings from lead-based paints, venereal diseases (e.g., syphilis), genetic diseases (e.g., Taysachs, phenylketonuria), nutritional diseases (e.g., pellegra), delinquency, or additions all illustrate this approach. In recent years, this approach has resulted in many improvements in the care of children and with a consequent decrease in wide variety of childhood disorders.

A third type of prevention program seeks to promote and enhance the overall psychosocial functioning of high risk children (e.g., poor and/or minority children). Programs following this approach are oriented toward building or strengthening parents' low-probability competencies in affective behaviors, cognitive and problem-solving abilities, and social skills.

A final type of prevention intervention provides children, parents, and teachers with experiences to ease the impact of traumatic developmental milestones or unavoidable life crises. For example, a program may focus on parenting skills for teenage expectant parents, problems of separation with school entrance, strategies for lessening the impact of divorce on young children, or minimizing problems associated with working parents. This approach seeks to place these positive educational interventions at strategic points in an individual's life cycle for the explicit purpose of enhancing coping skills to successfully navigate stressful life experiences.

Secondary Prevention. This approach to prevention focuses on the early detection of a problem and subsequent intervention before more intensive treatment is required. The approach may involve early and periodic development with concomitant treatment if required. The essential difference between primary and secondary prevention is that in primary prevention the focus is on the elimination of the root causes of a problem before the problem actually occurs; whereas, in secondary prevention, the goal is to reduce the problem (through treatment) before the problem worsens. For example, it is known that ingestion of lead can cause severe inflammation of the brain with resulting hemorrhage and lesions. Up to 20 years ago, lead poisoning was a severe problem among children who would become ill by chewing on furniture or window sills covered with paint containing lead. Once the relationship was established between lead poisoning and brain damage, laws were passed (i.e., primary prevention) restricting the manufacture and use of lead-based paints. This does not mean, however, that lead poisoning has been eliminated. It is known that children, mostly in poverty areas, still can eat the toxic substance in peeling paint from walls and window sills. Pediatricians, psychologists, and preschool educators, in their developmental assessment of young children from poverty areas, should be especially watchful of the problem of lead poisoning. Children who appear to be developmentally retarded in some aspect of their functioning may be suffering the consequences of lead ingestion. Accordingly, the screening may require a home visit, parent interview, and medical examination since the treatment (i.e., secondary prevention) of a child in the initial stages of lead poisoning differs from that of a child who shows signs of retardation not associated with lead poisoning.

Secondary prevention approaches seek to identify through various early screening procedures children who are demonstrating the initial signs of some physical or psychological dysfunction. Once identified, the second stage of the program is put into operation. This is the treatment phase, which aims to eliminate or curtail the problem(s) resulting from the dysfunction before they become severe enough to require tertiary prevention.

Tertiary Prevention.   In some respects, this type of prevention does not merit the term "prevention" at all. The focus here is on the rehabilitation through treatment of the individual once the dysfunction has reached such a magnitude that overall well-being is severely threatened or where the problem has reached the point where the individual must be institutionalized. Note that the central concept here is "rehabilitation." It should be obvious that much of this text focuses on the tertiary aspect of working with children. Despite the interest in primary and secondary prevention most child welfare programs and workers still devote the majority of their time and effort to tertiary prevention. There are many reasons for this. First, despite the lip service given to primary and secondary prevention, adequate support for true preventive programs has been largely lacking at the federal and state governmental levels. Second, primary prevention, because of its proactive stance of eliminating the root causes of mental disorders, is extremely difficult to carry to completion in most cases. Third, training in primary prevention techniques is sorely lacking in our educational programs. As a consequence, few specialists can be called upon to lend their expertise to problems requiring preventive approaches.

One aspect of tertiary prevention that requires comment and which if enacted upon can result in "rehabilitation" playing a more central role in child welfare concerns evaluation of treatment approaches. Throughout this book, we have discussed the various issues associated with child practice, including questions of assessment and the various treatment approaches. What we have not concentrated on is the issue of evaluation of our total approach to working with troubled children. By this, we mean that the child practitioner must apply rigorous methods to determine whether the assessment instruments and techniques are appropriate for the child being assessed. Similarly, the therapist must apply the same rigorous methods to evaluate the effectiveness of therapeutic intervention. What should be of prime concern is whether the child is making satisfactory gains in treatment, whether the improvement is long-lasting, and whether the improvement can be generalized to all facets of the child's life situation. Too often, "under the gun" of a heavy caseloads, practitioners are prone to put aside questions of evaluation of treatment. When evaluation of tertiary prevention is undertaken, this type of prevention becomes at least as important as the other approaches to prevention discussed above.

Family Crisis Prevention

Throughout this text, we have made reference to the critical role the family unit plays in childhood problems. Family crisis prevention can reduce stress that vulnerable children may feel. Primary prevention programs, to be most effective, relate to the family as a system and maximize relevant family program involvement (Lloyd & Sallee, 1994).

Broad prevention programs prevent multiple dysfunctional behaviors and can be applied to the general population as well as to targeted populations. The intervention timing in generic programs is generally "long before" the prevented problem is known to occur. Early research in generic prevention points to two ideal times to intervene in the family cycle: the preparent stage (example: high school parenting classes) and the stage when families have children zero to five years old (Sallee, D., 1982).

The existence of a dysfunctional family member is a stressor that may catalyze other family members to develop compensatory dysfunctional behavior. When an alcoholic, highly emotionally disturbed person, child abuser, or criminal is a family member, overall family functioning is highly disturbed. The primary intervention would best occur as soon after the problem emerges as possible.

Life passages such as childhood, puberty, menopause, old age, parenthood, and death are stressors which can trigger dysfunctional behavior. Other stressors such as divorce, unemployment, and poverty can be contributing factors (Sallee, D., 1982). In these cases, primary prevention intervention for individual family members or the entire family can be quite helpful.

A year-long consultation concerning prevention conducted with professionals from education, criminal justice, child care, medicine, mental health, and private child and family practitioners led to the development of policies and implementation strategies for family crisis prevention (Sallee & Downes, 1982). A summary of the recommendations follows:

1. Educational Services

   • Policies should promote family life education activities with suggested focus on curriculum and skill training.

   • A strong public information emphasis is endorsed, as well as a system of electronic information and referral services networking communities across the state.

2. Early Screening and Intervention Services

   • public health services

   • school-based programs

   • Medicaid-financed medical care

   • employees' assistance program

   • protective services

   • mental health services

   • law enforcement services

3. Support Services to Families

   • Comprehensive attention should be given to day-care services as a vehicle for family crisis prevention.

   • The economic stability of families is seen as a fundamental means of preventing family crises.

- Policies supporting the professionalism of the service providers to families should be promoted through training and certification.

- The role of homemaker services is a critical means of preventing family crises.

4. Funding

- A family-oriented philosophy should be promoted in the purchase of services through the state funding mechanisms.

- Policies must address more efficient coordination of state services to families, as well as a financial mechanism for funding such services.

- Adequate funding is needed to attract and support a high level of professional care.

The consultation demonstrated that child practitioners can play vital roles in improving policy which affects their clients. Implementing the policies is a long and ongoing process.

Overviewing Prevention

Professionals in the field of child welfare have been only nominally effective in designing preventive programs for children. As we suggested in the previous chapters, many vulnerable children remain undetected. Often, preventive measures for children are aimed at a secondary level of prevention, such as removing them from overcrowded classrooms or reducing the allowed length of time in foster care. Ideally, goals in preventive services for children should be twofold. First, we must strive to identify the contingencies that foster healthy development in children and families. Second, we should ensure that these conditions are maximally present in all homes, schools, and community environments that constitute the child's primary domain. In short, the child welfare worker should be an advocate for children and play the role of an "inspirator" in assisting the community to build upon existing resources to best foster the healthy development of children.

Cross-Culturally Competent Clinicians

Clinicians practicing with children often will be working cross-culturally. Given the diversity of ethnic groups in the United States, being culturally skilled has become critical to effective work with children and their families (Cohen, 1992). Characteristics of culturally competent practitioners include (1) becoming aware of their own assumptions, values, and biases; (2) understanding the world view of the culturally different client; and (3) knowing appropriate, culturally relevant intervention strategies and techniques (Sue & Sue, 1990). We will discuss each of these characteristics.

Self-assessment on a continuing basis is a tenet of most helping professions working with children, including psychology, counseling, and social work. Yet, the ability to critically examine our assumptions, values, and biases at an emotional level is very difficult and needs to be an ongoing process. Sue and Sue (1990) have identified five competencies of culturally skilled helping professionals:

1. Awareness of their own cultural heritage. Workers accept their group's cultural heritage such as traditions, rituals, language, and arts, with an acceptance of and respect for cultural differences. Practitioners do not impose their own values and standards on children or their family.

2. Awareness of their own values and biases and how they may impact on a minority child. The culturally competent child welfare worker is aware of the danger of prejudices and stereotyping of ethnic groups.

3. Comfort with differences between themselves and the child and his or her family concerning cultural beliefs and values. The worker is aware of differences and is not "color blind," but rather views diversity as a strength that may increase the number of options in working with a child.

4. Awareness of the need to refer a child and his or her family to another child welfare worker if they do not possess the knowledge of that culture or if they are biased. The worker should know his or her limits and see referral as an indication of professionalism in the best interest of the child.

5. Acknowledgment and awareness of racist attitudes, beliefs, and feelings. Culturally competent practitioners understand they may hold some biased beliefs and take responsibility for their racism.

The second area identified by Sue and Sue (1990), understanding the world view of the culturally different, addresses knowledge of broad systems which impact upon minority children. Of course, the practitioner must possess specific detailed knowledge of the child's ethnic group. The greater the knowledge, the more effective the clinician can be. The practitioner should be competent in the culture's use of verbal and nonverbal messages, customs, and traditions. Finally, the culturally competent child counselor is aware of institutional barriers which inhibit minorities from using child welfare and social services.

The culturally competent child welfare worker transforms the above knowledge into successful skills. A balance must be struck between recognizing the uniqueness of the child and the family and understanding group cultural norms. Different treatments do not necessarily imply discrimination; in fact, they may indicate a culturally sensitive worker.

The practitioner must exhibit a wide range of verbal and nonverbal responses accurate to the child's culture. Of course, a child welfare worker from another culture will be limited in his understanding of the culture to some extent, so it is important to know the impact of the worker's limitation on the child's treatment

As we discussed in Chapter 13, children's problems are not that they are Native American, African–American or Hispanic. Rather, the perception of differences and society's attitudes to minority groups prompt many cross-cultural concerns. Culturally competent child welfare workers view diversity as a strength and view the child within the cultural context. The culturally competent practitioner develops the knowledge and skills necessary to work with the child as a unique being who also is a member of a culture.

The Practitioner as Consultant

One of the primary ways in which the child welfare practitioner can effectively serve the community as a prevention specialist is through consultation with community organizations. Community based social service agencies often are very innovative in their approaches to children and family needs, however, often short-term governmental policies and funding practices do not allow for the blossoming of many of these innovative programs. Even with federal programs such as the Family Preservation and Support Act the implementation has been limited at best and very uneven (Lloyd, 1997). A basic difficulty is that not enough of the community affected by these programs is involved in their planning and implementation. A major role of the consultant, is to foster and guide interaction of involved parties so that innovative programs are prompted and pursued on a long-term basis if they prove effective.

The child welfare worker is a likely consultant for working with various groups involved in preventive family and children programs because of her or his knowledge about child development and skill in facilitating communication (Morales & Sheafor, 1983). The role of the child consultant differs from that of the child welfare worker. As consultant, the child specialist relies first and foremost upon communication skills. The consultant may provide some answers and ask critical questions. Primarily, the consultant attempts to uncover and process the wisdom of the group. The primary functions of the child consultant as summarized by Fullmer and Bernard (1972) are:

1. Provide in-service education functions for teachers, parents, and other children professionals.

2. Stimulate self-help organizations; that is, teach new approaches for relating children to teachers, parents, and other professionals so that they continue preventive child welfare measures.

3. Bring together persons of diverse roles and functions to engage in common tasks.

4. Improve communication and enhance information flow among significant persons in the milieu.

5. Extend the services of experts to the assigned task.

To successfully carry out the dual roles of consultant on child-related problems and advocate for children, numerous skills are required besides those of being a good child welfare worker. These skills fall into the following categories: consultant competencies, education and training competencies, and organizer competencies. Each of these categories is discussed below.

Consultant Competencies

The consultant must have an understanding of and skill in the consultative process so that he or she is perceived as a "friendly helper" who is nonthreatening, nonjudgmental, and willing to listen. In some respects, the required skills are the same as those deemed essential in a good therapist. However, some differences necessitate discussion. Insight into the knowledge and skills needed to function effectively as a consultant can be gleaned from a review of the literature, which suggests the importance of the following consultant competencies (Lloyd & Sallee, 1994; Morales & Sheafor, 1983; Rapoport, 1977; Caplan, 1970; Mannino, MacLennan & Shore, 1975; Williams, 1971;):

1. A thorough theoretical and practical understanding of the behavioral sciences.

2. Knowledge and use of authority for change in organizations.

3. Evaluation skills for both individuals and programs.

4. Ability to form relationships with other professionals based upon trust and knowledge.

5. Ability to plan and implement change with teams and community groups.

6. Ability to identify resources.

7. Possession of strong problem-solving skills.

8. Honesty, competence, strong values, maturity, and a strong ego.

From the list of required skills, it is clear that the consultant must simultaneously use both technical and interpersonal skills. Consultants must have excellent diagnostic, conceptual, and problem-solving abilities. They must be actively goal-directed: defining areas for consultation, suggesting ideas and alternatives to clients, referring clients to appropriate resources, and specifying desired outcomes. They must be knowledgeable about specific programs and how similar programs have resolved problems in the past. They must possess good communication skills, both oral and written, and must be able to both calmly assess difficult situations and "think on their feet." Moreover, consultants must develop the capacity to assess and influence an organization's readiness for consultation. Organization readiness refers to the organization's perceptions of the existence of a problem, its recognition of the need for consultation, and the clarity of its expectations for the consultant. Finally, and not surprisingly, consultation requires that all of the above be done in a tactful, friendly, yet professional manner, generating trust, remaining flexible and tolerant of ambiguity, showing a good sense of timing, and being able to handle both frustration and criticism.

Education and Training Competencies

In the role of child welfare consultants, workers must know how to plan and design training programs and be able to use a variety of educational and training techniques such as role-playing, simulations, and problem-solving exercises (Lloyd & Sallee, 1994). They must be able to use the media—radio, television, and newspapers. Knowledge of multiple information dissemination strategies (such as pamphlets, leaflets, posters, bumper stickers, public service announcements, mailings, speakers, workshops, colloquia, and retreats) is essential, as is knowledge of evaluation techniques for assessing the effectiveness of various educational or training programs.

As an educator, the advanced child welfare worker must be able to tailor different programs to specific populations. What may be effective with parents' groups may be inappropriate for teachers and vice versa. Similarly, a program designed for radio presentation may be ineffective on television. If all of this were not enough, the worker/educator must learn to overcome resistance to change within the targeted group.

Another function of the worker/educator in many situations is the need to identify and train natural helpers who can participate in the education and change process. Sometimes these helpers may be other professionals, but more often they are concerned parents. For example, parents of several autistic children in a community may seek the assistance of a worker in their efforts to obtain therapeutic and educational programs for their children from school officials or related social service agencies in the community. Other natural helpers may include community leaders (e.g., local elected officials, clergy, media personalities), business people, or any other individual recognized by members of the community as knowledgeable of the dynamics of the community and capable of moving people to action.

In sum, the worker/educator must be able to set clear objectives for educational efforts, to develop instructional materials, and to disseminate information that addresses identified needs. The person also must possess the energy and capacity to work with a diverse group of individuals on behalf of children.

Organizer Competencies

The child welfare workers functions as an organizer when in the task of instituting a prevention program for children, he or she attempts to develop networks and coalitions to address an identifiable problem, such as child abuse. Two specific skills required of the organizer can be identified: linking/outreach and group facilitation skills.

Linking/outreach skills are required when organizers move into the community. Organizers must have the ability to establish trust and a close working relationship with an ever-expanding network of individuals and groups brought together to achieve a common goal. Building trust, in turn, implies acting in a consistent and reliable manner with these frequently diverse constituencies. Organizers also must possess the ability to identify appropriate resources and to make them available to different client or consumer groups. To accomplish this, organizers must be able to access a range of resources (e.g., experts and sources of funds) as well as know how to put such resources in the hands of appropriate client groups. Finally, effective organizers must have good political skills which enable them to build coalitions and to employ strategies designed to shift the balance of power in the community.

It is essential to recognize that the key to organizing is skill at group facilitation. Facilitation skills enable the organizer to keep a group functioning effectively, achieving a balance between accomplishing group tasks and maintaining healthy interpersonal relationships among group members. Problem-solving skills also are required as the organizer assists the group(s) in creatively and effectively moving through the stages of problem identification, proposal and review of alternative solutions, selection of a plan of action, implementation of the plan, and evaluation of the overall problem-solving effort. The organizer must assist the group in moving through the problem-solving steps while maintaining open communication among members and seeking advice from the outside where necessary. Finally, the organizer must use both group facilitation and problem-solving skills in promoting the emergence of leadership within the group, so that future group activities will draw more heavily on the capacities of group members.

Overviewing Consultation Role

We have discussed the complexity involved in the consultative role. The child welfare worker who intends to advocate for children's rights must function in multiple roles. The skills required of the child welfare worker in each of these roles almost demand that the person be capable of "walking on water." The consultant must possess both technical and interpersonal competencies. In the role of consultant, practical experience is as essential as formal training. Nevertheless, without individuals willing to become engaged in the consultative role, many prevention programs for children would never have become instituted. This is especially true of many primary and secondary prevention programs set up for the well-being of children.

Viewing the Child Welfare Worker as Consultant

Let us now look more specifically at how a child welfare worker/consultant works in a preventive capacity with two different groups of individuals who are extremely influential in the development of a child. Obviously, we are speaking of parents and educators. The consultant role is becoming more common in child welfare practice, particularly in family preservation (Lloyd & Sallee, 1994).

Consultation with Parents.   The child welfare worker/consultant may work with parents individually or in groups. The exact structure of the consultation should be based on the goals defined by the involved parties. Regardless of the defined tasks, the child consultant will hold several broad goals. First, the consultant will attempt to aid the parents in gaining an objective view of their relationships with their children. Thus, the consultant helps the parents set realistic goals and appreciate their children's progress. Second, the consultant wants to help the parents understand their own motives in dealing with children. If the relationship between parent and child is highly dysfunctional or has potentially destructive elements, the consultant helps parents identify these patterns and begin to establish a more appropriate interaction pattern. Third, the consultant wants to facilitate the parents' empathy with the child. Once the parents can empathize with the child's stresses and conflicts, they are better able to identify appropriate child-rearing procedures. In order to sharpen parents' empathy, the consultant will provide information about child development. At times, it may be necessary for parents to deal with their own conflicts and repressions so that they will feel comfortable in identifying their children's stresses. In order to accomplish these goals, the consultant must take the parents' concerns seriously. The consultant's intense interest, as indicated by reflection and summarization of the parents' feelings and concerns, offers reassurance. The consultant will not surface the parents' possible role in the children's stresses too suddenly. If the parents feel they are being blamed, they are likely to become defensive. In this rigid state, the parents' abilities to be empathic with the child's dilemma is limited. The consultant should expect some stereotyping about her- or himself or transference from some parents. Some parents react to the consultant as a "bad parent," feeling that the consultant can do nothing but destroy hopes. Others respond as if the consultant is an omnipotent parent who can resolve any conflict (Freedman, Kaplan, & Sadock, 1976). The consultant will want to guard against providing excess advice as it may place the parent in a dependent position and reinforce the feeling that he or she is an inadequate parent.

In the role of consultant the professional provides information and advice and serves as a general resource person on issues pertaining to children. In consultation with parent groups, many of the same problems and resistances may occur that are seen in family therapy.

Parents will seek the aid of a child consultant for a variety of reasons. Of course in the child protective services the parent may be an involuntary client at first. Sometimes parents describe their children as experiencing "normal growing-up problems," but to the consultant, the problem may sound more serious (e.g., excessive stress reaction, learning disability, or even psychotic-like symptomatology); in these cases, the consultant should recommend that the child be seen by a therapist. Generally, if the parents' personal problems do not seem to interfere with their ability to empathize with the child, preventive consultation can be helpful. If the parents lack motivation to change their responses, if they are very narcissistic, or if their pathology interlocks with the child, family therapy and/or individual psychotherapy may be needed.

Parent groups can be conducted in a variety of ways. They may be open-ended discussion groups in which parents are encouraged to ask one another questions about child-rearing techniques. The consultant may semistructure these discussion groups by having parents write down and then discuss their approaches to specific dilemmas. Another approach is parent education programs, which focus upon discussion of a text or specific parenting material. Commonly employed procedures include the STEP Kit (Systematic Training for Effective Parenting) by Dinkmeyer & McKay (1976), humanistic approaches of Ginott

(1965), and communication techniques of Gordon (1970). A number of consultants are teaching parents in groups to conduct counseling with their children. For example, parents may watch the therapist/consultant conduct play therapy sessions with a child. Parents then attempt the play therapy approaches at home. Later parent group sessions are employed to discuss the effectiveness of the home play approach. In other programs, parents are instructed in behavior management techniques and then are encouraged to carry out these techniques in their own child-rearing practices (Kaplan & Girard, 1994).

Programs that encourage parents to be change agents of their own offspring's behavior are not new. Perhaps the classic case is that of "Little Hans," who was treated by his father following the directions for therapy received from Sigmund Freud (1955). Perhaps the two factors contributing to the growing interest in providing parents with the skills to change children's behavior stem from the large shortage in each of the helping professions and from the increasing demand for child and family intervention. Interest in child consultation ranges from single-parent groups to special-interest groups, such as parents of hyperactive, autistic, or children with mental retardation. Increased interest from parents in parenting skills and knowledge of child development will support that goal of primary prevention discussed earlier in the chapter.

Parents spend so much time with their children that they are the natural and most potent source for primary and secondary intervention. Clearly, consultation with parents is an important activity for most child welfare workers. An important task for the future will be to find ways to maximize the consultant role with parents.

Consulting with Educators.   A primary role for the child welfare workers is to consult with teachers. One of the primary functions of the school social worker is to provide support to educators. The teacher needs empathy and support for dealing with difficult children. By using effective communication skills, the child welfare worker directly or through the school social worker as a consultant can help the teacher clarify his or her teaching objectives so that he or she feels more confident in responding to children with child welfare issues (Freeman, 1995). It is easy for a consultant to become defensive if a teacher presents a very difficult case for assistance and the consultant feels that he or she lacks an answer to the dilemma. It is important for the consultant to recognize that the teacher possesses many skills and answers. Often, support and understanding may be all that are requested and needed.

The child consultant also can assist the teacher in working with special children (e.g., handicapped, gifted, and hyperactive). The consultant can conduct a systematic study of the child's behavior in the classroom, playground, and lunchroom so that appropriate reinforcers can be identified. Then, the consultant can work with the teacher to set up an effective management procedure. Often, the teacher is well versed in behavior management principles, but within the confines of the classroom may not be able to systematically observe a given child to identify problem behaviors and arrange for reinforcement contingencies for the shaping of new target behaviors. The consultant as a "free agent" can provide valuable individual assistance.

The child welfare worker as consultant may chair or participate in staff conferences about specific children. In these conferences, it is often the child consultant's responsibility to recommend or bring in other professionals that may be of assistance. It is important that the consultant follow up on the results of these case conferences to ensure that recommendations have been completed and that the consequences are desirable.

The consultant also may offer in-service training for school personnel. The consultant can educate teachers about new child abuse or child management and innovative materials for effective education in the areas of coping with divorce, death of a parent or other loved one, sexuality, adjusting to a handicap, and so on. It also may be necessary for the consultant to assist the school social worker or counselor in gaining the skills necessary to work with teachers on a wider basis.

Finally, the child welfare worker or school social worker as consultant can conduct groups with teachers to help them maximize their interpersonal skills and deal with their feelings of stress. Some teacher groups focus upon the teacher foster parent/biological parent interaction. In these groups, problems are identified. Teachers express their feelings about the problems and the ideas about the causes of the problems. They brainstorm possible solutions and develop techniques for measuring gain. Later meetings are used for assessing results and brainstorming modifications to the procedures. Clearly, ways must be sought to facilitate long-term stress reduction in teachers who find their jobs especially stressful. This is particularly true of teachers who work with severely emotionally disturbed or handicapped children, inner-city school teachers, and teachers employed by poor school districts who do not have access to many of the educational resources available in wealthier ones.

Overviewing Consultation

The child welfare worker possesses the skills to be of immense help to both parents and educators. The role of consultant is integral to successful prevention and service delivery. As a consultant, the practitioner lends his or her expertise to parents and teachers and attempts to facilitate their involvement with children by providing information on service interface, child development, behavioral management, and supportive problem solving. The ultimate goal of consultation is the promotion of positive relationships among children, parents, teachers, and any other individuals whose interests bring them into contact with children.

Child Welfare and the Legal System

Almost all child welfare workers are involved with the interfacing with the judiciary system. Theoretical questions such as what constitutes "in the best interest of the child" and what constitutes reasonable efforts require specific court actions such as whether a child should be returned home, placed in a foster home or a many other options. Thus, forensic work is concerned with legal ways of protecting a child's right to protection, development and emotional well-being. In recent years, the legal rights of children have become extremely important and demand discussion (Wineman, 1995)

In 1948, the Ohio Supreme Court (Haley vs. Ohio 332, US 5961) ruled that the rights guaranteed to adults also are applicable to children. However, the ruling has provoked some critical questions. Since children are developmentally different from adults, in what ways must the laws be modified to protect their rights? When do parents' rights conflict with the rights of children, and if they do, whose rights should be honored? Also, what rights are unique to children? We are only at the beginning stages of answering these questions. The child welfare worker interested in prevention will want to be familiar with the questions and tentative answers so that he or she can, when necessary, appeal to the judiciary system for children's betterment.

Some basic definitions of children's unique rights have emerged in the field of children's mental health. The joint Commission on the Mental Health of Children (1970) presented these rights as essential for children:

1. To be wanted

2. To be born healthy

3. To live in a healthy environment

4. To obtain satisfaction of basic needs

5. To receive continuous loving care

6. To acquire intellectual and emotional skills necessary to achieve individual aspirations

7. To cope effectively in our society

8. To receive care and treatment through facilities that are appropriate to children's needs

The commission's eight rights constitute a sublime list that we wish for all children, but enacting these rights is a monumental task. Enacting these rights requires an enormous thrust for children's prevention services. We already have discussed several ways of intervening for children's improved well-being. Let us add some legal ways of aiding children to ensure their rights to a healthy and productive life.

Precedent has been established for guaranteeing due process to children. According to the Gault decision (387, US 1, 1967), children and adolescents cannot be held for crimes (regardless of parents' testimony) without a due process hearing. Recently, the courts have upheld a child's right to privacy. One example of how this has been applied concerns the child's employment in research. Until the 1970s, parents could volunteer their institutionalized children for medical and behavioral studies. Now, these children must be asked if they wish to participate. If they cannot understand the request, an unbiased committee representing the child's best interests reviews the pros and cons of the research to be conducted (Koocher & Keith–Spiegel, 1990).

Some precedent in the disposition of child custody cases also has been established so that the child's needs are best protected. The doctrine of "best interest of the child," holds that the basis for a legal decision of a court custody case is:

- the nature of the child's relationship with each parent

- the capacity and willingness of each parent to care for the child

- the presence of a stable environment and length of time of the child in that environment
- the likelihood that the home will serve as a family unit
- the nature of the child's adjustment at school and in the community
- the moral fitness of each parent
- the physical and mental fitness of each parent
- the child's preference (Koocher & Keith–Spiegel, 1990)

Special guidelines have been set for dealing with legal offenses of minors. Children under 16 can be legally declared "persons in need of supervision." The children considered out of control by parents and authorities may be sanctioned by the courts for behaviors not considered criminal offenses if committed by adults (truancy, running away, glue-sniffing, and promiscuity are all considered legal offenses for minors, although they do not constitute adult illegal acts). A legal record of prosecutions under the doctrine of "persons in need of supervision" is not maintained if the child and parent participate in a social remediation program.

Special juvenile courts now handle the disposition of criminal acts by youth. These juvenile courts have been highly criticized for supporting ambiguous definitions of delinquency and for setting arbitrary penalties. Typically, a maximum of 15 minutes is spent on each case. In efforts to reach the "whole child," judges' decisions often are a curious mixture of punishment, parenting, and psychotherapy. New penal codes for youths has become more punitive, reflecting societies frustration with the increased violence by youth reported in the popular press. The codes concentrate on the criminal behavior and recommends specific penalties for particular acts. The new codes promise to correct the arbitrary nature of the present juvenile court system and places more responsibility upon the community to provide social remediation for acting-out youths.

The emerging precedence in juvenile courts suggests the need for child welfare consultants who specialize in forensic child welfare. This child specialist can play several crucial roles. He or she can serve as an expert witness in child custody cases or institutionalization of children. The child welfare worker/expert witness needs to be familiar with judicial rights of children as well as child and family assessment procedures and child development. The child consultant who is an expert in forensic child welfare also can serve as a child advocate. Children cannot initiate legal action on their own behalf. The child advocate insists that program and services are based upon sound child developmental knowledge. Child welfare advocates are involved in all cases of class action litigation (e.g., foster care, school segregation, and over representation of minority children in classes for the retarded) and legislative advocacy involving children. In some situations, the judiciary can be an important arm for implementing prevention strategies for children. Its effectiveness depends in part upon wise input from and wise use by informed child welfare clinicians.

Child welfare workers increasingly are being drawn in to the forensic arena. Their role can include expert witnesses concerning family matters including termination of parental rights, advocates for the child, and possible mediators between the child and family members. However, before agreeing to become involved in a forensic case, the practitioner should be certain he or she understands the legal principles, criteria, and processes bearing on that particular case. It is important that the practitioner carefully clarify the professional role including such factors as who the client is and what he or she is being asked to undertake. It also is important that the practitioner clearly communicate his or her role in the case with the clients and attorneys, including limits of areas of competency. When the practitioner's testimony is limited to legitimate areas of expertise, and the practitioner resists the temptation to speculate beyond the state of current accepted professional and scientific knowledge, the practitioner can be an objective and powerful advocate for the child (Koocher & Keith–Spiegel, 1990).

Clinical Practice Creates Policy

Child practitioners are involved in policy in many ways. The everyday practice decisions made by child practitioners create and evaluate policy (Schorr, 1985). Policy is defined as the set of regulations, laws, procedures, and implicit rules which guide how a practitioner functions outside of the intrapsychic realm. Any action a practitioner or child wants to take that is subject to external control reflects policy. The child welfare practitioner can exert some choice over the external arena that will in turn influence him or her. For example, the type of child referred to a practitioner is dictated by location of the office, the use of home visits, type of licensure, cases taken before, professional training, or use of appointments.

A practitioner's involvement in policy is viewed in three ways by Schorr (1985). The nature of professional practice is the first. The length of time in practice, theoretical base, or education and training provide a focus of the practice for most practitioners. Their view of the nature of practice with children shapes policy. For example, the adoption placement of minority children with white parents rarely took place before the mid-1960s. With the lower Anglo birthrate of unwanted babies because of effective contraceptives, Anglo families wanting to adopt turned to interracial adoptions. This sudden change in practice has raised serious policy questions, resulting in new laws such as the Indian Child Welfare Act (1978, P.L. 95-608), which requires tribal permission for placement with a non-Indian family.

Schorr's second point is how agency practice forms policy. The agency objectives, location, attitudes of staff and board, fee structure, choice of therapists, and intake procedures are policy-based decisions made in every agency and by many private practitioners. The client's perspective of the control the practitioner and agency have over her or him is not only a treatment constraint but also a policy and value choice. For example, until recently, minority and poor clients were often placed with short-term intervention programs, while Anglo and middle- to upper-class clients were more likely to be referred for long-term intervention (LeVine & Padilla, 1980). Societal change will be reflected in the cases that come to child welfare practitioners. The increased use of drugs by children or the increase of violent child abuse cases are indications of significant and changing social problems. Child welfare practitioners need to be sensitive to patterns of social change and assess their impact upon the family and the child. In that way, the practitioner can help formulate effective policy rather than reinforce existing social problems, such as prejudice and family violence.

Child welfare workers are engaged in policy formation and issues whenever they practice. We must be sensitive and better trained to understand and act on policy. From political involvement to testimony before legislative bodies to the location of our offices, we are making policy decisions. The choices we make affect more than the children we work with. The choices we make affect families, society, and future children.

The Future

In Chapter 2, an overview of the history of children in society, we asked our-selves, "How far have we progressed since the days when children had little importance in society?" As you read through the text, you may have felt that the answer to this question is mixed. We have discussed the high incidence of child-hood emotional problems and the confusion about etiology of childhood malad-justment. In contrast to the high incidence reports and confusion in some research, we also discussed a variety of therapeutic intervention strategies for working with children that are demonstrating increasing promise. We also have reviewed a wealth of information about vulnerable children that aids child welfare prac-titioners in being alert to who needs help, so that we are more attuned to listening to our children. Hopefully, you are as encouraged as we are about the advance-ments that have been made in listening to and working with children. Our final question in this text is, "With our increased understanding of child developmental processes and the application of intervention strategies for troubled children, how far can we go in assisting children to reach their full potential?" Obviously, we would like to eradicate crises in childhood, and we would like to create en-vironments that maximize children's physical, personal, and social development.

Both Freud and Watson proposed that experiences during early childhood exerted a powerful constraint on the topography of adult behavior. Further, before Freud, few if any credited children with sexual and aggressive emotions and conflicts. Similarly, before Watson, hereditary factors such as "degeneracy," seemed the obvious cause of delinquency, insanity, and mental retardation. Stimu-lated by these theories and the work of other developmental theorists, we now know a great deal about the genetic and environmental contributions to intelli-gence and abnormal behavior; new investigations have revealed much about the cognitive, linguistic, and social development of children; and research has shown us the importance of parent–infant bonding, to cite just a few of our important research findings with children. In short, we have accumulated a vast storehouse of information about children since the turn of the century.

Coupled with advances in our knowledge of child development, child thera-pists have provided us with many new techniques for working with children and families. We now are at the crossroads where we must use our knowledge about children and work diligently and constructively to create primary prevention programs for children. The President's Commission on Mental Health (1978) acknowledged that good care during pregnancy and childbirth can prevent some conditions that lead to later mental disability and can detect others early enough for effective treatment Also noted was the importance of detecting and correcting at the earliest stages problems of physical, emotional, and cognitive development that can lead to emotional maladjustment and learning difficulties. Our work leads us to continue to support areas of concern identified by consultants to the President's Commission.

Child welfare prevention programs will be the challenge of the future—a challenge for the following reasons:

1. There are yet few experts in the area of prevention.

2. Preventive programs are long-term ventures that often require years before they can be evaluated to determine their efficacy, and most practitioners do not have the luxury of time to wait to see if their preventive strategies have been effective.

3. Prevention programs are costly, and all indications point to fewer federal and state dollars for social service programs of any type.

4. The establishment of primary prevention programs usually takes place within a sociopolitical context of some type, and most child welfare workers are not expert in the political process.

A start in the direction of prevention and policy formation has been noted. Our task now is to continue the struggle for children's rights. Advocacy for children is essential. To listen deeply to our children and respond powerfully, our role for the future must be more than just that of a traditional child welfare practitioner who sits and talks with a child client behind a closed door. The practitioner of the future will consider meaningful contact with the child and their family, as well as significant others, agencies, and legislative bodies that affect children and their families an integral part of her or his role.

References

Abel, E. L. (1980). Fetal alcohol syndrome: Behavior teratology. *Psychological Bulletin, 87,* 29–50.

Abramowitz, C. V. (1976). The effectiveness of group psychotherapy with children. *Archives of General Psychiatry, 33,* 320–330.

Achenbach, T. (1974). *Developmental Psychopathology.* New York: Ronald Press.

Ack, M., Beale, E., and Ware, L. (1975). Parent guidance; Psychotherapy of the young child via the parent. *Bulletin of the Menninger Clinic, 39,* 436–447.

Ackerman, N. W. (1966a). Family psychotherapy today: Some areas of controversy. *Comprehensive Psychiatry, 7,* 375–378.

Ackerman, N. W. (1966b). *Treating the troubled family.* New York; Basic Books.

Ackerman, N. W. (1971). Prejudicial scapegoating and neutralizing forces in the family group. In J. G. Howells (Ed.), *Theory and practice of family psychiatry.* New York: Brunner/Mazel.

Adler, A. (1927). *Understanding human na*ture. New York: Greenberg.

Adler, A. (1958). *What life should mean to you.* New York: Capricorn.

Ahrons, C. (1980). Redefining the divorce family: A conceptual framework. *Social Work, 25* (6), 437–441.

Ainsworth, M. D. S. (1973). The development of infant–mother attachment. In B. Caldwell & H. Riccuiti (Eds.), *Review of child development research* (Vol. 3, pp. 1–94). Chicago: University of Chicago Press.

Alexander, D., Ehrhardt, A. A., and Money, J. (1966). Defective figure drawing, geometric and human, in Turner's syndrome. *Journal of Nervous and Mental Disease, 142,* 161–167.

Alexander, F. G., and Selesnick, S. T. (1966). *The history of psychiatry: An evaluation of psychiatric thought and practice from prehistoric times to the present.* New York: Harper and Row.

Allen, F. H. (1942). *Psychotherapy with children.* New York: W. W. Norton.

Allen, F. H. (1963). *Positive aspects of child psychiatry: As developed in the selective writings of Dr. Frederick H. Allen.* New York: W. W. Norton.

Alpern, G. D., and Boll, T. J. (1972). *Developmental profile.* Indianapolis: Psychological Development.

American Association on Mental Deficiency. (1973). Rights of the mentally handicapped. *Mental Retardation, 11* (5), 56.

American Association on Mental Retardation. (1992). *Mental retardation: Definition, Classification, and systems of supports* (9th ed.). Washington, DC: Author.

American Humane Association. (1985). *Highlights of official child neglect and abuse reporting for 1983.* Denver: Author.

American Psychiatric Association. (1980). *Diagnostic and statistical manual of mental disorders.* Washington, DC: Author.

American Psychiatric Association. (1987). *Diagnosis and statistical manual for mental disorders* (3rd Ed., Revised). Washington, DC.

American Psychiatric Association. (1994). *Diagnosis and statistical manual for mental disorders* (4th Ed.). Washington, DC.

Americans with Disabilities Act of 1990. P.L. 101-336, 104 Stat. 327.

Anastasi, A. (1976). *Psychological testing.* New York: Macmillan.

Anderson, H., and Goolishian, H. A. (1988). Human systems as linguistic systems: Preliminary and evolving ideas about the implications for clinical theory. *Family Process, 27,* 371–393.

Anderson, S. C., and Lauderdale, M. L. (1982). Characteristics of abusive parents: A look at self-esteem. *Child Abuse and Neglect 6,* 285–293.

Anonymous. (1972). Differentiation of self in one's family. In J. Framo (Ed.), *Family interaction.* New York: Springer.

Anthony, E. J. (1959). A group of murderous mothers. *Family interaction 7* (Supplement), 1–6.

Anthony, E. J. (1970). The behavior disorders of childhood. In P. H. Mussen (Ed.), *Carmichael's manual of child psychology* (Vol. II). New York: Wiley.

Aries, P. (1962). *Centuries of childhood: A social history of family life.* New York: Alfred A. Knopf.

Atwood, J. D. (1996). *Family scripts.* Washington, DC: Accelerated Development.

Austin, D. M., and Caragonne, P. (1981). *A comparative analysis of twenty two settings using case management components.* Austin: University of Texas at Austin School of Social Work.

Axline, V. (1969). *Play therapy* (Rev. ed.). Cambridge: Houghton Mifflin.

Azima, F. (1976). Group psychotherapy for latency-age children. *Canadian Psychiatric Association Journal 21*, 210–211.

Azrin, N. H., and Foxx, R. M. (1971). A rapid method of toilet training the institutionalized retarded. *Journal of Applied Behavior Analysis*, 4, 89–99.

Bandler, R., Grinder, R., and Satir, V. (1976). *Changing with families.* Palo Alto, CA: Science and Behavior Books.

Bandura, A. (1969). *Principles of Behavior Modification.* New York: Holt, Rinehart & Winston.

Bandura, A. (1977). *Social learning theory.* Englewood Cliffs, NJ: Prentice Hall.

Baratz, J. C., and Shuy, R. W. (Eds.). (1969). *Teaching Black children to read.* Washington, DC: Center for Applied Linguistics.

Barden, C. (1990). The effects of craniofacial deformity, chronic illness, and physical handicaps on patient and family adjustment. In B. Lahey & A. Kazdin (Eds.), *Advances in clinical child psychology,* Vol. XIII, (pp. 343–369). New York: Plenum Press.

Barkley, R. A. (1971). Stimulant drugs in the classroom. *School Psychology Digest 88,* 412–425.

Barkley, R. A. (1977). A review of stimulant drug research with hyperactive children. *Journal of Child Psychology and Psychiatry*, 18, 137–165.

Barnouw, V. (1963). *Culture and personality.* Homewood, IL: Dorsey Press.

Baroff, G. S. (1991). *Developmental disabilities: Psychosocial aspects.* Austin, TX: Pro-Ed.

Barrett, D. (1976). The effects of play therapy on the social and psychological adjustment of five-to nine-year-old children. *Dissertation Abstracts International, 36,* 5032A–5033A. (University Microfilms No. 76-4394).

Barth, R. P., and Berry, M. (1987). Outcomes of child welfare services under permanency planning. *Social Service Review, 61* (1), 71–90.

Barth, R. P., and Berry, M. (1988). *Adoption and disruption: Risks, rates, and responses.* Hawthorne, NY: Aldine de Gruyter.

Bateson, G. (1972). *Steps to an ecology of mind.* New York: Ballantine.

Bateson, G., Jackson, D. D., Haley, J., and Weakland, J. H. (1956). Toward a theory of schizophrenia. *Behavioral Science, 1,* 251–264.

Bayley, N. (1969). *Bayley Scales of Infant Development manual.* New York: Psychological Corporation.

Beck, A. (1982). Cognitive therapy of depression: New perspectives. In P. Clayton & J. Barrett (Eds.), *Treatment of depression: Old controversies and new approaches* (pp. 265–290). New York: Raven Press.

Belkin G. S. (1980). *Contemporary psychotherapies.* Chicago: Rand McNally.

Bell, J. E. (1964). The family group therapist: An agent of change. *International Journal of Group Psychotherapy, 14,* 72–83.

Bellak, L., and Bellak, S. S. (1971). *Children's Apperception Test.* Larchmont, NY: C. P. S.

Bem, S. L. (1974). The measurement of psychological androgeny. *Journal of Consulting and Clinical Psychology, 42,* 155–162.

Bem, S. L. (1975). Sex-role adaptability: One consequence of psychological androgyny. *Journal of Personality and Social Psychology, 31,* 634–643.

Bender, B. (1976). Self-chosen victims: Scapegoating behavior sequential to battering. *Child Welfare, 55,* 417–422.

Bender, L. (1938). *A visual motor gestalt test and its clinical use.* New York: American Orthopsychiatric Association.

Bender, L. (1947). Childhood schizophrenia: Clinical study of one hundred schizophrenic children. *American Journal of Orthopsychiatry, 17,* 40–56.

Bender, L. (1955). Twenty years of clinical research on schizophrenic children with special reference to those under six years of age. In G. Caplan (Ed.), *Emotional Problems of early childhood.* New York: Basic Books.

Bender, L. (1962). *A visual-motor gestalt test and its clinical use.* New York: American Orthopsychiatric Association.

Bender, L. (1974). Aggression in children. In S. Frazier (Ed.), *Aggression.* Baltimore: William & Wilkins.

Berger, K. S. (1988). *The developing person through the life span.* New York: Worth Pub, Inc.

Berkowitz, H. (1968). A preliminary assessment of

the extent of interaction between child psychiatric clinics and public schools. *Psychology in the Schools, 5,* 291–295.

Bernard, J. M. (1978). Divorce and young children: Relationships in transition. *School Guidance Counseling, 12* (3), 188–197.

Berry, M. (1991). Open adoption in a sample of 1296 families. *Children and Youth Services Review, 13,* 379–396.

Berry, M., and Barth, R. P. (1990). A study of disrupted adoptive placements of adolescents. *Child Welfare, 69* (3), 209–225.

Bessell, H., and Palomares, U. (1973). *Methods in human development.* La Mesa, CA: Human Development Training Institute.

Bettelheim, B. (1967). *The empty fortress: Infantile autism and the birth of the self.* New York: The Free Press.

Blackham, G. A., and Silberman, A. (1971). *Modification of child behavior.* Belmont, CA: Wadsworth.

Bloom, L. (1973). One word at a time: The use of a single word utterance before syntax. *Janua Linguarum; Series Minor,* 154.

Bloom, M. (1984). *Configurations of human behavior: Life span development in social environments.* New York: Macmillan.

Bloom, M. (1985). *Life span development: Basis for prevention and interventive helping* (2nd ed.). New York: Macmillan.

Boehm, A. E. (1971). *Boehm Test of Basic Concepts.* New York: Psychological Corporation.

Bohannan, P. (1970). *Divorce and after.* Garden City, NJ: Anchor Books.

Bohman, M. (1972). *Adopted children and their families—A follow up study of adopted children, their background environment and adjustment.* Stockholm: Proprius.

Borcherdt, B. (1996). *Making families work and what to do when they don't: Thirty guides for imperfect parents of imperfect children.* Binghamton, NY: The Haworth Press, Inc.

Bostow, D. E., and Barley J. B. (1969). Modification of severe disruptive and aggressive behavior using brief time-out and reinforcement procedures. *Journal of Applied Behavioral Analyses, 2,* 31–37.

Bott, E. (1971). *Family & social network.* New York: The Free Press.

Bowen, M. (1960). A family concept of schizophrenia. In D. Jackson (Ed.), *The etiology of schizophrenia.* New York: Basic Books.

Bowen, M. (1966). The use of family theory in clinical practice. *Comprehensive Psychiatry 7,* 345–374.

Bowker, J. P. (Ed.). (1983). Overview: Education for primary prevention in social work. *Education for Primary Prevention in Social Work* (pp. 1–7). New York: Council on Social Work Education.

Bowlby, J. (1951). Maternal care and mental health. *World Health Organization Monograph 2.* Geneva: World Health Organization.

Bowlby, J. (1969). Attachment and loss. *Attachment* (Vol. 1). New York: Basic Books.

Bracht, N. (1995). Prevention and wellness. In R. L. Edwards (Ed.-in-Chief), *Encycopedia of Social Work* (19th ed., Vol. 3, pp. 1879–1886). Washington, DC: National Association of Social Workers.

Braine, M. D. S. (1976). Children's first word combinations. *Monographs of the Society for Research in Child Development, 41* (1).

Brase, D., and Loh, H. (1975). Possible role of 5-hydroxytryptamine in minimal brain dysfunction. *Life Sciences, 16,* 1005–1015.

Brocune, A., and Finkelhor, D. (1986). Impact of child sexual abuse: A review of the research. *Psychological Bulletin, 99,* 6677.

Brodzinsky, D., Pappas, C., Singer, L., and Braff, A. (1981). Children's conception of adoption: A preliminary investigation. *Journal of Pediatric Psychology, 6,* 177–189.

Brodzinsky, D., Singer, L., and Braff, A. (1984). Children's understanding of adoption. *Child Development, 55,* 869–878.

Brown, D. (1976). Directive parental counseling: An appraisal to its effect on extraconditioning variables. *Dissertation Abstracts International, 36,* 4680B. (Microfiche available from National Library of Canada and Ottawa).

Brown, J. V., and Bakeman, R. (1977, March). *Antecedents of emotional involvement in mothers of premature and full-term infants.* Paper presented at the meeting of The Society for Research in Child Development, New Orleans.

Brown, K. (1983). *The effects of divorce on children.* Unpublished paper.

Brown, R. (1973). *A first language.* Cambridge, MA: Harvard University Press.

Bruner, J. S. (1964). The course of cognitive growth. *American Psychologist, 19,* 1–15.

Buck, J. N. (1950). *House-Tree-Person Test.* Beverly Hills, CA: Western Psychological Services.

Burchinal, L.A. (1964). Characteristics of adolescents from unbroken, broken and re-constituted families. *Journal of Marriage and the Family, 26,* (1), 44–51.

Burgemeister, B. B., Blum, L. H., and Lorge, I. (1972). *Columbia Mental Maturity Scale* (3rd ed.). New York: Harcourt Brace Jovanovich.

Burger, H. (1974). Ethnicity: An anthropological approach to ecstasy and sanity. *General Systems, 24*, 59–71.

Burks, H. F. (1969). *Burks' Behavior Rating Scale.* El Monte, CA: Arden Press.

Buros, 0. K. (Ed.). (1972). *Seventh mental measurements handbook.* Highland Park, NJ: Gryphon Press.

Cahn, K., and Johnson, P. (Eds.). (1993). *Children can't wait, reducing delays in out-of-home care.* Washington, DC: Child Welfare League of America, Inc.

Campbell, M., and Small, A. M. (1978). Chemotherapy. In B. B. Wolman, A. O. Ross, & J. Egan (Eds.), *Handbook of treatment of mental disorders in childhood and adolescence.* Engelwood Cliffs, NJ: Prentice Hall.

Campbell, S. (1986). Developmental issues in childhood anxiety. In R. Gittelman (Ed.), *Anxiety disorders of childhood* (pp. 24–57). New York: Guilford.

Caplan, G. (1970). *The theory and practice of mental health consultation.* New York: Basic Books.

Capper, L. (1996). *That's my child: Strategies for parents of children with disabilities.* Washington, DC: Child and Family Press.

Carkhuff, R. R., and Berenson, B. G. (1977). *Beyond counseling and therapy* (2nd Ed.). New York: Holt, Rinehart, & Winston.

Carkhuff, R. R., and Berenson, B. G. (1977). *Beyond counseling and therapy.* New York: Holt.

Caron, S. (1980, Dec.) *The case of the ill-tempered artist.* Unpublished case notes, Las Cruces, NM.

Carr, A. (1990). Failure in family therapy: A catalogue of engagement mistakes. *Journal of Family Therapy. 12*, 371–386.

Cattell, P. (1940). *The measurement of intelligence of infants and young children.* New York: Psychological Corporation.

Center for the Future of Children. (1994). *The future of children, 4 (1).*

Chambers, M. J. (1980, Nov.). The murder Of Robbie Wayne age six. *Reader's Digest,* pp. 216–251.

Chapman, S. B. (1995). Child abuse and neglect: Direct practice. In R. L. Edwards (Ed.-in-Chief), *Encyclopedia of Social Work* (19th ed., Vol. 1, pp. 353–366). Washington, DC: National Association of Social Workers.

Chase, N. F. (1975). *A child is being beaten.* New York: Holt, Rinehart & Winston.

Chess, S., and Hassibi, M. (1970). Behavior deviation in mentally retarded children. *Journal of the American Academy of Child Psychiatry, 9,* 282–297.

Chess, S., and Hassibi, M. (1978). *Principles and practice of child psychiatry.* New York: Plenum Press.

Chethik, M. (1989). *Techniques of child therapy: Psychodynamics strategies.* New York: Guilford.

Child Abuse Prevention and Treatment Act of 1974, SS 42 U.S.C. SS 5101.

Child Abuse Prevention, Adoption, and Family Services Act of 1992, P.L. 102–295, 106 Stat.187.

Child Abuse Prevention and Treatment Amendments of 1991. (Report 9740. Washington DC. U.S. House of Representatives.

Child sexual abuse: Incest, assault and sexual exploitation. (1981). Washington DC: National Center on Child Abuse and Neglect. (DHHS Publication No. (OHDS) 81-30166).

Children's Defense Fund. (1978). *Children Without Homes.* Washington DC: Author.

Chuda, R., and Sankar, D. (1976). Demographic studies in child psychiatry II—General data from second study. *Research communications in psychology, psychiatry and behavior, 3,* 478–483.

Cicchetti, D., Toth, S., and Bush, M. (1988). Developmental psychopathology and incompetence in childhood: Suggestions for intervention. In B. Lahey & A. Kazdin (Eds.), *Advances in clinical child psychology* Vol. 11, (pp. 1–59). New York: Plenum Press.

Cohen, A. H. (1979a). Effective treatment of child abuse and neglect. *Social Work, 24* (6), 513–519.

Cohen, A. H. (1979b). An evaluation of three demonstration child abuse and neglect treatment programs. *Journal of American Academy of Child Psychiatry,* 18, 283–291.

Cohen, J. S., and Westhues, A. (1990). *Well-functioning families for adptive and foster children.* Toronto: University of Toronto Press.

Cohen, L. B. (1979). Our developing knowledge of infant perception and cognition. *American Psychologist,* 34, 894–899.

Cohen, N. A. (Ed.) (1992). *Child welfare: A multicultural focus.* Boston: Allyn and Bacon.

Cohen, S. M., Allan, M. G., Pollin, W., and Hrubec, Z. (1972). Relationship of schizo-affective psychosis to manic depressive psychosis and schizophrenia. *Archives of General Psychiatry, 26* (6), 539–545.

Cohen, T. (1983). The incestuous family revisited. *Social Casework 63* (3), 154–161.

Colletta, N. D. (1979). The impact of divorce: Father absence or poverty? *Journal of Divorce, 3* (1), 27–35.

Combrinck–Graham, L. (Ed.). (1995). *Children in families at risk.* New York: The Guilford Press.

Committee on the Family Group for the Advancement of Psychiatry. (1970). *Treatment of families in conflict: The clinical study of family process.* New York: Jason Aronson.

Compton, B., and Galaway, B. (1984). *Social Work Processes* (3rd ed.). Homewood IL: Dorsey Press.

Conners, C. K., and Rothschild, G. H. (1968). Drugs and learning in children. In J. Hellmuth (Ed.), *Learning disorders* (Vol. III). Seattle: Special Child Publications.

Connolly, A. J., Nachtman, W., and Pritchett, E. M. (1973). *Key Math Diagnostic Arithmetic Test.* Circle Pines, MN: American Guidance Service.

Conte, J. R. (1984). Progress in treating the sexual abuse of children. *Social Work, 29* (3), 258–263.

Conte, J. R. (1995). Child sexual abuse overview.. In R. L. Edwards (Ed.-in-Chief), *Encyclopedia of Social Work* (19th ed., Vol. 1, pp. 402–408). Washington, DC: National Association of Social Workers.

Coopersmith, S. (1967). *The antecedents of self-esteem.* San Francisco: W. H. Freeman.

Cornell, D. G. (1983). Gifted children: The impact of positive labeling on the family system. *American Journal of Orthopsychiatry, 53* (2), 322–335.

Costin, L. B. (1979). *Child welfare: Policies and practice.* New York: McGraw-Hill.

Council of the American Academy of Child and Adolescent Psychiatry. (1988). Perspective: Guidelines for the clinical evaluation of child and adolescent sexual abuse. *American Academy of Child and Adolescent Psychiatry, 88,* 655–657.

Coyne, A., and Brown, M. E. (1985). Developmentally disabled children can be adopted. *Child Welfare LXIV* (6), 607–616.

Crabtree, M. (1963). *Houston Test for Language Development.* Houston: Houston Test.

Daniel, R. M. (1977). Father–child intimacy in divorced families (Doctoral dissertation, California School of Professional Psychology). *Dissertation Abstracts International 38* (6-B), 2854.

Davidson, W. S., and Seidman, E. (1974). Studies of behavior modification and juvenile delinquency: A review, methodological critique, and social perspective. Ps*ychological Bulletin, 81,* 998.–1011.

Deblinger, E., Lippmann, J., Stauffer, L., and Finkel, M. (1994). Personal responses to child sexual abuse allegations. *Child Abuse and Neglect, 18* (8), 679–682.

Department of Health, Education and Welfare, Office of Child Development. *Report of the conference on the use of stimulant drugs in the treatment of behaviorally disturbed young school children.* Washington, DC: Author.

Derevensky, J. L. (1979). Children's fears: A developmental comparison of normal and exceptional children. *Journal of Genetic Psychology, 135,* 11–21.

deShazer, S. (1986). An indirect approach to brief therapy. Indirect Approaches. Rockville, MD: Aspen.

Deutsch, M., and Brown, B. (1964). Social influences in Negro and white intelligence differences. *Journal of Social Issues, 20* (2), 24–35.

DeWeaver, K. L. (1995). Developmental disabilities: Definitions and policies. In R. L. Edwards (Ed.-in-Chief), *Encyclopedia of Social Work* (19th ed., Vol. 1, pp. 712–720). Washington, DC: National Association of Social Workers.

Diaz–Guerrero, R. (1975). *Psychology of the Mexican: Culture and personality.* Austin, TX: University of Texas Press.

Dickerson, M. U. (1981). *Social work practice with the mentally retarded.* New York: The Free Press.

Dimick, K., and Huff, V. (1970). *Child counseling.* Dubuque, IA: W. C. Brown.

Dinkmeyer, D., and Caldwell, E. (1970). *Developmental counseling and guidance.* New York: McGraw-Hill.

Dinkmeyer, D., and McKay, G. (1976). *Systematic training for effective parenting.* Circle Pines, MN: American Guidance Services.

Doll, E. (1965). *The Vineland Social Maturity Scale: Manual of directions.* Minneapolis: American Guidance Service.

Donofrio, A. (1976). Parent education vs child psychotherapy. *Psychology in the Schools, 13,* 175–180.

Donovan, D. and McIntyne, D. (1990). *Healing the hurt child.* New York: W. W. Norton.

Douglas, J. W. B. and Mulligan, D. C. (1961). Emotional adjustment and educational achievement—the preliminary results of a longitudinal study of a national sample of children. *Proceedings of the Royal Society of Medicine, 54,* 885–891.

Dreikurs, R., and Soltz, V. (1964). *Children: The challenge.* New York: Hawthorne.

Drillien, C. M. (1970). Complications of pregnancy and delivery. In J. Wortis (Ed.), *Mental retardation.: An annual review* (Vol. 1). New York: Grune & Stratton.

Dunn, L. M. (1965). *Expanded manual for the Peabody Picture Vocabulary Test.* Minneapolis: American Guidance Service.

Durost, W. N., Bixler, H. H., Writestone, J. W., Prescott, G. A., and Balow, I. (1971). *Metropolitan Achievement Test.* New York: Harcourt Brace Jovanovich.

Durrell, D. D. (1955). *Durrell analysis of reading difficulty.* New York: Harcourt Brace Jovanovich.

Duvall, E. M. (1971). *Family Development* (4th ed.). Philadelphia: J. B. Lippincott.

Edelman, M. W. (1990). Speech: Children's Defense Fund President.

Edwards, H., and Thompson, B. (1971). Who are the fatherless? *New Society, 17* (436), 192–193.

Egeland, B. (1988). The consequences of physical and emotional neglect on the development of young children. In National Center on Child Abuse and Neglect (Ed.), *Research symposium on child neglect.* Washington, DC: National Center on Child Abuse and Neglect.

Eimas, P. D. (1974). Auditory and linguistic processing of cues for places of articulation by infants. *Perception and Psychophysics, 16,* 513–521.

Eimas, P. D. (1975). Auditory and phonetic coding of the cues for speech: *Perception and Psychophysics, 18,* 341–347.

Elkind, D. (1974). *Children and adolescents: Interpretive essays on Jean Piaget.* New York: Oxford University Press.

Ellis, A. (1962). *Reason and emotion in psychotherapy.* New York: Lyle Stuart.

Ellison, R., and LeVine, E. (1982). *Counseling children of divorce.* Unpublished manuscript.

Elwell, M. E. (1979). Sexually assaulted children and their families. *Social Casework, 60* (4), 227–235.

Erickson, M. T. (1978). *Child psychopathology: Assessment, etiology, and treatment.* Englewood Cliffs, NJ: Prentice Hall.

Erikson, E. H. (1963). *Childhood and society* (2nd ed.). New York: W. W. Norton.

Ervin–Tripp, S. M. (1973). Imitation and structural change in children's language. In C. A. Ferguson & D. I. Slobin (Eds.), *Studies of child language development.* New York: Holt, Rinehart & Winston.

Espenshade, T. J. (1979). The economic consequences of divorce. *Journal of Marriage and the Family, 41* (3), 615–625.

Evaluation of child abuse & neglect: Demonstration projects 1974–1977 (1977, Dec.). Vol. 6: Child client impact: Final report (PB 178-448). Washington, DC: U.S. Department of Commerce.

Evans, I. M., and Nelson, R. O. (1977). Assessment of child behavior problems. In A. R. Ciminero, A. R. Calhoun, K. S. Calhoun, & H. E. Adams (Eds.), *Handbook of behavioral assessment* (pp. 603–681). New York: Wiley.

Everett, J. E. (1995). Child foster care.. In R. L. Edwards (Ed.-in-Chief), *Encycopedia of Social Work* (19th ed., Vol. 1, pp. 375–389). Washington, DC: National Association of Social Workers.

Ewing, C. (1976). Family crisis intervention and traditional child guidance: A comparison of outcomes and factors related to success in treatment. *Dissertation Abstracts International, 36, 4686B.* (University Microfilm No. 76-5933).

Families First. Atlanta: GA, (Pamphlet, 1994).

Fanshel, D., and Shinn, E. B. (1978). *Children in foster care: A longitudinal investigation.* New York: Columbia University Press.

Feigelson, C. I. (1974). Play in child analysis. *Psychoanalytic Study of the Child, 29,* 21–26.

Feldman, D. (1979). Toward a nonelitist conception of giftedness. *Phi Delta Kappan, 60,* 660–663.

Finkelhor, D. (1979). *Sexually victimized children.* New York: The Free Press.

Finkelhor, D. (1984). *Child sexual abuse: New theory and research.* New York: The Free Press.

Finkelhor, D., Hotaling, G., Lewis, I. A., and Smith, C. (1990). Sexual abuse in a national survey of adult men and women: Prevalence, characteristics, and risk factors. *Child Abuse and Neglect, 14,* 19–28.

Fisher, J., and Gochros, H. L. (1975). *Planned behavior change: Behavior modification in social work.* New York: The Free Press.

Flango, V. E., and Flango, C. R. (1993). Adoption statistics by state. *Child Welfare, 72,* 311–319.

Framo, J. L. (1979). Family theory and therapy. *American Psychologist, 34,* 988–992.

Frankel, S. (1977). The management aspect of psychotherapy with aggressive children. *Child Psychiatry and Human Development, 7,* 169–185.

Frankenburg, W. K., and Dodds, J. B. (1970). *Denver Developmental Screening Test.* Denver: University of Colorado Medical Center.

Frankl, S. (1963). *Man's search for meaning.* New York: Washington Square Press.

Fraser, M. W. (Ed.). (1997). *Risk and resilience in childhood: An ecological perspective.* Washington, DC: NASW Press.

Frazier, D., and LeVine, E. (1983). Reattachment therapy: Intervention with the very young physically abused child. *Psychotherapy, Research and Practice, 20* (10), 90–100.

Freedman, A. M., Kaplan, H., and Sadock, B. (1976). *Modern synopsis of comprehensive textbook of psychiatry II.* Baltimore: Williams & Wilkins.

Freeman, E. (1995). School social work overview. In R. L. Edwards (Ed.-in-Chief), *Encyclopedia of Social Work* (19th ed., Vol.. 3, pp. 983–991). Washington, DC: National Association of Social Workers.

Freud, A. (1928). Introduction to the technique of child analysis. *Nervous and Mental Disease Monograph No. 48.* New York.

Freud, A. (1965). *Normality and pathology in childhood: Assessment of development.* New York: International Universities Press.

Freud, S. (1953). Three essays on the theory of sexuality. *The standard edition of the complete psychological works of Sigmund Freud* (Vol. 7). London: Hogarth Press.

Freud, S. (1955). *Analysis of a phobia of a five-year-old boy.* London: Hogarth Press.

Freundlich, D. J. (1987). The gifted: An underserved minority population. *Social-Work-in-Education, 10* (1), 43–59.

Frey, J. III, Heckel, R. V., Salzberg, H. C., and Wackwitz, J. (1976). Demographic variables as predictors of outcome in psychotherapy with children. *Journal of Clinical Psychology, 32,* 713–721.

Friedman, E. C., and Barclay, A. (1963). The discriminative validity of certain psychological tests as indices of brain damage in the mentally retarded. *Mental Retardation, 1,* 291–293.

Friedman, R. (1997). What's working in family-based services?—or, what's left to believe in during a time of such doubt? *Family Preservation Journal, 2,* (1), 9–19.

Friedrich, W. N., and Borinskin, J. A. (1976). The role of the child in abuse: A review of the literature. *American Journal of Orthopsychiatry, 46* (4), 580–590.

Friedrich, W. N., Einbender, A. J., and Luecke, W. J. Cognitive and behavioral characteristics of physically abused children. *Journal of Consulting and Clinical Psychology, 51* (2), 313–314.

Frisk, M. (1964). Identity problems and confused conceptions of the genetic ego in adopted children during adolescence. *Acta Paedo Psychiatrics, 31,* 6–12.

Frostig, M., Lefever, D. W., and Whittlesey, J. R. B. (1964). *The Marianne Frostig Development Test of Visual Perception.* Palo Alto, CA: Consulting Psychologists Press.

Fuller, J. (1977). Duo therapy case studies: Process and techniques. *Social Casework, 56,* 84–91.

Fullmer, D. W., and Bernard, H. W. (1972). *The school counselor-consultant.* Boston: Houghton Mifflin.

Furgeson, J. (1981, Feb.). *The case of the unsure, angry, eight-year-old.* Unpublished case notes, New Mexico State University, Las Cruces.

Furman, S., Sweat, L. and Corcetti, G. (1965). Social class factors in the flow of children to outpatient psychiatric facilities. *American Journal of Public Health, 55,* 385–392.

Gagnon J. (1965). Female child victims of sex offenses. *Sociological Problems, 13,* 176–192.

Gambrill, E. D. (1961). A behavioral perspective of families. In E. R. Tolson & W. J. Reid (Eds.), *Models of family treatment.* New York: Columbia University Press.

Gammen, C. (1990). Cognitive approaches to depression in children: Current findings and new directions. In B. Lahey & A. Kazdin (Eds.), *Advances in child clinical psychology* Vol. 13 (pp. 139–168). New York: Plenum.

Gannon, W. J. (1972). *The effects of the gestalt oriented group approach on the interpersonal contact attitudes of selected high school students.* Unpublished doctoral dissertation, Case Western Reserve University, Ann Arbor. (University microfilms No. 72-26).

Gardner, R. A. (1970). *The boys and girls book about divorce.* New York: Science House.

Gardner, R. A. (1971). *Therapeutic communication with children: The mutual storytelling technique.* New York: Science House.

Gardner, R. A. (1975). *Psychotherapeutic approaches to the resistant child.* New York: Jason Aronson.

Gardner, R. A. (1976). *Psychotherapy with children of divorce.* New York: Jason Aronson.

Gardner, R. A. (1977). *Parents book about divorce.* New York: Doubleday.

Gardner, R. A. (1979). *The objective diagnosis of minimal brain dysfunction.* Cresskill, NJ: Creative Therapeutics.

Garfield, S. (1978). Research on client variables in psychotherapy. In S. L. Garfield and A. E. Bergin (Eds.), *Handbook of psychotherapy and behavior change* (2nd ed.). New York: Wiley.

Garfield, S. (1980). *Psychotherapy: An eclectic approach.* New York: Wiley.

Garmezy, N. (1981). Children under stress: Perspectives on antecedents and correlates of. vulnerability and resistance to psychopathology. In R. A. Zucken & A. I. Rabin (Eds.), *Further explorations in personality.* New York: Wiley.

Gates, A. I., and Russell, D. H. (1962). *Diagnostic and Remedial Spelling Manual.* New York: Bureau of Publications, Teachers College, Columbia University.

In re Gault 387 U.S. 1428 (1967).

Gelles, R. G., and Straus, M. A. (1985, Nov. 11). Child abuse shows sharp decline. *Las Cruces Sun-News* (AP).

Germain, C. B., and Gitterman, A. (1980). *The life model of social work practice.* New York: Columbia University Press.

Giardino, A. P., Christian, C. W., and Giardino, E. R. (1997). *A practical guide to the evaluation of child physical abuse and neglect.* Thousand Oaks, CA: Sage Publications, Inc.

Giaretto, H. (1976). Humanistic treatment of father–daughter incest. In R. E. Helfer & C. H. Kempe (Eds.), *Child abuse and neglect: The family and the community.* Cambridge, MA: Ballinger.

Gil, D. G. (1970). *Violence against children: Physical child abuse in the U.S.* Cambridge, MA: Harvard Press.

Gilligan, Carol. (1982). *In a different voice: Psychological theory and women's development.* Cambridge: Harvard University Press.

Ginott, H. G. (1961). *Group psychotherapy with children: The theory and practice of play therapy.* New York: McGraw-Hill.

Ginott, H. G. (1965). *Between parent and child: New solutions to old problems.* New York: Macmillan.

Giovannoni, J. M. (1995). Childhood. In R. L. Edwards (Ed.-in-Chief), *Encyclopedia of Social Work* (19th ed., Vol. 1, pp. 433–441). Washington, DC: National Association of Social Workers.

Glasser, W. (1965). *Reality therapy. A new approach to psychiatry.* New York: Harper and Row.

Glucksberg, S., Krauss, R., and Higgins E. T. (1975). The development of referential communication skills. In F. D. Horowitz (Ed.), *Review of child development research* (Vol. 4), 305–347. Chicago, University of Chicago Press.

Glueck, S., and Glueck, E. T. (1950). *Unraveling delinquency.* New York: Commonwealth Fund.

Glueck, S., and Glueck, E. T. (1952). *Delinquents in the making.* New York: Harper.

Golden, C. J. (1981). The Lunia-Nebraska's children's battery: Theory and formulation. In G. Hynd & J. Obrzut (Eds.), *Neuropsychological Assessment and School-Age Child: Issues and Perspectives* (pp. 277–302). New York: Grune & Staston.

Goldfarb, W. (1961). *Childhood schizophrenia.* Cambridge, MA: Harvard University Press.

Goldfarb, W. (1970). Childhood psychosis. In P. H. Mussen (Ed.), *Carmichael's manual of child psychology* (3rd ed., Vol. 2). New York: Wiley.

Goldman, J., and Coane, J. (1977). Family therapy after the divorce: Developing a strategy. *Family Process, 16* (3), 357–362.

Goldstein, J., Freud, A., and Solnit, A. (1979). *Beyond the best interests of the child.* London: The Free Press.

Goldstein, K. M., Caputo, D. V., and Taub, H. B. (1976). The effects of parental and perinatal complications on development at one year of age. *Child Development, 47,* 613–621.

Goldstein, S. E. (1978). A national perspective. In D. G. Forgays (Ed.), *Primary prevention of psychopathology series, Vol. 2: Environmental influences* (pp. 25–36). New Hampshire: University of New England Press.

Gongola, P. A. (1977). Social relationships after marital separation: A study of women with children (Doctoral dissertation. Case Western Reserve University). *Dissertation Abstracts International, 30* (9-A), 5742.

Gonso, J. L. (1977). The effects of divorce on children (Doctoral dissertation, Indiana University). *Dissertation Abstracts International, 38* (11-B), 5568.

Goodenough, F. L. (1926). *Measurement of intelligence by drawings.* Yonkers on Hudson, NY: World Book.

Goodenough, F., and Harris, D. (1963). *Goodenough–Harris Drawing Test.* New York: Harcourt Brace Jovanovich.

Goodman, J. D., and Sours, J. A. (1967). *The child mental status examination.* New York: Basic Books.

Gordon, T. (1970). *Parent effectiveness training.* New York: Wydene.

Gottesman, I. I., and Shields, J. (1972). *Schizophrenia and genetics.* New York: Academic Press.

Gough, H. G. (1969). *California Psychological Inventory.* Palo Alto, CA: Consulting Psychologists Press.

Gowan, J. C. (1960). The organization of guidance for the able. *Personnel and Guidance Journal 4*, 275–279.

Grabe, P. V. (1990). *Adoption resources for mental health professionals*. New Brunswick: Transaction Publishers.

Graham, F. G., Ernhart, C. B., Craft, M., and Berman, P. W. (1963). Brain injury in the preschool child: Some developmental considerations. *Monographs, 77* (Whole 10 & 11).

Graham, F. G., Ernhart, C. B., Thurston D., and Craft M. (1961). Development three years after perinatal anoxia and other potentially damaging new born experience. *Psychological Monographs, 76* (Whole 522).

Gray, W. S., and Robinson, H. M. (Eds.), *(1967). Gray Oral Reading Test*. Indianapolis: Bobbs-Merrill.

Green, A. H. (1978). Self-destructive behavior in battered children. *American Journal of Psychiatry, 135*, 579–582.

Greenbert, H.S. (1989). Psychological functioning in 8 16-year-old cancer survivors and their parents. (DSW dissertation, University of Pennsylvania).

Gregg, G. S., & Elmer, E. (1969). Infant injuries: Accident or abuse. *Pediatrics, 44*, 434–439.

Grenier, C. E., Dawson, S. E., and Gray, V. (1989). Parenting skills intervention program for parents of gifted preschool children. *Social-Work-in-Education, 11* (4), 251–259).

Griggs, S. A. (1984). Counseling the gifted and talented based on learning styles. *Exceptional Children, 50* (5), 429–432.

Grollman, E. A. (1975). *Talking about divorce: A dialogue between parent and child*. Boston: Beacon Press.

Grossman, H. (Ed.). (1977). *Revised manual on terminology and classification in mental retardation*. Washington, DC: American Association on Mental Deficiency.

Guerney, B., Jr. (1964). Filial therapy: Description and rationale. *Journal of Consulting Psychology, 28*, 304–310.

Guerney, L. F. (1979). Play therapy with learning disabled children. *Journal of Clinical Child Psychology, 8*, 242–244.

Guilford, J. P. (1968). *Intelligence, creativity, and their educational implications*. San Diego: Robert R. Knapp.

Guilford, J. P. (1975). Creativity: A quarter century of progress. In I. A. Taylor and J. W. Getzels (Eds.), *Perspectives in creativity*. Chicago: Aldine.

Haley, J. *(1963). Strategies of psychotherapy*. New York: Grune & Stratton.

Haley v. Ohio, 332 U.S. 5961 (1948).

Hall, C. S., and Lindzey, G. (1970). *Theories of Personality* (2nd ed.). New York: Wiley.

Hall, R. V., Panyon, M., Rabon, D., and Broden, M. (1972). The effective use of punishment to modify behavior in the classroom. In K. D. O'Leary and S. O'Leary (Eds.), *Classroom manager. The successful use of behavior modification*. Elensford, NY: Pergamon Press.

Halpern, F. (1953). *A clinical approach to the children's Rorschach*. New York: Grune & Stratton.

Hammill, D. D., and Larsen, S. C. (1974). The effectiveness of psycholinguistic training. *Exceptional Children, 41*, 5–14.

Hansen, J., Niland, T., and Zani, L. (1969). Model reinforcement in group counseling with elementary school children. *Personnel and Guidance Journal, 47*, 741–744.

Hardcastle, D. (1977). A mother–child, multiple-family counseling program: Procedures and results. *Family Process, 16*, 67–74.

Harlow, H. (1958). The nature of love. *American Psychologist, 13*, 673–685.

Harrell, R. F., Woodyard, E., and Gates, A. I. (1955). *The effects of mother's diet on the intelligence of offspring*. New York: Teachers College.

Harrington, R. (1984). A holistic approach to the assessment of emotionally disturbed children. In M. Fine (Ed.). *Systematic intervention with disturbed children* (pp. 203–227). New York: S.P. Medical & Scientific Books.

Harris, D. B. (1963). *Children's drawings as measures of intellectual maturity*. New York: Harcourt, Brace & World.

Harris, T. A. (1969). *I'm O.K. You're O.K.* New York: Harper and Row.

Harrison, S., McDermott, J., Wilson, P., and Schrager, J. (1965). Social class and mental illness in children. *Archives of General Psychiatry, 13*, 411–417.

Harry, J., and DeVall, W. B. (1978). *The social organization of gay males*. New York: Praeger.

Hartman, A. (1978). Diagramatic assessment of family relationships. *Social Casework 59* (8), 465–476.

Hartman, A. (1979). The extended family as a resource for change. In C. B. Germain (Ed.), *Social work practice: People and environments*. New York: Columbia University Press.

Hartman, A. (1981). Bowen Family Systems: Theory & practice. In E. R. Tolson and W. J. Reid (Eds.), *Models of family treatment*. New York: Columbia University Press.

Hartman, A. and Laird, J., (1983). *Family-centered social work practice*. New York: The Free Press.

Hartman, A. (1995). Family Therapy. In R. L. Edwards (Ed.-in-Chief), *Encycopedia of Social Work* (19th ed., Vol. 2, pp. 983–991). Washington, DC: National Association of Social Workers.

Harvald, B., and Hauge, M. (1965). Hereditary factors elucidated by twin studies. In J. V. Neel, M. S. Shaw, & W. J. Schull (Eds.), *Genetics and the epidemiology of chronic diseases*. Washington, DC: U.S. Department of Health, Education and Welfare.

Haworth, M. (1964). *Child psychotherapy: Practice and theory*. New York: Basic Books.

Haynes, K. S., and Holmes, K. A. (1994). *Invitation to social work*. White Plains, NY: Longman.

Heath, A. (1981, Feb.). *Never insult the cook before you eat*. Unpublished case study, Family Research Institute, Purdue University, West Lafayette, IN.

Heatherington, E. M. (1966). Effects of paternal absence on sex-typed behavior in Negro and white preadolescent males. *Journal of Personality and Social Psychology, 4* (1), 87–91.

Heatherington, E. M., Cox, M., & Cox, R. (1976). Divorced fathers. *The family coordinator, 24,* 416–428.

Heatherington, E. M., Cox, M., & Cox, R. (1979). Family interaction in the social emotional and cognitive development of children following divorce. In V. Vaughn & T. B. Brazelton (Eds.), *The family: Setting priorities*. New York: Science and Medicine.

Heatherington, E. M., & Deur, J. (1971). The effects of father absence on child development. *Young Children, 26,* 233–248.

Heatherington, E. M., Stouwie, R. J., & Ridberg, E. H. (1971). Patterns of family interaction and child-rearing attitudes related to three dimensions of juvenile delinquency. *Journal of Abnormal Psychology, 78,* 160–176.

Heber, R. (1959, Sept.). A manual on terminology and classification in mental retardation. *American Journal of Mental Deficiencies, 64* (Monograph Supplement).

Heim, R., and Trosman, H. (1960). Initial expectations of the doctor–patient interaction as a factor in continuance in psychotherapy. *Psychotherapy, 23,* 272–275.

Helfer, R. E. (1987). The developmental basis of child abuse and neglect: An epidemiological approach. In R. E. Helfer and R. S. Kempe (Eds.), *The battered child (*4th ed., pp. 60–80). Chicago: University of Chicago Press.

Hepler, J. B. (1991). Evaluating the clinical significance of a group approach for improving the social skills of children. *Social Work with Groups, 14* (2), 87–104.

Herzog, E., and Sudia, C. E. (1973). Children of fatherless families. In B. M. Caldwell & H. N. Ricciuti (Eds.), *Review of child development research* (Vol. III). Chicago: University of Chicago Press.

Hess, R. D., and Camara, K. A. (1979). Post-divorce family relationships as mediating factors in the consequences of divorce for children. *Journal of Social Issues, 35* (4), 79–96.

Hewett, F. M., and Forness, S. R. (1977). *Education of exceptional learners* (2nd ed.). Boston: Allyn and Bacon.

Hill, D. (1952). EEG in episodic psychiatric and psychopathic behavior. *Electroencephalography and Clinical Neurophysiology, 4,* 419.

Hill, R. (1949). *Families under stress. New* York: Harper.

Hill, R. B. (1972). *The strengths of black families*. New York, NY: National Urban League.

Hitchfield, E. M. (1973). *In search of promise*. London: Longman Group.

Hoffman, K. S., and Sallee, A. L. (1994). *Social work practice: Bridges to change*. Boston, MA: Allyn and Bacon.

Hoffman, L. (1985). Beyond power and control: Toward a second order family systems therapy. *Family Systems Medicine, 3,* 381–396.

Holdahl, S., and Casperson, P. (1977). Children of family change: Who's helping them now? *Family Coordinator, 26* (4), 473–477.

Hooper–Briar, K., Broussard, C. A., Ronnau, J., and Sallee, A. L. (1996). *Family Preservation Journal*. Las Cruces, NM: New Mexico State University, Department of Social Work, Family Preservation Institute.

Hoorwitz, A. N. (1983). Guidelines for treating father–daughter incest. *Social Casework, 63* (11), 515–524.

Howells, J. G. (1971). *Theory and practice of family psychiatry*. New York: Brunner/Mazel.

Howells, J. G. (1975). *World history of psychiatry*. New York: Brunner/Mazel.

Hozman, T. L., and Froiland, D. J. (1976). Families in divorce: A proposed model for counseling children. *The Family Coordinator, 25* (3), 271–276.

Hubbell, R. (1981). *Foster care and families. Conflicting values and policies.* Philadelphia: Temple University Press.

Hug–Hellmuth, H. (1962). Aus dem seelenhen des kindes. In L. Kanner (Ed.), *Child Psychiatry* (3rd ed.). Springfield, IL: Charles C. Thomas. (Original work published: Leipzig, Deuticke, 1913).

Hunt, J. McV. (1975). Reflections on a decade of early education. The *Journal of Abnormal Child Psychology, 3,* 275–330.

Hunt, R. (1988). Attention deficit disorder and hyperactivity (pp. 519–562). In C. Kestenbaum & D. Williams (Eds.) *Handbook of Clinical Assessment of Children and Adolescents,* Vol. II. New York: New York University Press.

Hunter, R. S., Kilstrom, N., Kraybill, E. N., and Loda, F. (1978). Antecedents of child abuse and neglect in premature infants: A prospective study in a newborn intensive care unit. *Pediatrics, 61* (4), 629–635.

Hurlock, E. B. (1942). *Child development.* New York: McGraw-Hill.

Hutchinson, J. R., and Nelson, K. E. (1985, June). How public agencies can provide family-centered services. *Social Casework 66.6,* 367–371.

Hynd, G., Snow, J., Becker, M. (1986). Neuropsychological assessment in clinical child psychology, Vol. IX. In B. Lahey & A. Kazdin (Eds.), *Advances in clinical child psychology* (pp. 35–76). New York: Plenum Press.

Inhelder, B., and Piaget, J. (1958). *The growth of logical thinking from childhood to adolescence.* New York: Basic Books.

Jackson, D. D. (1959). Schizophrenic symptoms and family interaction. *Archives of General Psychiatry, 1,* 618–621.

Jackson, H., and Nuttall, R. (1994). Effects of gender, age, and history of abuse on social workers' judgments of sexual abuse allegations. *Social Work Research, 30* (2), 105–113.

Jacobson, D. S. (1979). The impact of marital separation/divorce on children: Parent–child separation and child adjustment. *Journal of Divorce, 1* (4), 314–360.

Janzen, C., and Harris, O. (1997). *Family treatment in social work practice.* (3rd. ed) Itasca, IL: F.E. Peacock.

Jastak, J. F., Jastak, S. R., and Bijou, S. W. (1965). *The Wide Range Achievement Test manual of instructions.* Wilmington, DE: Guidance Associates.

Jennings, R., and Davis, C. (1977). Attraction-enhancing client behaviors: A structured learning approach for "Non-Yavis, Jr." *Journal of Counseling and Clinical Psychology, 45,* 135–144.

Jensen, A. R. (1969). How much can we boost IQ and scholastic achievement? *Harvard Educational Review, 39,* 1–123.

Johnson, H. W., and contributors. (1990). *The social services: An introduction.* 3rd ed. Itasca, IL: Peacock.

Johnson, P. J. (1965). Case Management. in A. Fink, J. H. Pfouts, and A. W. Doblestein (Eds.), *The field of social work* (8th ed.). Beverly Hills, CA: Sage.

Joint Commission on Mental Health of Children. (1970). *Crisis in child mental health: Challenge for the seventies.* New York: Harper and Row.

Jones, M. C. (1926). *Development of early behavior patterns in young children.* Berkeley, CA: Author.

Justice, B., and Justice, R. (1976). *The Abusing Family.* New York: Human Science Press.

Kabcenell, R. (1974). On countertransference. *Psychoanalytic Study of the Child, 29,* 27–33.

Kaczmarek, M., and LeVine, E. (1980). Expansion training: A counseling stance for the withdrawn rigid child. *Elementary School Guidance and Counseling, 15,* 31–47.

Kadushin, A. (1980). *Child welfare services: An introduction.* (3rd ed.). New York: Macmillan.

Kallmann, P. (1953). *Heredity in health and mental disorder.* New York: Norton.

Kalter, N. (1990). *Growing up with divorce: Helping your child avoid immediate and later emotional problems.* New York: Free Press.

Kamerman, S. B. (1985). Young, poor, and a mother alone: Problems and possible solutions. In H. McAdoo & J. Pardham (Eds.), *Service to young families* (pp. 1–38). Washington, DC: American Public Welfare Association.

Kanner, L. (1962a). *Child psychiatry* (3rd ed.). Springfield, IL: Charles C. Thomas.

Kanner, L. (1962b). Emotionally disturbed children: A historical review. *Child Development, 33,* 97–102.

Kanner, L (1973). *Childhood psychosis: Initial studies and new insights.* New York: Wiley.

Kaplan, E., and Kaplan, G. (1971). The prelinguistic child. In J. Elliot (Ed.), *Human development and cognitive processes.* (pp. 359–381). New York: Holt, Rinehart and Winston.

Kaplan, L., and Girard, J. L. (1994). *Strengthening high-risk families: A handbook for practitioners.* New York: Lexinton Books.

Karls, J. M., and Wandrei, K. E. (Eds.) (1994). *Person-in-environment system: The PIE classification system for social functioning problems.* Washington, DC: NASW Press.

Karnes, F. A., and Collins, E. C. (1978). State definitions of gifted and talented: A report and analysis. *Journal for the Education of the Gifted, 1,* 44–62.

Karnes, F. A., and Wherry, N. (1981). Wishes of fourth and seventh grade students. *Psychology in the Schools, 2,* 238–242.

Kazdin, A. E. (1977). *The token economy. A review and evaluation.* New York: Plenum Press.

Keat, D. II (1974). *Fundamentals of child counseling.* Boston: Houghton Mifflin.

Keat, D. II (1979). *Multimodal therapy with children.* New York: Pergamon Press.

Kelly, R., and Berg, B. (1978). Measuring children's reactions to divorce. *Journal of Clinical Psychology, 34,* 215–221.

Kempe, C. H., and Helfer, R. E. (1980). *The battered child.* Chicago: University of Chicago Press.

Kempe, C. H., Silverman, F. N., Steele, B. F., Droegemueller, W., and Silver, H. K. (1962). The battered child. *Journal of the American Medical Association, 181,* 17–24.

Kempe, R., and Kempe, C. H. (1976). Assessing family pathology. In R. E. Helfer & C. H. Kempe (Eds.), *Child abuse and neglect. The family and the community.* Cambridge, MA: Ballinger.

Kempe, R., and Kempe, C. H. (1978). *Child abuse.* Cambridge, MA: Harvard University Press.

Kennell, J. H., Jerauld, R., Wolfe, H., Chesler, D., McAlpine, W., Kreger, N. C., Steffa, M., and Klaus, M. H. (1974). Maternal behavior one year after early and extended postpartum contact. *Developmental Medicine and Child Neurology, 16,* 172–179.

Keeney, B. F., and Ross, J. M. (1985). *Mind in therapy.* New York: Basic Books.

Kent, J. T. (1976). A follow up study of abused children. *Journal of Pediatric Psychology, 1,* 25–31.

Kinard, E. M.. (1980). Mental health needs of abused children. *Child Welfare, 59* (8), 451–462.

Kinard, E. M. (1980). Emotional development in physically abused children. *American Journal of Orthopsychiatry, 50* (4), 686–696.

Kirk, S. A., McCarthy, J. J., and Kirk, W. D. (1968). *Illinois Test of Pscholinguistic Abilities* (Rev. ed.). Urbana, IL: University of Illinois Press.

Kissel, S. (1974). Mothers and therapists evaluate long-term and short-term therapy. *Journal of Clinical Psychology, 30,* 296–299.

Klein, D. C., and Goldston S. E. (Eds.). (1977). *Primary prevention: An idea whose time has come.* Washington, DC: U.S. Government Printing Office.

Klein, M. (1937). *The psychoanalysis of children* (2nd ed.). London: Hogarth Press.

Klein, M. (1960). *The psychoanalysis of children.* New York: Grove Press.

Klein, M., and Stern L. (1971). Low birth weight and battered child syndrome. *American Journal of Diseases of Children, 122,* 15–18.

Knights, R. M., and Hinton, G. G. (1969). The effects of methylphenidate (Ritalin) on the motor skills and behavior of children with learning problems. *The Journal of Nervous and Mental Disease, 148,* 643–653.

Knopf, I. J. (1979). *Childhood psychopathology. A developmental approach.* Englewood Cliffs, NJ: Prentice Hall.

Kohlberg, L. (1966). A cognitive developmental analysis of children's sex-role concepts and attitudes. In E. Maccoby (Ed.), *The development of sex differences.* Stanford, CA: Stanford University Press.

Kohlberg, L. (1968). The child as a moral philosopher. *Psychology Today, 2,* 25–30.

Kohlberg, L. (1969). *Stages in the development of moral thought and action.* New York: Holt, Rinehart and Winston.

Koocher, G., and Keith–Spiegel, P. (1990). *Children, ethics and the law.* Lincoln: University of Nebraska Press.

Kopiewicz, H., and Williams, D. (1988). Psychopharmacological treatment. In C. Kestenbaum & D. Williams (Eds.), *Handbook of clinical assessment of children and adolescents,* Vol. II. New York: New York University Press.

Koppitz, E. M. (1964). *The Bender Gestalt Test for Young Children.* New York: Grune and Stratton.

Koppitz, E. M. (1968). *Psychological evaluation of children's human figure drawings.* New York: Grune and Stratton.

Kovacs, M., Feinberg, T., Cruse–Novac, M., Pauluskas, S. and Finkelstein, R. (1984). Depressive disorders in childhood II. A longitudinal study of the risk for a subsequent major depression. *Archives of General Psychiatry, 41,* 643–649.

Kraft, A. D., Palombo, J., Mitchell D. L., Woods, P. K., Schmidt, A. W., and Tucker, N. G. (1985). Some theoretical considerations on confidential adoptions. Part III: The adopted child. *Child and Adolescent Social Work, 2* (3), 139–153.

Kreisberg, M. (1967). Rearing children for educational achievement in fatherless families. *Journal of Marriage and the Family, 29,* 288.–301.

Kukla, R. A., and Weingarten, H. (1979). The long term effects of parental divorce in childhood on adult adjustment. *Journal of Social Issues, 35* (4), 50–78.

Ladd, E. T. (1973). Pills for classroom peace? In A. Davis (Ed.), *Issues in abnormal child psychology.* Monterey, CA: Brooks/Cole.

Lang, D. M., Papenfuhs, R., and Walters, J. (1976). Delinquent females perceptions of their fathers. *The Family Coordinator, 25* (4), 475–481.

Lang, F. (1975). Effects of maternal group counseling on the academic achievement of high risk first grade children. *Dissertation Abstracts International, 36,* 1309A. (University Microfilms No. 75-20, 925)

Langner, T., Herson, J., Greene, E., Jameson, J., and Goff, J. (1970). Children of the city: Affluence, poverty, and mental health. In V. L. Allen (Ed.), *Psychological factors in poverty.* Chicago: Markham.

Lansky, L. M. (1967). The family structure also affects the model: Sex-role attitudes in parents of preschool children. *Merrill–Palmer Quarterly, 13,* 139–150.

Lapouse, R., and Monk, M. (1959). Fears and worries in a representative sample of children. *American Journal of Orthopsychiatry, 29,* 803–818.

Laterza, P. (1983). An eclectic approach to group work with the mentally retarded. In F. J. Turner (Ed.), *Differential diagnosis and treatment in social work* (3rd ed., pp. 520–529). New York: Free Press.

Lawton, J. J., and Gross, S. F. (1964). Review of psychiatric literature on adopted children. *Archives of General Psychiatry, 11,* 635–644.

Lazarus, A. (1966). Behavioral rehearsal vs. non-directive therapy vs. advice in effecting behavior change. *Behavior Research and Therapy, 4,* 209–210.

Lazarus, A. (1976). *Multimodal behavioral therapy.* New York: Springer.

Lazarus, A., Davison, G. C., and Polefka, D. A. (1965). Classical and operant factors in the treatment of a school phobia. *Journal of Abnormal Psychology, 70,* 225–229.

Ledwidge, B. (1978). Cognitive behavior modification: A step in the wrong direction? *Psychological Bulletin, 70,* 225–220.

Lee, E. (Ed.). (1997). *Working with asian americans: A guide for clinicians.* New York: The Guilford Press.

Leifer, A. D., Leiderman, P. H., Barnett, C. R., and Williams J. A. (1972). Effects of mother–infant separation on maternal behavior. *Child Development, 43,* 1203–1218.

Leiter, R. G. (1959). Part I of the manual for the 1948 revision of the Leiter International Performance Scale: Evidence of the reliability and validity of the Leiter Tests. *Psychological Service Center Journal, 11,* 1–72.

Leland, H., and Smith, D. (1974). *Mental retardation: Present and future perspectives.* Worthington, OH: Charles A. Jones.

Lenneberg, E. H. (1967). *Biological foundations of language.* New York: Wiley.

Lemer, J. W. (1971). *Children with learning disabilities: Theories, diagnosis and teaching strategies.* Boston: Houghton Mifflin.

LeRoy, J., and Derdeyn, A. (1976). Drawings as a therapeutic medium: The treatment of separation anxiety in a 4-year-old boy. *Child Psychiatry and Human Development, 16,* 155–169.

Lesser, S. R., and Easser, B. R. (1972). Personality differences in the perceptually handicapped. *American Academy of Child Psychiatry, 11,* 458–466.

Lester, B. M., Kotelchuck, M., Spelke, E., Sellers, M. J., and Klein, R. E. (1974). Separation protest in Guatemalan infants: Cross-cultural and cognitive findings. *Developmental Psychology, 10,* 79–85.

Lester, E. P. (1975). Language behavior and child psychotherapy. *Canadian Psychiatric Association Journal, 20,* 175–181.

Lever, J. (1976). Sex differences in the games children play. *Social problems, 23.*

LeVine, E. (1980). Indirect suggestions through personalized fairy tales for the treatment of childhood insomnia. *American Journal of Clinical Hypnosis 23,* 57–63.

LeVine, E. (1984). The challenge of the creative child: Implementing their divergency in the service of therapy. *Psychotherapy: Research & Practice, 21,* 31–39.

LeVine, E., and Padilla, A. (1980). *Crossing cultures in therapy: Pluralistic counseling for the Hispanic.* Monterey, CA: Brooks/Cole.

LeVine, E., and Ruiz, R. A. (1984). Refining the goals of pluralistic therapy from the Hispanic–Anglo experience. In J. L. Martinez, Jr. & Richard Mendoza (Eds.), *Child psychology* (2nd Ed.). Orlando: Academic Press.

LeVine, R. A. (1973). *Culture, behavior and personality.* Chicago: Aldine.

LeVine, W. (1985). *Personal communication.* Wichita: University of Kansas Medical School.

Levitin, T. E. (1979). Children of Divorce. *Journal of Social Issues, 35* (4), 1–25.

Lewis, H. (1954). *Deprived children.* London: Oxford University Press.

Lewis, J. M., Beavers, W. R., Gossett, J. T., & Phillips, V. A. (1976). *No single thread: Psychological health in family systems.* New York: Brunner/Mazel.

Lincoln, A. L. (1955). *Lincoln Diagnostic Spelling Tests.* Indianapolis: Bobbs-Merrill.

Lipman, R. S. (1970). The use of psychopharmacological agents in residential facilities for the retarded. In F. J. Menolascino (Ed.), *Psychiatric approaches to mental retardation.* New York: Basic Books.

Littner, N. (1971). The importance of the national parents to the child in placement. *Preliminary Conference Report of the First Conference of Foster Parents.* Washington DC: U.S. Department of Health, Education and Welfare. (Dept. of H.E.W., Publication No. 72-5).

Lloyd, J. C. (1984). *Basic family-centered curriculum for family service workers and parent aides.* Iowa: National Resource Center on Family Based Services, University of Iowa.

Lloyd, J. (1997). Conceptual bases of the planning process in family preservation/family support State plans. *Family Preservation Journal, 2* (1), 47–56.

Lloyd, J. C., and Sallee, A. L. (1994). The challenge and potential of family preservation services in the public child welfare system. *Protecting children, 10* (3), 3–6.

Longres, J. E. (1995). *Human behavior in the social environment.* (2nd. ed.). Itasca, Il.: F.E. Peacock Publishers, Inc.

Lorian, R. P., and Lounsbury, J. W. (1992) Conceptual and methodological considerations in evaluating prevention interventions. In W. R. Trash & G. Stahler (Eds.), *Innovative approaches to mental health evaluation.* New York: Academic Press.

Lovaas, O. I., and Bucher, B. D. (Eds.). (1974). *Perspectives in behavior modification with deviant children.* Englewood Cliffs, NJ: Prentice Hall.

Lovaas, O. I., Koegel, R., and Schreibman, L. (1979). Stimulus overselectivity in autism: A review of research. *Psychological Bulletin, 86,* 1236–1254.

Lovaas, O. I., Koegel, R., Simmons, J. Q., and. Stevens–Long, J. (1973). Some generalization and follow-up measures on autistic children in behavior therapy. *Journal of Applied Behavior Analysis 6,* 131–166.

Luepnitz, D. A. (1982). *Child custody: A study of families after divorce.* Lexington, MA: D. C. Health.

Luria, A. R. (1961). *The role of speech in the regulation of normal and abnormal behavior.* New York: J. B. Lippincott.

Luria, A. R. (1963). *The mentally retarded child.* New York: Pergamon Press.

Lutey, C. (1977). *Individual intelligence testing: A manual and sourcebook.* Greeley, Colorado: Author.

Maccoby, E. (1980). *Social Development.* New York: Harcourt, Brace and Jovanovich.

MacFarlane, J. W., Allen, L, and Honzik, M. P. (1954). *A developmental study of the behavior problems of normal children.* Berkeley: University of California.

MacFarlane, K., Waterman, J., Conerly, S., Damon, L., Durfee, M., and Long, S. (1986). *Sexual abuse of young children.* New York: The Guilford Press.

MacGregor, R. (1962). Multiple impact psychotherapy with families. *Family Process, 1,* 15–29.

MacGregor, R., Ritchie, A. M., Serrario, A. C., and Schuster, F. P. (1964). *Multiple impact therapy with families.* New York: McGraw-Hill.

Machover, K. (1949). *Personality projection in the drawing of the human figure.* Springfield, IL: Charles C. Thomas.

Machover, K. (1953). Human figure drawings of children. *Journal of Projective Techniques, 17,* 85–91.

MacKinnon, D. W. (1962). The nature and nurture of creative talent. *American Psychologist, 17,* 484–495.

McIntyre, L. J., and Sussman, M. B. (Eds.) (1995). *Families and law.* New York: The Haworth Press.

Maguire, L. (1984). Networking for self-help: An empirically based guideline. In F. M. Cox, J. L. Erlich, J. Rothman, and J. E. Tropman (Eds.), *Tactics and techniques of community practice.* (pp. 198–208). Itasca, IL F. E. Peacock.

Mahler, M. (1968). *On human symbiosis and the vicissitudes of individuation: Infantile psychosis.* New York: International Universities Press.

Mahler, M., Pine, F., and Bergman, A. (1975). *The psychological birth of the human infant: Symbiosis and individuation.* New York: Basic Books.

Mahoney, M. (1974). *Cognition and behavior modification.* Cambridge, MA: Ballinger.

Maluccio, A. N. (1995). Children: Direct Practice. In R. L. Edwards (Ed.-in-Chief), *Encycopedia of Social Work* (19th ed., Vol. 1, pp. 442–447). Washington, DC: National Association of Social Workers.

Mandelbaum, A. (1977). Mental health and retardation. In J. B. Turner (Ed.), *Encyclopedia of social work* (17th issue, Vol. 2). Washington, DC: National Association of Social Workers.

Mannino, F. V., MacLennan, B. W., and Shore, M. F. (1975). (Eds.). *The practice of mental health consultation.* Adelphi, MD: National Institute of Mental Health.

Mantell, D. M. (1988). Clarifying erroneous child sexual abuse allegations. *American Journal of Orthopsychiatry, 58* (4), 618–621.

Margolin, F. (1973). An approach to resolution of visitation disputes post-divorce: Short-term counseling. *Dissertation Abstracts International, 34,* 1754B (University Microfilms No. 73-22, 680).

Marcos, L. R. (1976). Linguistic dimensions in the bilingual patient. *American Journal of Psychoanalysis, 36,* 347–354.

Marland, S. P. (1972). *Education of the gifted and talented: A report submitted to the citizens of the United States by the Commissioner of Education.* Washington, DC: U.S. Department of Education.

Marshall, R. J. (1976). "Joining techniques" in the treatment of resistant children and adolescents: A learning theory rationale. *American Journal of Psychotherapy, 30,* 73–84.

Martin, H. P. (Ed.). (1976). *The abused child: A multidisciplinary approach to development issues and treatment.* Cambridge, MA: Ballinger.

Martin, H.P. (1980). The consequences of being abused and neglected: How the child fares. In C. H. Kempe & R. E. Helfer (Eds.), *The battered child.* Chicago: University of Chicago Press.

Maudsley, H. (1880). *The pathology of the mind.* New York: Appleton.

Maurer, R., Cadoret, R. J., & Cain, C. (1980). Cluster analysis of childhood temperament data on adoptees. *American Journal of Orthopsychiatry, 50* (3), 522–534.

Maximus, Inc. (1984). *Child welfare statistical fact book. 1984: Substitute care and adoption.* Washington, DC: Office of Human Development Series.

Mayfield, J., and Neil J. B. (1983). Group treatment for children in substitute care. *Social Casework, 64* (10), 579–584.

Mayhall, P. D., and Eastlack–Norgard, K. (1983). *Child abuse and neglect: Sharing responsibility.* New York: Wiley.

McBroom, E. (1976). Socialization through small groups. In R. W. Roberts & H. Northern (Eds.), *Theories of social work with groups* (pp. 272–299). New York: Columbia University.

McConville, B. J. (1976). Opening moves and sequential strategies in child psychotherapy. *Canadian Psychiatric Association Journal, 21,* 295–301.

McCoy, S. A. (1976). Clinical judgements of normal childhood behavior. *Journal of Consulting and Clinical Psychology, 44,* 710–714.

McDermott, J. F. (1970). Divorce and its psychiatric sequelae in children. *Archives of General Psychiatry, 23,* 421–427.

McDowell, R. (1976). Parent counseling: The state of the art. *Journal of Learning Disabilities, 9,* 614–619.

McGoldrick, M., and Gerson, R. (1985). *Genograms in family assessment.* New York: W. W. Norton.

McGoldrick, M., Giordano, J., and Pearce, J. K. (1996). *Ethnicity and family therapy.*(2nd ed.) New York, NY: The Guilford Press.

McKay, H., Sinisterra, L., McKay, A., Gomez H., and Lioreda, P. (1978). Improving cognitive ability in chronically deprived children. *Science* (200) 270–278.

McLaren, J., and Bryson, S. E. (1987). Review of recent epidemiological studies of mental retardation: Prevalence, associated disorders, and etiology. *American Journal of Mental Retardation, 92* (3), 243–254.

McRoy, R. G., Grotevant, H. D. and Zurcher, Louis A. Jr. (1968). *Emotional disturbance in adopted adolescent: Origins and development.* New York: Praeger.

Mead, G. H. (1934). *Mind, self and society.* Chicago: University of Chicago Press.

Meadow, K. (1976). Personality and social development of deaf persons. *Journal of Rehabilitation of the Deaf, 9,* 1–12.

Mech, E. H. (1973). Adoption: A policy perspective. In B. Caldwell & H. Riccuitti (Eds.), *Review of child development research* (Vol. 3, pp. 467–508). Chicago: University of Chicago Press.

Meezan, W., and McCroskey, J. (1996). Improving family functioning through family preservation services: Results of the Los Angeles experiment. *Family Preservation Journal,* (Winter), 9–29.

Meichenbaum, D. (1977). *Cognitive-behavior modification: An integrative approach.* New York: Plenum Press.

Meier, M. (1974). Some challenges for clinical neuropsychology. in R. Reitan & L. Davison (Eds.), *Clinical neuropsychology: Current status and application.* New York: John Wiley.

Meiselman, K. C. (1978). *Incest. A psychological study of causes and effect with treatment and recommendation.* San Francisco: Jossey Bass.

Mellsop, G. W. (1972). Psychiatric patients seen as children and adults: Childhood predictors of adult illness. *Journal of Child Psychology & Psychiatry, 13,* 91–101.

Mengeot, S. W. (1982). The impact of cumulative trauma in infancy: Some treatment techniques. *Clinical Social Work Journal, 10* (4), 265–274.

Mikkelsen, M., and Stene, J. (1970). Genetic counseling in Down's syndrome. *Human Heredity, 20,* 457–464.

Milazzo–Sayre, L. *Changes in the age and sex composition of first admissions to state and county mental hospitals, United States 1962–1975.* (Mental Health Statistical Note No. 145.) U.S. Department of Health, Education and Welfare: National Institute of Mental Health.

Milazzo–Sayre, L. *Changes in the age, sex, and diagnostic composition of additions to state and county mental hospitals, United States 1969–1975.* (Mental Health Statistical Note No. 148.) U.S. Department of Health, Education and Welfare: National Institute of Mental Health.

Milazzo–Sayre, L. *Changes in the age, sex, and diagnostic composition of the resident population of state and county mental hospitals, United States 1965–1975.* (Mental Health Statistical Note No. 146.) U.S. Department of Health, Education and Welfare: National Institute of Mental Health.

Miller, W., and Ervin, S. (1970). *The development of grammar in child language, in cognitive development in children* (pp. 309–334). Chicago: University of Chicago Press.

Minskoff, E. (1975). Research on psycholinguistic training: Critique and guidelines. *Exceptional Children, 42,* 136–147.

Minton, C., Kagan, J., and Levine, J. A. (1971). Maternal control and obedience in the two-year-old. *Child Development, 42,* 1873–1894.

Minuchin, S. (1974). *Families and family therapy.* Cambridge, MA: Harvard University Press.

Minuchin, S., and Fishman, H. C. (1981). *Family therapy techniques.* Cambridge, MA: Harvard University Press.

Minuchin, S. Montalvo, B., Guerney, B. G. Jr., Rosman, B. L., & Schurmer, F. (1967). *Families of the slums.* New York: Basic Books.

Mischel, W. (1968). *Personality and assessment.* New York: Wiley.

Mitchell, Susan. (1995). "The next baby boom." *American Demographics.* Ithaca, NY: American Demographics, Inc.

Morales, A., and Sheafor, B. W. (1983). *Social work: A profession of many faces* (3rd Ed.). Newton, MA: Allyn and Bacon.

Morrison, T. L., and Newcomer, B. L. (1975). Effects of directive vs. nondirective play therapy with institutionalized mentally retarded children. *American Journal of Mental Deficiency, 79,* 666–669.

Moustakes, C. (1959). *Psychotherapy with children: The living relationship.* New York: Ballantine.

Moustakes, C. (1973a). *Children in play therapy.* New York: Jason Aronson.

Moustakes, C. (1973b). The dying self within the living self. In C. Moustakes (Ed.), *The child's discovery of himself* (pp. 9–29). New York: Jason Aronson.

Moustakes, C. (1975). *Who will Listen?* New York: Ballantine.

Mowrer, 0. H., and Mowrer, W. M. (1938). Enuresis: A method for its study and treatment. *American Journal of Orthopsychiatry, 8,* 436–459.

Murray, H. A. (1943). *Thematic Apperception Test Manual.* Boston, MA: Harvard College.

Myklebust, H. (1965). *Picture Story Language Test: The development and disorders of written language* (Vol. 1), New York: Grune and Stratton.

Nagi, S. (1977). *Child malnutrition in the United States: A challenge to social institutions.* New York: Columbia University Press.

Narabayashi, H. (1972). Stereotaxic amagdelectomy. In B. E. Eleftheriou (Ed.), *The neurobiology of the amydala.* New York: Plenum Press.

National Institute of Mental Health. "Introduction to Tabular Material Prepared on Children, Adolescents, and Young Adults (Age Groups Under 25 Years) Under Care in Mental Health Treatment Facilities/Services," by Redick, R. R. Unpublished report to the Institute, 1979.

National Institute of Mental Health. 1986 Client Survey. Inpatient Admissions in State/County Mental Hospitals Prior Mental Health Service by Age Groups (l) and Sex.

National Institute of Mental Health. Additions and Resident Patients at End of Year, State and

County Mental Hospitals, by age and diagnosis, by state, United States, 1989. Rockville, MD: The Institute, 1991.

National Institute of Mental Health. (1990). *Research on children and adolescents with mental, behavioral, and developmental disorder.* Rockville, MD: National Institute of Mental Health.

National Research Council. (1993). *Understanding child abuse and neglect.* Washington, DC: National Academy Press.

Nay, W. R. (1979). Parents as real life reinforcers: The enhancement of parent training effects across conditions other than training. In A. P. Goldstein & F. H. Kanfer (Eds.), *Maximizing treatment gains' transfer enhancement in psychotherapy.* New York: Academic Press.

Neely, M. (1982). *Counseling and guidance practices with special education students.* Homewood, IL: Dorsey Press.

Newcomer, B. L., and Morrison, T. L. (1974). Play therapy with institutionalized mentally retarded children. *American Journal of Mental Deficiency, 78,* 727–733.

Newman, M. N., and Newman, P. R. (1995). *Development through life: A psychosocial approach.* Pacific Grove, CA: Brooks/Cole.

Nichols, J., and Early, B. P. (1996). The family partners credit card: A token economy system. Adapted for intensive family preservation services to enable families to manage difficult behavior of adolescents, (Winter), 59–74.

Nichols, M. P. (1984). *Family therapy concepts and methods.* New York: Gardner.

Nichols, M. P., and Schwartz, R. C., (1995). *Family therapy concepts and methods.* Needham Heights, MA: Simon & Schuster.

Nihira, K., Foster, R., Shellhaas, M., and Leland, H. (1974). *Adaptive Behavior Scale.* Washington, DC: American Association on Mental Deficiency.

Northen, H. (1995). *Clincal social work: Knowledge and skills.* New York: Columbia University Press.

Norvell, M., and Guy, R. (1977). A comparison of self-concept in adopted and nonadopted adolescents. *Adolescence, 12* (47).

Nye, F. J. (1975). Child adjustment in broken and in unhappy un-broken homes. *Marriage and Family Living, 19,* 356–361.

Oaklander, V. (1978). *Windows to our children: A gestalt therapy approach to children and adolescents.* Moab, UT: Real People Press.

Oates, R. K., Davis, A. A., Ryan M. G., and Stewart, L. F. (1978). Factors associated with child abuse. *Abstracts. Second International Congress on Child Abuse & Neglect.* London: Pergamon Press.

O'Brien, S. (1983). *Child Pornography.* Dubuque, IA: Kendal/Hunt.

Okun, B. F. (1996). *Understanding diverse families: What practitioners need to know.* New York, NY: The Guilford Press.

O'Malley, J. E., Koocher, G., Foster, D., and Slavin L. (1979). Psychiatric sequelae of surviving childhood cancer. *American Journal of Orthropsychiatry, 49* (4), 608–616.

O'Neal P., and Robins, L. N. (1959). Childhood patterns predictive of adult schizophrenia: A thirty year follow-up study. *American Journal of Psychiatry, 115,* 385–391.

Omnibus Budget Reconciliation Act of 1993. P.L. 103-66, 107 Stat.312.

Opler, M. (1967). *Culture and social psychiatry.* New York: Atherton Press.

Ornstein, A. (1976). Making contact with the inner world of the child. *Comprehensive Psychiatry, 17,* 3–36.

O'Rourke, J. (1963). Field laboratory: The decision making behavior of family groups in two experimental conditions. *Sociometry, 26,* 422–534.

Palmer, J. O. (1970). *The psychological assessment of children.* New York: Wiley.

Pasamanick, B., and Knobloch, H. (1966). Retrospective studies on the epidemiology of reproductive causality: Old and New. *Merrill Palmer Quarterly, 12,* 7–29.

Passons, W. (1975). *Gestalt approaches in counseling.* New York: Holt, Rinehart and Winston.

Patterson, G. R. (1971). *Families.* Champaign, IL: Research Press.

Perlman, H. H. (1957). *Social casework: A problem solving process.* Chicago: University of Chicago Press.

Perls, F. (1969). *Gestalt therapy verbatim.* Lafayette, CA: Real People Press.

Piaget, J. (1951). *The child's perception of the world.* New York: Humanities Press. (Originally published in French in 1926).

Piaget, J. (1976). *The grasp of consciousness: Action and concept in the young child.* Cambridge, MA: Harvard University Press. (Originally published in French in 1974).

Piers, E. V., and Harris, D. B. (1969). *The Piers–Harris Children's Self Concept Scale (The way I feel about myself)*. Nashville: Counselor Recordings & Tests.

Pillari, V. (1988). *Human behavior in the social evironment*. Pacific Grove, CA: Brooks/Cole.

Pinkston, E. M., Levitt, J. L., Green, G. R., Linsk, N. L., and Rzepnicki, T. L. (1982). *Effective social work practice*. San Francisco: Jossey Bass.

Popple, P. R., and Leighninger, L. (1996). *Social work, social welfare, and american society*. (3rd. ed.). Needham Heights, MA: Simon & Schuster.

Portner, D. (1981). Clinical aspects of social group work with the deaf. *Social Work with Groups* (Vol. 4), 123–133.

Prasad, Rajen. (1988). *Foster care research: Emerging practice principles*. King George, VA: American Foster Care Resources, Inc.

Presidents Commission on Mental Health. (1978). *Task Panel Reports* (Volume II–IV). Washington, DC: U.S. Government Printing Office.

Pritchard, M., and Graham, P. (1966). An investigation of a group of patients who have attended both the child and adult departments of the same psychiatric hospital. *British Journal of Psychiatry, 112,* 603–612.

Proctor, E. K., (1983). New Directions for work with parents of retarded children. In F.J. Turner (Ed.), *Differential diagnosis and treatment in social work* (3rd. ed., pp. 511–519). New York: The Free Press.

Procter, E. K., Davis, L. E., and Vosler, N. R. (1995). Families: Direct practice.. In R. L. Edwards (Ed.-in-Chief), *Encycopedia of Social Work* (19th ed., Vol. 2, pp. 941–950). Washington, DC: National Association of Social Workers.

Quinn, B., and Goldberg, S. (1977, March). *Feeding and fussing. Parent–infant interaction as a function of neonatal medical status*. Paper presented at a meeting of the Society for Research on Child Development, New Orleans.

Quinn, P. O., and Rapoport, J. L. (1975). One year followup of hyperactive boys treated with imipramine or methylphenidate. *American Journal of Psychiatry 32*, 241–245.

Radbill S. X. (1980). Children in a world of violence: A history of child abuse. In C. H. Kempe & R. E. Helfer (Eds.), *The battered child*. Chicago: University of Chicago.

Rapoport J. (1989). Summary. In J. L. Rapoport (Ed.) *Obsessive-compulsive disorder in children and adolescents* (pp. 347–350). Washington, DC: Psychiatric Press.

Rapoport, J. L., Mikkelson, E. J., and Zavadil, A. (1980). Childhood enueresis II: Psychopathology tricyclic concentration in plasma, and antineuretic effect. *Archives of General Psychiatry, 37,* 1146–1152.

Rapoport, L. (1977). Consultation in social work. In J. B. Turner (Ed.), *Encyclopedia of social work* (pp. 193–196). Washington, DC: National Association of Social Workers.

Raschick, M. (1977). A multi-faceted, intensive family preservation program evaluation. *Family Preservation Journal, 2* (2), 33–52.

Reaffirming our roots: Resource book. Ninth National Conference on Child Abuse and Neglect U.S. Department of Health and Human Services. Denver Colorado, September 14–17, 1991.

Redl, F., (1972). The concept of "therapeutic milieu." In J. K. Whittaker & A. E. Trieschman (Eds.), *Children away from home. A source book of residential treatment*. Chicago IL: Atherton.

Regier, D. A., Goldberg, I. D., and Taube, C. A. (1978). The de facto U.S. Mental Health Services System. *Archives of General Psychiatry, 35,* 685–693.

Reiss, D. (1980). Pathways to assessing the family: Some choice points and a sample route. *The Family: Proceedings of the 1979 Annual Meeting of the American College of Psychiatrists*. New York: Brunner/Mazel.

Reitan, R. (1964). *Manual for administering and scoring the Reitan-Indiana Neuroupsychology: Battery for Children (Aged 5 through 8)*. Indianapolis: University of Indiana Medical Center.

Reitan, R., and Davison, L. (Eds.). (1974). *Clinical neuropsychology: Current status and application*. New York: Wiley.

Renaud, H., and Estess, F. (1961). Life history interviews with one hundred normal American males: "Pathogenicity" of childhood. *American Journal of Orthopsychiatry, 31*, 786–802.

Resnick, P. (1969). Child murder by parents: A psychiatric review of filicide. *American Journal of Psychiatry, 126*, 325–334.

Ribble, M. (1945). Anxiety in infants and its disorganizing effects. In N. Lewis (Ed.), *Trends in child psychiatry*. New York: International Universities Press.

Richardson, E. H. (1981). Cultural and historical perspectives in counseling American Indians. In D. W. Sue (Ed.), *Counseling the culturally different*. New York: John Wiley & Sons.

Richmond, M. E. (1917). *Social Diagnosis.* New York: Russell Sage Foundation.

Robinson, H. B., and Robinson, N. M. (1970). Mental retardation. In P. H. Mussen (Ed.), *Carmichael's manual of child psychology* (Vol. II). New York: Wiley.

Roe, A. (1976). Psychological approaches to creativity in science. In A. Rothenberg & C. R. Hausman (Eds.), *The creativity questions.* Durham, NC: Duke University Press.

Rogers, C. (1951). *Client-centered therapy.* Boston: Houghton Mifflin.

Roll, S., Lockwood, J., and Roll, E. J. (1980). *P.A.S.I.: Parent attachment structured interview.* Albuquerque, NM: Authors.

Ronnau, J. P. (1991). Assessing and using family strengths. Video training tape. Las Cruces, NM: Family Preservation Institute, New Mexico State University.

Ronnau, J. P. (1990). A strengths approach to helping family caregivers. *Today, 19,* (6), 24–27.

Ronnau, J. P., Lloyd, J. C., Sallee, A. L., and Shannon, P. J. (1990). Family preservation skills with Native Americans. In M. Mannes (Ed.), *Family preservation and Indian child welfare* (pp. 79–99).

Rose, S. M. (1992). *Case management & social work practice.* New York: Longman.

Rose, S. M., and Moore, V. L. (1995).Case Management. In R. L. Edwards (Ed.-in-Chief), *Encycopedia of Social Work* (19th ed., Vol. 1, pp. 335–340). Washington, DC: National Association of Social Workers.

Rosenzweig, S. (1950). Levels of behavior in psychodiagnosis with special reference to the Picture Frustration Study. *American Journal of Orthopsychiatry, 20,* 63–72.

Ross, H. L, & Sawhill, I. V. (1975). *Time of transition.* Washington, DC: The Urban Institute.

Rotter, J. B., Rafferty, J. E., and Schachtitz, E. (1965). Validation of the Rotter Incomplete Sentence Test for College Screening. In B. I. Murstein (Ed.), *Handbook of projective techniques.* New York: Basic Books.

Routh, D. K. (1979, Fall). Activity, attention, and aggression in learning disabled children. *Journal of Clinical Child Psychology,* 183–186.

Rubel, A. J. (1964). The epidemiology of a folk illness: Susto in Hispanic America. *Ethnology, 3,* 268–283.

Ruiz, R. A. (1977). The delivery of mental health and social change services for Chicanos: Analysis and recommendations. In J. Martinez (Ed.), *Chicano psychology.* New York: Academic Press.

Russell, D. (1983). Incidence and prevalence of intrafamilial and extrafamilial sexual abuse of female children. *Child Abuse and Neglect, 7,* 133–146.

Rutter, M., Izard, C. and Read, P. (1986). *Depression in young people.* New York: Guilford.

Rutter, M., Tome, A., and Lann, I. (1988). *Assessment and diagnosis in child psychopathology.* New York: Guilford.

Sabatini, S. (1976). An investigation of play group counseling. *Dissertation Abstracts International, 36,* 7875A. (University Microfilms No. 76-13, 496).

Safer, D. J., Allen, R., and Barr, E. (1972). Depression of growth in hyperactive children on stimulant drugs. *New England Journal of Medicine, 287,* 217–232.

Sallee, A. (1991). National trends in family preservation: Implications for Region VI. Working paper for the Family Preservation Institute, New Mexico State University.

Sallee, A. L., and Lloyd, J. C. (1990). Family preservation: Papers from the Institute for Social Work Educators. Riverdale, IL: National Association for Family-Based Services.

Sallee, A. L., and Downes, B. (1982). *A report to the Governor on family crisis prevention: Policy recommendations and implementation strategies.* Sante Fe, NM: Governor's Office.

Sallee, A. L., and LeVine, E. (1985, August 9). *Identity crisis of adopted children at adolescence.* Paper presented at the meeting of the North American Council on Adoptable Children, Albuquerque, NM.

Sallee, D. K. (1982, June 22). *Family crisis prevention: An explanation.* Keynote address to Governor's Forum on Family Crisis Prevention, Albuquerque, NM.

Sallee, D. K. (1991). A genogram of family therapy. Unpublished.

Sanford, L. T. (1980). *The silent children.* Garden City, NY: Anchor Doubleday Press.

Santrock, J. (1976). Father absence, perceived maternal behavior, and moral development in boys. *Child Development 46* (3), 753–757.

Santrock, J. (1977). Effects of father absence on sex-typed behaviors in male children: Reason for absence and age of onset of absence. *Journal of Genetic Psychology, 130,* 3–10.

Sapir, E. (1921). *Language.* New York: Harcourt Brace (reprinted in 1958).

Satir, V. (1967). *Conjoint family therapy* (Rev. ed.). Palo Alto, CA: Science and Behavior Books.

Satir, V. (1972). *People Making.* Palo Alto, CA: Science and Behavior Books.

Sattler, J. M. (1974). *Assessment of children's intelligence.* Philadelphia: Saunders.

Schaffer, H. R., and Emerson, P. E. (1964). The development of social attachment in infancy. *Monographs of the Society for Research in Child Development, 29* (94).

Schechter, M. (1964, Feb.). Emotional problems of the adoptee. *General Archives of Psychiatry, 10.*

Schneider, C., Hoffmeister, J., and Helfer, R. (1976). A predictive screening questionnaire for potential problems in mother–child interaction. In R. Helfer & C. Kempe (Eds.), *Child abuse and neglect: The family and the community.* Cambridge, MA: Ballinger.

Schopler, J. H., and Galinsky, M. J. (1995). Group practice overview. In R. L. Edwards (Ed.-in-Chief), *Encyclopedia of Social Work* (19th ed., Vol. 2, pp. 1129–1142). Washington, DC: National Association of Social Workers.

Schorr, A. L. (1985). Professional practice as policy. *Social Service Review, 59* (2), 178–196.

Schorr, A. L. (1997). *Passion and policy.* Cleveland, OH: David Press.

Schriver, J. M. (1995). *Human behavior and the social environment: Shifting paradigms in essential knowledge for social work practice.* Boston, MA: Allyn and Bacon.

Schwartz, A., and Goldiamond, I. (1975). *Social casework: A behavioral approach.* New York: Columbia University Press.

Sedlak, A. J., and Broadhurst, D. D. (1996). *Executive summary of the third national incidence study of child abuse and neglect.* Washington, DC: Administration for Children and Families.

Selye, H. (1950). *The psychology and pathology of exposure to stress.* Montreal: Acta.

Shepherd, M., Oppenheim, A. N., and Mitchell, S. (1966). Childhood behavior disorders and the child guidance clinic: An epidemiological study. *Journal of Psychology and Psychiatry, 7,* 39–52.

Sheridan, M. S., and Kline, K. (1978). Psychosomatic illness in children. *Social Casework, 59* (4), 227–232.

Sherman, S. N. (1981). A social work frame for family therapy. In E. R. Tolson, & W. J. Reid (Eds.), *Models of family treatment* (pp. 7–32). New York: Columbia University Press.

Shinn, M. (1978). Father absence and children's cognitive development. *Psychological Bulletin, 85* (2), 295–324.

Shofield, W. (1964). *Psychotherapy: The purchase of friendship.* Englewood Cliffs, NJ: Prentice Hall.

Shore, M. F. (1979). Legislation, advocacy, and the rights of children and youth. *American Psychologist, 34,* 1017–1019.

Shostrom E. H. (1967). *Man, the manipulator, The inner journey from manipulation to actualization.* Nashville: Abingdon Press.

Simeonsson, R. J. (1994). *Risk resilience & prevention: Promoting the well-being of all children.* Baltimore, MD: Paul H. Brookes Pub. Co.

Shulman, L. (1979). *The skills of helping: Individuals and groups.* Itasca, IL: F. E. Peacock.

Shulman, L. (1992). *The skills of helping individuals, families and groups* (3rd ed.). Itasca, IL.: F.E. Peacock.

Shyne, A. W., and Schroeder, A. (1978). *National study of social services to children and their families.* Rockville, MD: Westat.

Simon, R. (1987). Good-bye paradox, hello invarient prescription: An interview with Mara Selvini Palazzoli. Family Therapy Networker, 11(5), 16–33.

Skinner, B. F. (1938). *The behavior of organisms.* New York: Appleton Century Crofts.

Sloane, R. B., Staples, F. R., Cristol, A. H., Yorkston, N. J., and Whipple, K. (1975). *Psychotherapy versus behavior change.* Cambridge: Harvard University Press.

Slossum, R. L. (1963). *Slossum Intelligence Test.* East Aurora, NY: Slossum Education.

Smalley, R. E. (1971). Social casework: The functional approach. In R. Morris (Ed.), *Encyclopedia of social work.* New York: National Association of Social Workers.

Smirnoff, V. (1971). *The scope of child analysis.* New York: International Universities Press.

Smith, C., and Nylund, D. (Eds.). (1997.) *Narrative therapies with children and adolescents.* New York: The Guilford Press.

Smith, D., Jr. (1976). Effects of modeling/role playing counseling technique on second-grade socially withdrawn children. *Dissertation Abstracts International 36,* 414OB–4141B. (University Microfilms No. 76-4416).

Snapper, K. J. (1976). The American legacy. In H. E. Grotberg (Ed.), *200 years of children* (pp. 13–38). Washington, DC: U.S. Department of Health, Education and Welfare, Office of Human Development (DWEW Publication No. OHD 77-30103)

Snow, C. (1972). Mothers' speech to children learning language. *Child Development, 43,* 549–565.

Solomon, M. A. (1973). A developmental, conceptual premise for family therapy. *Family Process, 12,* 179–188.

Sorosky, A. D., Baran, A., and Pannor R. (1978). *The adoption triangle: The effects of the sealed record on adoption, birth parents and adoptive parents.* Garden City, NY: Anchor Books.

Specht, H. (1981). Professionalism: Weighed and found wanting: An opinion by Harry Specht. *Public Welfare, 39* (3), 8–9.

Speck, R. V. (1967). Psychotherapy of the social network of a schizophrenic family. *Family Process, 6,* 208–214.

Speer, D., Fossom, M., Lippman, H., Schwartz, R., and Slocum, B. (1968). A comparison of middle- and lower-class families in treatment at a child guidance clinic. *American Journal of Orthopsychiatry, 38,* 814–822.

Spence, J. T., and Helmreich, R. L. (1978). *Masculinity and femininity: Their psychological dimensions, correlates and antecedents.* Austin: University of Texas Press.

Spiegel, J. P. (1981). An ecological model with an emphasis on ethnic families. In S. R. Tolson & J. R. Williams, (Eds.), *Models of family treatment.* New York: Columbia University Press.

Spock B. (1960). *Baby and child care.* New York: Affiliated Publishers.

Sprague, R. L. (1977). Psychopharmacotherapy with children. In M. McMillan & S. Henao (Eds.), *Child Psychiatry Treatment and research.* New York: Bruner/Mazel.

Starr, R. H. (1979). Child Abuse. *American Psychologist, 34,* 872–878.

Stehno, S. M. (1982). Differential treatment of minority children in service systems. *Social Work 27* (1), 39–45.

Stein, M. (1976). Therapeutic initiatives with inaccessible preschoolers. *American Academy of Child Psychiatry, 15,* 385–394.

Stein, T. J. (1998). *The social welfare of women and children with HIV and AIDS legal Protections, policy, and programs.* New York: Oxford University Press.

Steinhauer, P. D. (1991). *The least detrimental alternative.* Toronto: University of Toronto Press.

Stewart, A. J., Copeland, A. P. Chester, N. L., Malley, J. E., and Barenbaum, N. B. (1997). *Separating together: how divorce transforms families.* New York: The Guilford Press.

Stolberg, A. L., and Bloom, M. (1992). Child development and functioning during the divorce adjustment process: Bases of preventive helping. In Bloom (Ed.), *Changing lives: Studies in Human development and professional helping.* Columbia, SC: University of South Carolina Press.

Stone, L. J., and Church, J. (1973). *Childhood and adolescence.* New York: Random House.

Straus, M. A., Gelles, R. J., and Steimetz, S. K. (1979). *Behind closed doors: Violence in the American family.* Garden City, NY: Doubleday.

Straus, M. A., and Tallman, I. (1971). SIMFAM: A technique for observational measurement and experimental study of families. In J. Aldous (Ed.), *Family problem solv*ing. Hinsdale, IL: Dryden Press.

Sudia, C. E., and Herzog, E. (1973). Children in fatherless families. In C. Anderson (Ed.), *Review of child development research* (Vol. 3, pp. 233–282). Chicago: University of Chicago Press.

Tatara, T. (1993). *Characteristics of children in substitute and adoptive care.* Washington, DC: Voluntary Cooperative Information System, American Public Welfare Association.

Taylor, C. W., and Holland, J. (1964). Predictors of creative performance. In C. W. Taylor (Ed.), *Creativity, Progress and potential.* New York: McGraw-Hill.

Terman, C. M., and Oden, M. (1959). *Genetic studies of genius* (Vols. 1–5). Stanford, CA: Stanford University Press.

Terman, L. M., and Merrill, M. A. (1973). *Stanford–Binet Intelligence Scale Manual for the third revision, form L-M.* Boston: Houghton Mifflin.

Thomas, A. (1968). Children with absent fathers. *Journal of Marriage and the Family, 30* (1), 89–96.

Thomas, A., Birch, H. G., Chess, S., and Hertzig, M. E. (1960). A longitudinal study of primary reaction patterns in children. *Comprehensive Psychiatry, 1,* 103.

Thomas, E. J. (1967). *The socio-behavioral approach and application to social work.* New York: Council on Social Work Education.

Thomas, E. J. (1977). Social casework and social groupwork: The behavior modification approach. In J. B. Turner (Ed.), *Encyclopedia of social work.* Washington DC: National of Social Workers.

Thompson, S. K. (1975). Gender labels and early sex roles development. *Child Development, 46,* 339–347.

Thorndike, E. L. (1896). Animal intelligence: An experimental study of the associative process in animals. *Psychological Review* (Monograph Supplement), (Whole 80).

Thornman, G. (1967). Helping Troubled Families. In C. B. Truiax & R. R. Carkhuff (Eds.), *Toward effective counseling and psychotherapy: Training and practice.* Chicago: Aldine.

Thornman, G. (1982). *Helping troubled families: A social work perspective.* New York: Aldine.

Tiegs, E. W., and Clark, W. W. (1970). *California Achievement Test.* Hightown, NJ: CTB/McGraw-Hill.

Tolor, A., and Schulberg, H. (1963). *An evaluation of the Bender–Gestalt Test.* Springfield, IL: Thomas.

Tooley, K. M. (1977). The young child as victim of sibling attack. *Social Casework, 58* (1), 25–28.

Torrance, E. P. (1962). *Guiding creative talent.* Englewood Cliffs, NJ: Prentice Hall.

Torrance, E. P. (1975). Creativity research in education is still alive. In. I. A. Taylor and J. W. Getzels (Eds.), *Perspectives in Creativity.* Chicago: Aldine.

Torrance, E. P., and Mourad, S. (1978). Some creativity and style of learning and thinking correlates of Guglielmino's Self-Directed Learning Readiness Scale. *Psychological Reports, 43,* 1167–1171.

Torrey, E. F. (1972). *The mind game: Witchdoctors and psychiatrists.* New York: Emerson Hall.

Tower, C. C. (1996). *Understanding child abuse and neglect.* (3rd ed.). Needham Heights, MA: Allyn and Bacon.

Trehub, S. E. (1973). Infants' sensitivity to vowel and tonal contrasts. *Developmental Psychology, 9,* 91–96.

Trehub, S. E., & Rabinovitch, M. S. (1972). Auditory-linguistic sensitivity in early infancy. *Developmental Psychology, 6,* 74–77.

Trevarthen, C. (1977). Descriptive analyses of infant communicative behavior. In H. R. Schaffer (Ed.), *Studies in mother infant interaction.* London: Academic Press.

Truax, C. B., and Carkhoff, R. R. (1967). *Toward effective counseling and psychotherapy: Training and practice.* Chicago: Aidine.

Unger, C, Dwarshuis, G., and Johnson, E. (1977). *Chaos, madness and unpredictability.* Chelsea, MI: Spaulding for Children.

Urie, R. G. (1975). Effects of preparing children for psychotherapy. *Dissertation Abstracts International, 36,* 924B–925B. (University Microfilms No. 75-17, 691).

U.S. Bureau of the Census. (1978). *Special studies* (Series p-23, No. 75). Washington, DC: U.S. Government Printing Office.

U.S. Bureau of the Census (1979a). *Characteristics of the population below the poverty level.* (Series p-20, No. 119). Washington, DC: U.S. Government Printing Office.

U.S. Bureau of the Census. (1979b). *Current population reports.* (Series p-20, No. 338). Washington, DC: U.S. Government Printing Office.

U.S. Bureau of the Census. (1979c). *Population Profile of the United States.* 1978. (Series p-20, No. 336). Washington, DC: U.S. Government Printing Office.

U.S. Bureau of the Census. (1983). Marital and living arrangements: March, 1982. *Current population reports* (Series p-20, No. 380). Washington, DC: U.S. Government Printing Office.

U.S. Bureau of the Census. (1984). *Statistical abstracts of the United States 1985* (105 ed.). Washington, DC: U.S. Government Printing Office.

U.S. Bureau of the Census. Current Population Reports, (Series p-25, No. 1018). Projections of the Population in U.S., By Age, Sex, Race: 1988–2080, By Gregory Spenser, U.S. Gov. Printing Office, Washington, DC, 1989.

U.S. Bureau of the Census. Current Population Report. (1989). (Series p-23, No. 163). "Changes in American Family Life." U.S. Washington, DC: Government Printing Office.

U.S. Bureau of the Census. Current Population Reports, P23-181. *Households, Families, and Children: a 30-Year Perspective.* By Terry Lugaila, U.S. Government Printing Office, Washington, DC, November 1992.

U.S. Bureau of the Census. (1992). *Living arrangements of children differ by race and Hispanic origin.* C3.186: P23-181

U.S. Bureau of the Census. Current Population Reports, P60-185. *Poverty in the United States.* U.S. Government Printing Office, Washington, DC, 1993.

U.S. Congress, Office of Technology Assessment. (1986, Dec.). *Children's mental health: Problems and services—a background paper,* (OYA-BP-H-33) Washington, DC: U.S. Government Printing Office.

U.S. Department of Health and Human Services. (1980). *The status of children.* Washington, DC: Office of Human Services (DHHS Publication No. (OHDS) 80302740).

U.S. Department of Health and Human Services. (1981). *Study finding: Natural study of the incidence and severity of child abuse and neglect.* Washington, DC: U.S. Government Printing Office. (DHHS Publication No. (OHDS) 81-30325).

U.S. Department of Health and Human Services. (1997). *Child Maltreatment 1995: Reports from the states to the National Child Abuse and Neglect Data System.* Washington, DC: U.S. Government Printing Office.

U.S. Department of Health and Human Services. (1997). *New state reports show continued high level of child abuse and neglect.* Press Release, April 8, 1997.

U.S. National Center for Health Statistics. (1978). In J. A. Weed (Ed.), *Trends in divorce: Implications for family health.* Hyattsville, MD: Author.

Visher, E. B., and Visher, J. S. (1979). *Stepfamilies: A Guide to working with stepparents and stepchildren.* New York: Brunner/Mazel.

Vygotsky, L. S. (1962). *Thought and language.* Cambridge, MA: MIT Press.

Wallace, A. F. C. (1970). *Culture and personality* (2nd. ed.). New York: Random House.

Wallach, M. A., and Kogan, N. (1965). *Modes of thinking in young children.* New York: Holt, Rinehart and Winston.

Wallerstein, J. S. (1987). Children of divorce: Report of a ten-year follow-up of early latency-age children. *American Journal of Orthopsychiatry, 57* (2), 199–211.

Wallerstein, J. S. (1984). Children of divorce: Preliminary report of a ten-year follow-up of young children. *American Journal of Orthopsychiatry, 54,* 444–458.

Wallerstein, J. S., and Kelly, J. B. (1975). The effects of parental divorce: Experiences of the preschool child. *Journal of the American Academy of Child Psychiatry, 14* (4), 600–616.

Wallerstein, J. S., and Kelly, J. B., (1976). The effects of parental divorce: Experiences of the child in later latency. *American Journal of Orthopsychiatry, 46* (2), 256–269.

Wallerstein, J. S., and Kelly, J. B. (1979). Children of divorce: A review. *Social Work 24* (6), 468–475.

Wallerstein, J. S., and Kelly, J. B. (1980). California's children of divorce. *Psychology Today, 13* (8), 66–76.

Wallerstein, J., and Lewis, J. Research presented in San Francisco to the Second World Congress on Family Law and the Rights of Children & Youth, June, 1997.

Walsh, G. S. (1975). *Creativity and intelligence: A personality approach.* Chapel Hill, NC: Institute for Research on Social Sciences, University of North Carolina at Chapel Hill.

Warshak, R. A., and Santrock, J. W. (1980). Children of divorce: Impact of custody disposition on social development. In E. J. Callahan, and K. A. McCluskey (Eds.), *Life developmental psychology: Nonnormative life events.* New York: Academic Press.

Wechsler, D. (1944). *The Measurement of adult intelligence.* Baltimore: Williams & Wilkins.

Wechsler, D. (1967). *Manual for the Wechsler Preschool and Primary Scale of Intelligence.* New York: Psychological Corporation.

Wechsler, D. (1974). *Manual for the Wechsler Intelligence Scale for Children—Revised.* New York: Psychological Corporation.

Weir, R. (1972). *Language in the crib.* The Hague, Netherlands: Mouton.

Weiss, A. (1984). Parent–child relationships of adopted adolescents in a psychiatric hospital. *Adolescence XIX* (73), 77–88.

Weissbourd, R. (1996). *The vulnerable child: What really hurts america's children and what we can do about it.* Reading, MA; Addison-Wesley Pub. Co.

Weissman, H. N. (1975). The mental health team as a differential decision-maker for child patients: A national survey. *Psychological Reports, 37,* 643–650.

Wells, S.J . (1995). Child abuse and neglect overview. In R. L. Edwards (Ed.-in-Chief), *Encyclopedia of Social Work* (19th ed., Vol. 1, pp. 346–353). Washington, DC: National Association of Social Workers.

Wepman, J. (1958). *Auditory Discrimination Test.* Chicago: Language Research Association.

Westman, J. C., Cline, D. W., Swift, W. J., and Kramer, D. J. (1970). Role of child psychiatry in divorce. *Archives of General Psychiatry, 23,* 416–420.

Whitaker, C. (1958). Psychotherapy with couples. *American Journal of Psychotherapy, 12,* 18–23.

Whitaker, C. (1976). A family is a four dimensional relationship. In P.J. Guerin (Ed.), *Family therapy: Theory and practice.* New York: Gardner.

Whitaker, C. (1980, Dec. 3–8) *Conversation Hour.* At the First International Conference on Ericksonian Hypnosis and Suggestive Therapy, Phoenix, AZ.

Whitaker, J. K. (1995). Children: Group Care. In *Encyclopedia of Social Work*, 19th Edition, Volume 1. Washington, DC: National Association of Social Work Press.

White, M. (1989). Selected Papers. Adelaide, Australia: Dulwich Center Publications.

Whitmore, J. R. (1980). *Giftedness, conflict and underachievement*. Boston: Allyn and Bacon.

Whorf, B. L. (1956). *Language, thought, and reality*. New York: MIT Press Wiley.

Williams, M. (1971, July). The problem profile technique in consultation. *Social Work, 16*, 52–59.

Wineman, D. (1995). Children's rights. In R. L. Edwards (Ed.-in-Chief), *Encycopedia of Social Work* (19th ed., Vol. 1, pp. 465–475). Washington, DC: National Association of Social Workers.

Winnicott, D. W. (1971). *Therapeutic consultations in child psychiatry*. New York: Basic Books.

Wolkenstein, A. (1977). The fear of committing child abuse: A discussion of eight families. *Child Welfare, 16*, 249–257.

Wolking, W. D., Quast, W., and Lawton, J. J. (1966). MMPI profiles of parents of behaviorally disturbed children and parents from the general population. *Journal of Clinical Psychology, 22*, 39–48.

Wolpe, J. (1961). The systematic desensitization treatment of neuroses. *Journal of Nervous and Mental Diseases, 132*, 189–203.

Wolpe, J. (1969). *The practice of behavior therapy*. New York: Pergamon Press.

Woodcock, R. W. (1973). *Woodcock Reading Mastery Tests*. Circle Pines, MN: American Guidance Services.

Woods, T. (1975). Comments on the dynamics and treatment of disfigured children. *Clinical Social Work Journal, 3 (1)*, 16–23.

World Health Organization. (1978). *International classification of disease*, (9th Ed.) Geneva.

Wynne, L. C. (1961). The study of intrafamilial alignments and splits in exploratory family therapy. In F. L. Beatman & S. N. Sherman (Eds.), *Exploring the base for family therapy*. New York: Family Services.

Young, T. M., Pappenfort, D. M., and Marlow, C. R. (1983). *National Survey of Residential Group Care Facilities: Residential group care, 1966 and 1981 facilities for children and youth with special problems and needs*. Chicago: University of Chicago, School of Social Service Administration.

Zigler, E. F., and Stevenson, M. F. (1993.). *Children in a changing world: Development and social issues*. (2nd. ed.). Pacific Grove, CA: Brooks/ Cole Pub. Co.

Zuckerman, E. (1983). *Child welfare*. New York: The Free Press.

Index